D1003713

Thank you for picking up Haikyu!! volume 25! Kageyama is on the cover of this volume! He was also on the promotional poster I did for the January 2017 Spring Tournament (last year's featured Hinata, by the way). Both the part of the story I'm working on in *Weekly Shonen Jump* and the touch-ups I did for this volume focus on Kageyama. It's practically "Kageyama Month" for me right now! The thing is, drawing Kageyama is pretty rough. Well...the gloss for his hair is anyway...

TOP OF...

HIS HEAD!

BRUSH PEN

HARUICHI FURUDATE began his manga career when he was 25 years old with the one-shot *Ousama Kid* (King Kid), which won an honorable mention for the 14th Jump Treasure Newcomer Manga Prize. His first series, *Kiben Gakuha, Yotsuya Sensei no Kaidan* (Philosophy School, Yotsuya Sensei's Ghost Stories), was serialized in *Weekly Shonen Jump* in 2010. In 2012, he began serializing *Haikyu!!* in *Weekly Shonen Jump*, where it became his most popular work to date.

HAIKYU!!
VOLUME 25
SHONEN JUMP Manga Edition

Story and Art by
HARUICHI FURUDATE

Translation  **ADRIENNE BECK**
Touch-Up Art & Lettering ❷ **ERIKA TERRIQUEZ**
Design ❸ **JULIAN [JR] ROBINSON**
Editor ❹ **MARLENE FIRST**

HAIKYU!! © 2012 by Haruichi Furudate
All rights reserved.
First published in Japan in 2012 by SHUEISHA Inc., Tokyo.
English translation rights arranged by SHUEISHA Inc.

The stories, characters and incidents mentioned
in this publication are entirely fictional.

Printed in Canada

Published by VIZ Media, LLC
P.O. Box 77010
San Francisco, CA 94107

10 9 8 7 6 5 4 3 2 1
First printing, July 2018

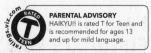

SHONEN**JUMP** MANGA

HAIKYU!!

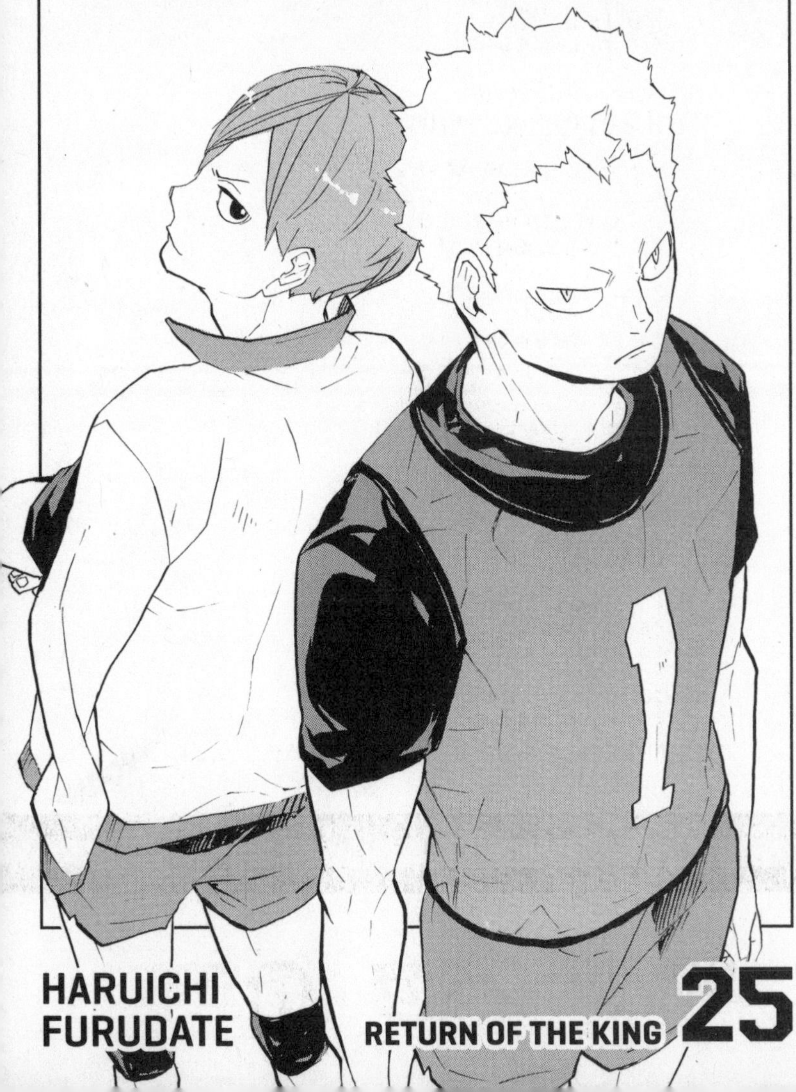

HARUICHI
FURUDATE

RETURN OF THE KING 25

Karasuno High School Volleyball Club

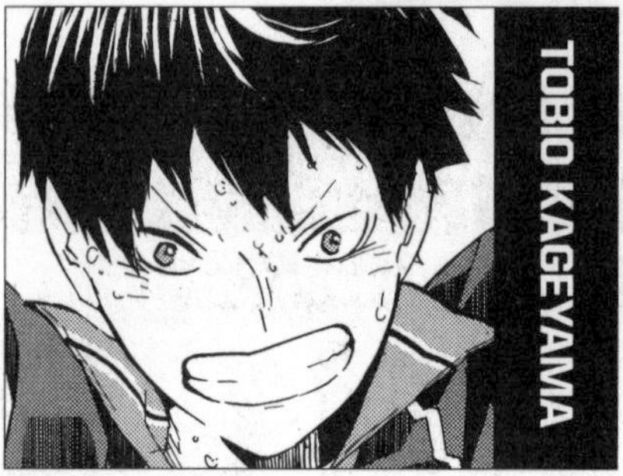
TOBIO KAGEYAMA

1ST YEAR / SETTER

His instincts and athletic talent are so good that he's like a "king" who rules the court. Demanding and egocentric.

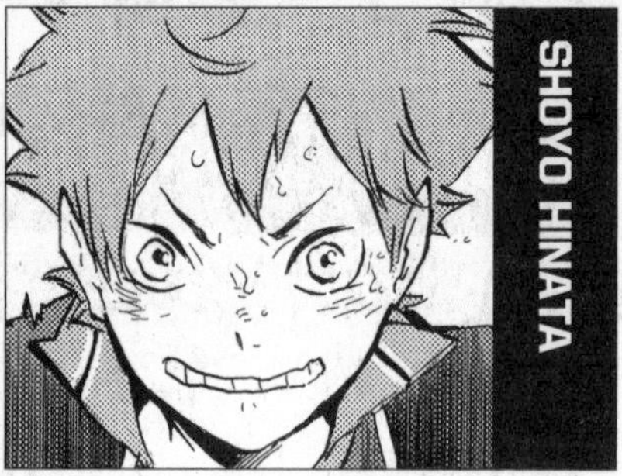
SHOYO HINATA

1ST YEAR / MIDDLE BLOCKER

Even though he doesn't have the best body type for volleyball, he is super athletic. Gets nervous easily.

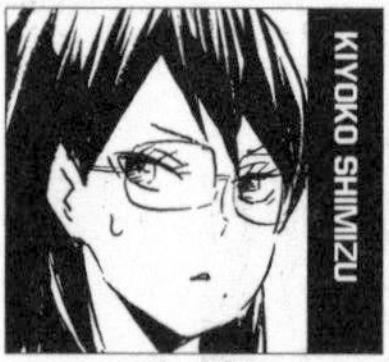
KIYOKO SHIMIZU

3RD YEAR
MANAGER

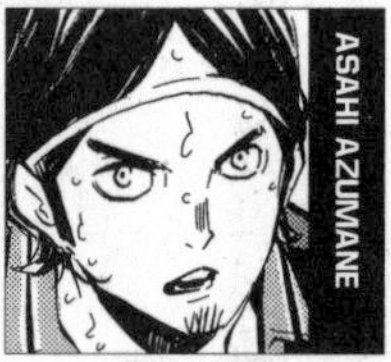
ASAHI AZUMANE

3RD YEAR
WING SPIKER

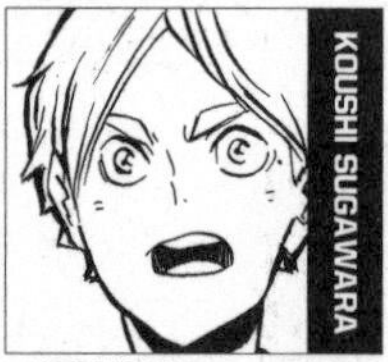
KOUSHI SUGAWARA

3RD YEAR (VICE CAPTAIN)
SETTER

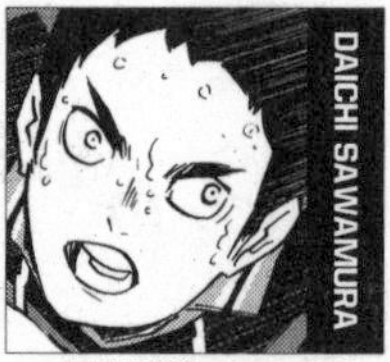
DAICHI SAWAMURA

3RD YEAR (CAPTAIN)
WING SPIKER

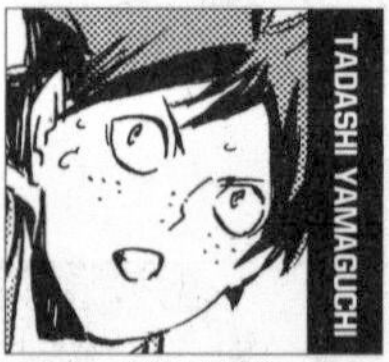
TADASHI YAMAGUCHI

1ST YEAR
MIDDLE BLOCKER

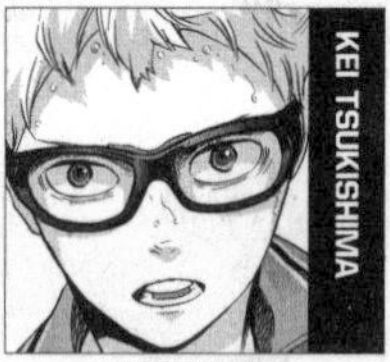
KEI TSUKISHIMA

1ST YEAR
MIDDLE BLOCKER

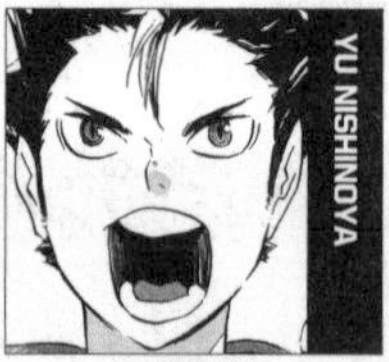
YU NISHINOYA

2ND YEAR
LIBERO

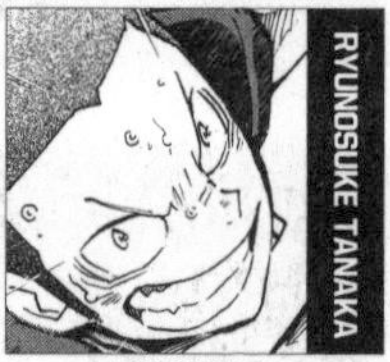
RYUNOSUKE TANAKA

2ND YEAR
WING SPIKER

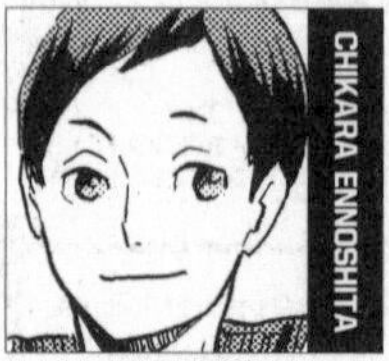
CHIKARA ENNOSHITA

2ND YEAR
WING SPIKER

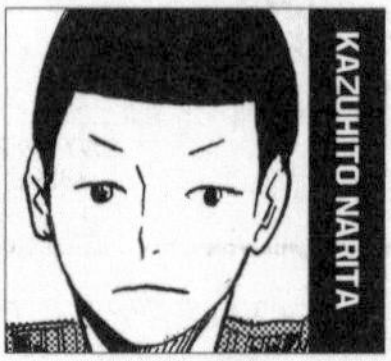
KAZUHITO NARITA

2ND YEAR
MIDDLE BLOCKER

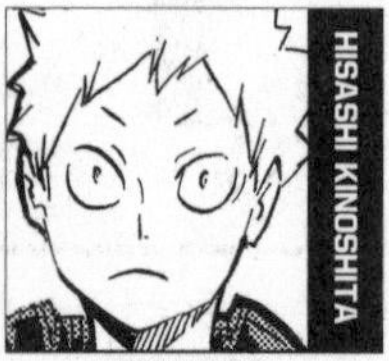
HISASHI KINOSHITA

2ND YEAR
WING SPIKER

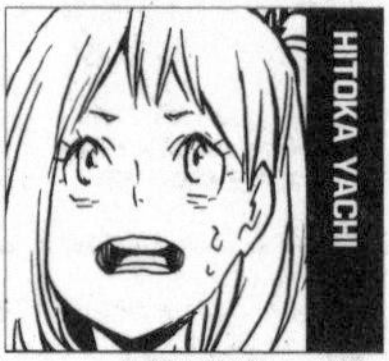
HITOKA YACHI

1ST YEAR
MANAGER

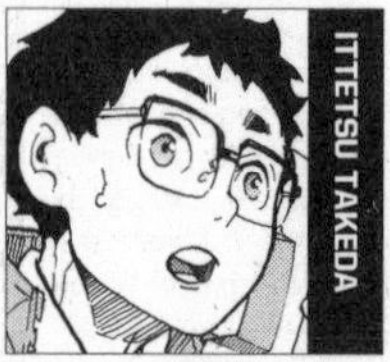
ITTETSU TAKEDA

ADVISER

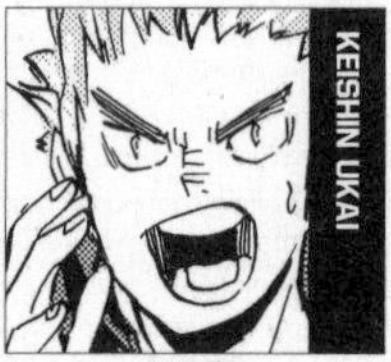
KEISHIN UKAI

COACH

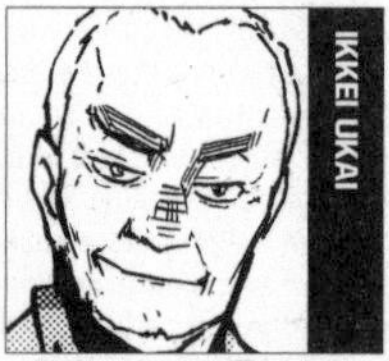
IKKEI UKAI

FORMER HEAD COACH

CHARACTERS

THE TRAINING CAMP ARC

Miyagi Prefecture Rookie Select Training Camp

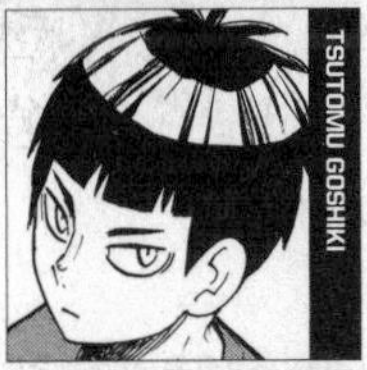
TSUTOMU GOSHIKI
SHIRATORIZAWA 1ST YEAR
WING SPIKER

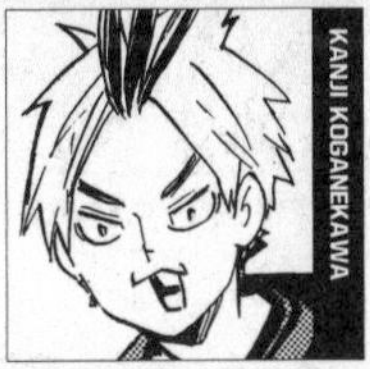
KANJI KOGANEKAWA
DATE TECH 1ST YEAR
SETTER

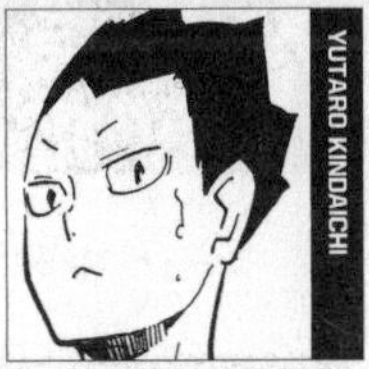
YUTARO KINDAICHI
AOBA JOHSAI 1ST YEAR
MIDDLE BLOCKER

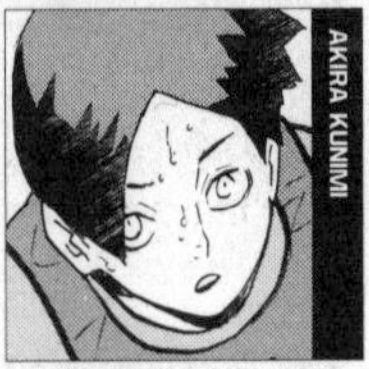
AKIRA KUNIMI
AOBA JOHSAI 1ST YEAR
WING SPIKER

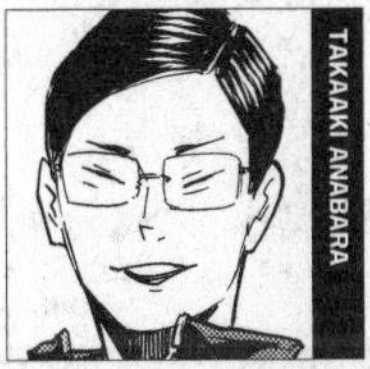
TAKAAKI ANABARA
JOHZENJI HEAD COACH

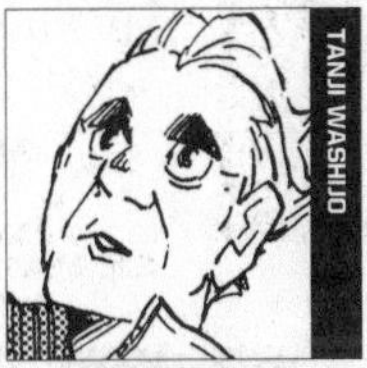
TANJI WASHIJO
SHIRATORIZAWA
HEAD COACH

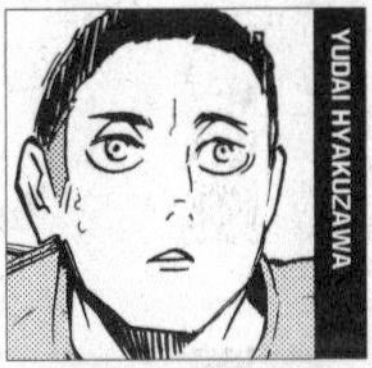
YUDAI HYAKUZAWA
KAKUGAWA 1ST YEAR
WING SPIKER

All-Japan Youth Training Camp

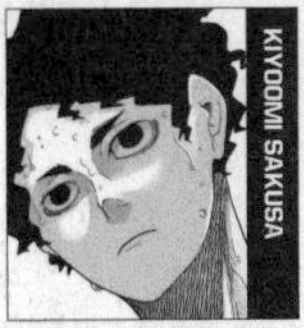
KIYOOMI SAKUSA
ITACHIYAMA 2ND YEAR
MIDDLE BLOCKER

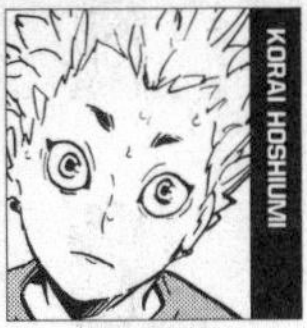
KORAI HOSHIUMI
2ND YEAR
WING SPIKER

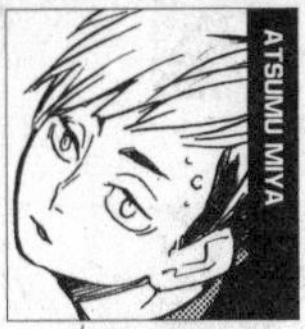
ATSUMU MIYA
2ND YEAR
SETTER

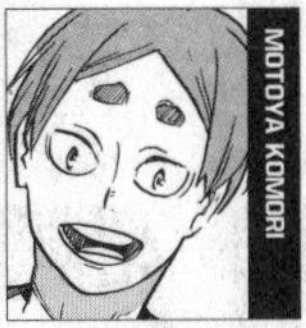
MOTOYA KOMORI
2ND YEAR
LIBERO

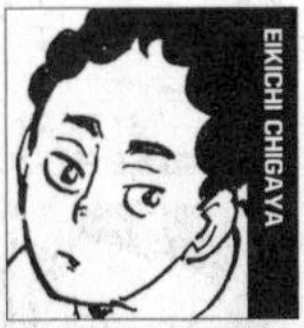
EIKICHI CHIGAYA
SHINZEN 1ST YEAR
MIDDLE BLOCKER

Ever since he saw the legendary player known as "the Little Giant" compete at the national volleyball finals, Shoyo Hinata has been aiming to be the best volleyball player ever! He decides to join the volleyball club at his middle school and gets to play in an official tournament during his third year. His team is crushed by a team led by volleyball prodigy Tobio Kageyama, also known as "the King of the Court." Swearing revenge on Kageyama, Hinata graduates middle school and enters Karasuno High School, the school where the Little Giant played. However, upon joining the club, he finds out that Kageyama is there too! The two of them bicker constantly, but they bring out the best in each other's talents and become a powerful combo. After a long and bitterly fought game, Karasuno finally defeats Shiratorizawa and wins the Miyagi Prefecture Qualifiers! With the Spring Tournament only a month away, Kageyama gets invited to the All-Japan Youth Camp. Frustrated at being left behind, Hinata decides to crash the prefectural rookie camp that Tsukishima has been invited to. Once there, he gets stuck being a ball boy! Left on the sidelines, Hinata discovers that he can learn all kinds of things simply by watching the other players. Meanwhile, at the All-Japan Youth Camp, Kageyama gets called a Goody-Two-shoes by Miya, another setter there. And for some reason, it's driving Kageyama crazy!

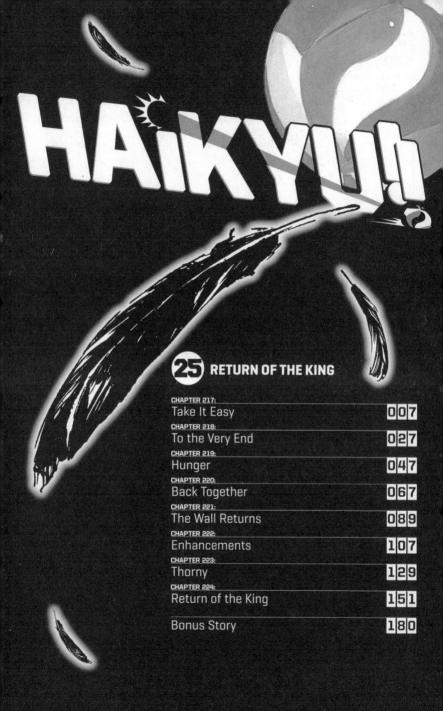

HAIKYU!!

25 RETURN OF THE KING

CHAPTER 217: Take It Easy

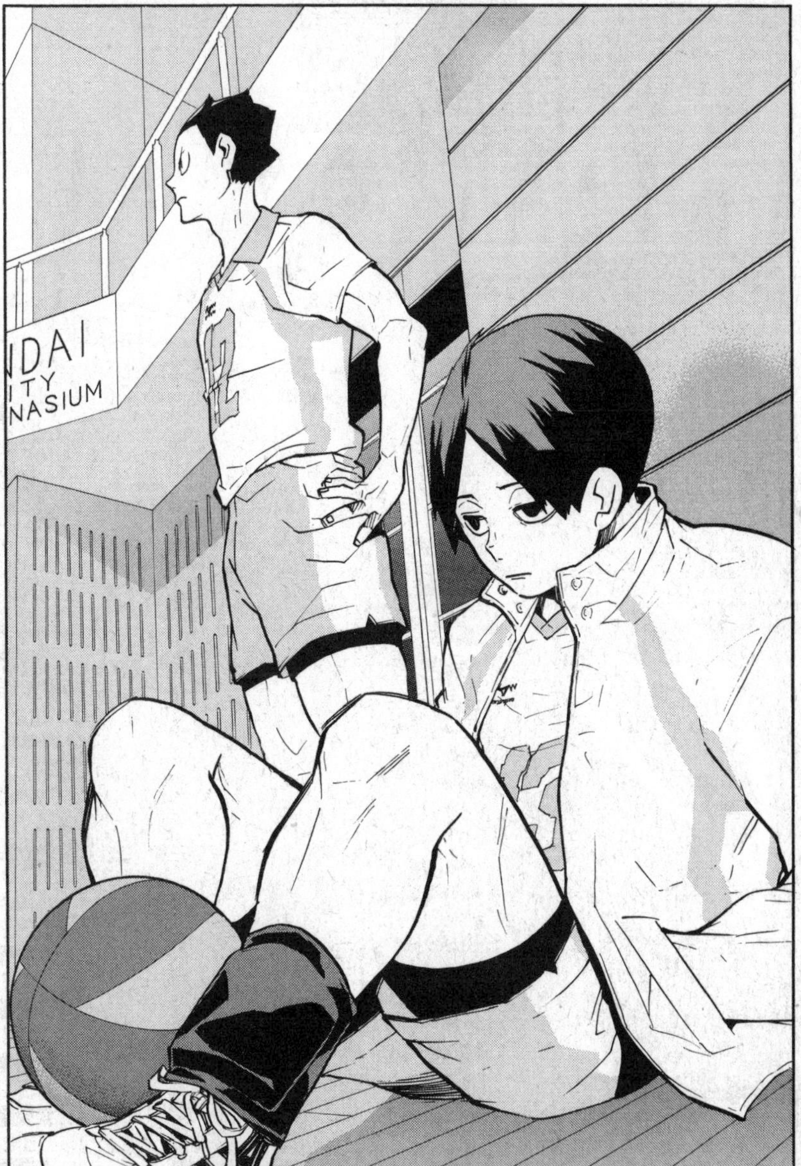
NDAI
ITY
NASIUM

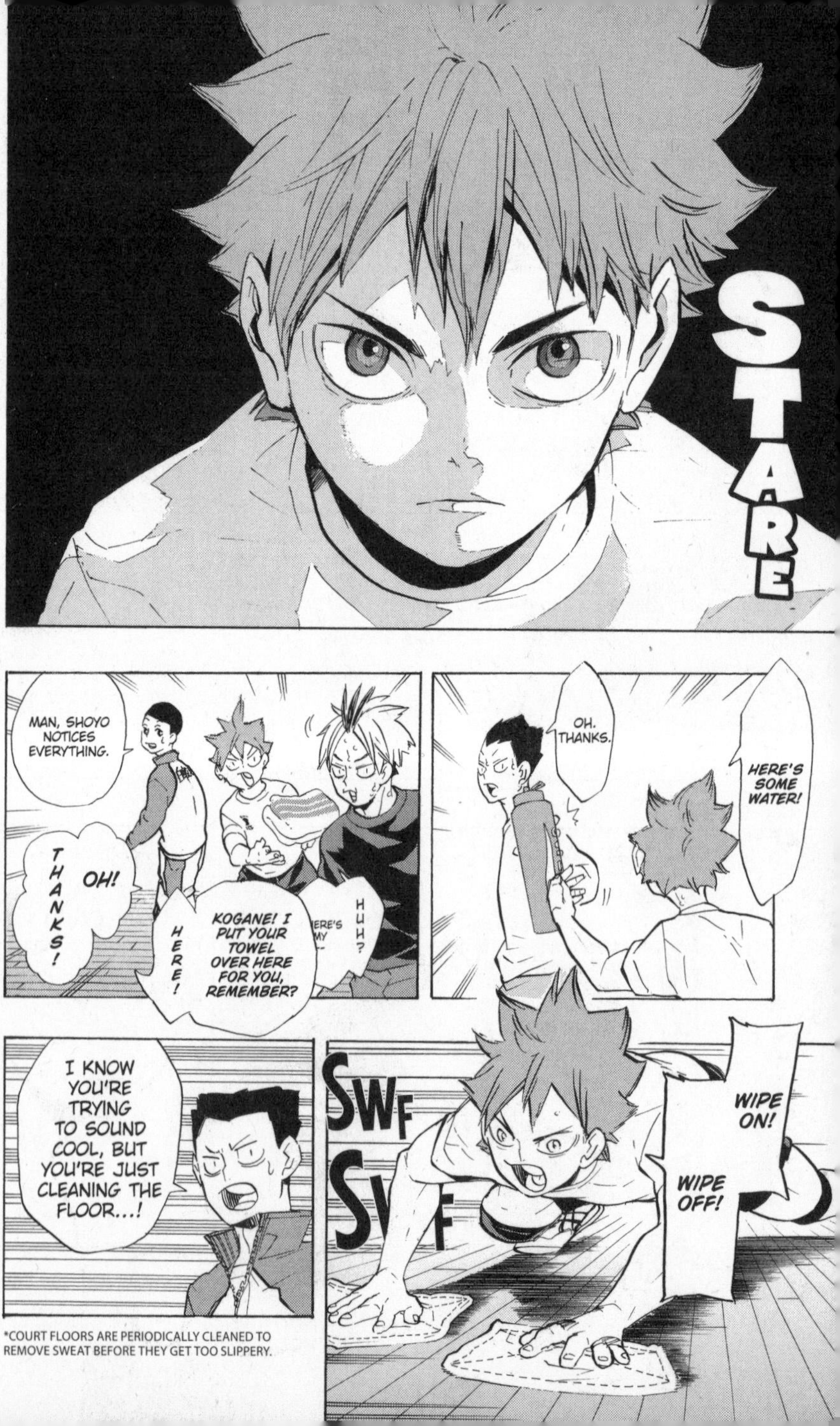
STARE
HERE'S SOME WATER!
OH. THANKS.
HUH?
KOGANE! I PUT YOUR TOWEL OVER HERE FOR YOU, REMEMBER?
HERE!
OH!
THANKS!
MAN, SHOYO NOTICES EVERYTHING.
WIPE ON!
WIPE OFF!
SWF
SWF
I KNOW YOU'RE TRYING TO SOUND COOL, BUT YOU'RE JUST CLEANING THE FLOOR...!

*COURT FLOORS ARE PERIODICALLY CLEANED TO REMOVE SWEAT BEFORE THEY GET TOO SLIPPERY.

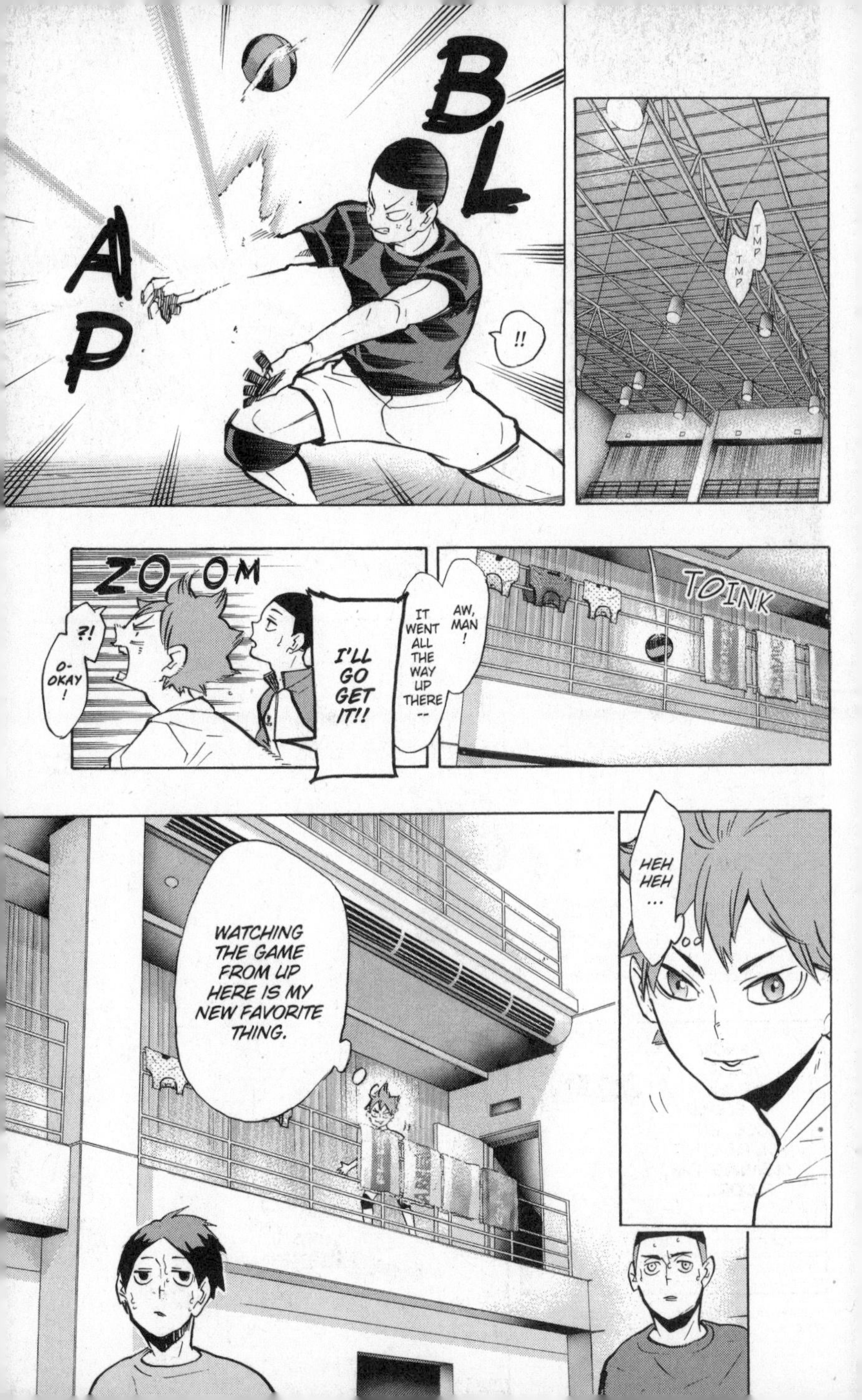
TMP TMP TMP
BLAP
!!
TOINK
AW, MAN!
IT WENT ALL THE WAY UP THERE --
I'LL GO GET IT!!
ZO OM
?!
O-OKAY!
HEH HEH ...
WATCHING THE GAME FROM UP HERE IS MY NEW FAVORITE THING.

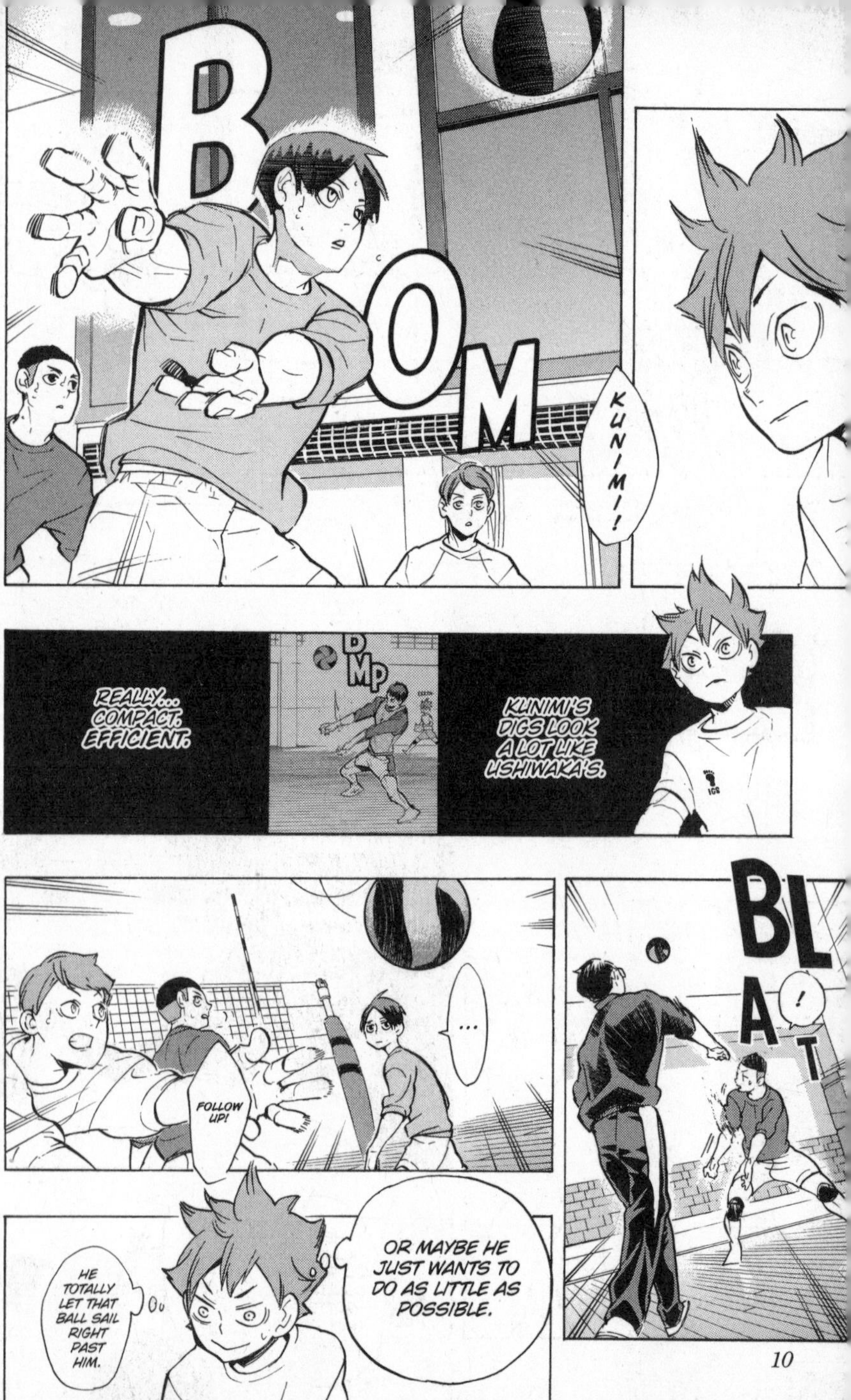
BOOM
KUNIMI!
KUNIMI'S DIGS LOOK A LOT LIKE USHIWAKA'S.
REALLY... COMPACT. EFFICIENT.
BLAT
!
...
FOLLOW UP!
OR MAYBE HE JUST WANTS TO DO AS LITTLE AS POSSIBLE.
HE TOTALLY LET THAT BALL SAIL RIGHT PAST HIM.

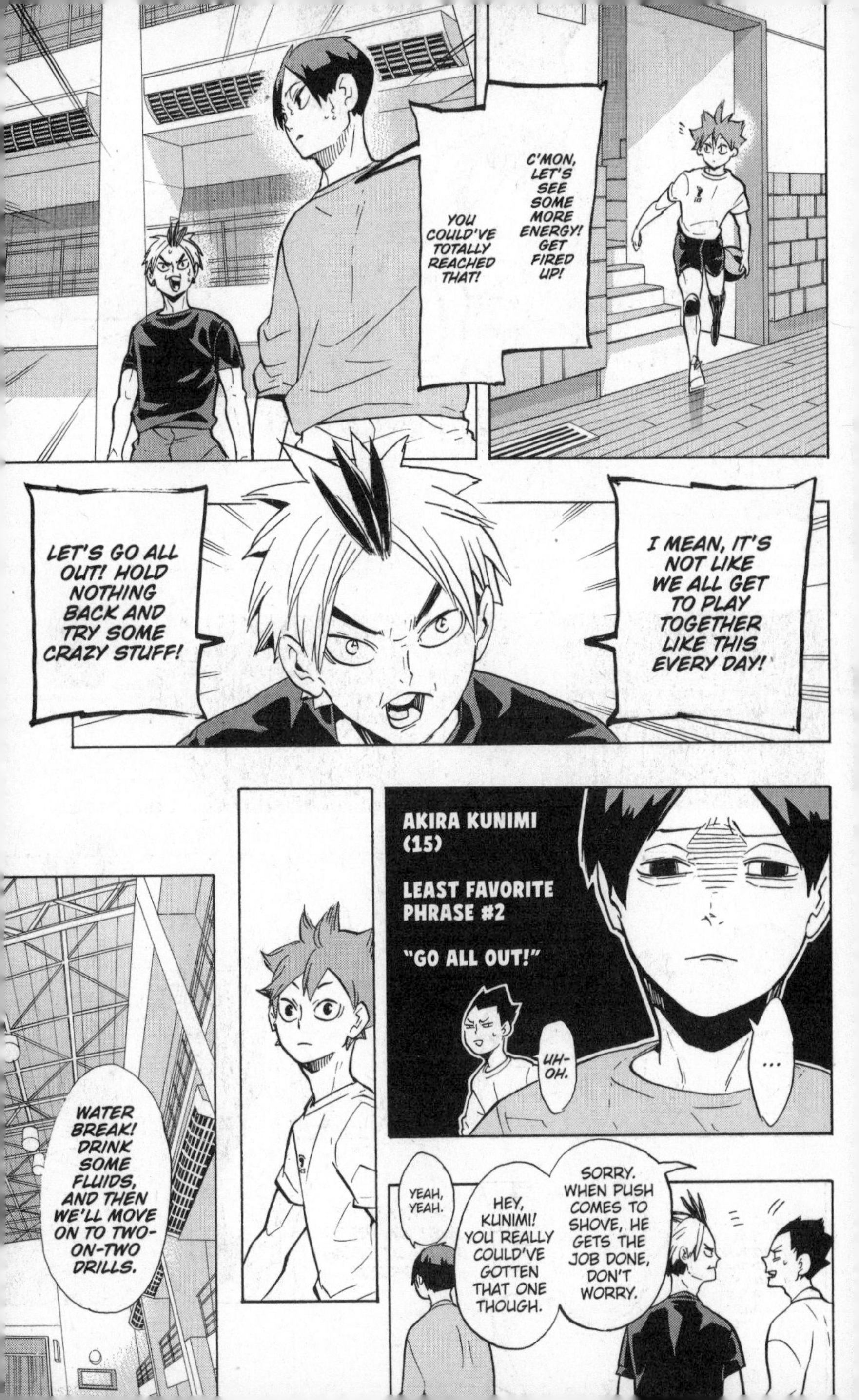
C'MON, LET'S SEE SOME MORE ENERGY! GET FIRED UP!
YOU COULD'VE TOTALLY REACHED THAT!
I MEAN, IT'S NOT LIKE WE ALL GET TO PLAY TOGETHER LIKE THIS EVERY DAY!
LET'S GO ALL OUT! HOLD NOTHING BACK AND TRY SOME CRAZY STUFF!
AKIRA KUNIMI (15)
LEAST FAVORITE PHRASE #2
"GO ALL OUT!"
...
UH-OH.
SORRY. WHEN PUSH COMES TO SHOVE, HE GETS THE JOB DONE, DON'T WORRY.
HEY, KUNIMI! YOU REALLY COULD'VE GOTTEN THAT ONE THOUGH.
YEAH, YEAH.
WATER BREAK! DRINK SOME FLUIDS, AND THEN WE'LL MOVE ON TO TWO-ON-TWO DRILLS.

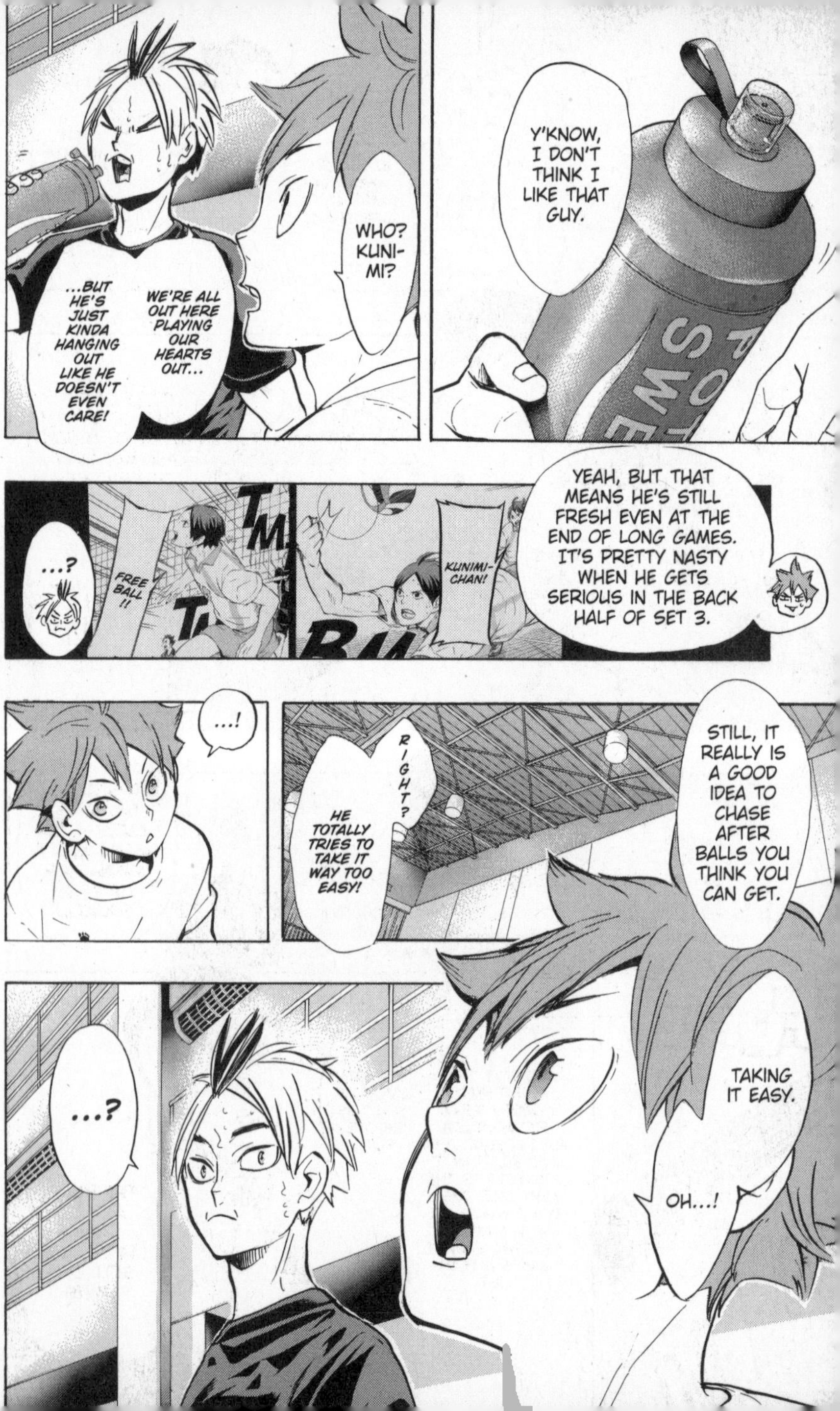

Y'KNOW, I DON'T THINK I LIKE THAT GUY.
WHO? KUNIMI?
WE'RE ALL OUT HERE PLAYING OUR HEARTS OUT...
...BUT HE'S JUST KINDA HANGING OUT LIKE HE DOESN'T EVEN CARE!
YEAH, BUT THAT MEANS HE'S STILL FRESH EVEN AT THE END OF LONG GAMES. IT'S PRETTY NASTY WHEN HE GETS SERIOUS IN THE BACK HALF OF SET 3.
KUNIMI-CHAN!
FREE BALL !!
...?
STILL, IT REALLY IS A GOOD IDEA TO CHASE AFTER BALLS YOU THINK YOU CAN GET.
RIGHT?
HE TOTALLY TRIES TO TAKE IT WAY TOO EASY!
...!
TAKING IT EASY.
OH...!
...?

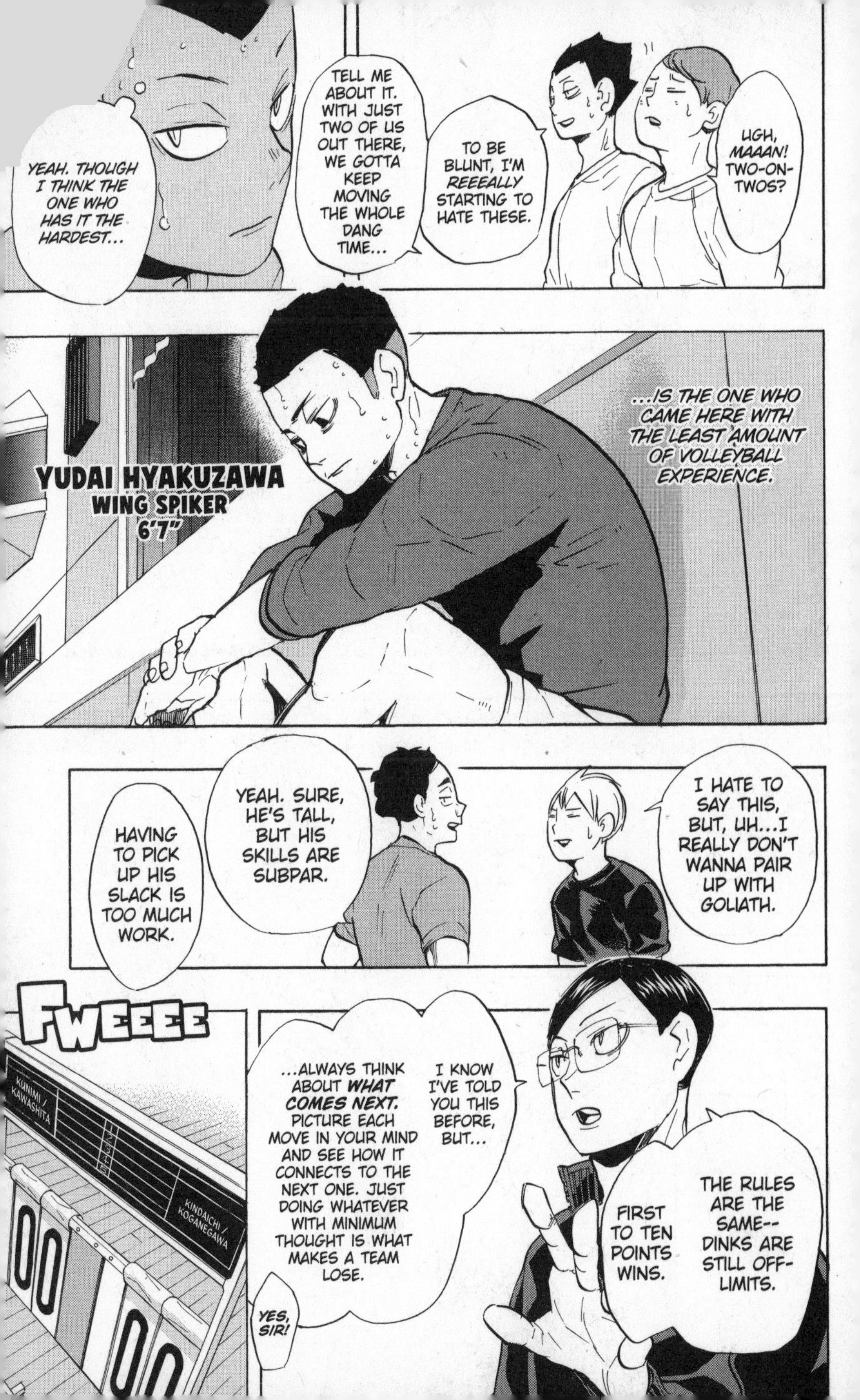
UGH, MAAAN! TWO-ON-TWOS?
TO BE BLUNT, I'M REEEALLY STARTING TO HATE THESE.
TELL ME ABOUT IT. WITH JUST TWO OF US OUT THERE, WE GOTTA KEEP MOVING THE WHOLE DANG TIME...
YEAH. THOUGH I THINK THE ONE WHO HAS IT THE HARDEST...
...IS THE ONE WHO CAME HERE WITH THE LEAST AMOUNT OF VOLLEYBALL EXPERIENCE.
YUDAI HYAKUZAWA
WING SPIKER
6'7"
I HATE TO SAY THIS, BUT, UH...I REALLY DON'T WANNA PAIR UP WITH GOLIATH.
YEAH. SURE, HE'S TALL, BUT HIS SKILLS ARE SUBPAR.
HAVING TO PICK UP HIS SLACK IS TOO MUCH WORK.
I KNOW I'VE TOLD YOU THIS BEFORE, BUT...
...ALWAYS THINK ABOUT WHAT COMES NEXT. PICTURE EACH MOVE IN YOUR MIND AND SEE HOW IT CONNECTS TO THE NEXT ONE. JUST DOING WHATEVER WITH MINIMUM THOUGHT IS WHAT MAKES A TEAM LOSE.
THE RULES ARE THE SAME--DINKS ARE STILL OFF-LIMITS.
FIRST TO TEN POINTS WINS.
YES, SIR!
FWEEEE
KUNIMI / KAWASHITA
KINDAICHI / KOGANEGAWA
00
00

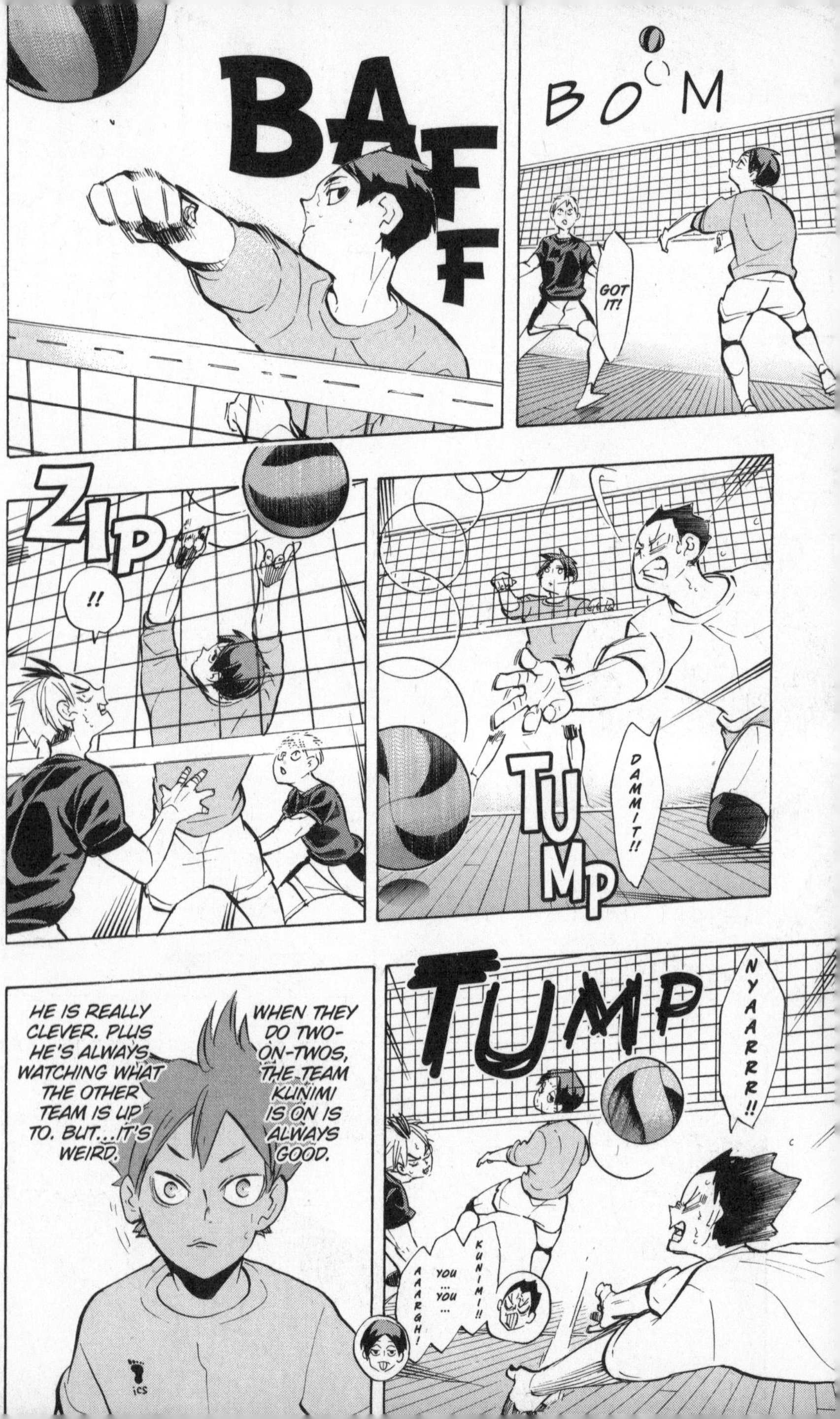
BOOM
GOT IT!
BAFF
DAMMIT!!
TUMP
ZIP
!!
TUMP
NYAARRR!!
KUNIMI!!
YOU ... YOU ...
AAARGH!
HE IS REALLY CLEVER. PLUS HE'S ALWAYS WATCHING WHAT THE OTHER TEAM IS UP TO. BUT...IT'S WEIRD.
WHEN THEY DO TWO-ON-TWOS, THE TEAM KUNIMI IS ON IS ALWAYS GOOD.

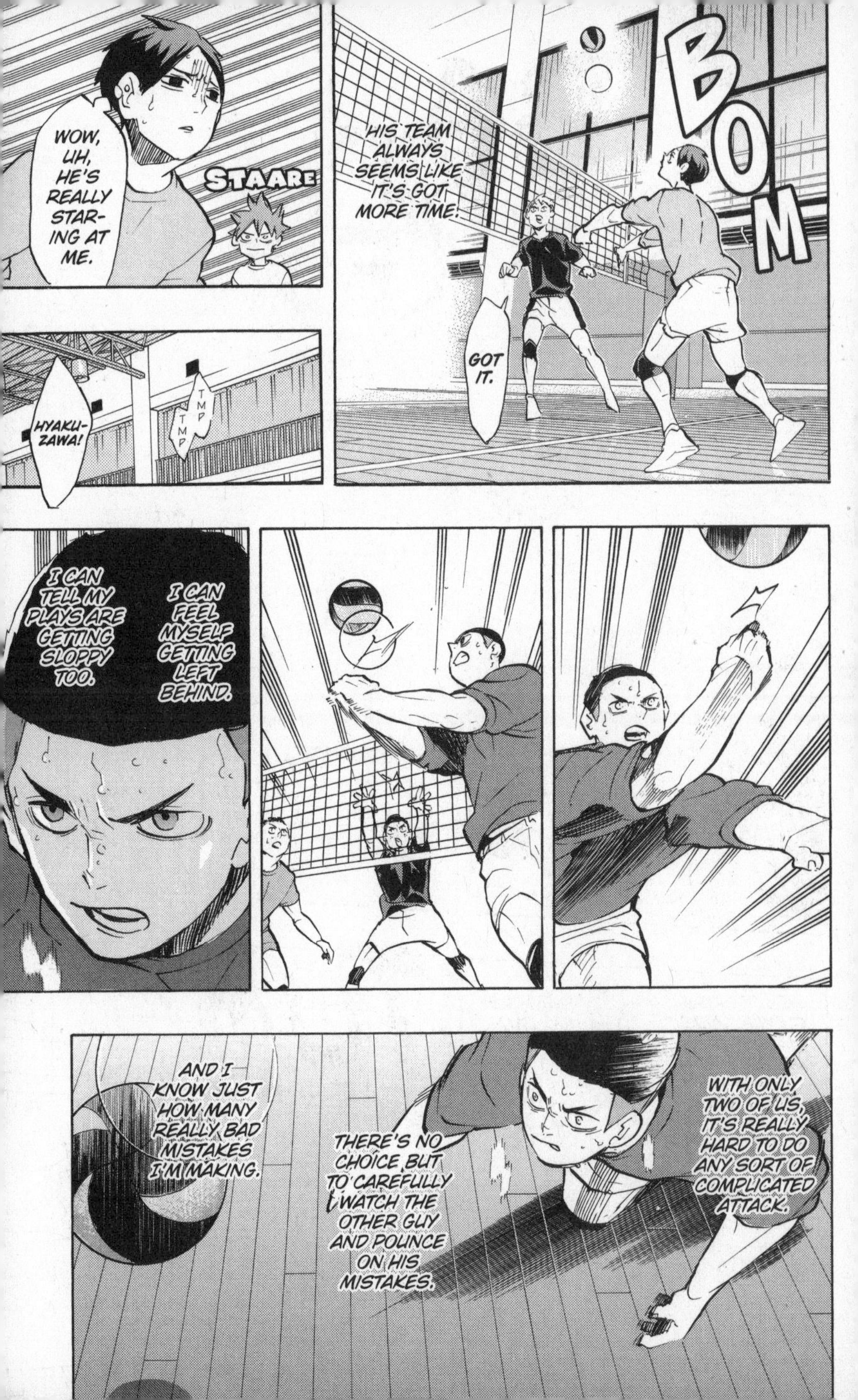
BOM
HIS TEAM ALWAYS SEEMS LIKE IT'S GOT MORE TIME.
GOT IT.
WOW, UH, HE'S REALLY STAR-ING AT ME.
STAARE
HYAKU-ZAWA!
TMP TMP
I CAN FEEL MYSELF GETTING LEFT BEHIND.
I CAN TELL MY PLAYS ARE GETTING SLOPPY TOO.
WITH ONLY TWO OF US, IT'S REALLY HARD TO DO ANY SORT OF COMPLICATED ATTACK.
THERE'S NO CHOICE BUT TO CAREFULLY WATCH THE OTHER GUY AND POUNCE ON HIS MISTAKES.
AND I KNOW JUST HOW MANY REALLY BAD MISTAKES I'M MAKING.

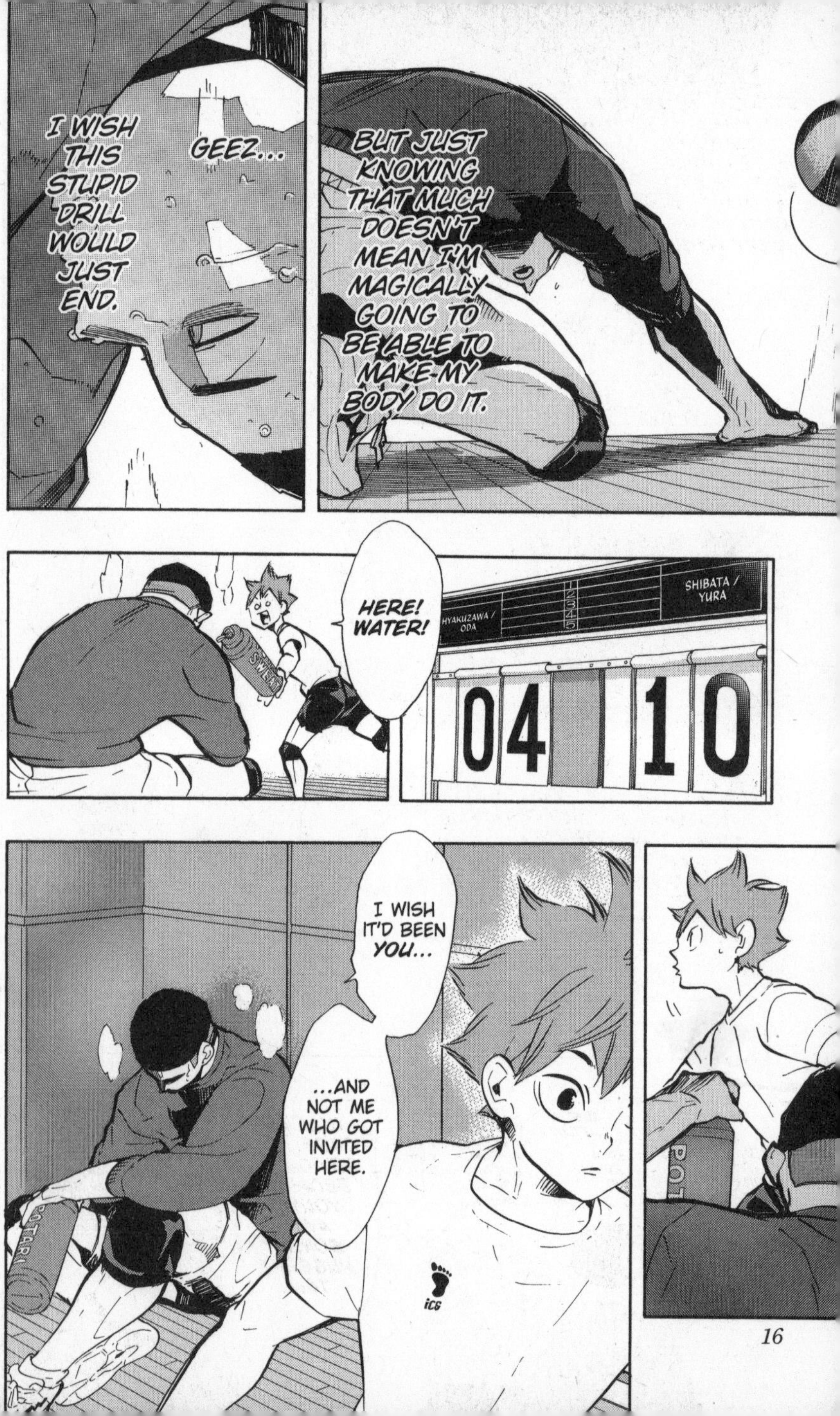
BUT JUST KNOWING THAT MUCH DOESN'T MEAN I'M MAGICALLY GOING TO BE ABLE TO MAKE MY BODY DO IT.
GEEZ...
I WISH THIS STUPID DRILL WOULD JUST END.
SHIBATA / YURA
1 2 3 4 5
HYAKUZAWA / ODA
04 10
HERE! WATER!
SWEAT
I WISH IT'D BEEN *YOU*...
...AND NOT ME WHO GOT INVITED HERE.
POTARI

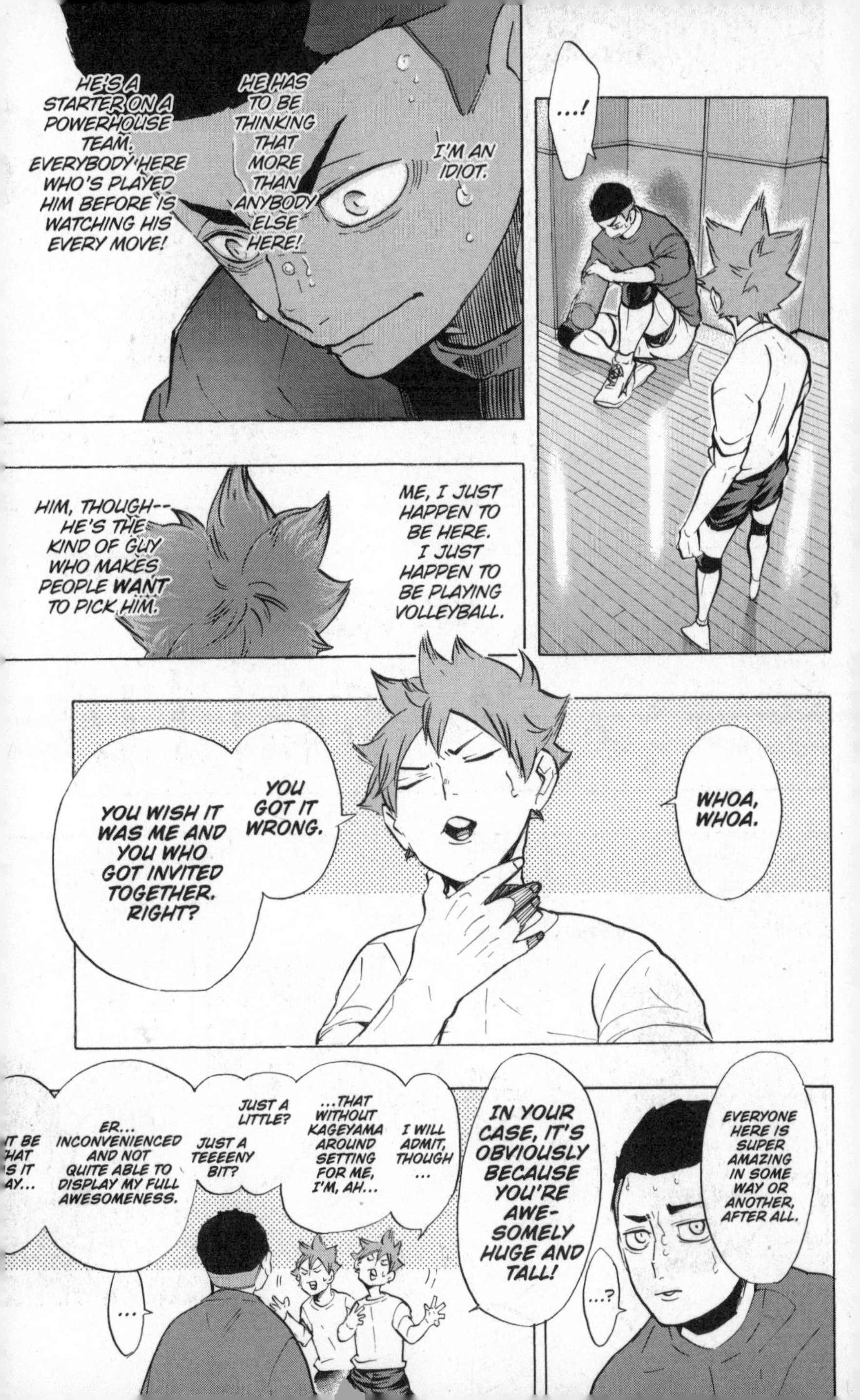
...!
I'M AN IDIOT.
HE HAS TO BE THINKING THAT MORE THAN ANYBODY ELSE HERE!
HE'S A STARTER ON A POWERHOUSE TEAM. EVERYBODY HERE WHO'S PLAYED HIM BEFORE IS WATCHING HIS EVERY MOVE!
ME, I JUST HAPPEN TO BE HERE. I JUST HAPPEN TO BE PLAYING VOLLEYBALL.
HIM, THOUGH-- HE'S THE KIND OF GUY WHO MAKES PEOPLE WANT TO PICK HIM.
WHOA, WHOA.
YOU GOT IT WRONG.
YOU WISH IT WAS ME AND YOU WHO GOT INVITED TOGETHER. RIGHT?
EVERYONE HERE IS SUPER AMAZING IN SOME WAY OR ANOTHER, AFTER ALL.
...?
IN YOUR CASE, IT'S OBVIOUSLY BECAUSE YOU'RE AWE-SOMELY HUGE AND TALL!
I WILL ADMIT, THOUGH...
...THAT WITHOUT KAGEYAMA AROUND SETTING FOR ME, I'M, AH...
JUST A LITTLE?
JUST A TEEEENY BIT?
ER... INCONVENIENCED AND NOT QUITE ABLE TO DISPLAY MY FULL AWESOMENESS.
...

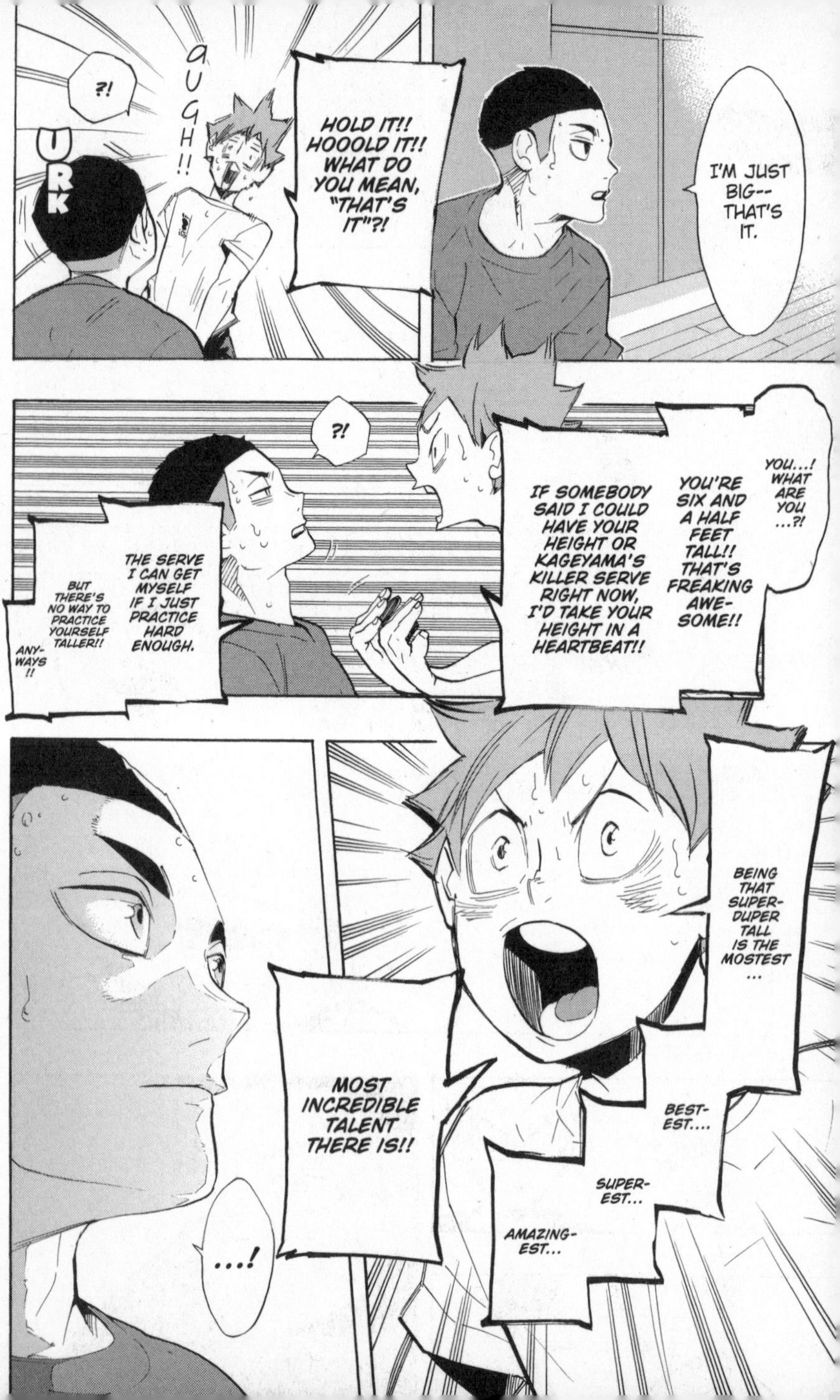
I'M JUST BIG-- THAT'S IT.
HOLD IT!! HOOOLD IT!! WHAT DO YOU MEAN, "THAT'S IT"?!
AUGH!!
URK
?!
YOU...! WHAT ARE YOU ...?!
YOU'RE SIX AND A HALF FEET TALL!! THAT'S FREAKING AWESOME!!
IF SOMEBODY SAID I COULD HAVE YOUR HEIGHT OR KAGEYAMA'S KILLER SERVE RIGHT NOW, I'D TAKE YOUR HEIGHT IN A HEARTBEAT!!
?!
THE SERVE I CAN GET MYSELF IF I JUST PRACTICE HARD ENOUGH.
BUT THERE'S NO WAY TO PRACTICE YOURSELF TALLER!!
ANYWAYS!!
BEING THAT SUPER-DUPER TALL IS THE MOSTEST...
BEST-EST....
SUPER-EST...
AMAZING-EST...
MOST INCREDIBLE TALENT THERE IS!!
...!

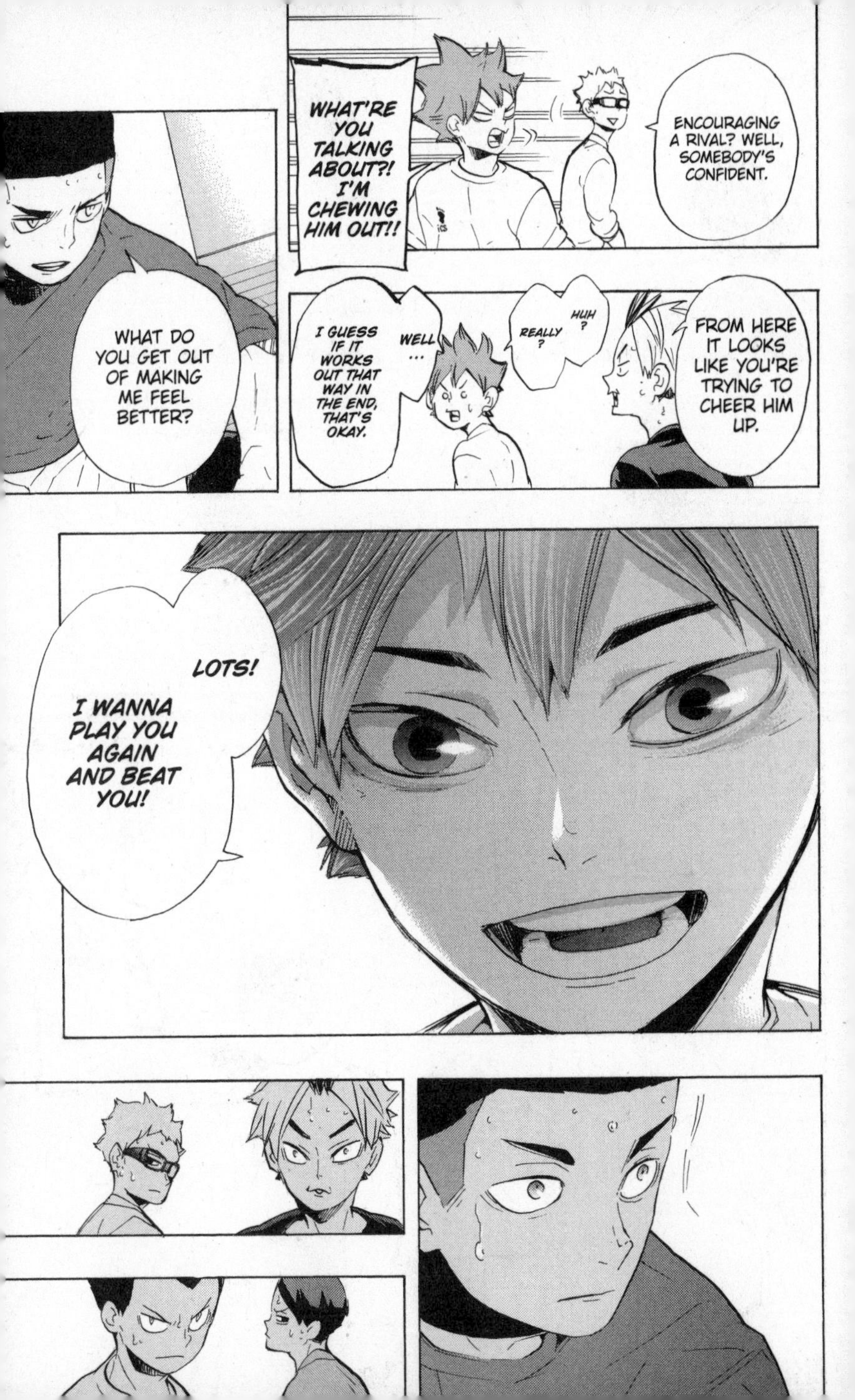
ENCOURAGING A RIVAL? WELL, SOMEBODY'S CONFIDENT.
WHAT'RE YOU TALKING ABOUT?! I'M CHEWING HIM OUT!!
FROM HERE IT LOOKS LIKE YOU'RE TRYING TO CHEER HIM UP.
HUH?
REALLY?
WELL...
I GUESS IF IT WORKS OUT THAT WAY IN THE END, THAT'S OKAY.
WHAT DO YOU GET OUT OF MAKING ME FEEL BETTER?
LOTS!
I WANNA PLAY YOU AGAIN AND BEAT YOU!

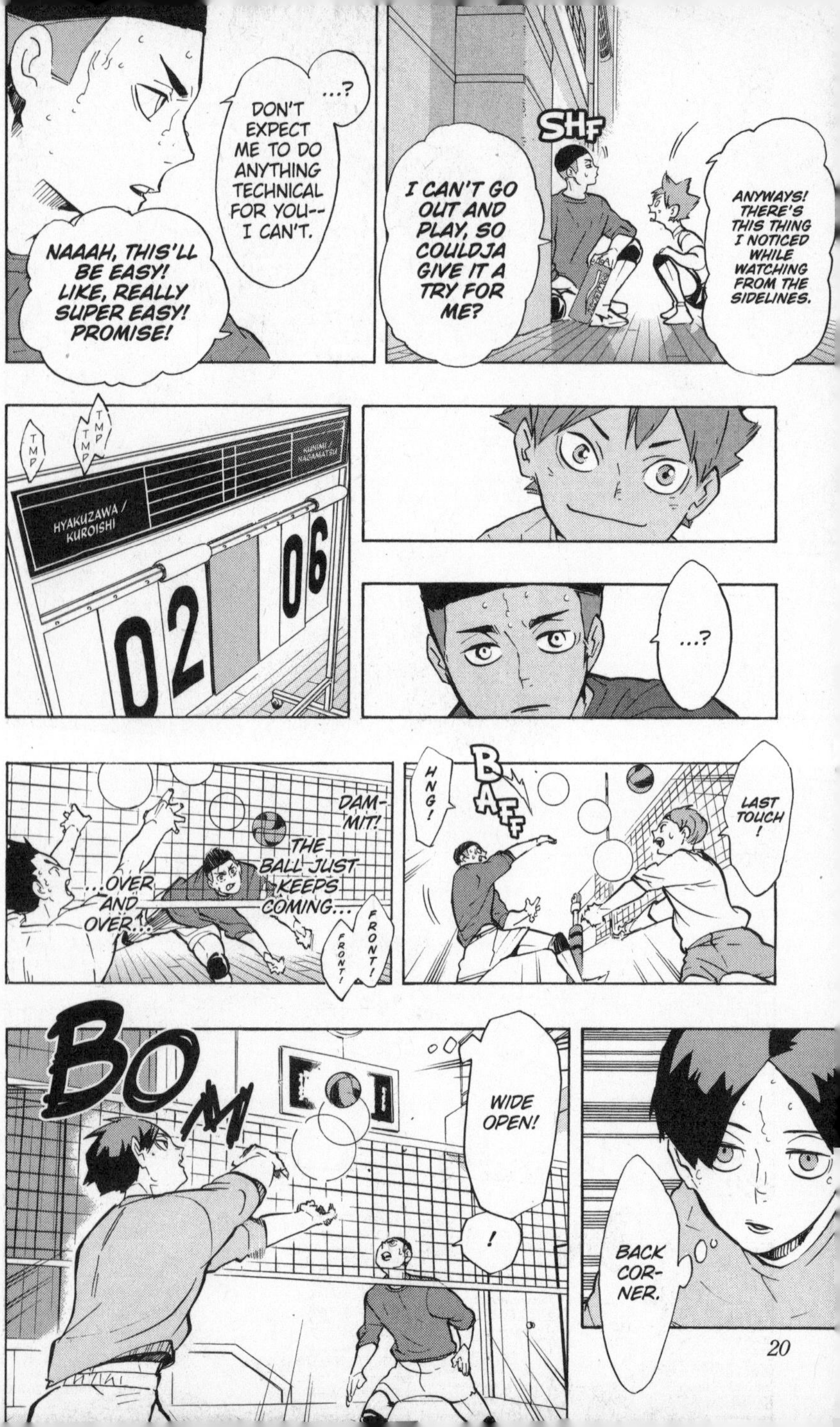
SHF
ANYWAYS! THERE'S THIS THING I NOTICED WHILE WATCHING FROM THE SIDELINES.
I CAN'T GO OUT AND PLAY, SO COULDJA GIVE IT A TRY FOR ME?
...?
DON'T EXPECT ME TO DO ANYTHING TECHNICAL FOR YOU-- I CAN'T.
NAAAH, THIS'LL BE EASY! LIKE, REALLY SUPER EASY! PROMISE!
...?
TMP
TMP
TMP
HYAKUZAWA / KUROISHI
KUNIMI / NAGAMATSU
02
06
LAST TOUCH!
BAFF
HNG!
DAM-MIT!
THE BALL JUST KEEPS COMING...
...OVER AND OVER...
FRONT!
FRONT!
BACK COR-NER.
WIDE OPEN!
!
BOOM

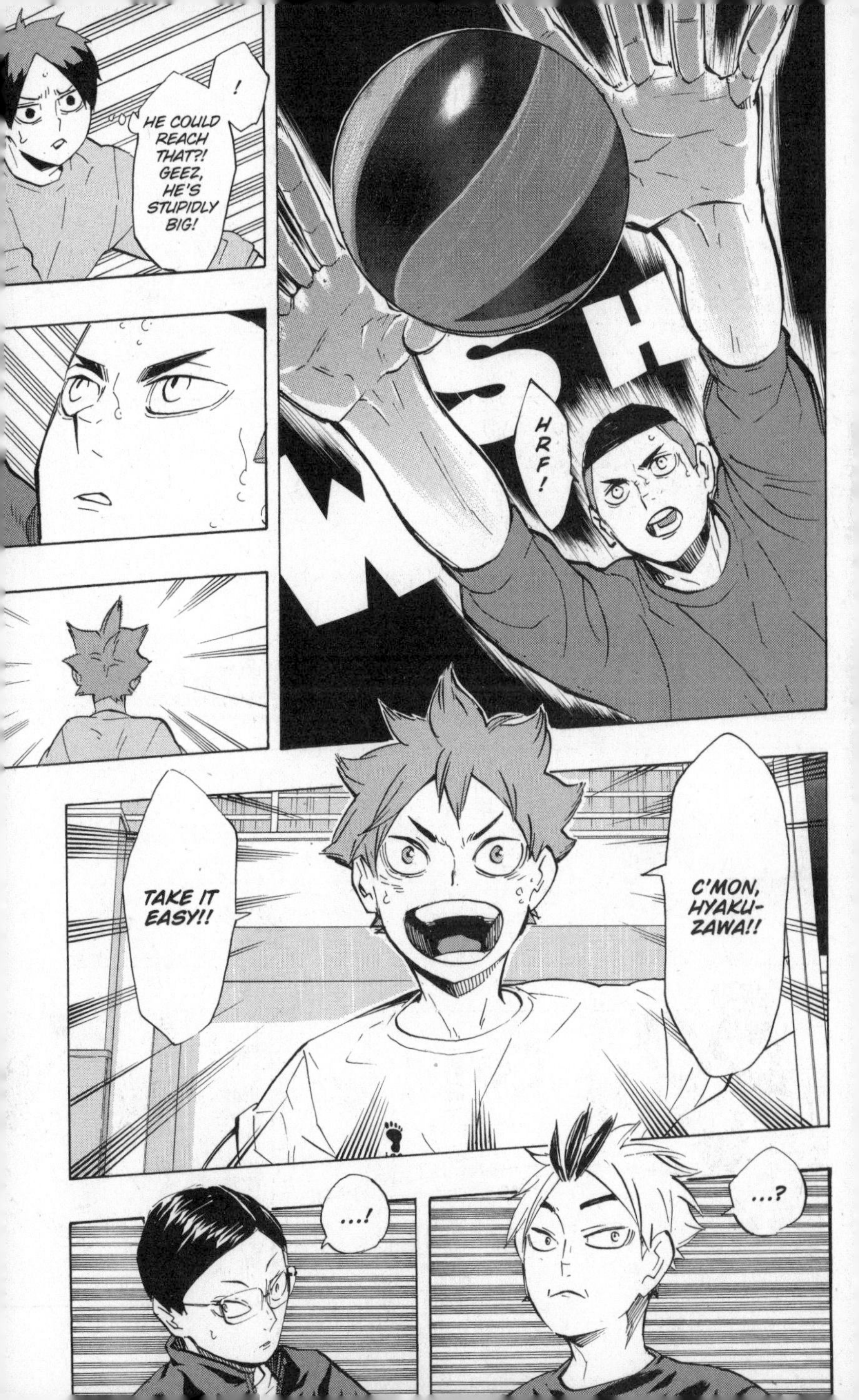
WSH
HRF!
!
HE COULD REACH THAT?! GEEZ, HE'S STUPIDLY BIG!
C'MON, HYAKU-ZAWA!!
TAKE IT EASY!!
...?
...!

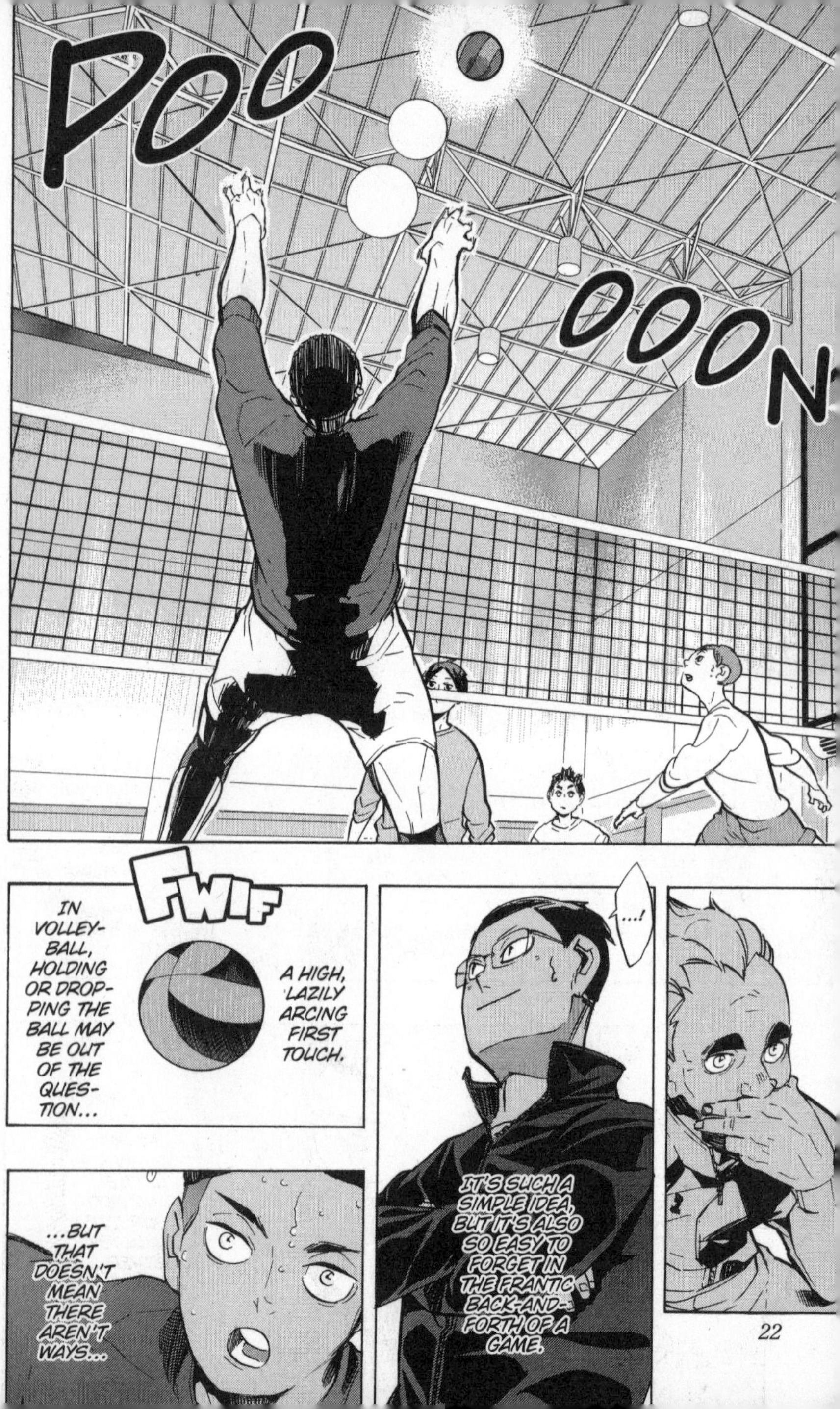
POOOOON
...!
IT'S SUCH A SIMPLE IDEA, BUT IT'S ALSO SO EASY TO FORGET IN THE FRANTIC BACK-AND-FORTH OF A GAME.
A HIGH, LAZILY ARCING FIRST TOUCH.
FWIF
IN VOLLEY-BALL, HOLDING OR DROP-PING THE BALL MAY BE OUT OF THE QUES-TION...
...BUT THAT DOESN'T MEAN THERE AREN'T WAYS...

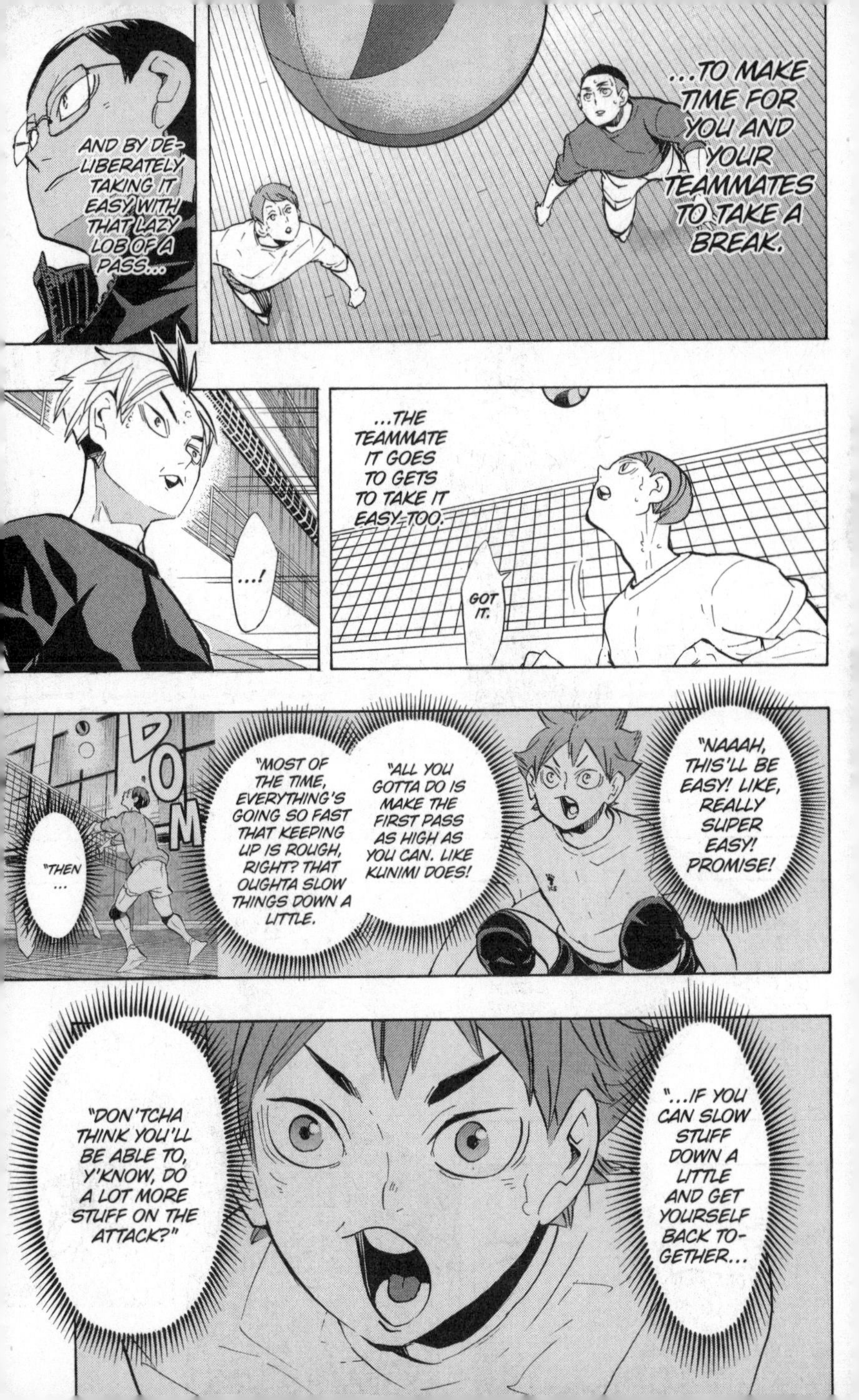
...TO MAKE TIME FOR YOU AND YOUR TEAMMATES TO TAKE A BREAK.
AND BY DE-LIBERATELY TAKING IT EASY WITH THAT LAZY LOB OF A PASS...
...THE TEAMMATE IT GOES TO GETS TO TAKE IT EASY TOO.
GOT IT.
...!
"NAAAH, THIS'LL BE EASY! LIKE, REALLY SUPER EASY! PROMISE!
"ALL YOU GOTTA DO IS MAKE THE FIRST PASS AS HIGH AS YOU CAN. LIKE KUNIMI DOES!
"MOST OF THE TIME, EVERYTHING'S GOING SO FAST THAT KEEPING UP IS ROUGH, RIGHT? THAT OUGHTA SLOW THINGS DOWN A LITTLE.
DOM
"THEN ...
"...IF YOU CAN SLOW STUFF DOWN A LITTLE AND GET YOURSELF BACK TO-GETHER...
"DON'TCHA THINK YOU'LL BE ABLE TO, Y'KNOW, DO A LOT MORE STUFF ON THE ATTACK?"

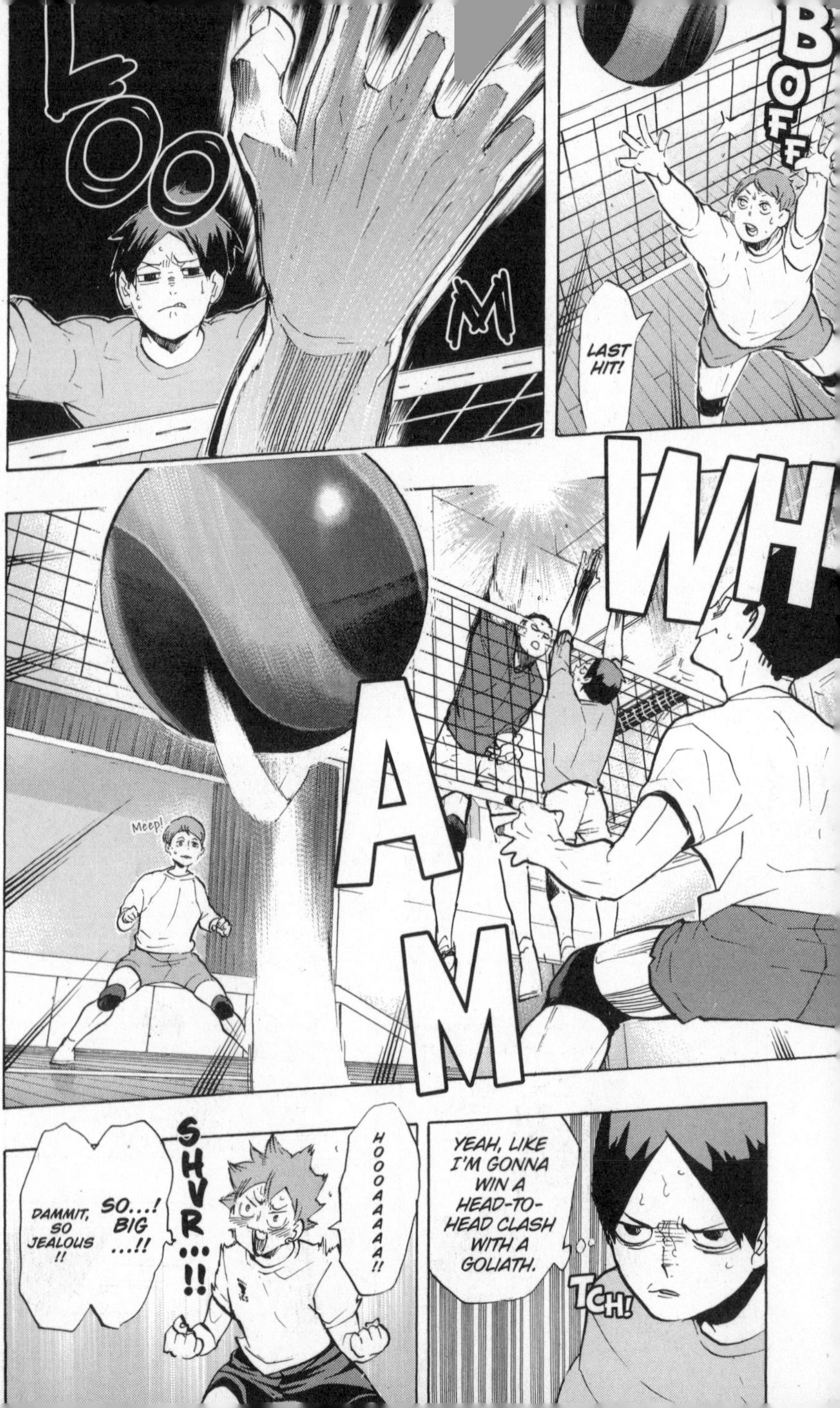
BOFF
LAST HIT!
LOOOM
WHAM
Meep!
YEAH, LIKE I'M GONNA WIN A HEAD-TO-HEAD CLASH WITH A GOLIATH.
TCH!
HOOOAAAAAA!!
SHVR...!!
SO...! BIG ...!!
DAMMIT, SO JEALOUS !!

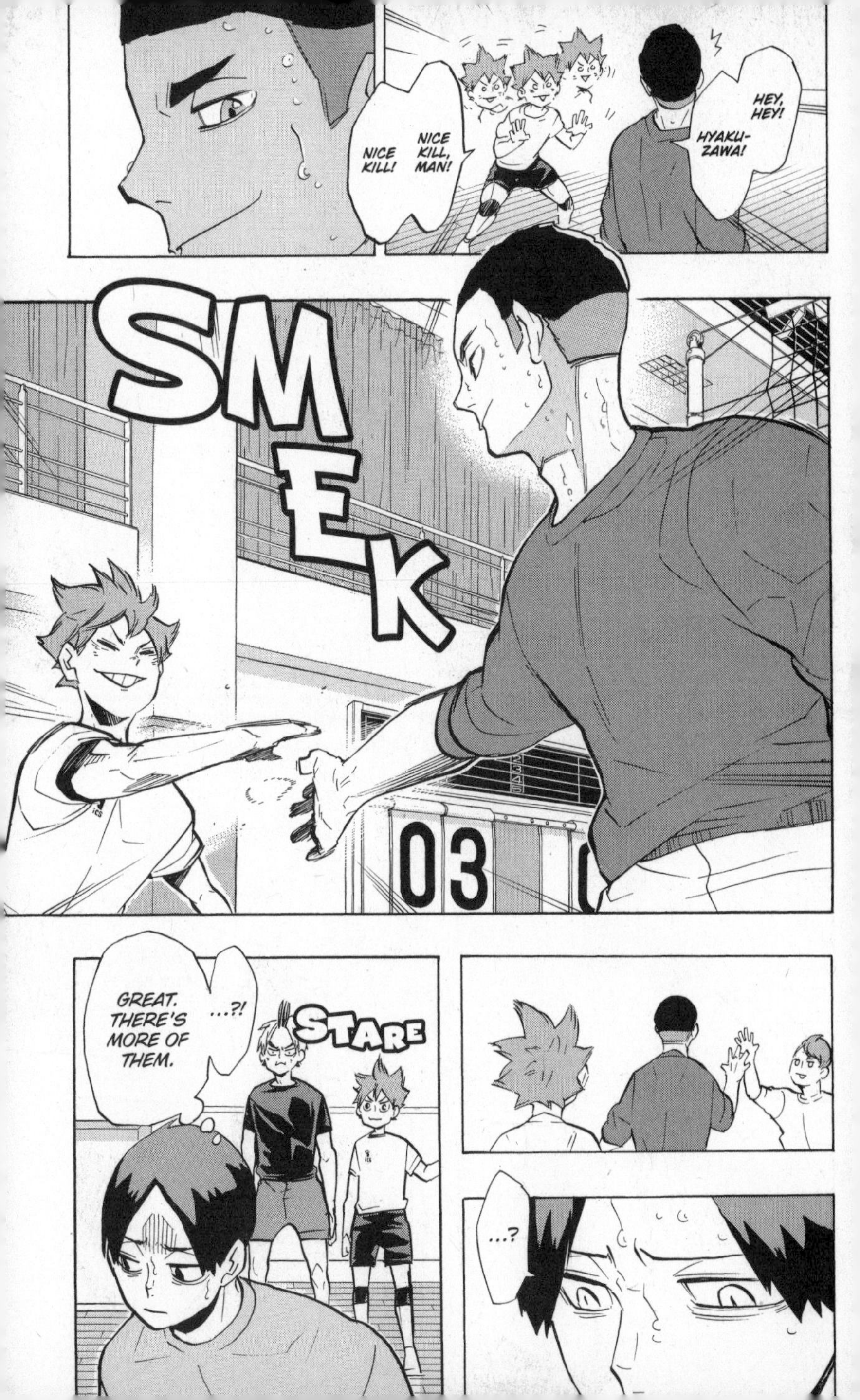
HEY, HEY! HYAKU-ZAWA!
NICE KILL, MAN! NICE KILL!
SMEK
...?
STARE
...?!
GREAT. THERE'S MORE OF THEM.

AKIRA KUNIMI (15)

LEAST FAVORITE PHRASE #1

"SO PITIFUL!"

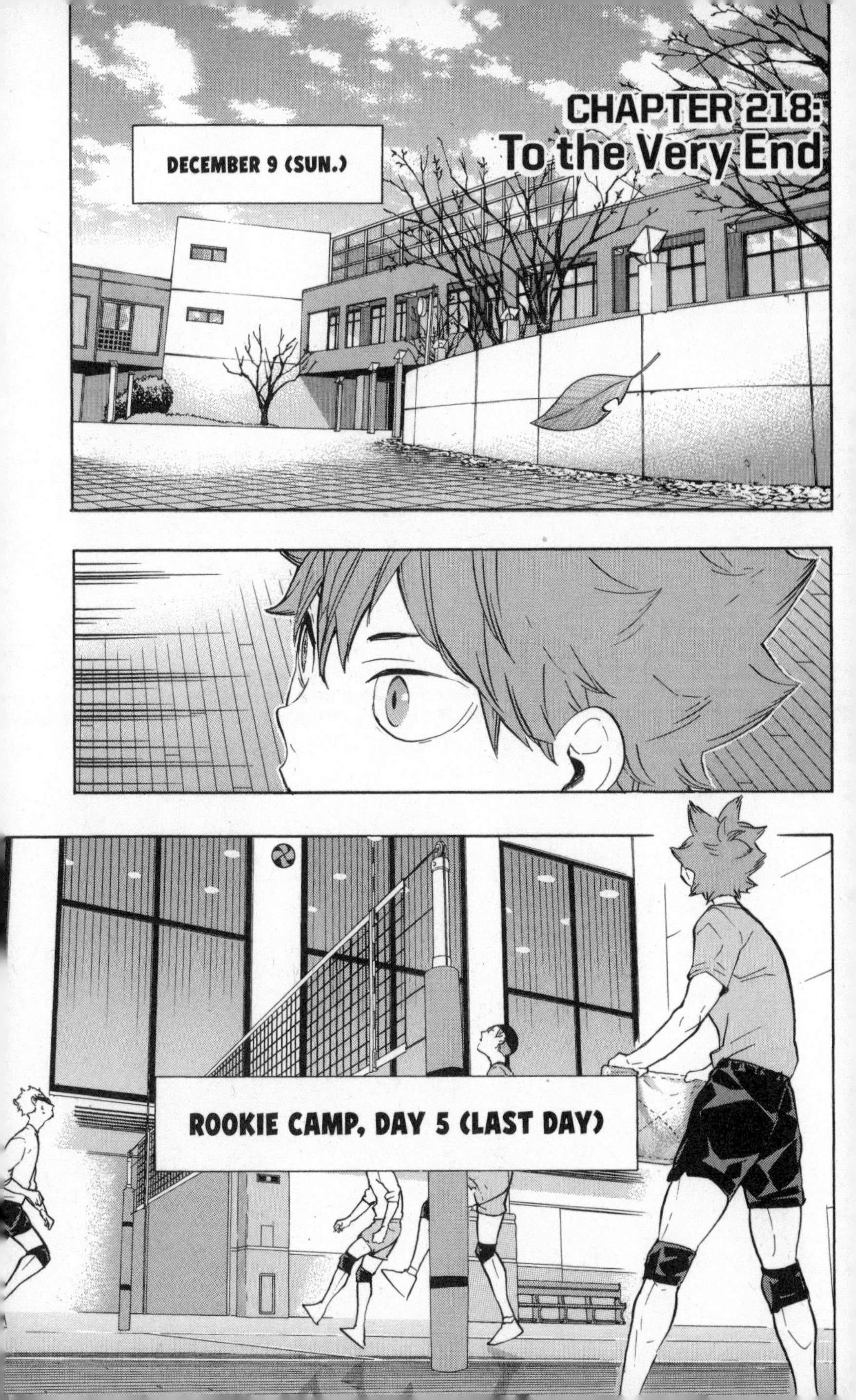
CHAPTER 218:
To the Very End
DECEMBER 9 (SUN.)
ROOKIE CAMP, DAY 5 (LAST DAY)

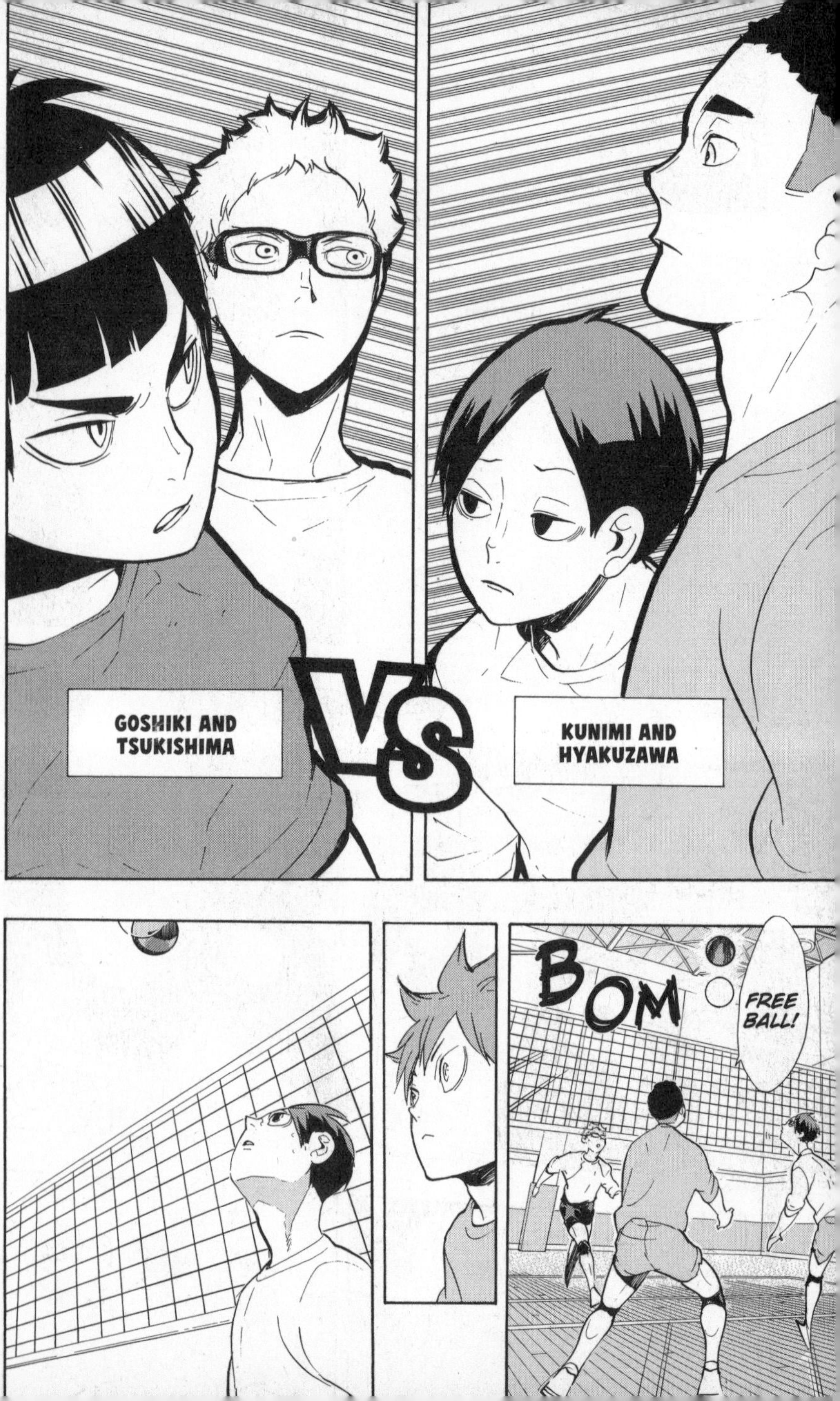
KUNIMI AND HYAKUZAWA
VS
GOSHIKI AND TSUKISHIMA
BOM
FREE BALL!

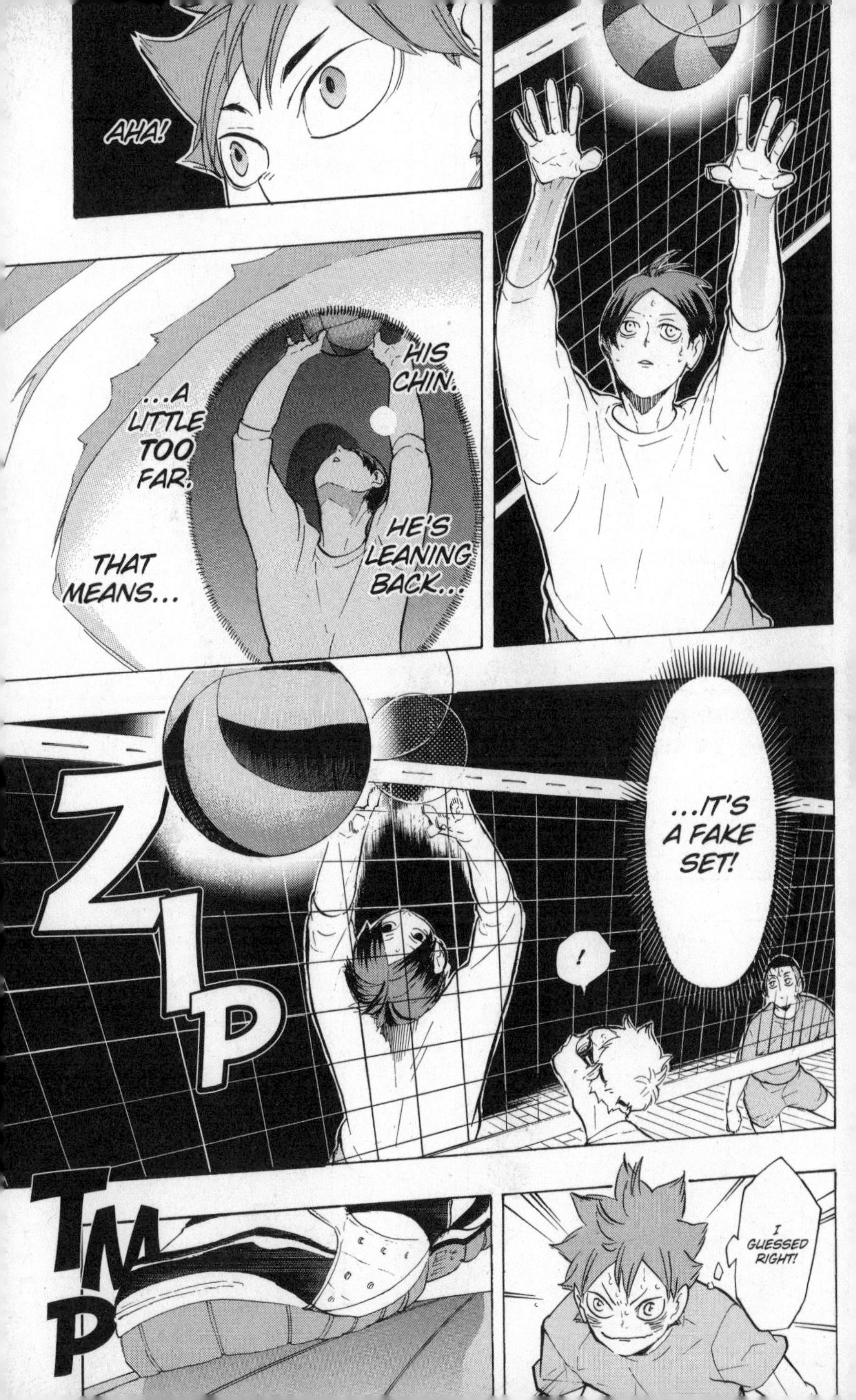
AHA!
HIS CHIN.
HE'S LEANING BACK...
...A LITTLE TOO FAR.
THAT MEANS...
...IT'S A FAKE SET!
!
ZIP
I GUESSED RIGHT!
TMP

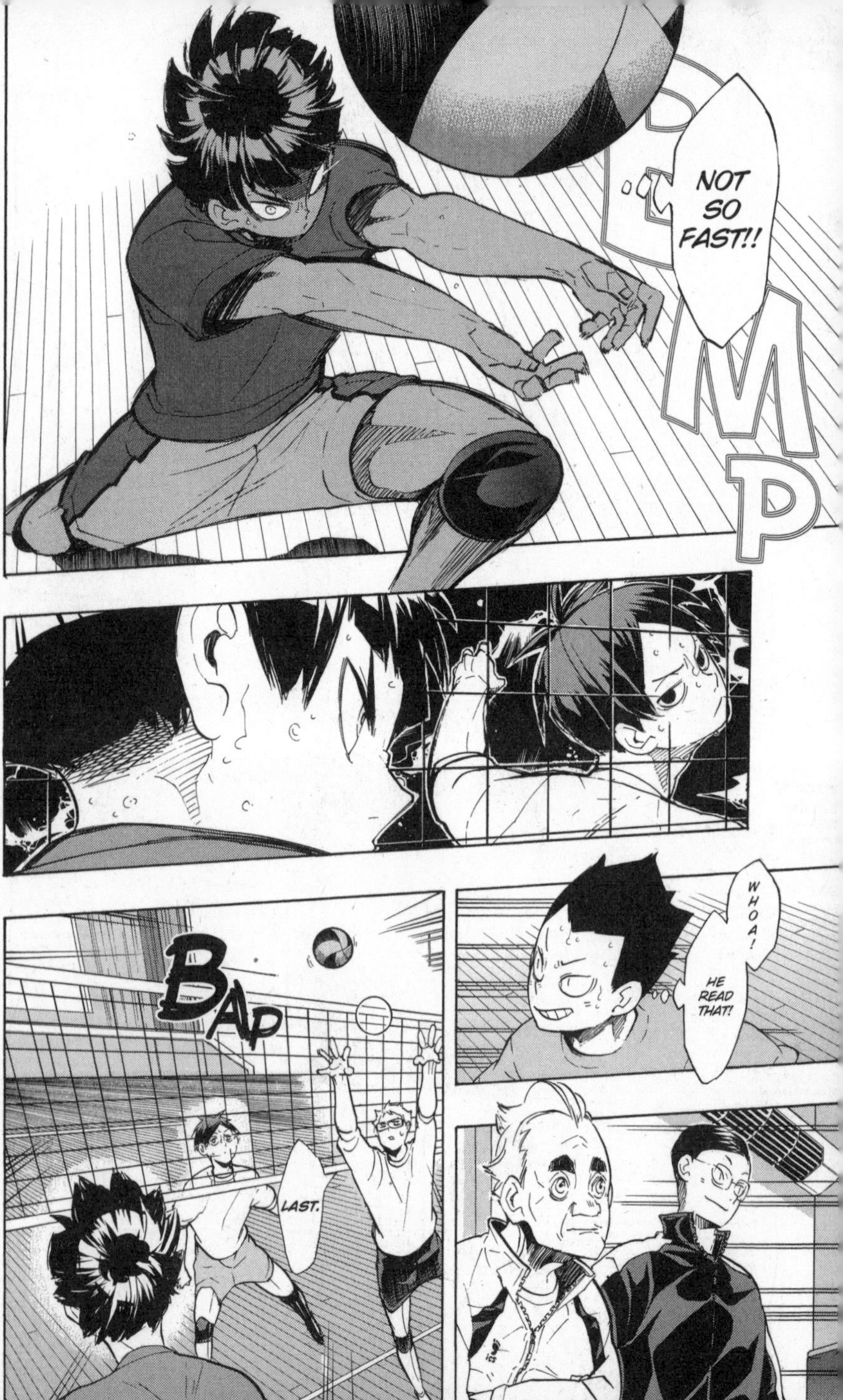
NOT SO FAST!!
WHOA!
HE READ THAT!
BAP
LAST.

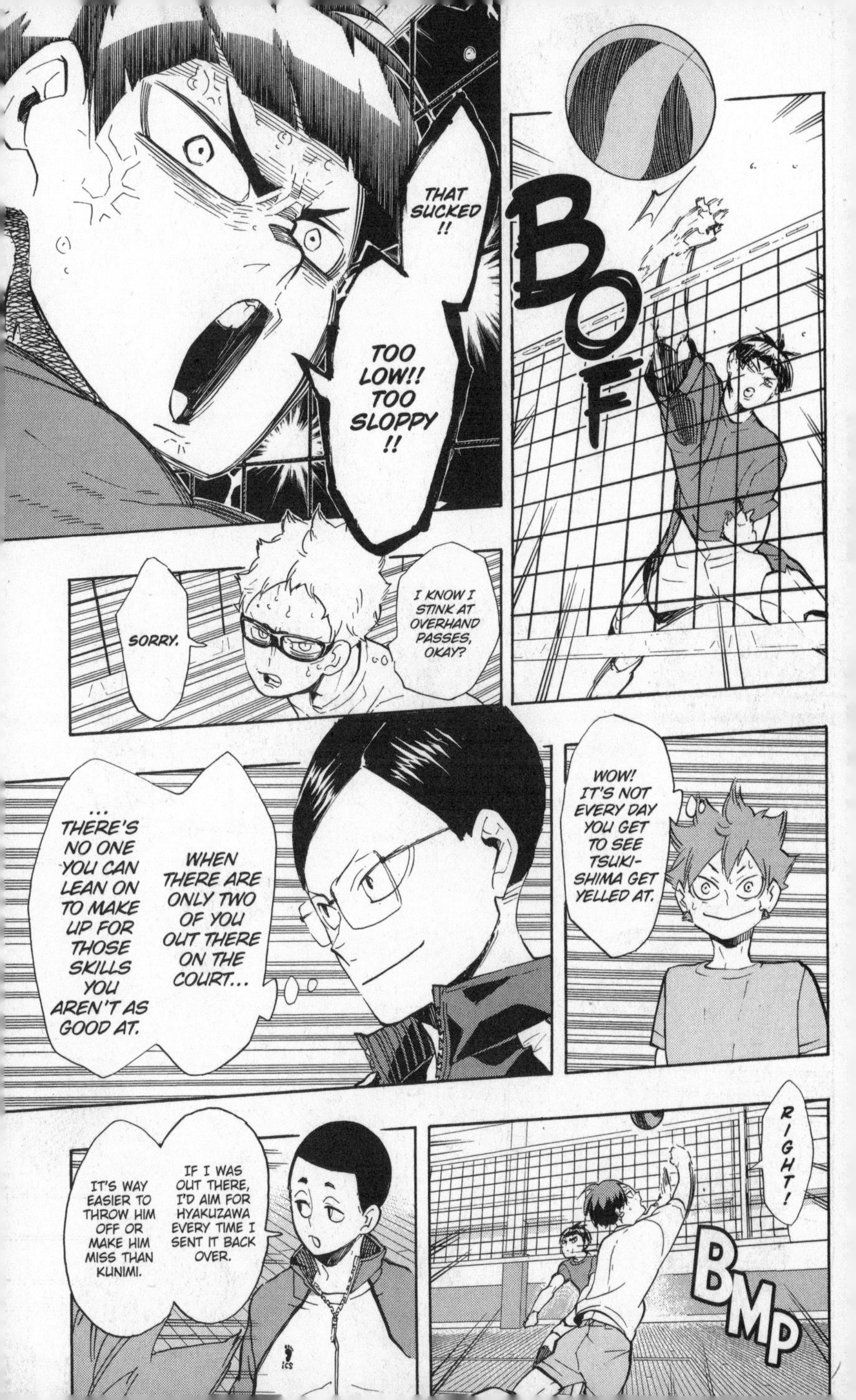
BOF
THAT SUCKED!!
TOO LOW!! TOO SLOPPY!!
I KNOW I STINK AT OVERHAND PASSES, OKAY?
SORRY.
WOW! IT'S NOT EVERY DAY YOU GET TO SEE TSUKISHIMA GET YELLED AT.
WHEN THERE ARE ONLY TWO OF YOU OUT THERE ON THE COURT...
... THERE'S NO ONE YOU CAN LEAN ON TO MAKE UP FOR THOSE SKILLS YOU AREN'T AS GOOD AT.
RIGHT!
BMP
IF I WAS OUT THERE, I'D AIM FOR HYAKUZAWA EVERY TIME I SENT IT BACK OVER.
IT'S WAY EASIER TO THROW HIM OFF OR MAKE HIM MISS THAN KUNIMI.

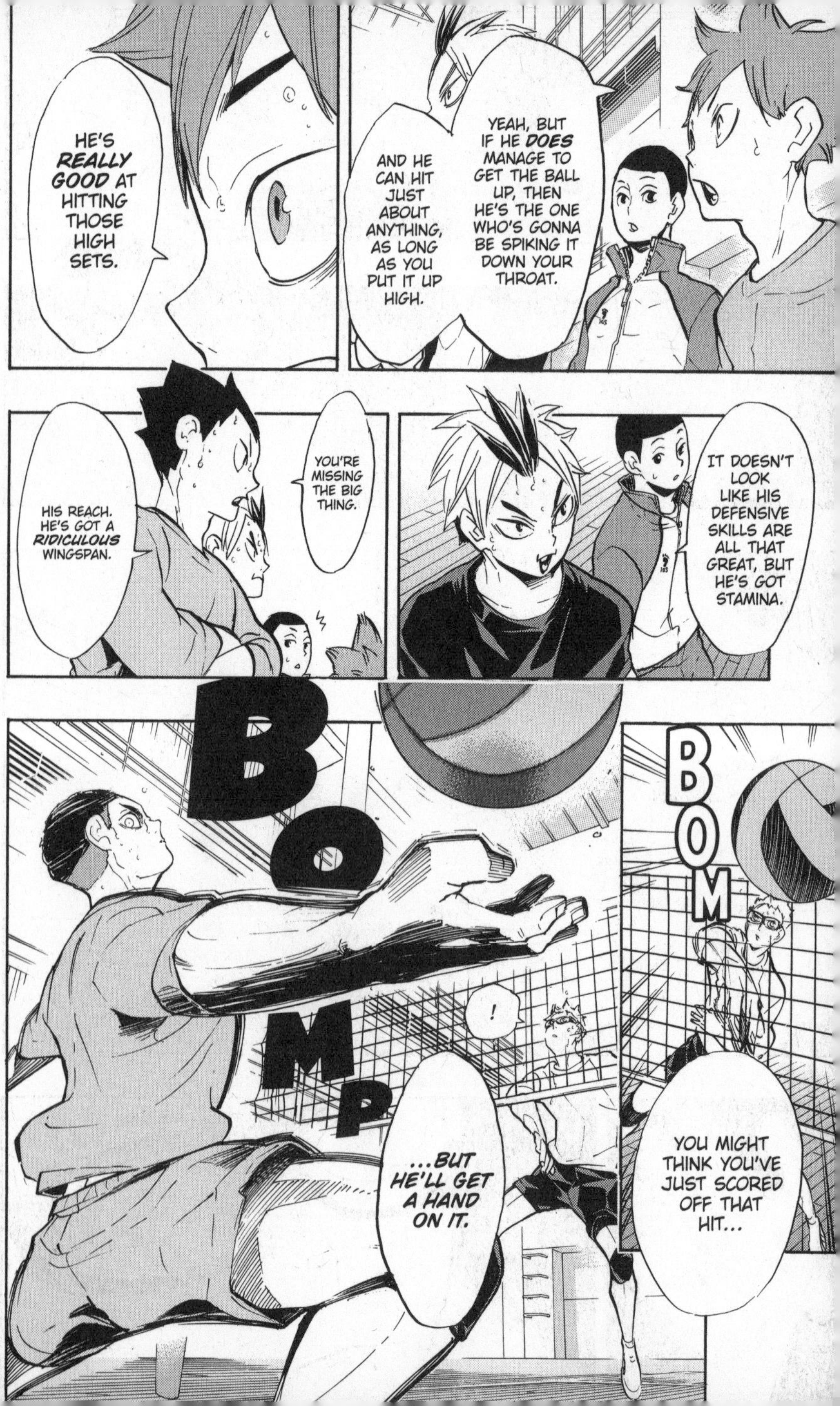
YEAH, BUT IF HE DOES MANAGE TO GET THE BALL UP, THEN HE'S THE ONE WHO'S GONNA BE SPIKING IT DOWN YOUR THROAT.
AND HE CAN HIT JUST ABOUT ANYTHING, AS LONG AS YOU PUT IT UP HIGH.
HE'S REALLY GOOD AT HITTING THOSE HIGH SETS.
IT DOESN'T LOOK LIKE HIS DEFENSIVE SKILLS ARE ALL THAT GREAT, BUT HE'S GOT STAMINA.
YOU'RE MISSING THE BIG THING.
HIS REACH. HE'S GOT A RIDICULOUS WINGSPAN.
BOM
YOU MIGHT THINK YOU'VE JUST SCORED OFF THAT HIT...
BOMP
!
...BUT HE'LL GET A HAND ON IT.

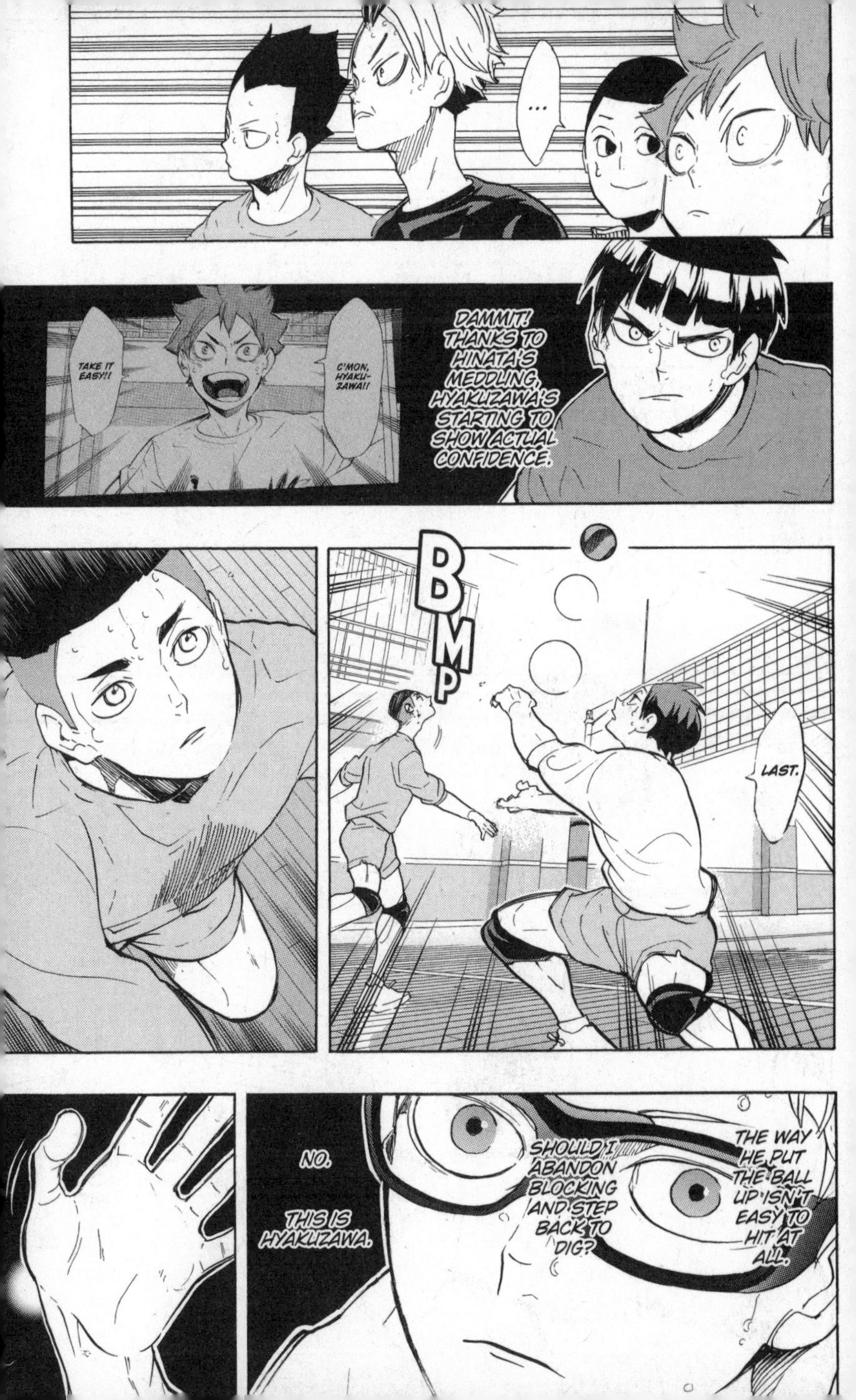
...
DAMMIT! THANKS TO HINATA'S MEDDLING, HYAKUZAWA'S STARTING TO SHOW ACTUAL CONFIDENCE.
C'MON, HYAKU-ZAWA!!
TAKE IT EASY!!
BUMP
LAST.
THE WAY HE PUT THE BALL UP ISN'T EASY TO HIT AT ALL.
SHOULD I ABANDON BLOCKING AND STEP BACK TO DIG?
NO.
THIS IS HYAKUZAWA.

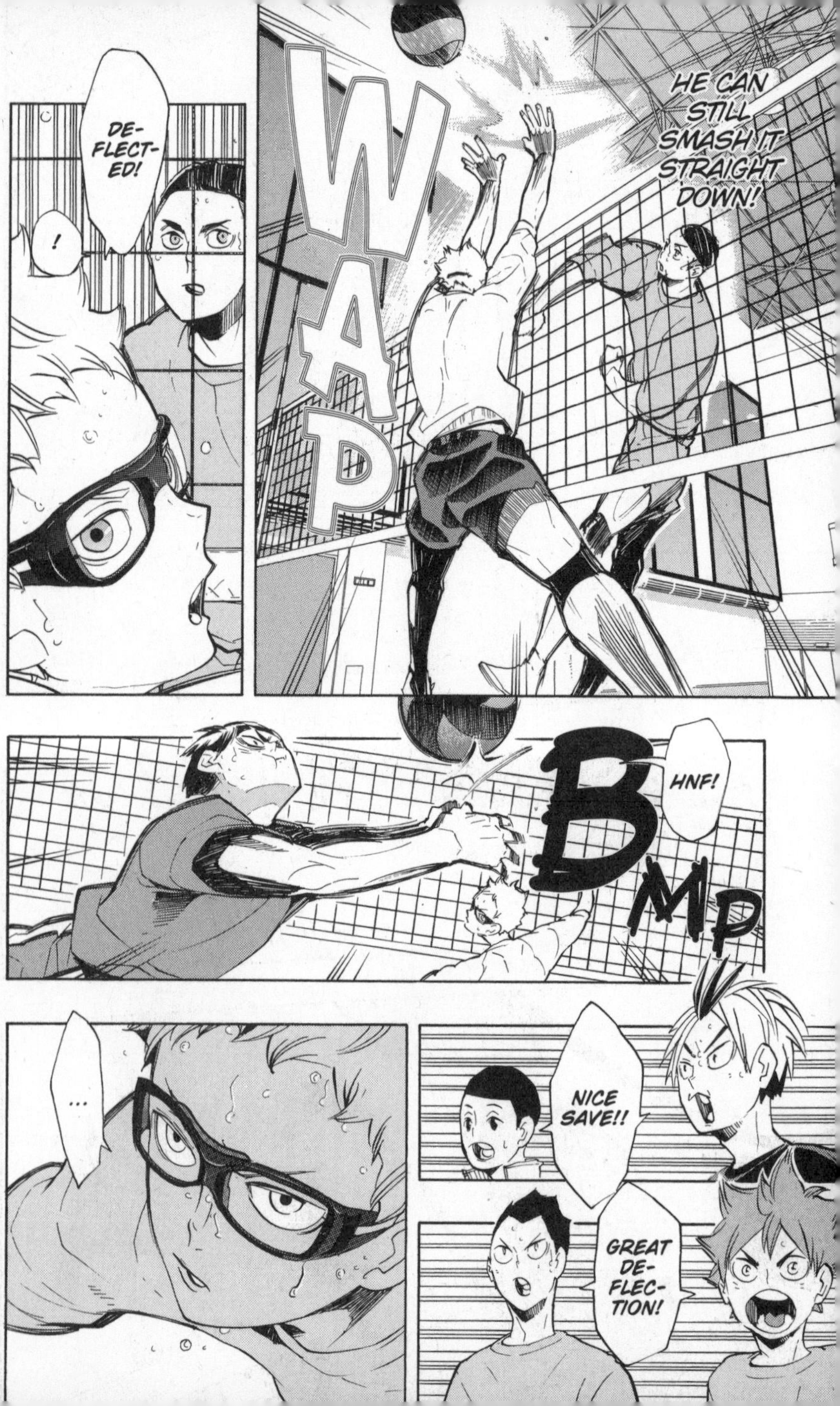
HE CAN STILL SMASH IT STRAIGHT DOWN!
WAP
DE-FLECT-ED!
!
HNF!
BMP
NICE SAVE!!
GREAT DE-FLEC-TION!
...

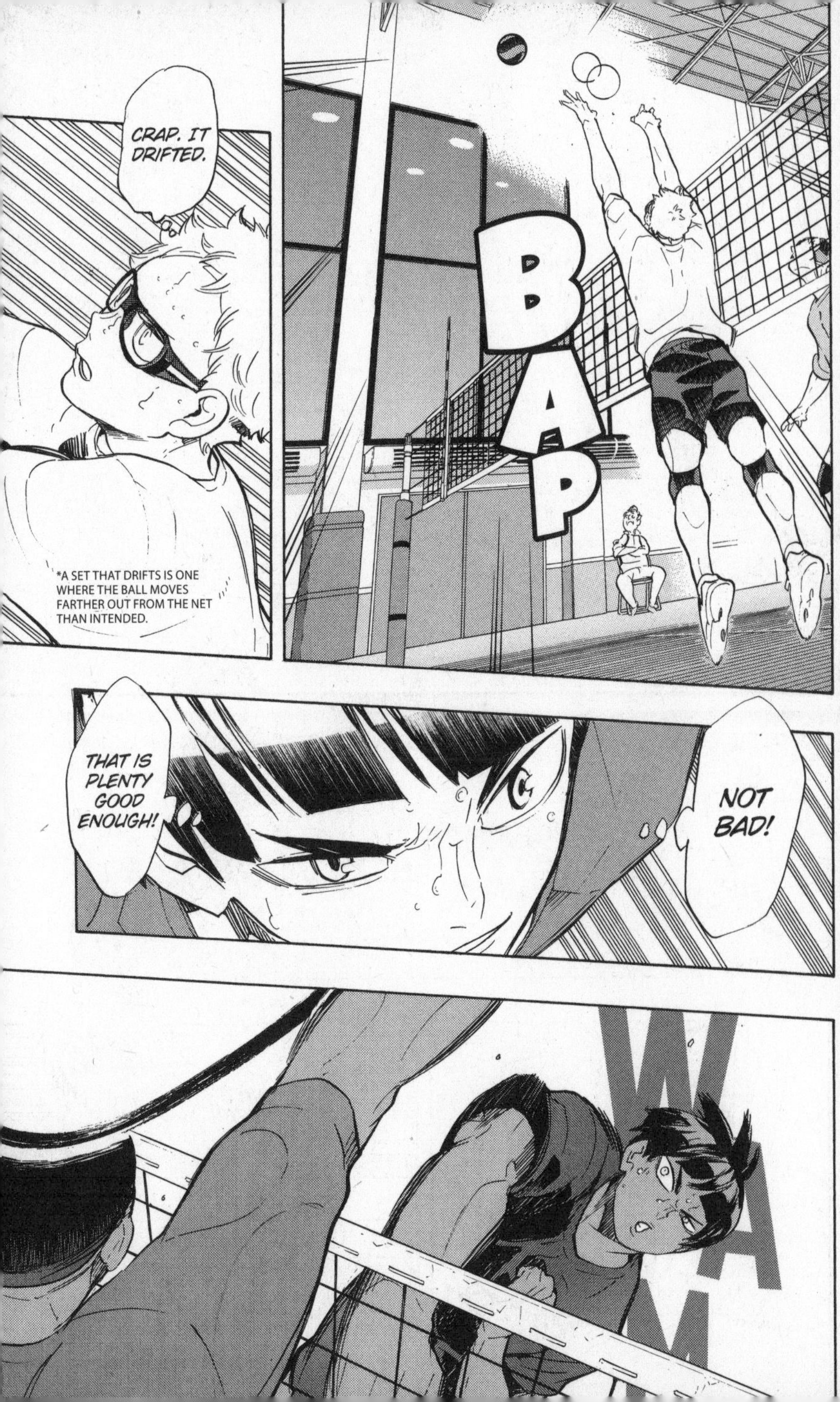
BAP
CRAP. IT DRIFTED.
*A SET THAT DRIFTS IS ONE WHERE THE BALL MOVES FARTHER OUT FROM THE NET THAN INTENDED.
NOT BAD!
THAT IS PLENTY GOOD ENOUGH!
WAM

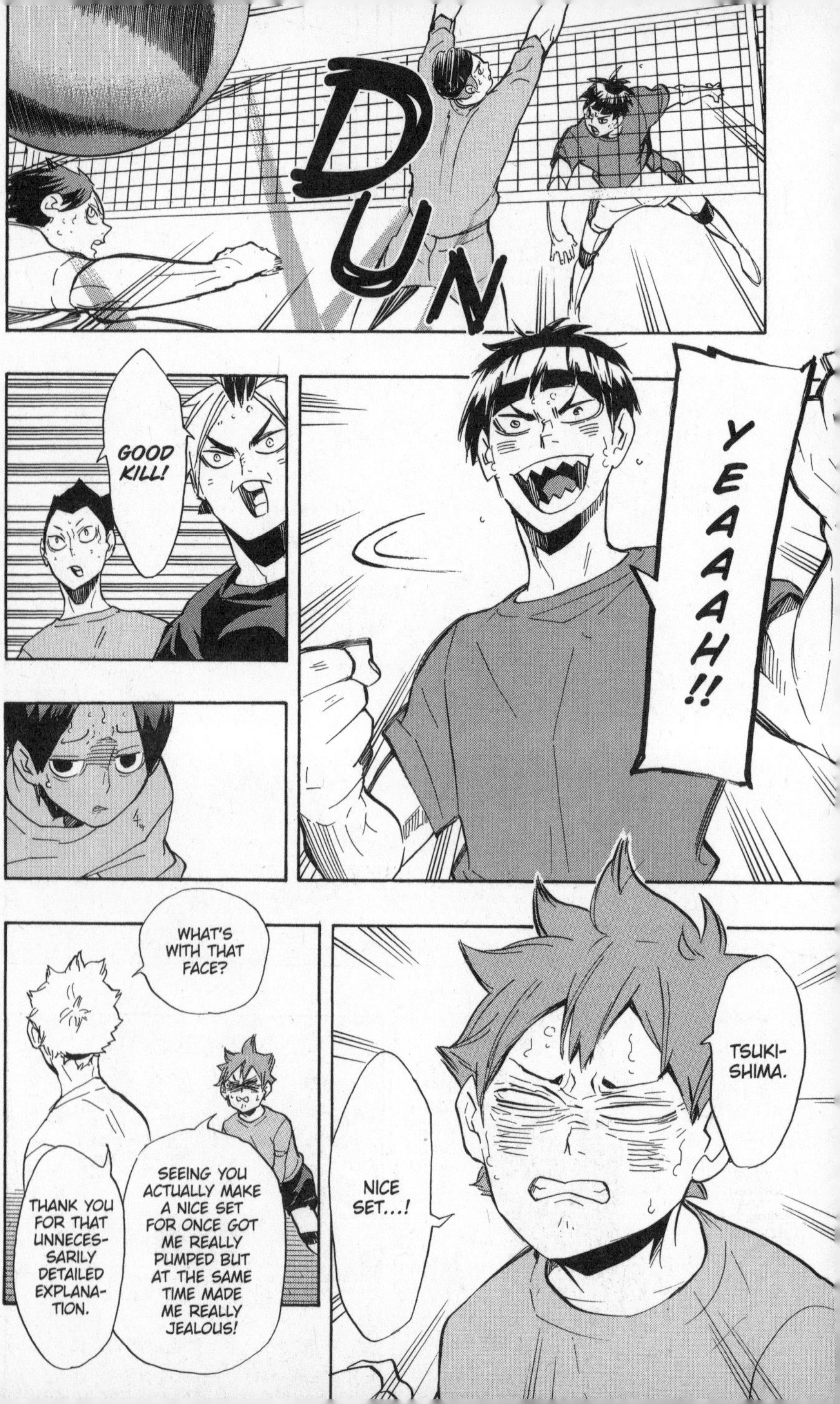
DUN
YEAAAAH!!
GOOD KILL!
TSUKI-SHIMA.
NICE SET...!
WHAT'S WITH THAT FACE?
SEEING YOU ACTUALLY MAKE A NICE SET FOR ONCE GOT ME REALLY PUMPED BUT AT THE SAME TIME MADE ME REALLY JEALOUS!
THANK YOU FOR THAT UNNECES-SARILY DETAILED EXPLANA-TION.

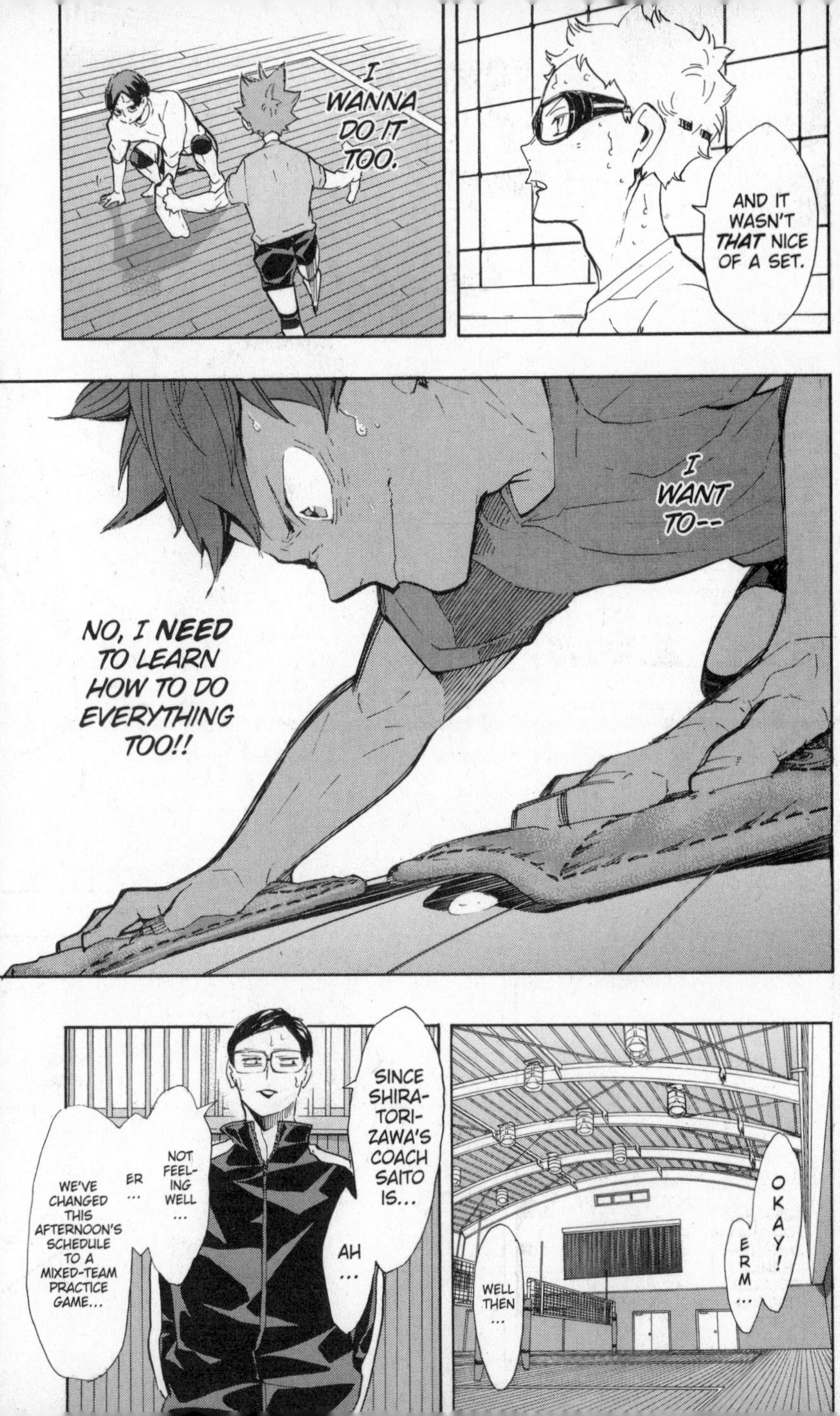
AND IT WASN'T *THAT* NICE OF A SET.
I WANNA DO IT TOO.
I WANT TO--
NO, I **NEED** TO LEARN HOW TO DO EVERYTHING TOO!!
OKAY!
ERM...
WELL THEN...
SINCE SHIRATORIZAWA'S COACH SAITO IS...
AH...
NOT FEELING WELL...
ER...
WE'VE CHANGED THIS AFTERNOON'S SCHEDULE TO A MIXED-TEAM PRACTICE GAME...

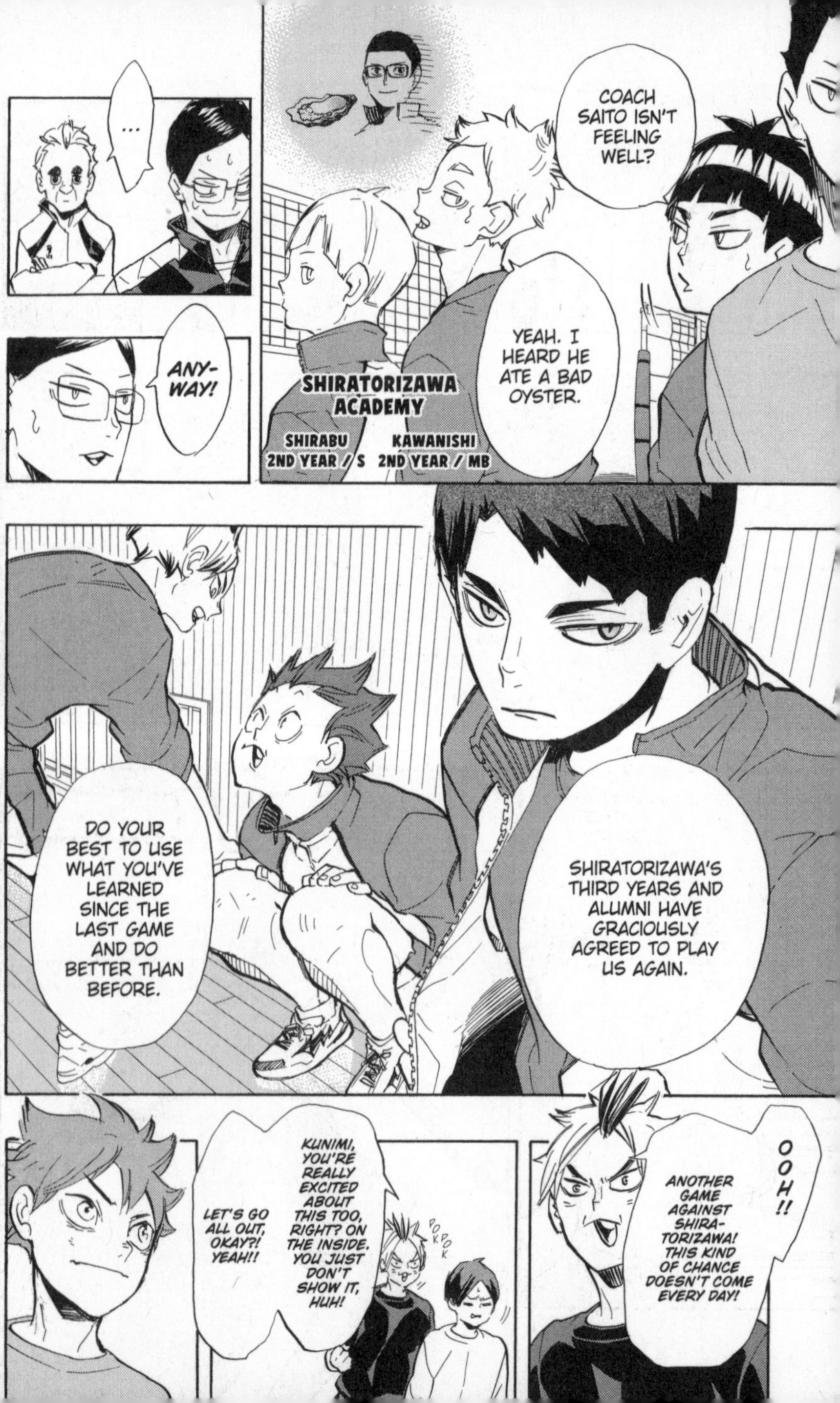
COACH SAITO ISN'T FEELING WELL?
YEAH. I HEARD HE ATE A BAD OYSTER.
SHIRATORIZAWA ACADEMY
KAWANISHI 2ND YEAR / MB
SHIRABU 2ND YEAR / S
...
ANY-WAY!
SHIRATORIZAWA'S THIRD YEARS AND ALUMNI HAVE GRACIOUSLY AGREED TO PLAY US AGAIN.
DO YOUR BEST TO USE WHAT YOU'VE LEARNED SINCE THE LAST GAME AND DO BETTER THAN BEFORE.
OOOH!!
ANOTHER GAME AGAINST SHIRA-TORIZAWA! THIS KIND OF CHANCE DOESN'T COME EVERY DAY!
KUNIMI, YOU'RE REALLY EXCITED ABOUT THIS TOO, RIGHT? ON THE INSIDE. YOU JUST DON'T SHOW IT, HUH!
POK POK
LET'S GO ALL OUT, OKAY?! YEAH!!

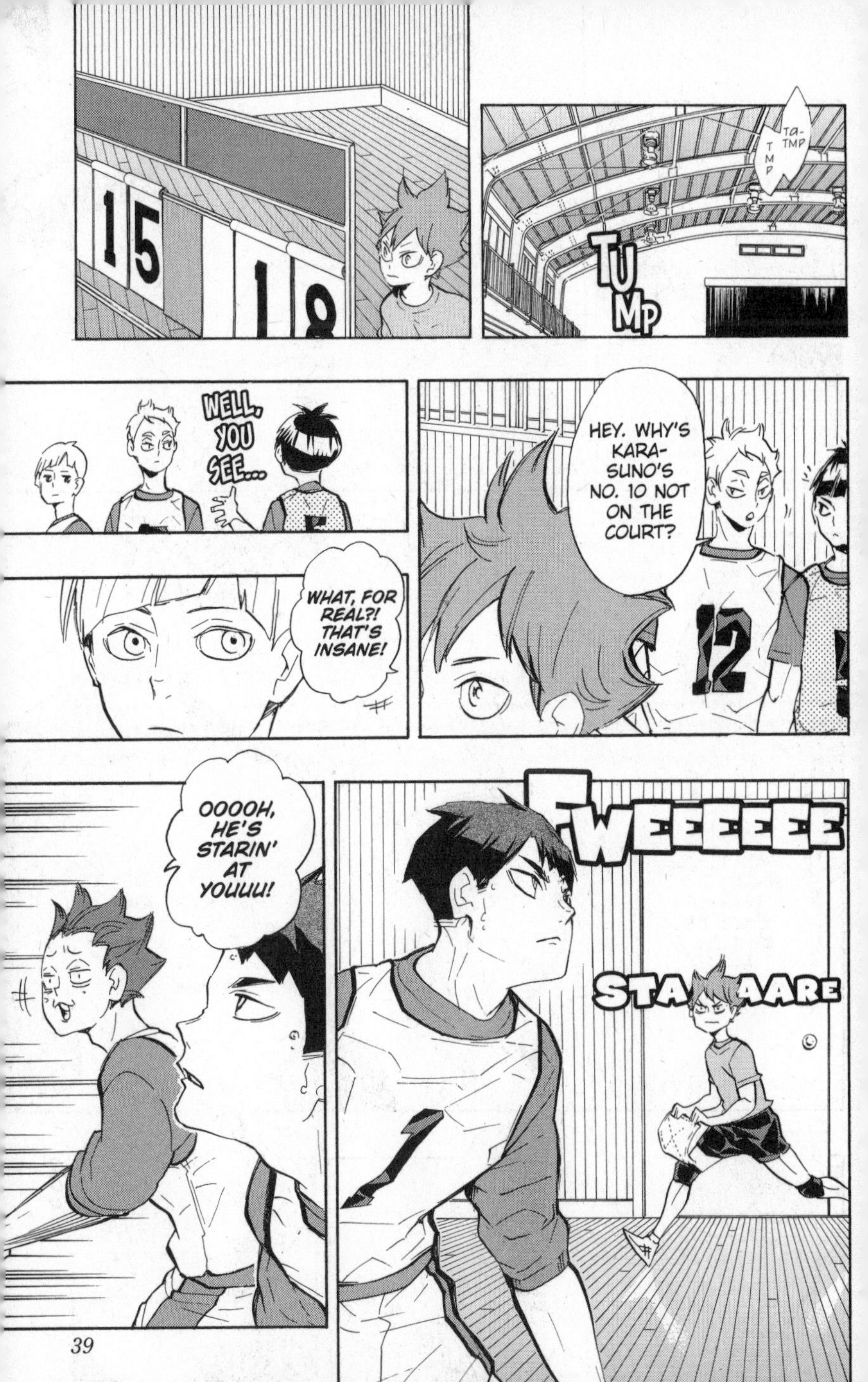
TA-TMP
TMP
TUMP
HEY. WHY'S KARASUNO'S NO. 10 NOT ON THE COURT?
WELL, YOU SEE...
WHAT, FOR REAL?! THAT'S INSANE!
FWEEEEEE
STA AARE
OOOOH, HE'S STARIN' AT YOUUU!

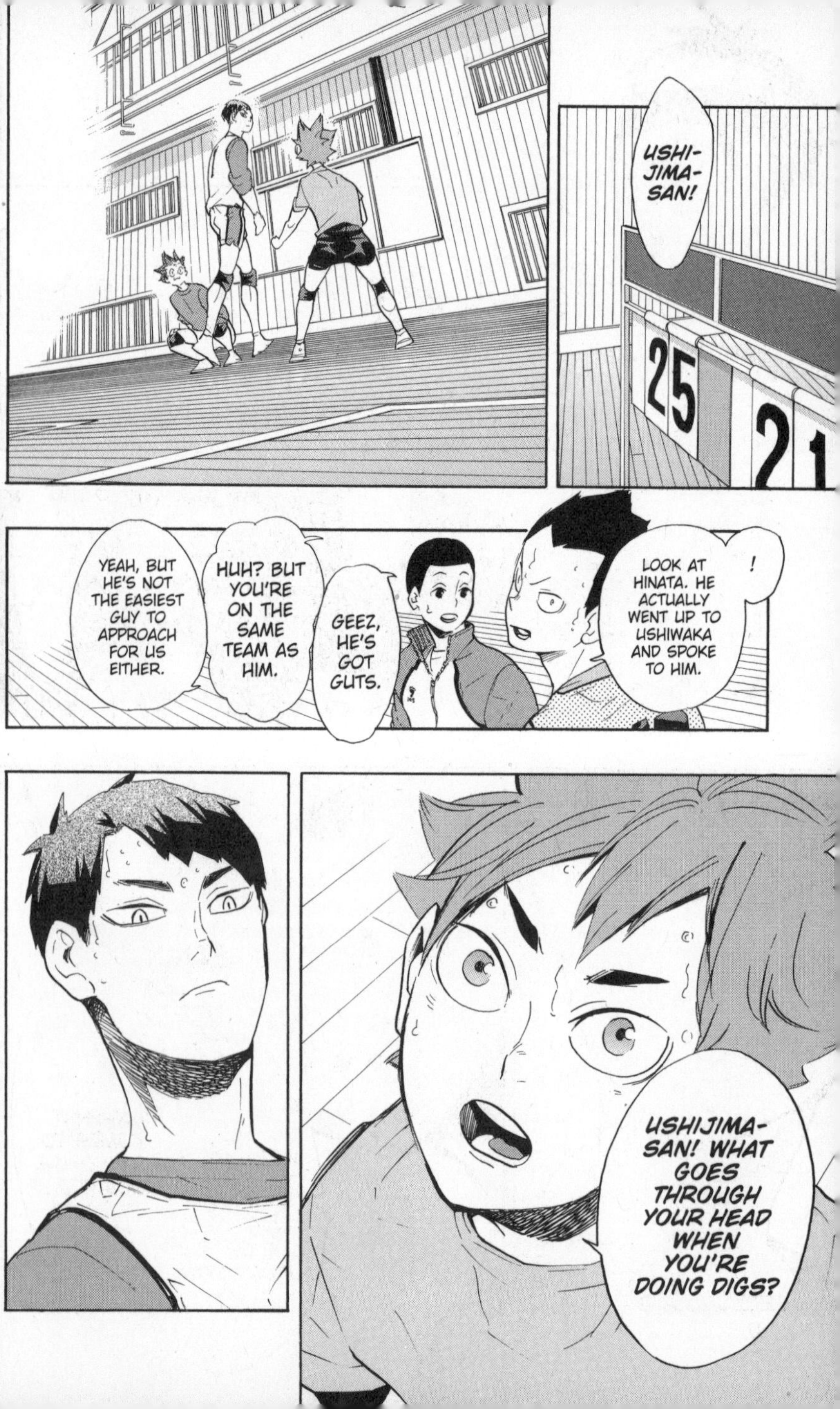
USHI-JIMA-SAN!
25
21
!
LOOK AT HINATA. HE ACTUALLY WENT UP TO USHIWAKA AND SPOKE TO HIM.
GEEZ, HE'S GOT GUTS.
HUH? BUT YOU'RE ON THE SAME TEAM AS HIM.
YEAH, BUT HE'S NOT THE EASIEST GUY TO APPROACH FOR US EITHER.
USHIJIMA-SAN! WHAT GOES THROUGH YOUR HEAD WHEN YOU'RE DOING DIGS?

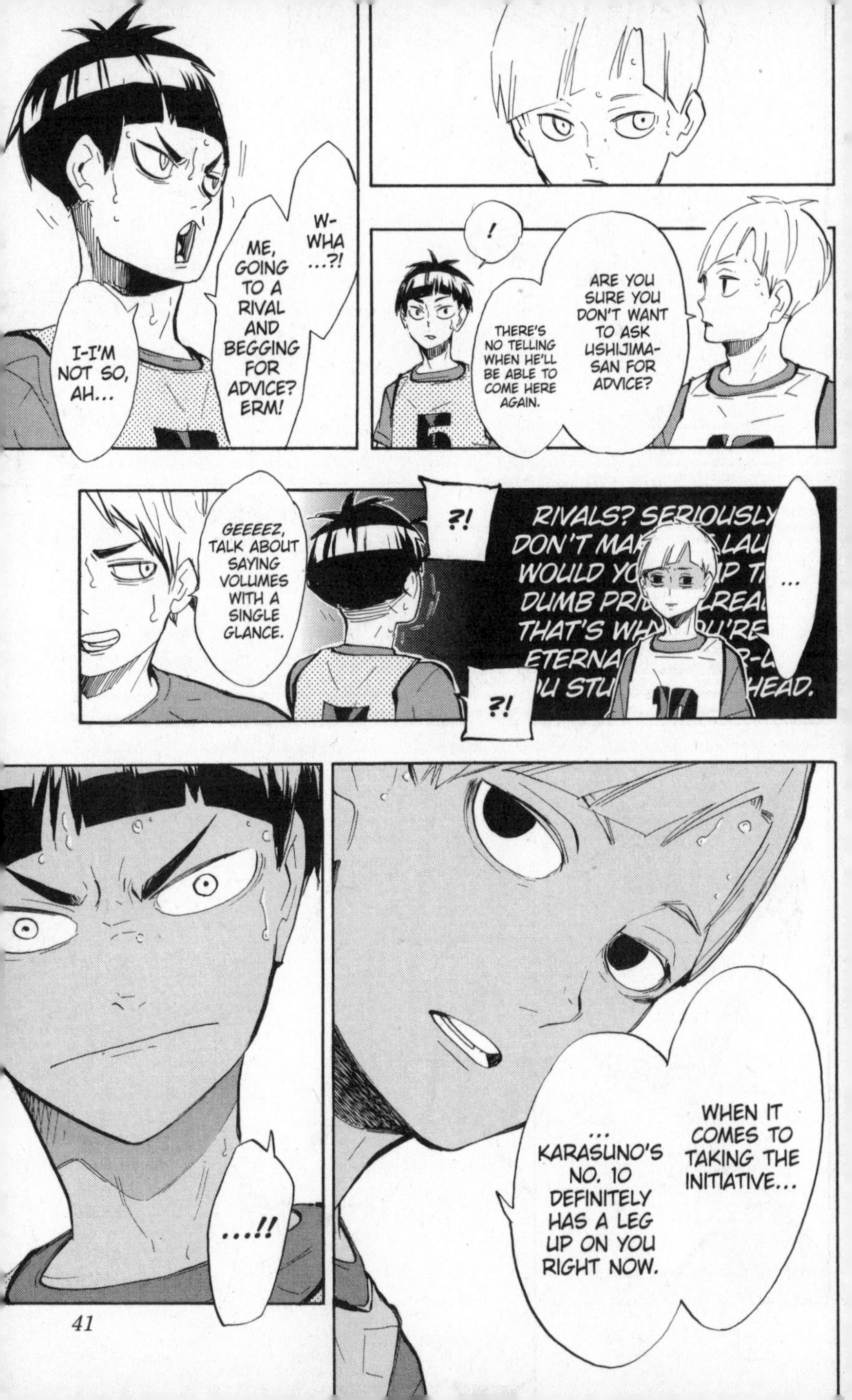
!
ARE YOU SURE YOU DON'T WANT TO ASK USHIJIMA-SAN FOR ADVICE?
THERE'S NO TELLING WHEN HE'LL BE ABLE TO COME HERE AGAIN.
W-WHA ...?!
ME, GOING TO A RIVAL AND BEGGING FOR ADVICE? ERM!
I-I'M NOT SO, AH...
...
RIVALS? SERIOUSLY
DON'T MA LAU
WOULD YO IP T
DUMB PRI LREA
THAT'S WH OU'RE
ETERNA R-U
OU STU HEAD.
?!
?!
GEEEEZ, TALK ABOUT SAYING VOLUMES WITH A SINGLE GLANCE.
WHEN IT COMES TO TAKING THE INITIATIVE...
... KARASUNO'S NO. 10 DEFINITELY HAS A LEG UP ON YOU RIGHT NOW.
...!!

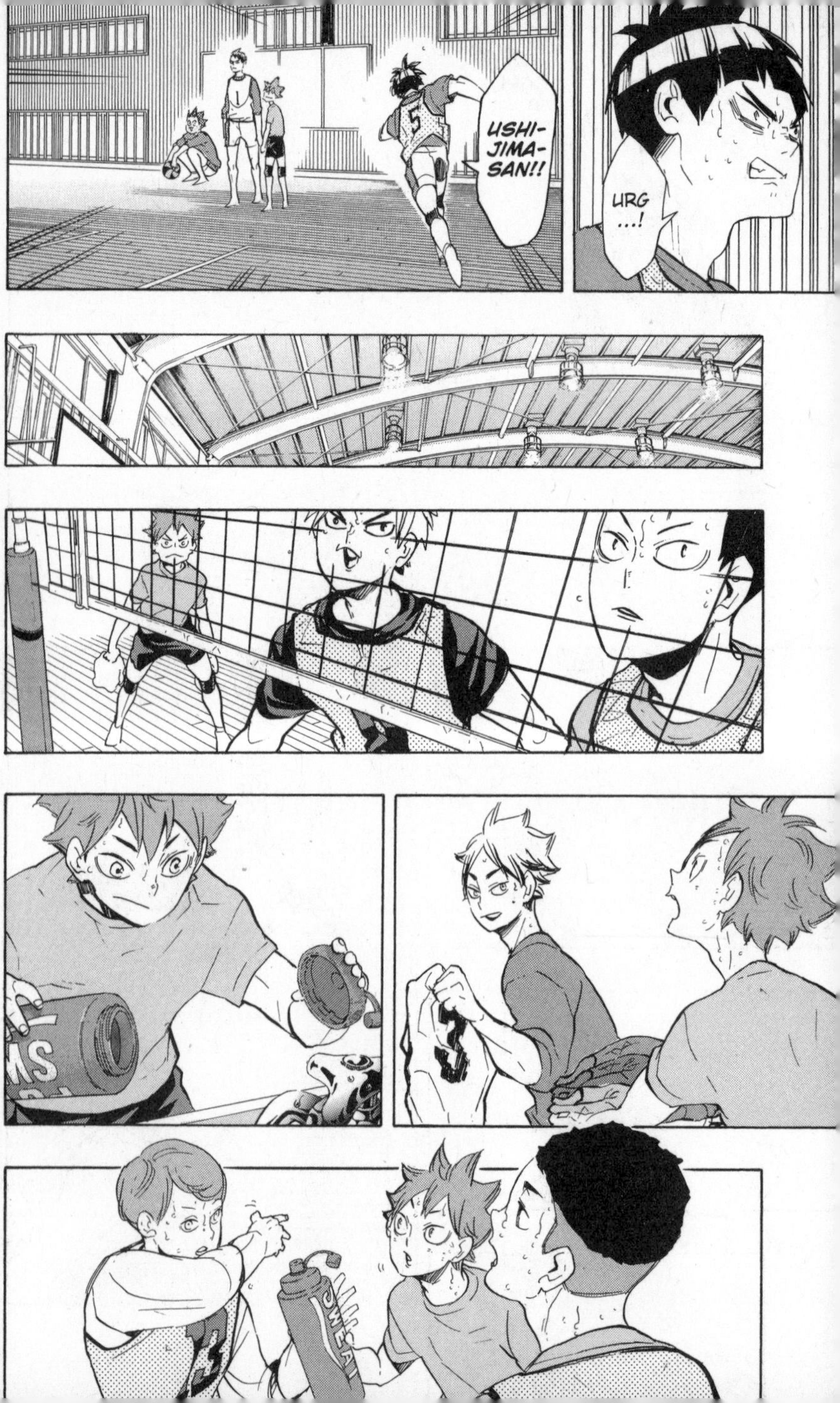
URG ...!
USHI-JIMA-SAN!!

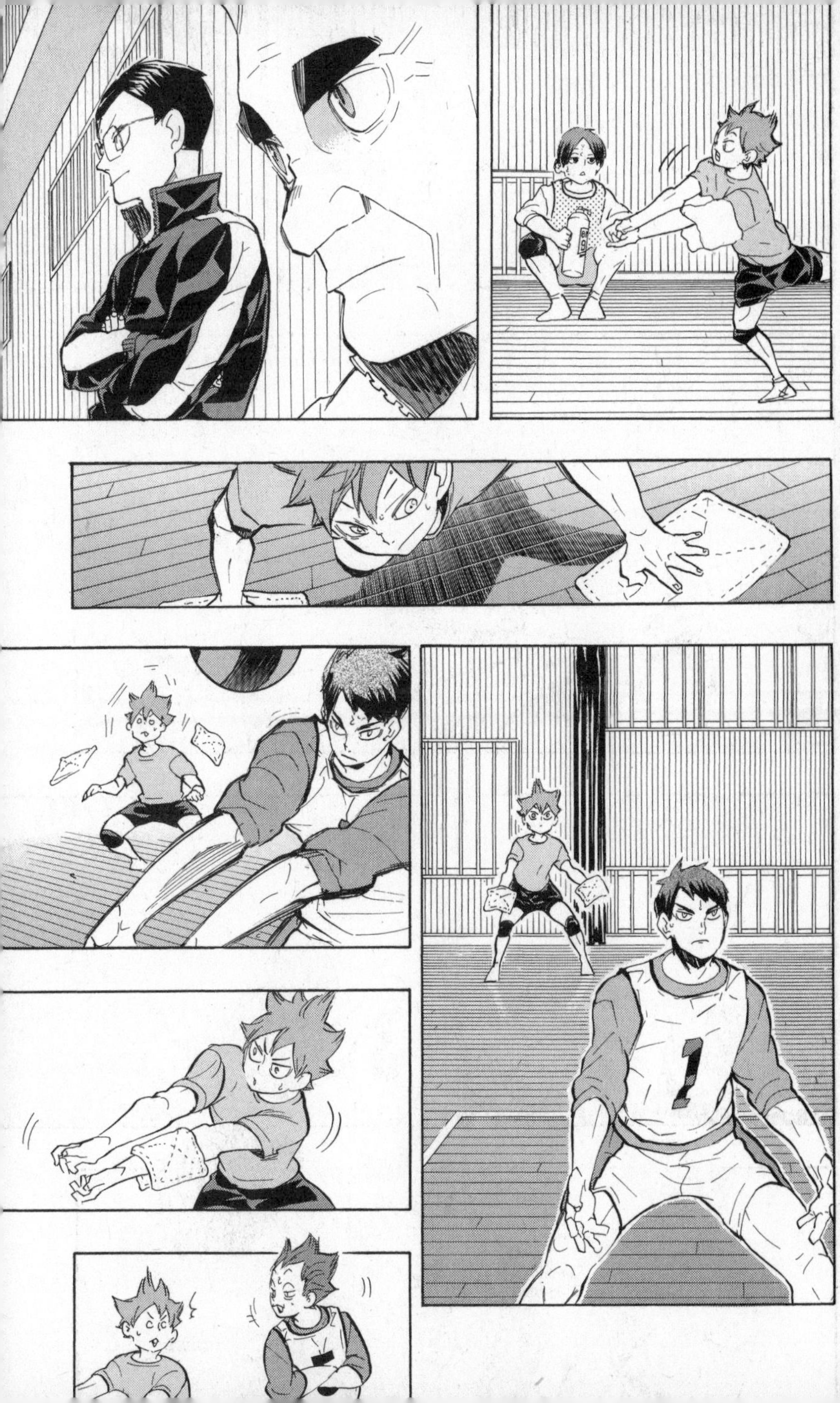

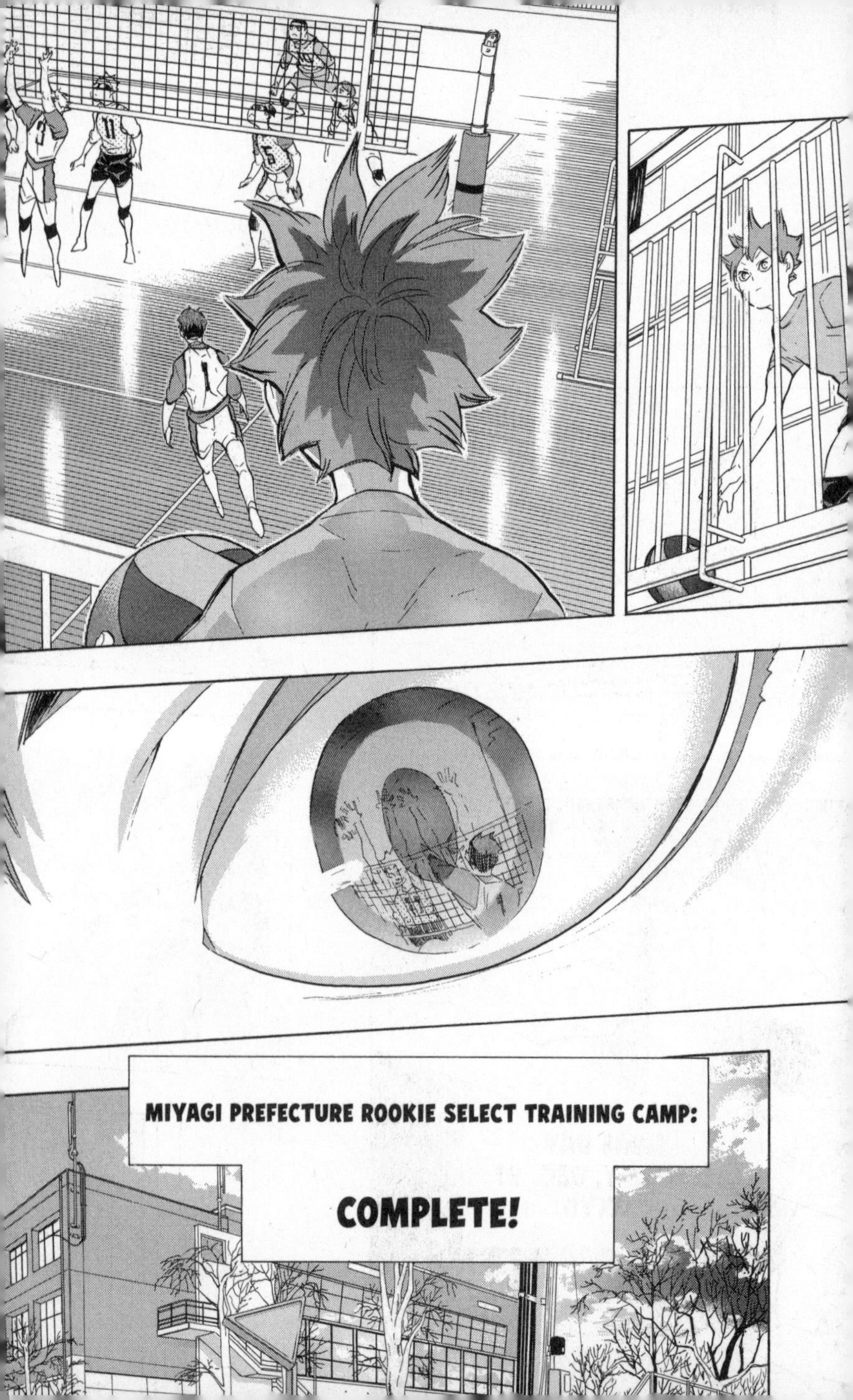
MIYAGI PREFECTURE ROOKIE SELECT TRAINING CAMP:
COMPLETE!

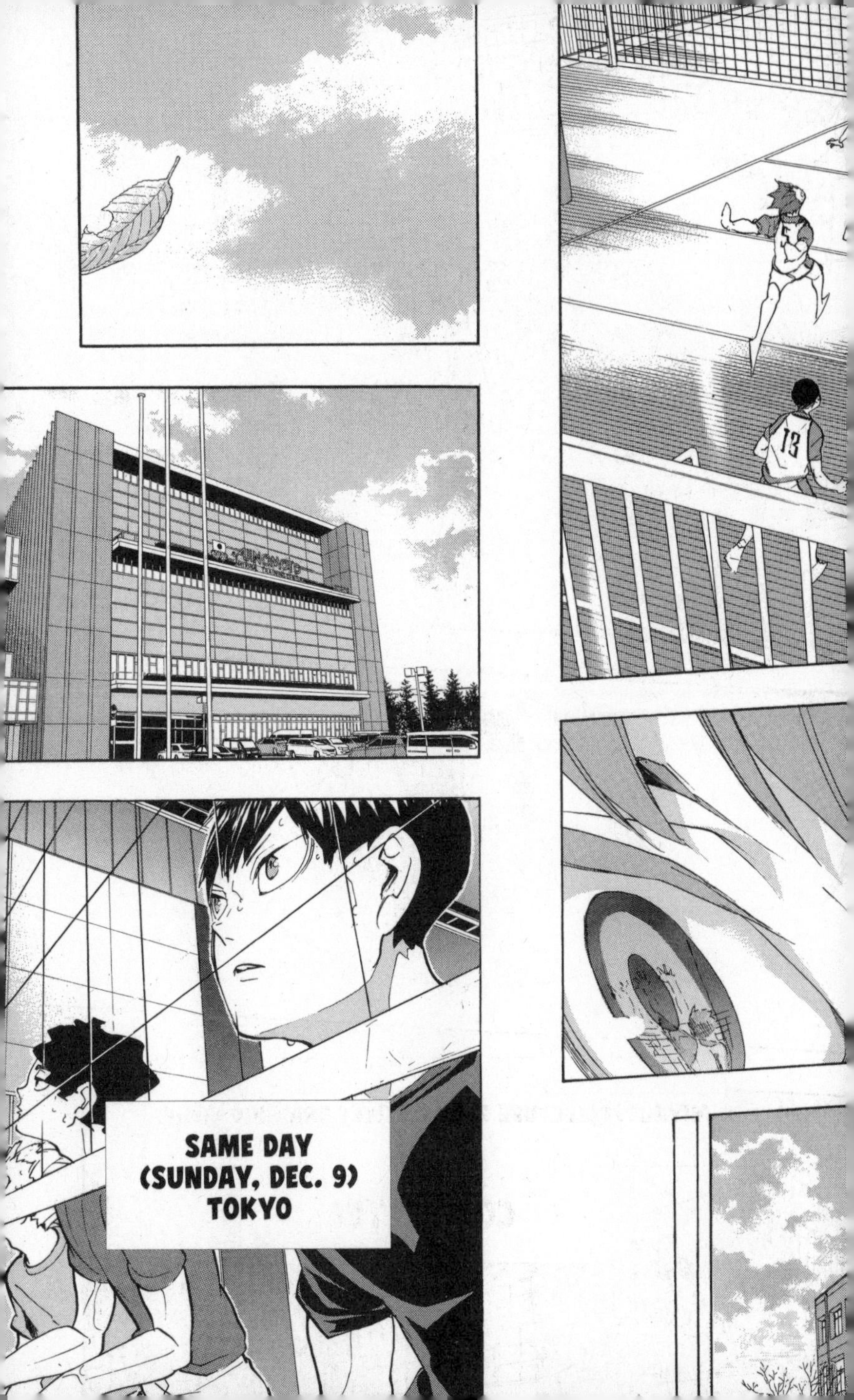
SAME DAY
(SUNDAY, DEC. 9)
TOKYO

CHAPTER 219: Hunger

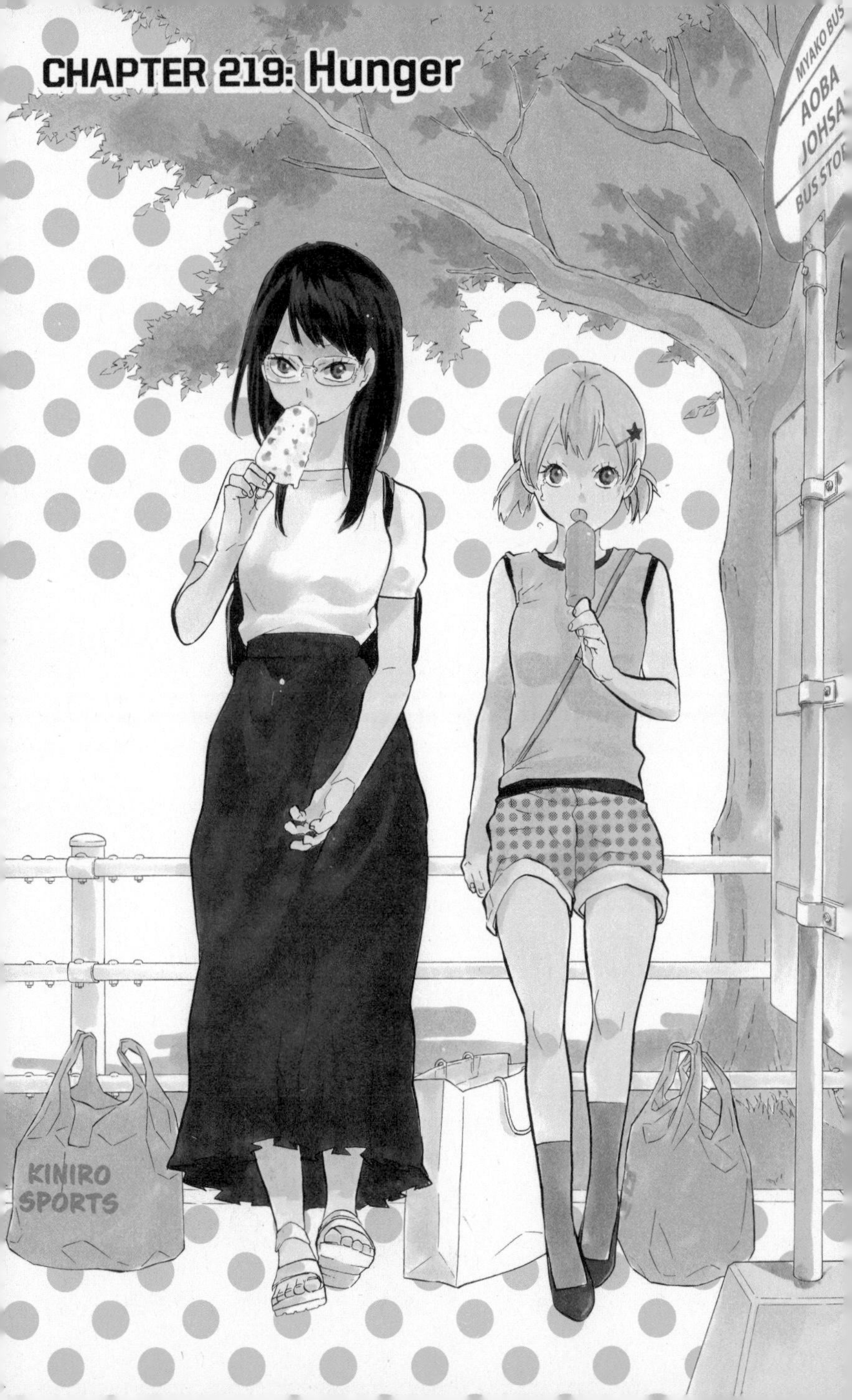
MYAKO BUS
AOBA
JOHSA
BUS STOP
KINIRO SPORTS

HAIKYU!!

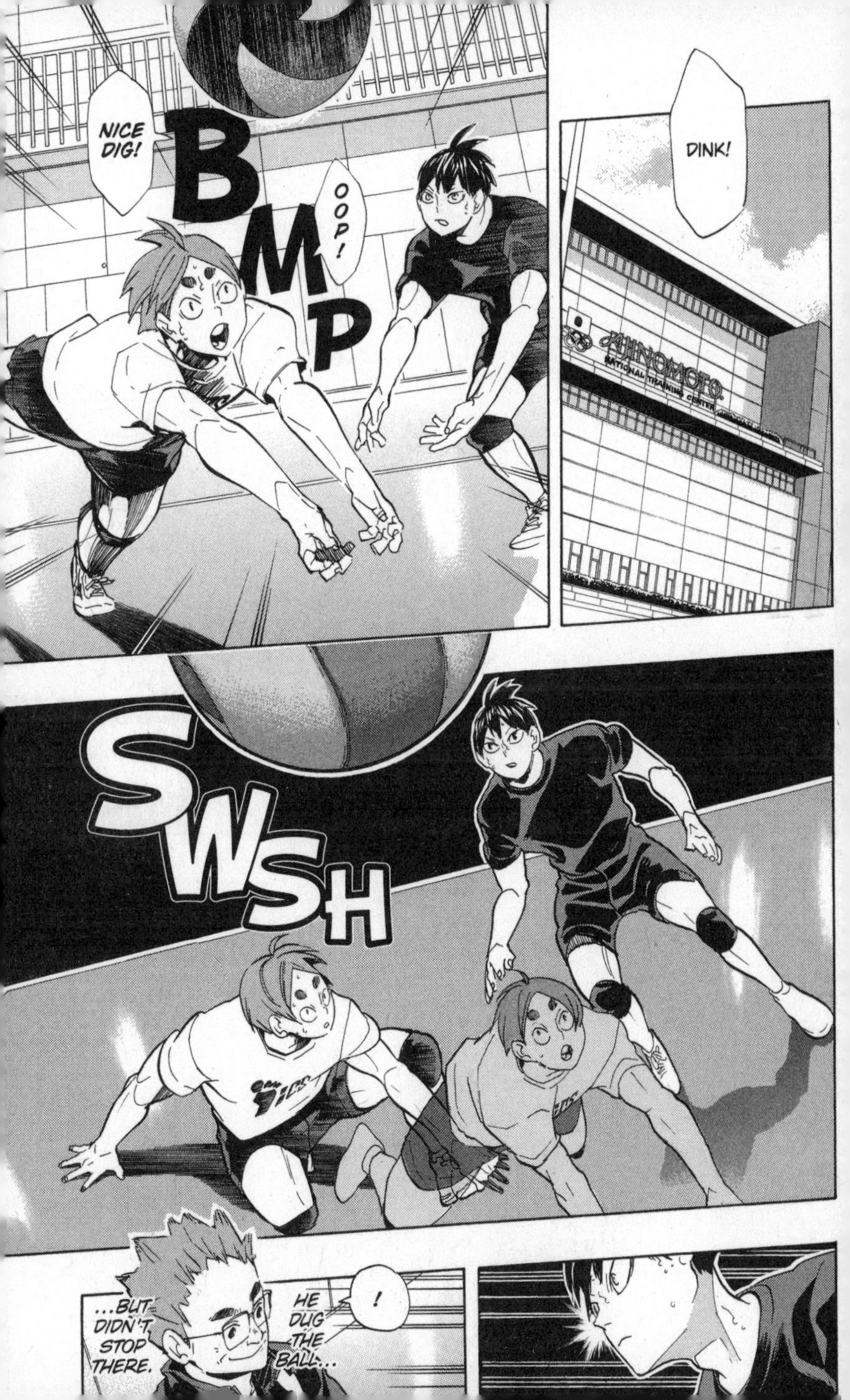
DINK!
BMP
OOP!
NICE DIG!
SWSH
!
HE DUG THE BALL...
...BUT DIDN'T STOP THERE.

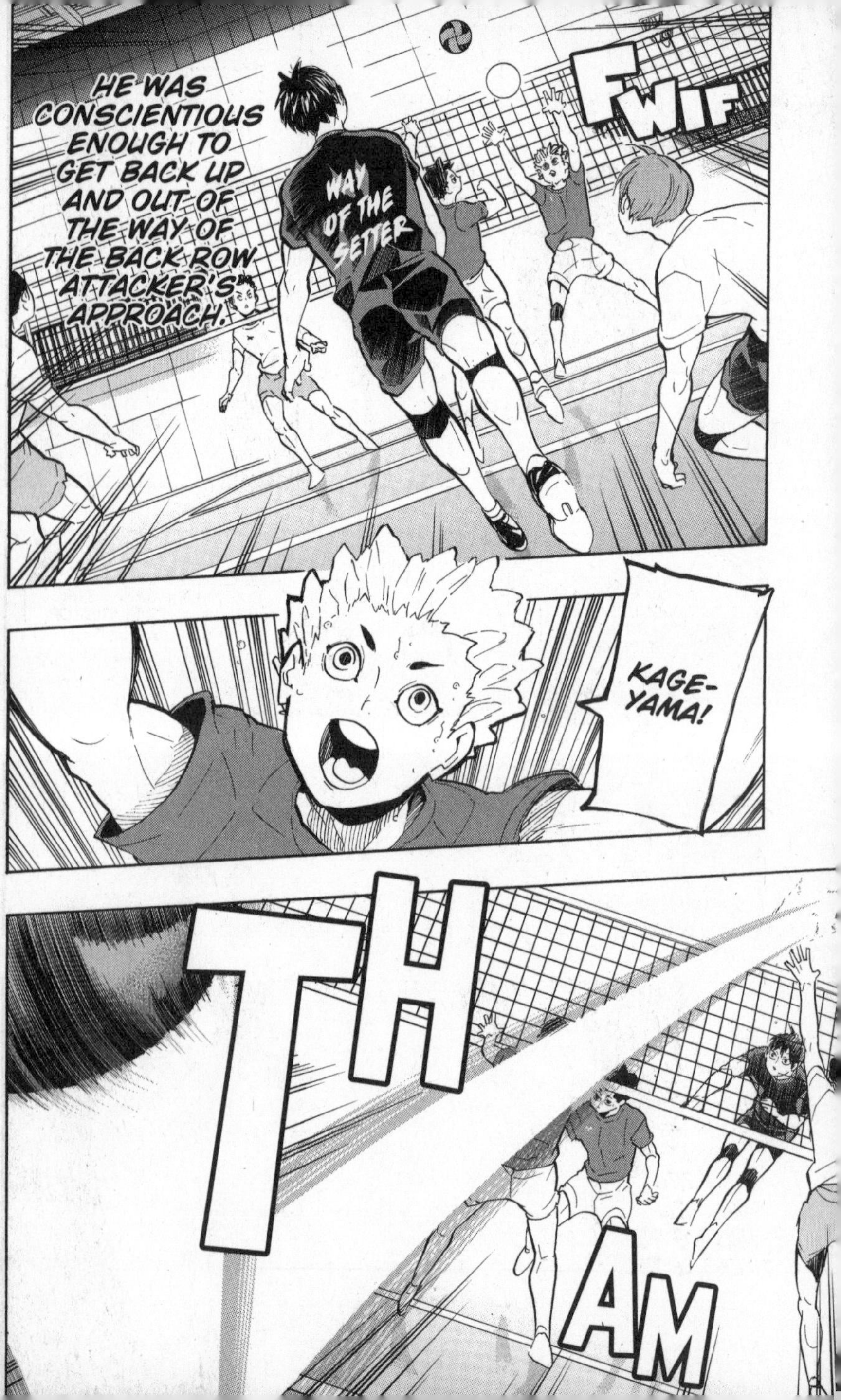
HE WAS CONSCIENTIOUS ENOUGH TO GET BACK UP AND OUT OF THE WAY OF THE BACK ROW ATTACKER'S APPROACH.
FWIF
WAY OF THE SETTER
KAGE-YAMA!
THAM

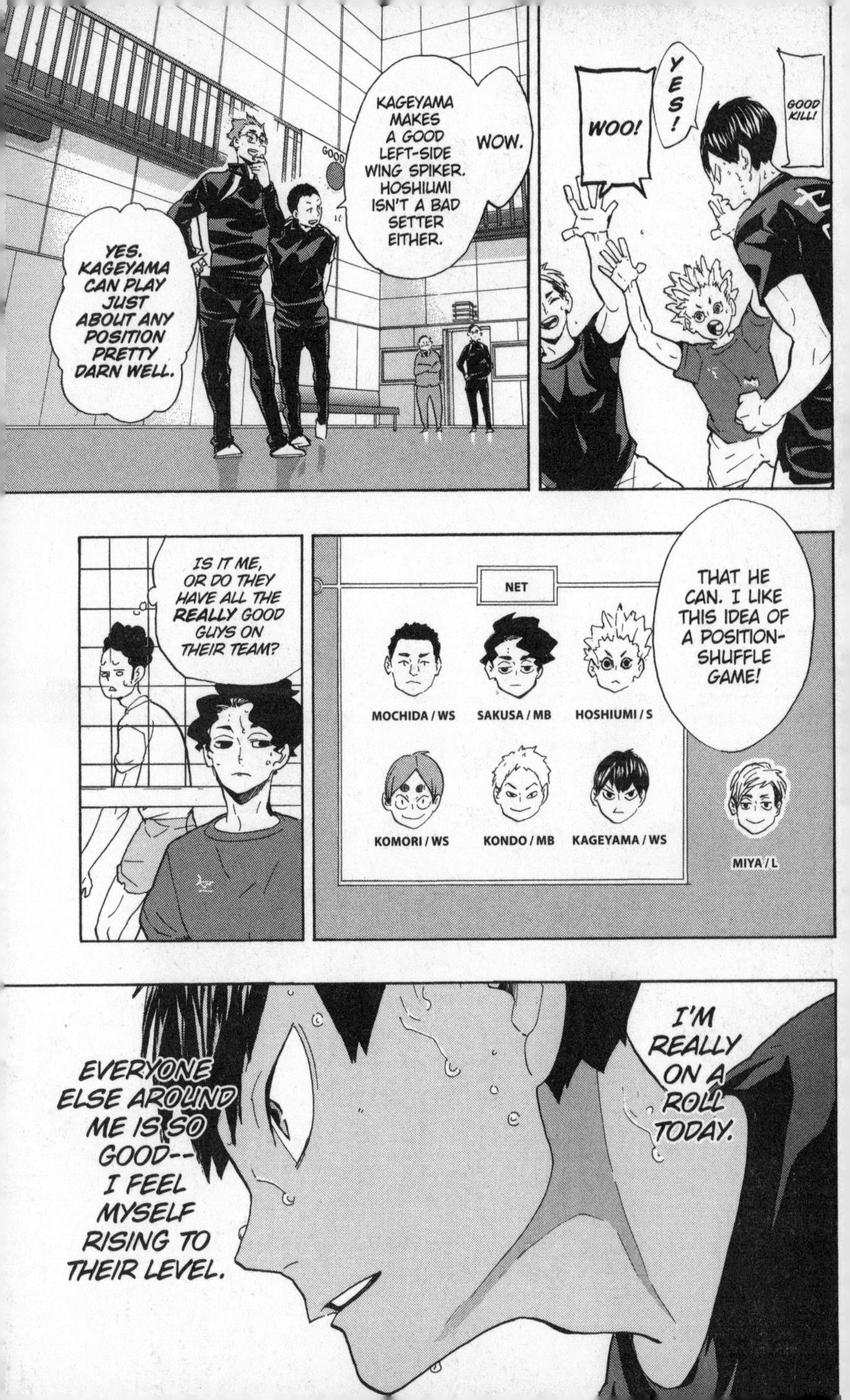
GOOD KILL!
YES!
WOO!
WOW.
KAGEYAMA MAKES A GOOD LEFT-SIDE WING SPIKER. HOSHIUMI ISN'T A BAD SETTER EITHER.
GOOD
YES. KAGEYAMA CAN PLAY JUST ABOUT ANY POSITION PRETTY DARN WELL.
THAT HE CAN. I LIKE THIS IDEA OF A POSITION-SHUFFLE GAME!
NET
MOCHIDA / WS
SAKUSA / MB
HOSHIUMI / S
KOMORI / WS
KONDO / MB
KAGEYAMA / WS
MIYA / L
IS IT ME, OR DO THEY HAVE ALL THE REALLY GOOD GUYS ON THEIR TEAM?
I'M REALLY ON A ROLL TODAY.
EVERYONE ELSE AROUND ME IS SO GOOD-- I FEEL MYSELF RISING TO THEIR LEVEL.

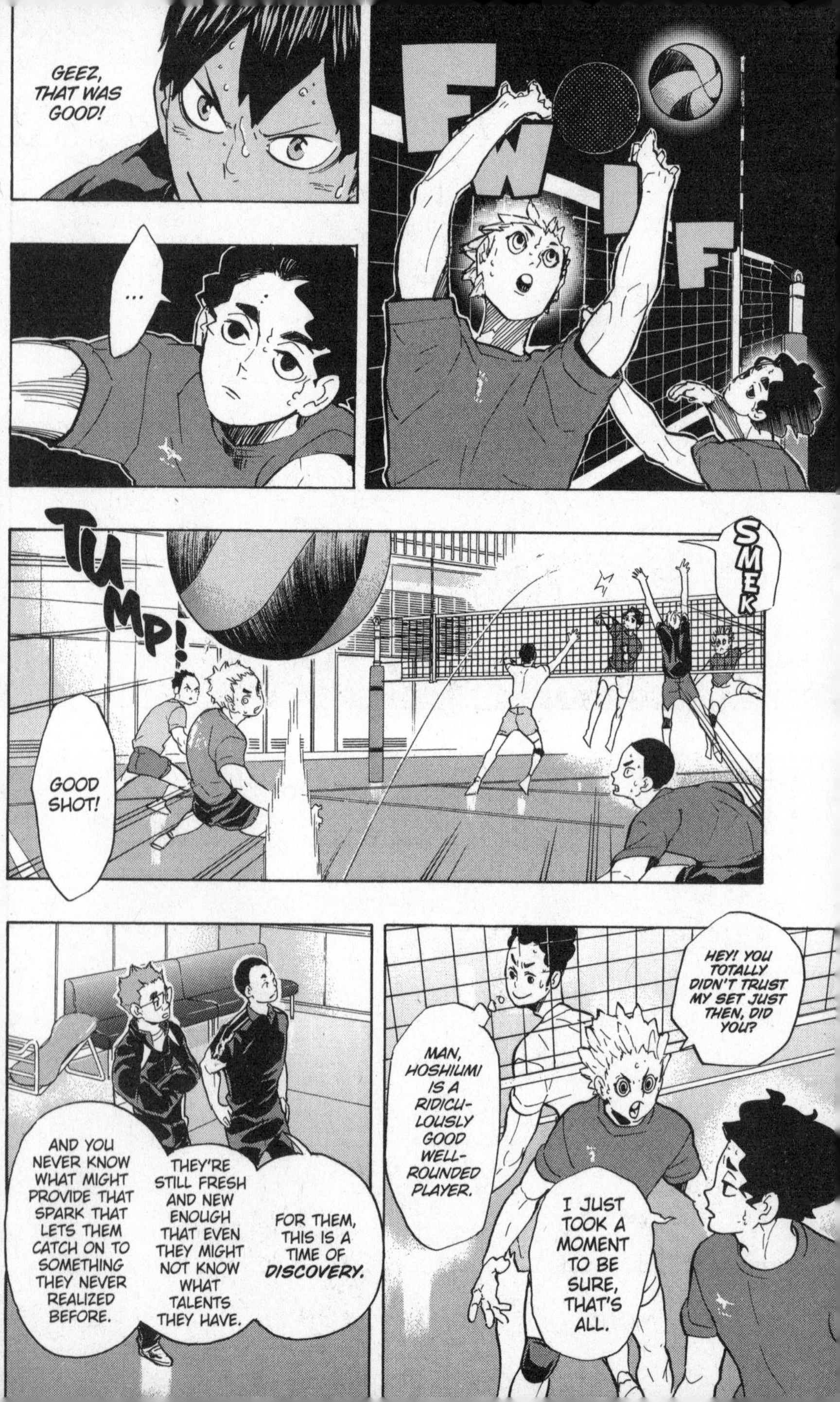
FWIFF
GEEZ, THAT WAS GOOD!
...
SMEK
TUMP!
GOOD SHOT!
HEY! YOU TOTALLY DIDN'T TRUST MY SET JUST THEN, DID YOU?
MAN, HOSHIUMI IS A RIDICULOUSLY GOOD WELL-ROUNDED PLAYER.
I JUST TOOK A MOMENT TO BE SURE, THAT'S ALL.
FOR THEM, THIS IS A TIME OF *DISCOVERY.*
THEY'RE STILL FRESH AND NEW ENOUGH THAT EVEN THEY MIGHT NOT KNOW WHAT TALENTS THEY HAVE.
AND YOU NEVER KNOW WHAT MIGHT PROVIDE THAT SPARK THAT LETS THEM CATCH ON TO SOMETHING THEY NEVER REALIZED BEFORE.

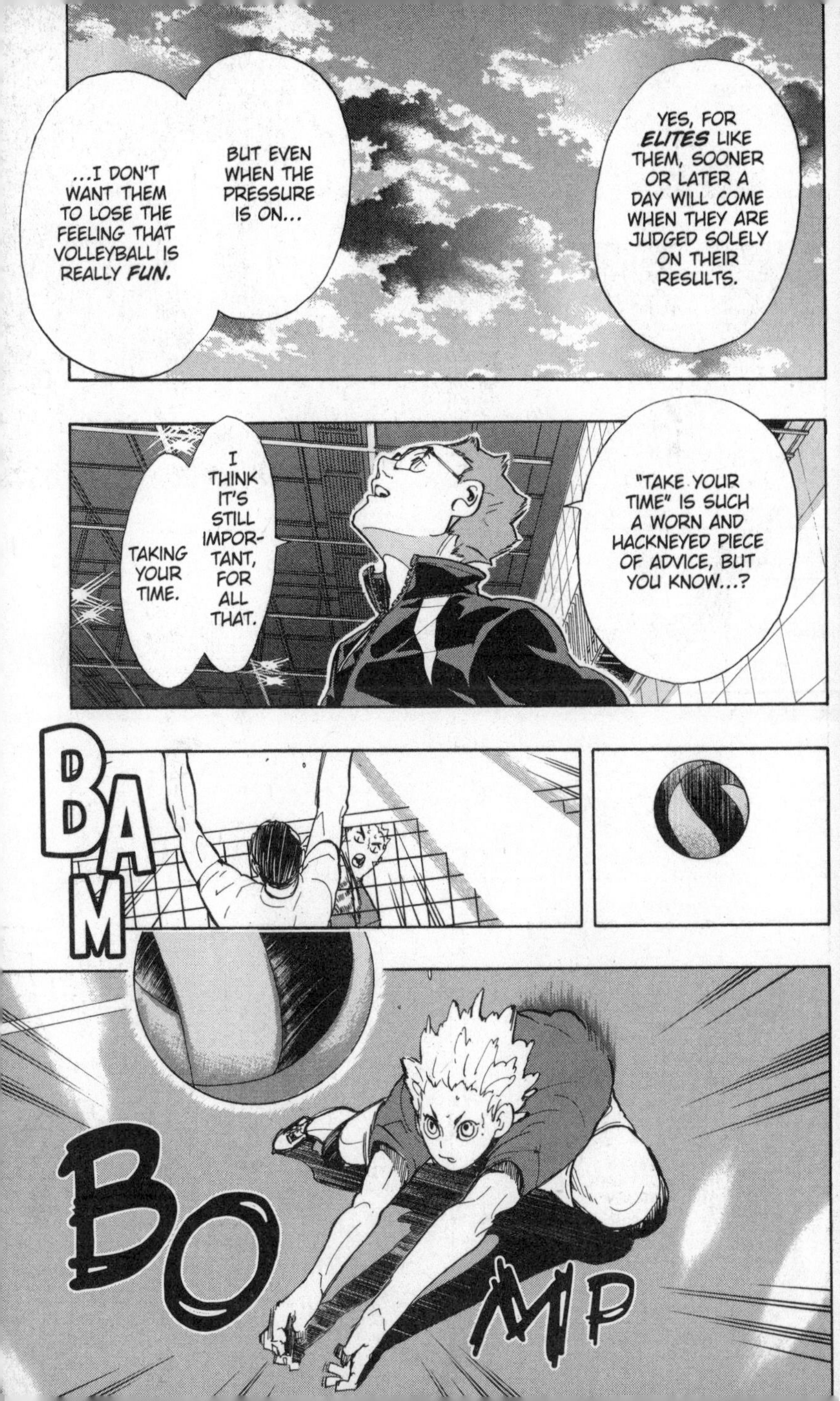
YES, FOR ELITES LIKE THEM, SOONER OR LATER A DAY WILL COME WHEN THEY ARE JUDGED SOLELY ON THEIR RESULTS.
BUT EVEN WHEN THE PRESSURE IS ON...
...I DON'T WANT THEM TO LOSE THE FEELING THAT VOLLEYBALL IS REALLY FUN.
"TAKE YOUR TIME" IS SUCH A WORN AND HACKNEYED PIECE OF ADVICE, BUT YOU KNOW...?
I THINK IT'S STILL IMPORTANT, FOR ALL THAT.
TAKING YOUR TIME.
BAM
BOOMP

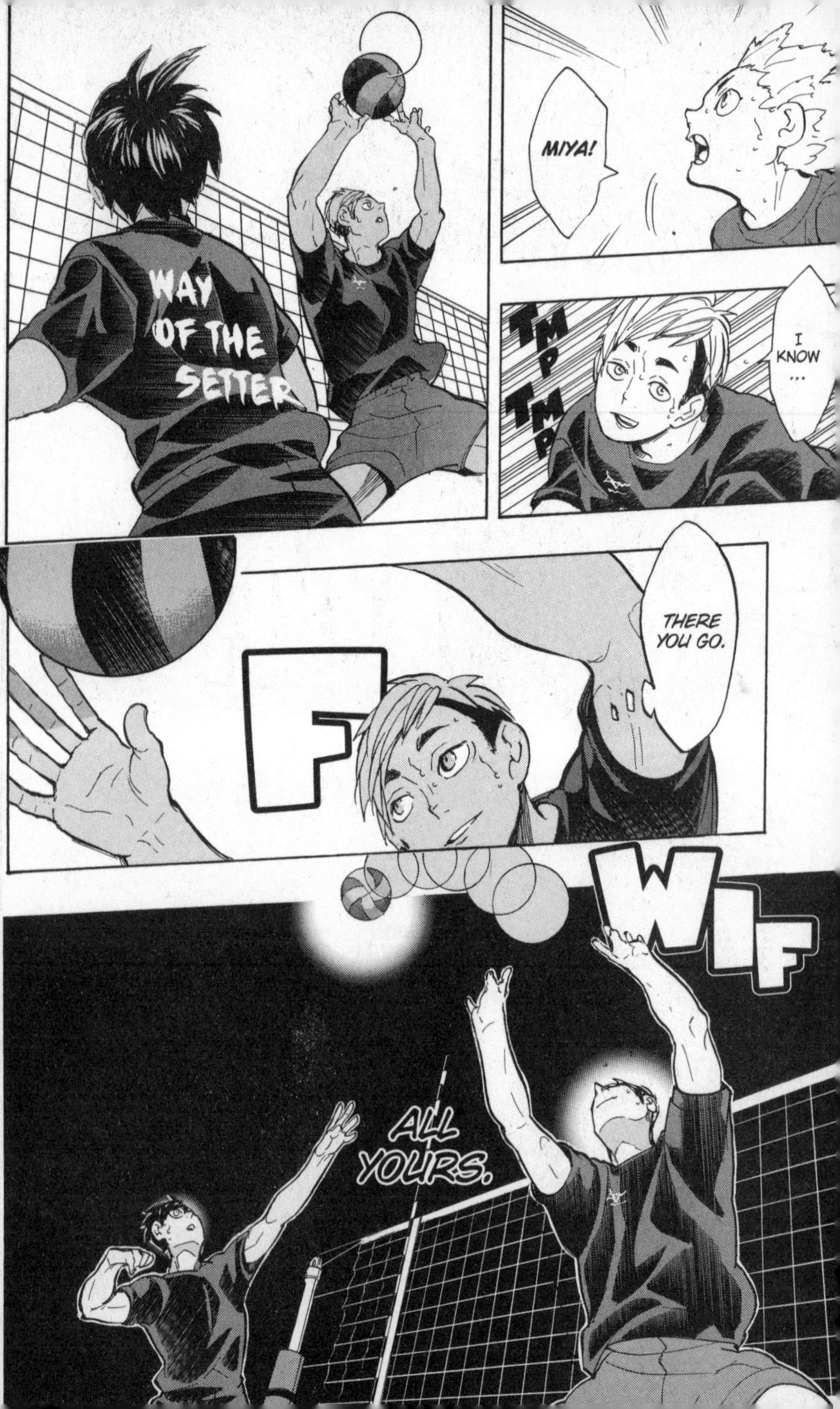
MIYA!
I KNOW...
TMP TMP
WAY OF THE SETTER
THERE YOU GO.
F
WIF
ALL YOURS.

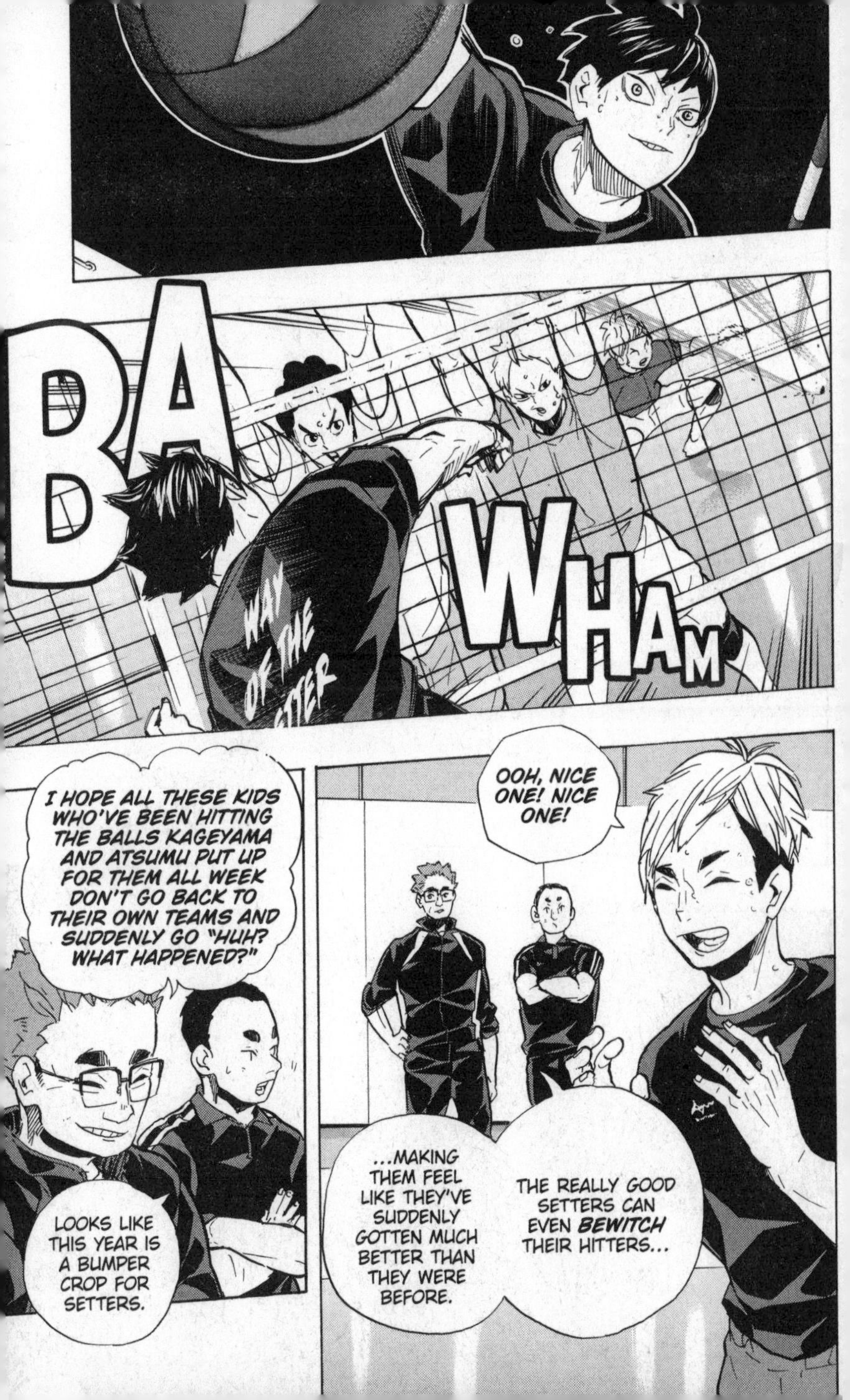
WHAM
BADD
OOH, NICE ONE! NICE ONE!
THE REALLY GOOD SETTERS CAN EVEN *BEWITCH* THEIR HITTERS...
...MAKING THEM FEEL LIKE THEY'VE SUDDENLY GOTTEN MUCH BETTER THAN THEY WERE BEFORE.
I HOPE ALL THESE KIDS WHO'VE BEEN HITTING THE BALLS KAGEYAMA AND ATSUMU PUT UP FOR THEM ALL WEEK DON'T GO BACK TO THEIR OWN TEAMS AND SUDDENLY GO "HUH? WHAT HAPPENED?"
LOOKS LIKE THIS YEAR IS A BUMPER CROP FOR SETTERS.

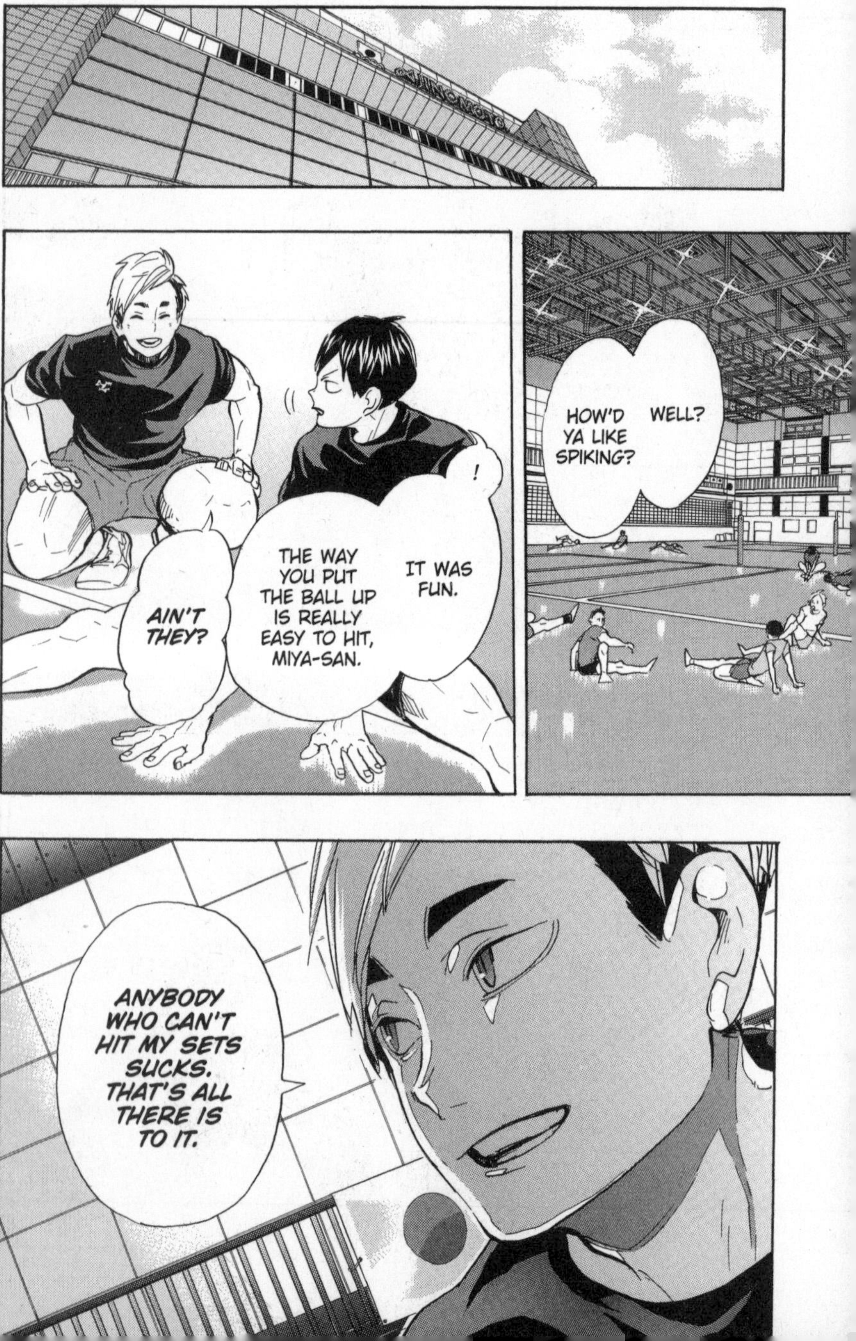
WELL?
HOW'D YA LIKE SPIKING?
!
IT WAS FUN.
THE WAY YOU PUT THE BALL UP IS REALLY EASY TO HIT, MIYA-SAN.
AIN'T THEY?
ANYBODY WHO CAN'T HIT MY SETS SUCKS. THAT'S ALL THERE IS TO IT.

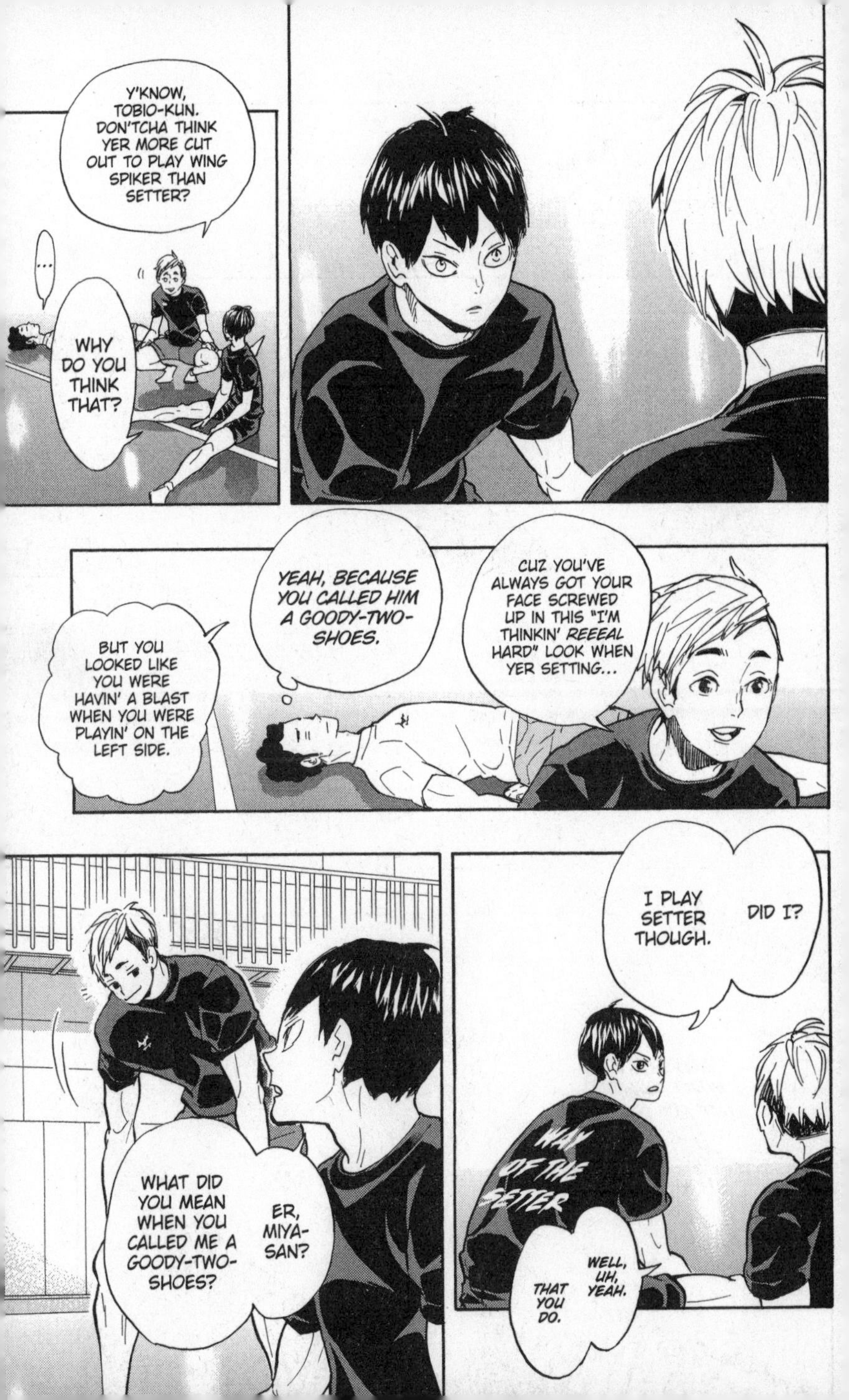
Y'KNOW, TOBIO-KUN. DON'TCHA THINK YER MORE CUT OUT TO PLAY WING SPIKER THAN SETTER?
...
WHY DO YOU THINK THAT?
CUZ YOU'VE ALWAYS GOT YOUR FACE SCREWED UP IN THIS "I'M THINKIN' *REEEAL* HARD" LOOK WHEN YER SETTING...
YEAH, BECAUSE YOU CALLED HIM A GOODY-TWO-SHOES.
BUT YOU LOOKED LIKE YOU WERE HAVIN' A BLAST WHEN YOU WERE PLAYIN' ON THE LEFT SIDE.
DID I?
I PLAY SETTER THOUGH.
WAY OF THE SETTER
WELL, UH, YEAH.
THAT YOU DO.
ER, MIYA-SAN?
WHAT DID YOU MEAN WHEN YOU CALLED ME A GOODY-TWO-SHOES?

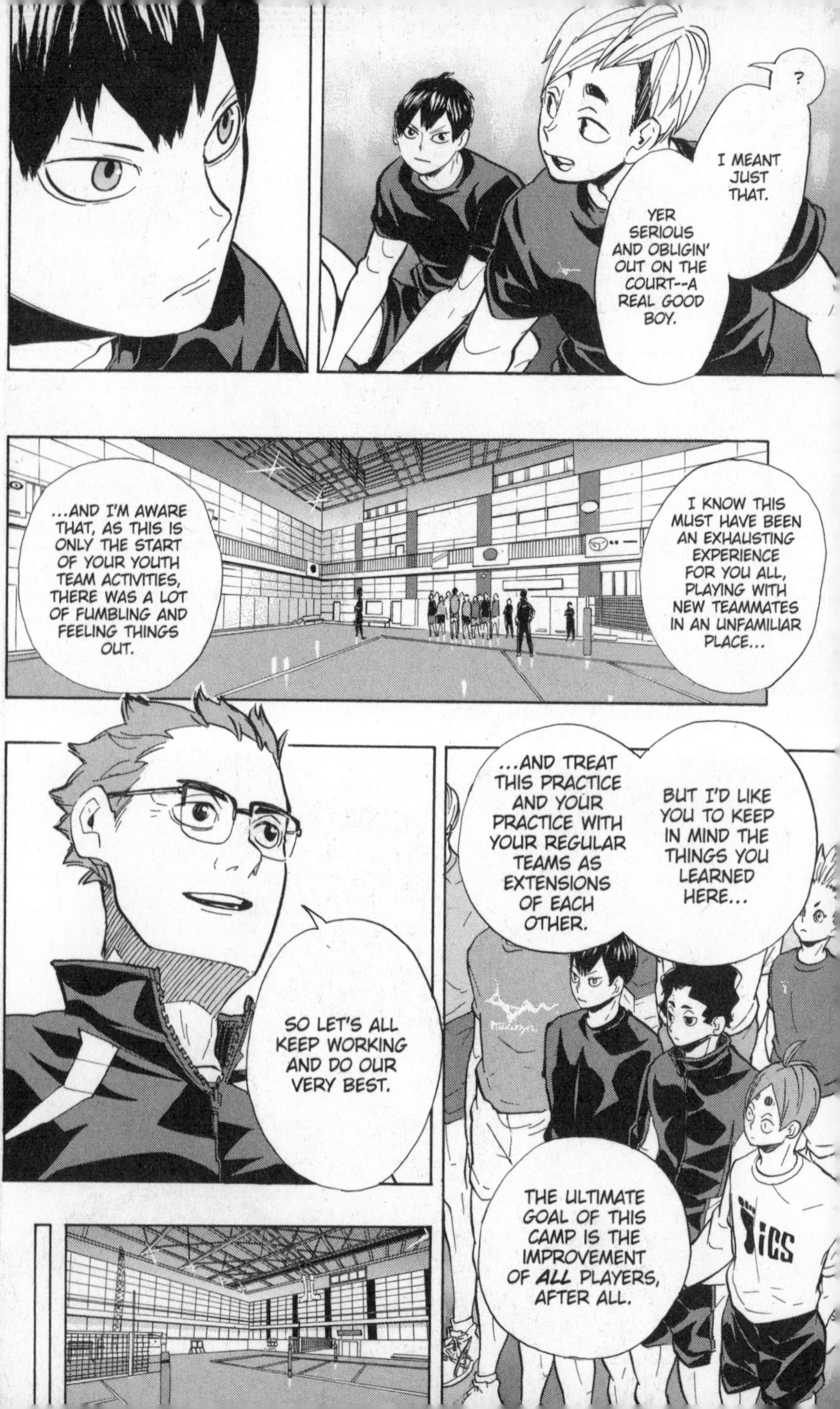
?
I MEANT JUST THAT.
YER SERIOUS AND OBLIGIN' OUT ON THE COURT--A REAL GOOD BOY.
I KNOW THIS MUST HAVE BEEN AN EXHAUSTING EXPERIENCE FOR YOU ALL, PLAYING WITH NEW TEAMMATES IN AN UNFAMILIAR PLACE...
...AND I'M AWARE THAT, AS THIS IS ONLY THE START OF YOUR YOUTH TEAM ACTIVITIES, THERE WAS A LOT OF FUMBLING AND FEELING THINGS OUT.
BUT I'D LIKE YOU TO KEEP IN MIND THE THINGS YOU LEARNED HERE...
...AND TREAT THIS PRACTICE AND YOUR PRACTICE WITH YOUR REGULAR TEAMS AS EXTENSIONS OF EACH OTHER.
THE ULTIMATE GOAL OF THIS CAMP IS THE IMPROVEMENT OF *ALL* PLAYERS, AFTER ALL.
SO LET'S ALL KEEP WORKING AND DO OUR VERY BEST.

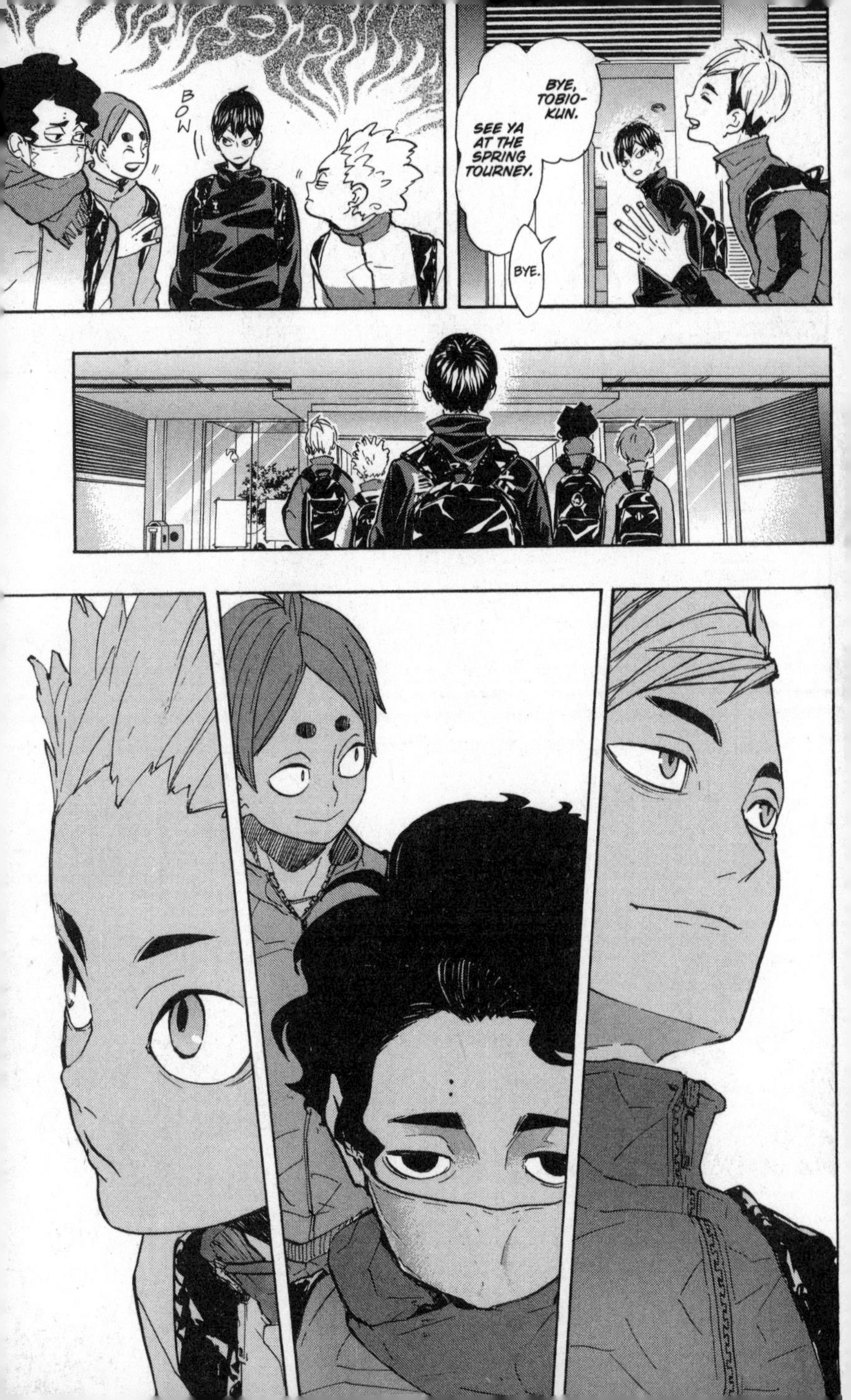
BYE, TOBIO-KUN.
SEE YA AT THE SPRING TOURNEY.
BYE.
BOW

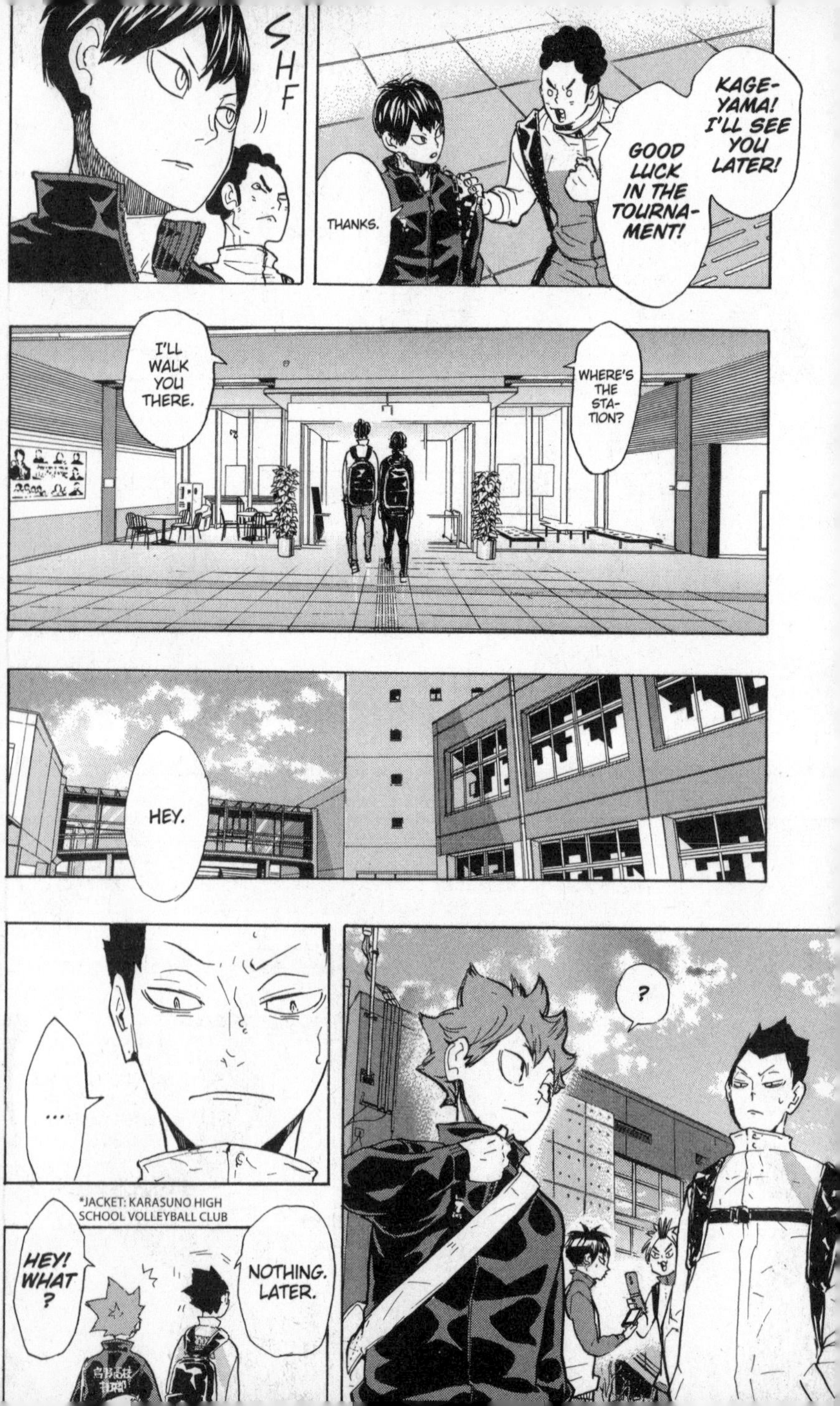
KAGE-YAMA! I'LL SEE YOU LATER!
GOOD LUCK IN THE TOURNA-MENT!
THANKS.
SHF
WHERE'S THE STA-TION?
I'LL WALK YOU THERE.
HEY.
?
...
*JACKET: KARASUNO HIGH SCHOOL VOLLEYBALL CLUB
NOTHING. LATER.
HEY! WHAT?

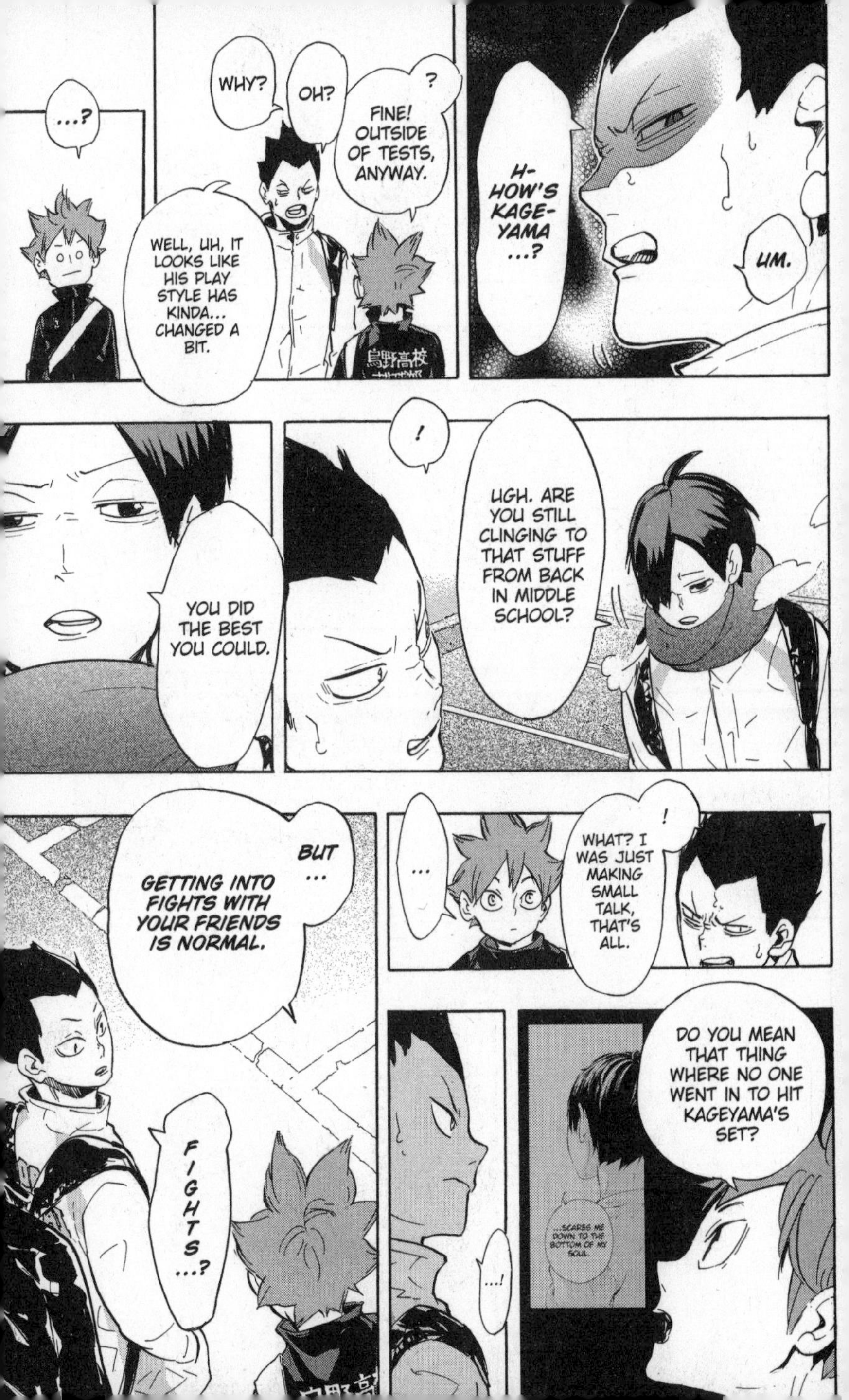
UM.
H-HOW'S KAGE-YAMA ...?
?
FINE! OUTSIDE OF TESTS, ANYWAY.
OH?
WHY?
WELL, UH, IT LOOKS LIKE HIS PLAY STYLE HAS KINDA... CHANGED A BIT.
...?
!
UGH. ARE YOU STILL CLINGING TO THAT STUFF FROM BACK IN MIDDLE SCHOOL?
YOU DID THE BEST YOU COULD.
!
WHAT? I WAS JUST MAKING SMALL TALK, THAT'S ALL.
...
DO YOU MEAN THAT THING WHERE NO ONE WENT IN TO HIT KAGEYAMA'S SET?
...SCARES ME DOWN TO THE BOTTOM OF MY SOUL
...!
BUT ...
GETTING INTO FIGHTS WITH YOUR FRIENDS IS NORMAL.
FIGHTS ...?

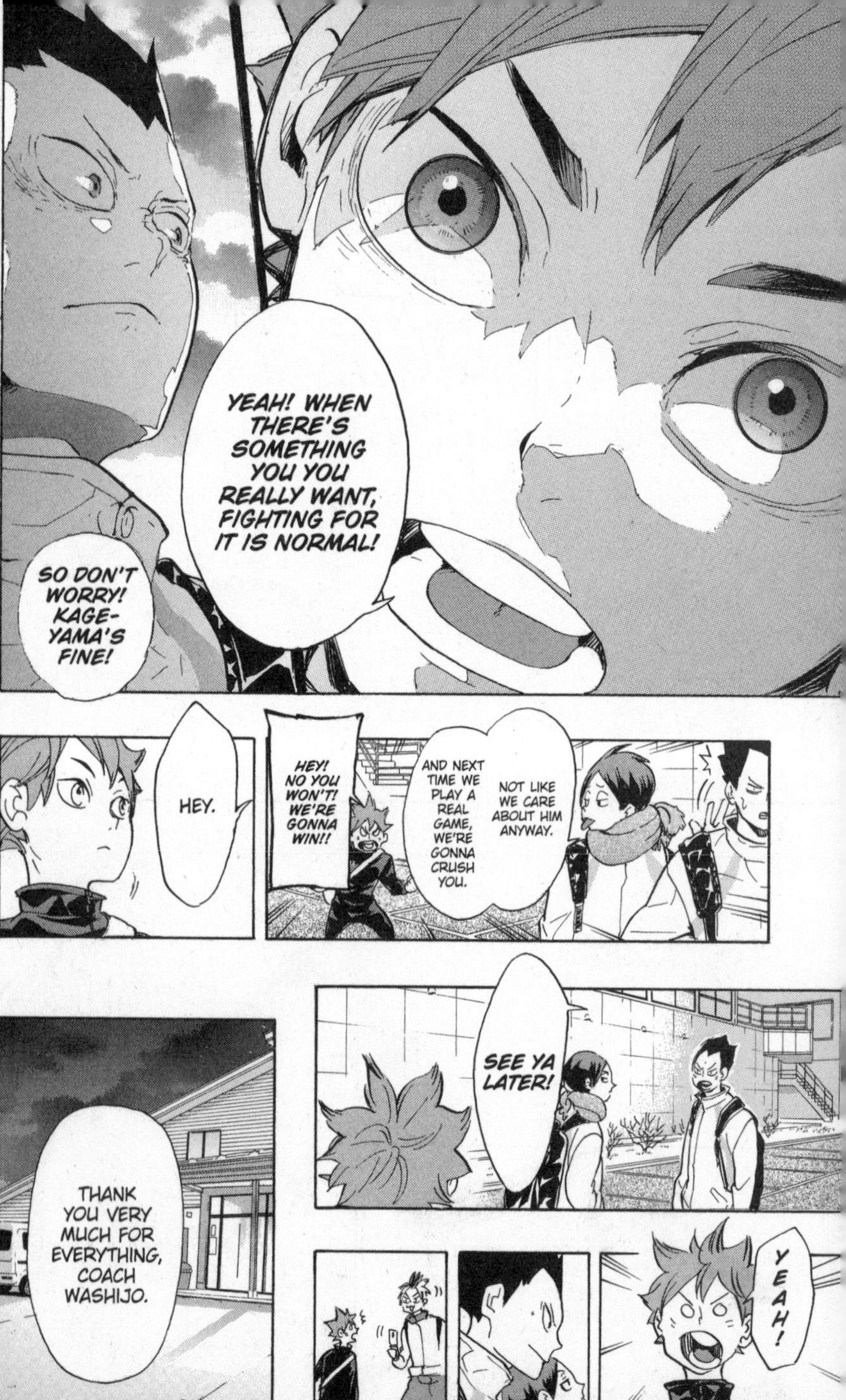
YEAH! WHEN THERE'S SOMETHING YOU YOU REALLY WANT, FIGHTING FOR IT IS NORMAL!
SO DON'T WORRY! KAGE-YAMA'S FINE!
NOT LIKE WE CARE ABOUT HIM ANYWAY.
AND NEXT TIME WE PLAY A REAL GAME, WE'RE GONNA CRUSH YOU.
HEY! NO YOU WON'T! WE'RE GONNA WIN!!
HEY.
SEE YA LATER!
YEAH!
THANK YOU VERY MUCH FOR EVERYTHING, COACH WASHIJO.

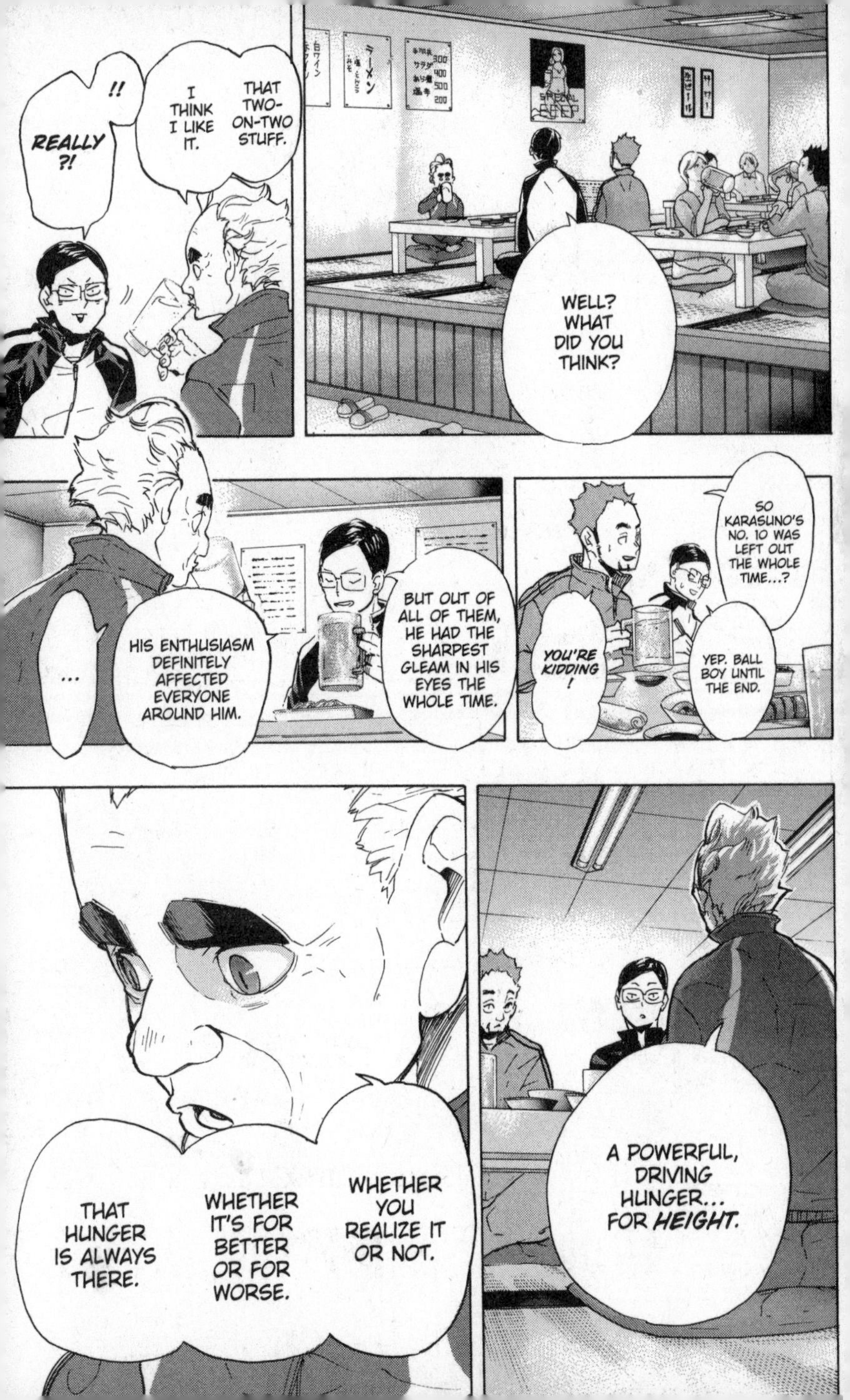
WELL? WHAT DID YOU THINK?
THAT TWO-ON-TWO STUFF.
I THINK I LIKE IT.
!!
REALLY ?!
SO KARASUNO'S NO. 10 WAS LEFT OUT THE WHOLE TIME...?
YEP. BALL BOY UNTIL THE END.
YOU'RE KIDDING!
BUT OUT OF ALL OF THEM, HE HAD THE SHARPEST GLEAM IN HIS EYES THE WHOLE TIME.
HIS ENTHUSIASM DEFINITELY AFFECTED EVERYONE AROUND HIM.
...
A POWERFUL, DRIVING HUNGER... FOR HEIGHT.
WHETHER YOU REALIZE IT OR NOT.
WHETHER IT'S FOR BETTER OR FOR WORSE.
THAT HUNGER IS ALWAYS THERE.

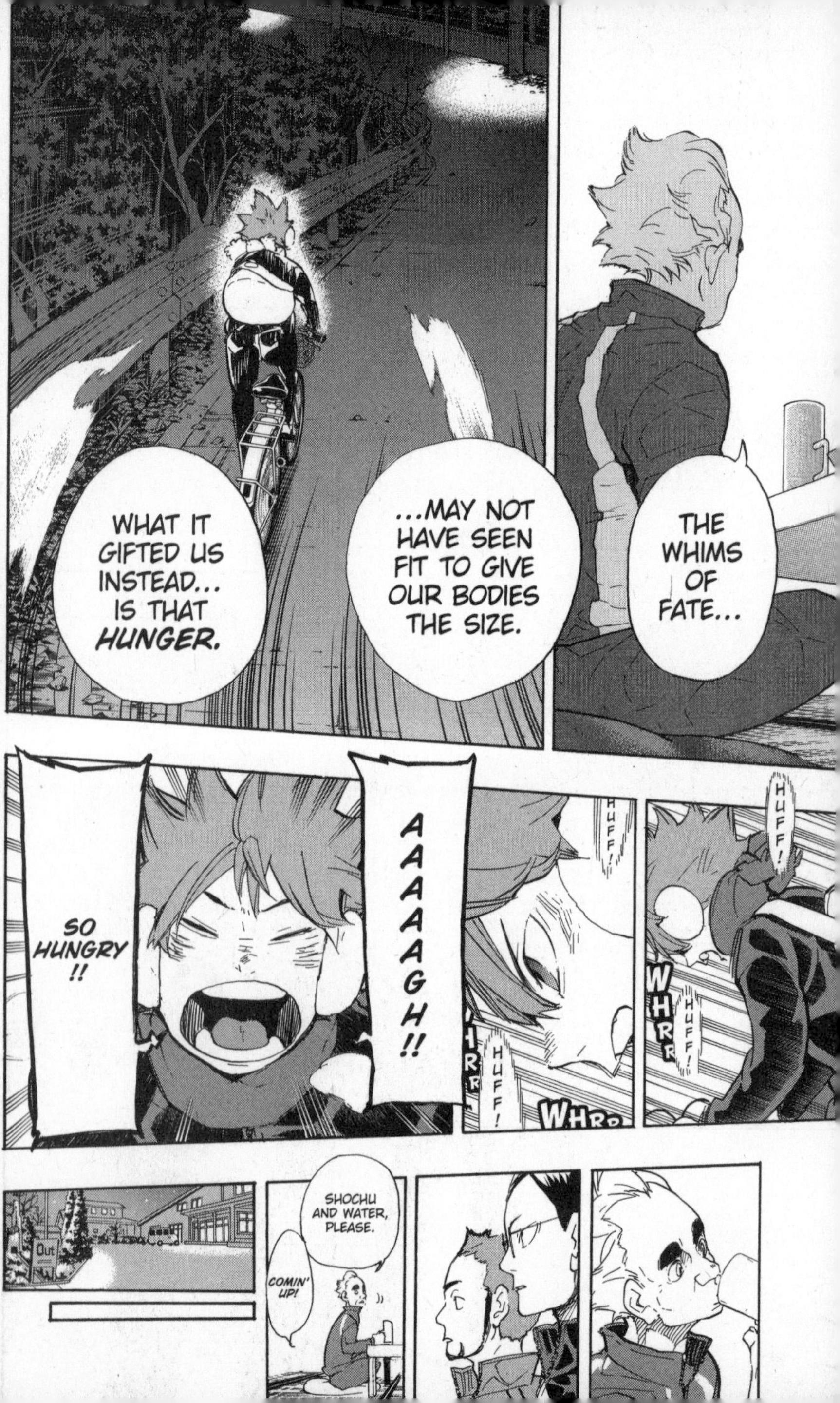
THE WHIMS OF FATE...
...MAY NOT HAVE SEEN FIT TO GIVE OUR BODIES THE SIZE.
WHAT IT GIFTED US INSTEAD... IS THAT *HUNGER.*
HUFF!
WHRR
HUFF!
HUFF!
HUFF!
WHRR
WHRR
AAAAAAAGH!!
SO HUNGRY!!
SHOCHU AND WATER, PLEASE.
COMIN' UP!
Out

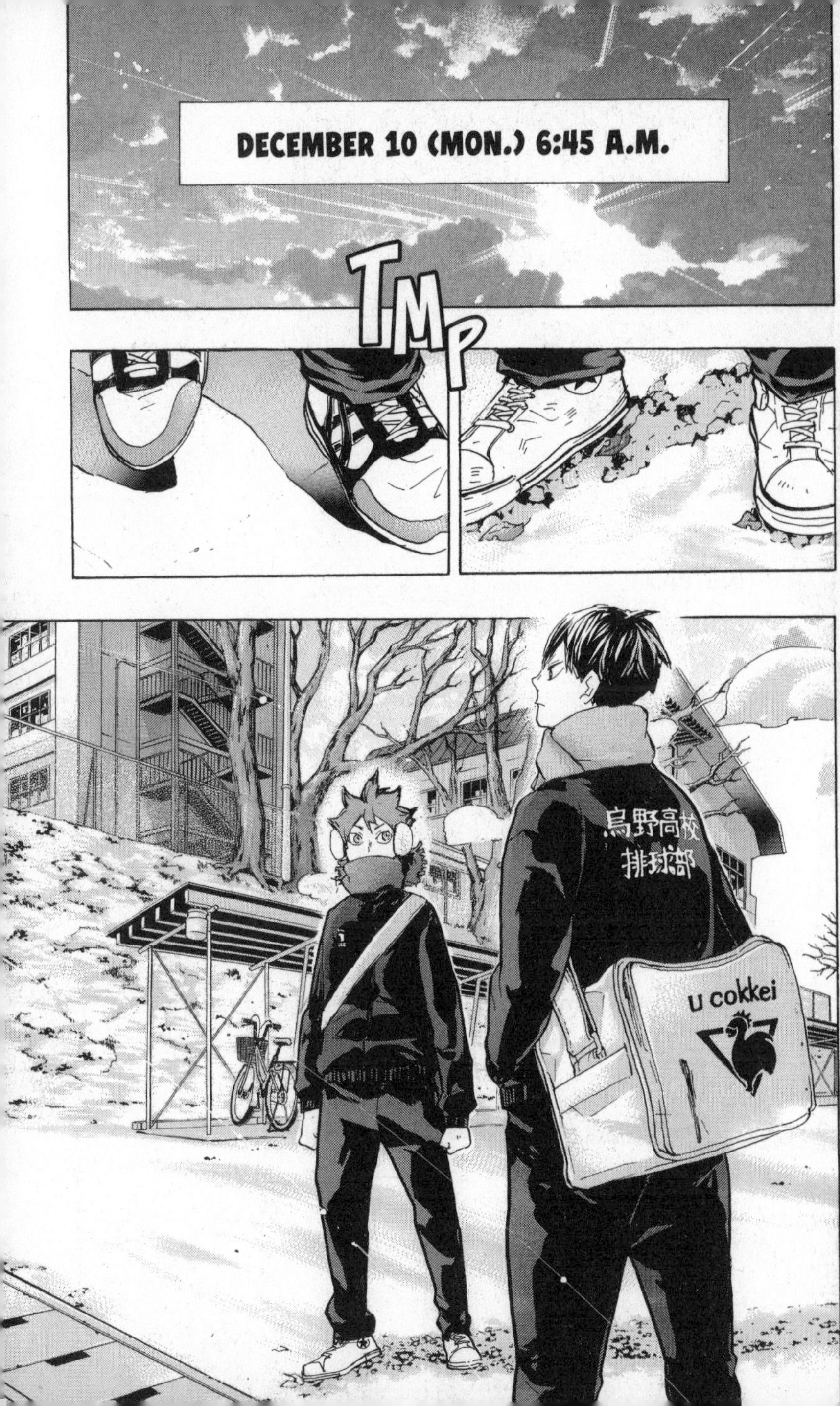
DECEMBER 10 (MON.) 6:45 A.M.
TMP
烏野高校
排球部
U cokkei

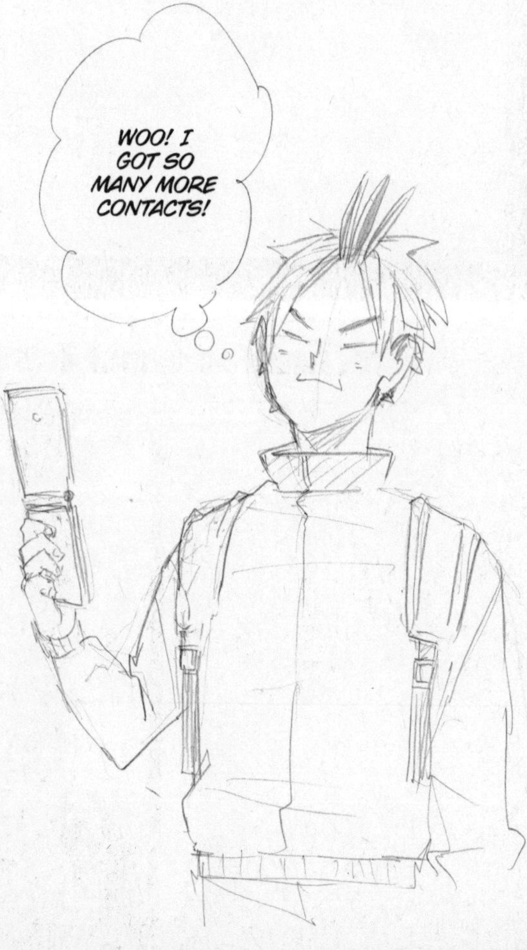
WOO! I GOT SO MANY MORE CONTACTS!

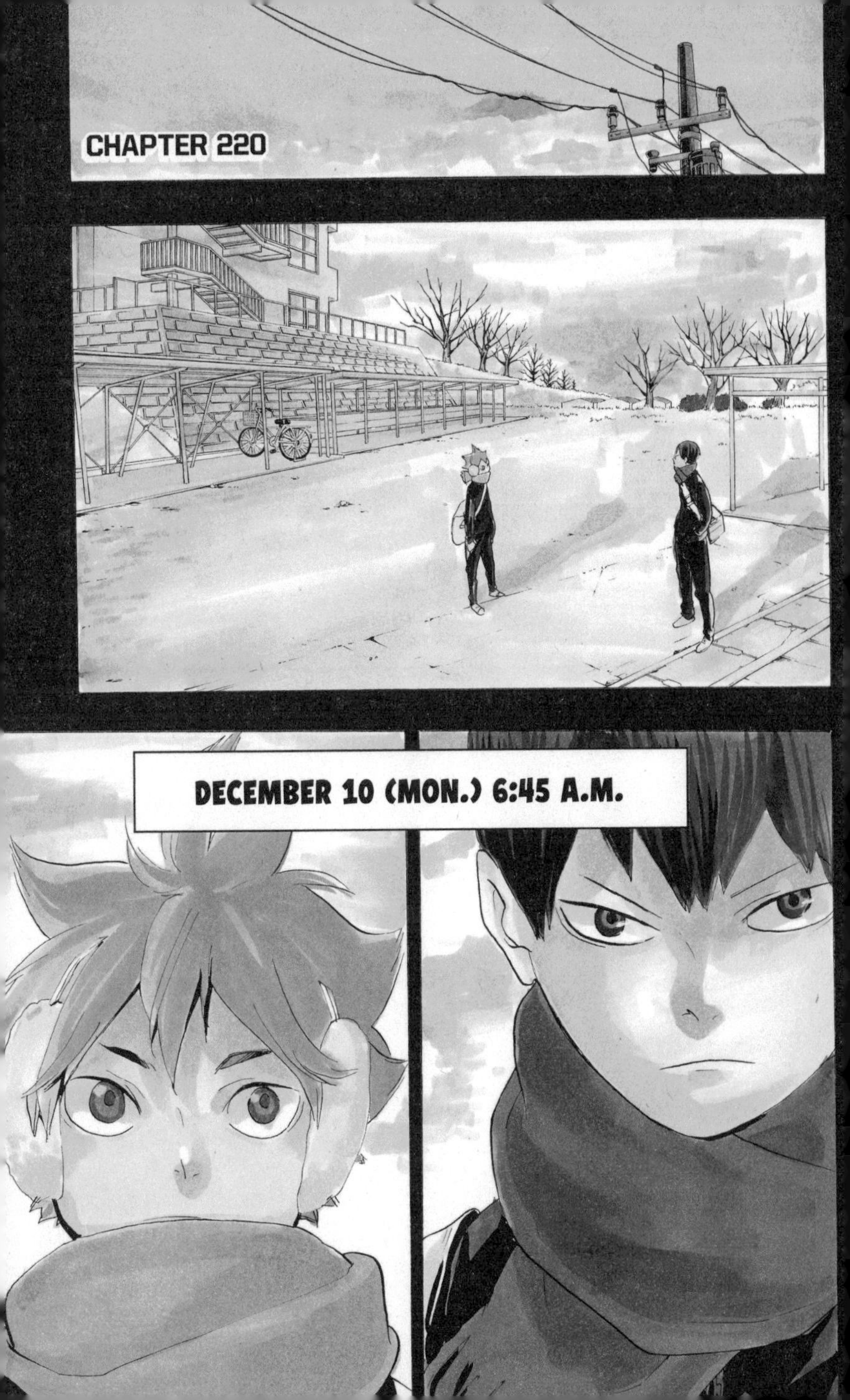
CHAPTER 220
DECEMBER 10 (MON.) 6:45 A.M.

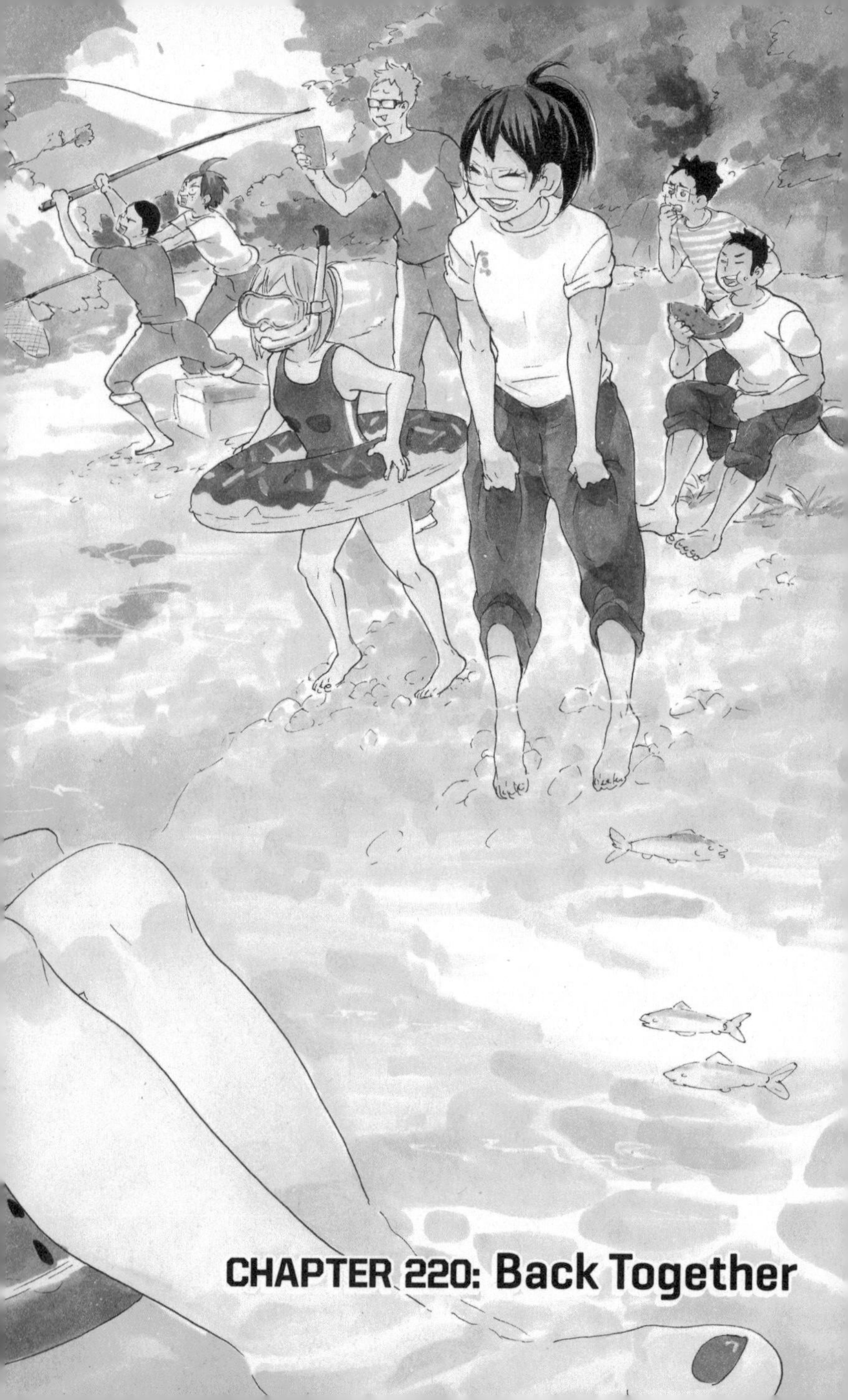
CHAPTER 220: Back Together

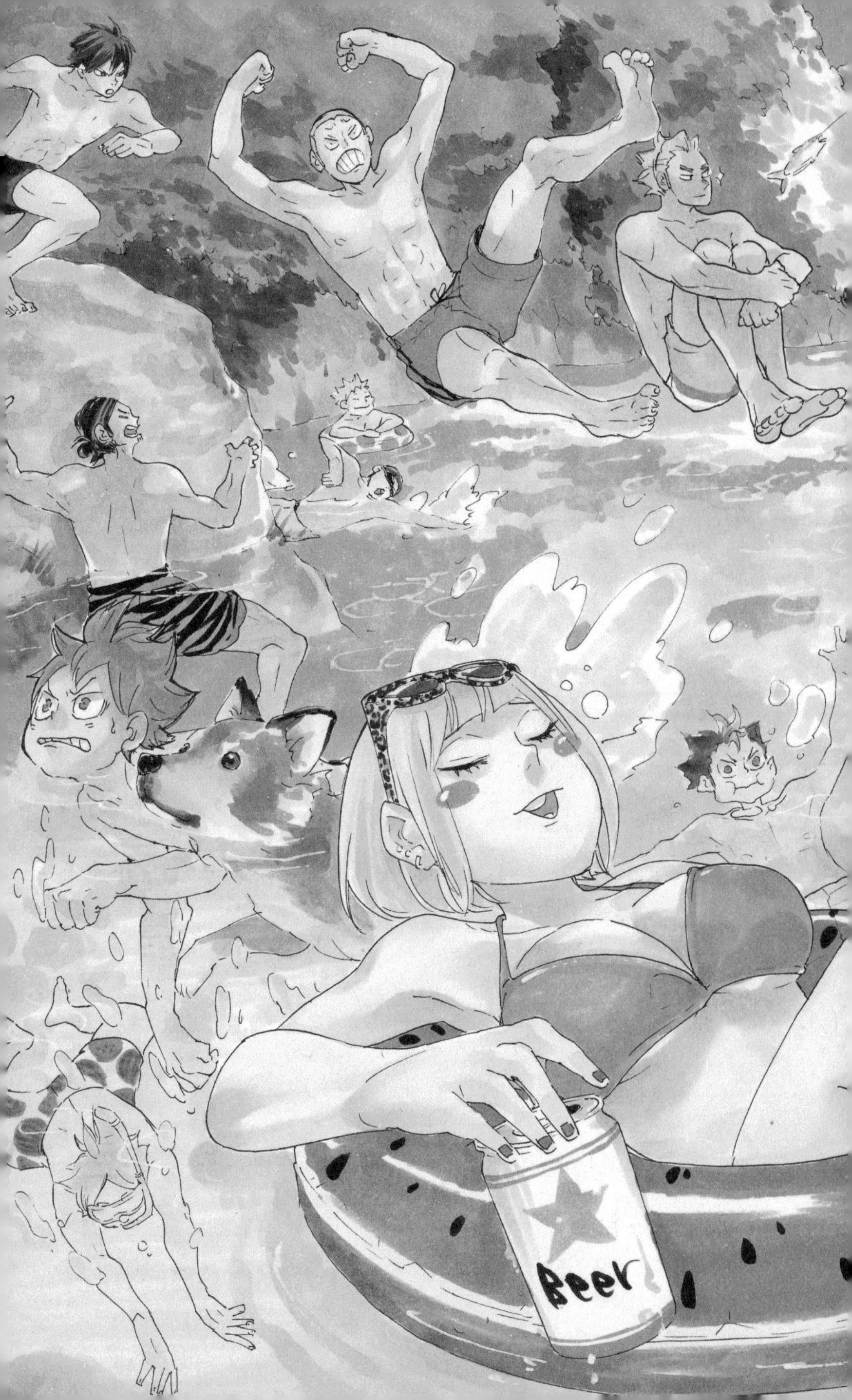
Beer

HAIKYU!!

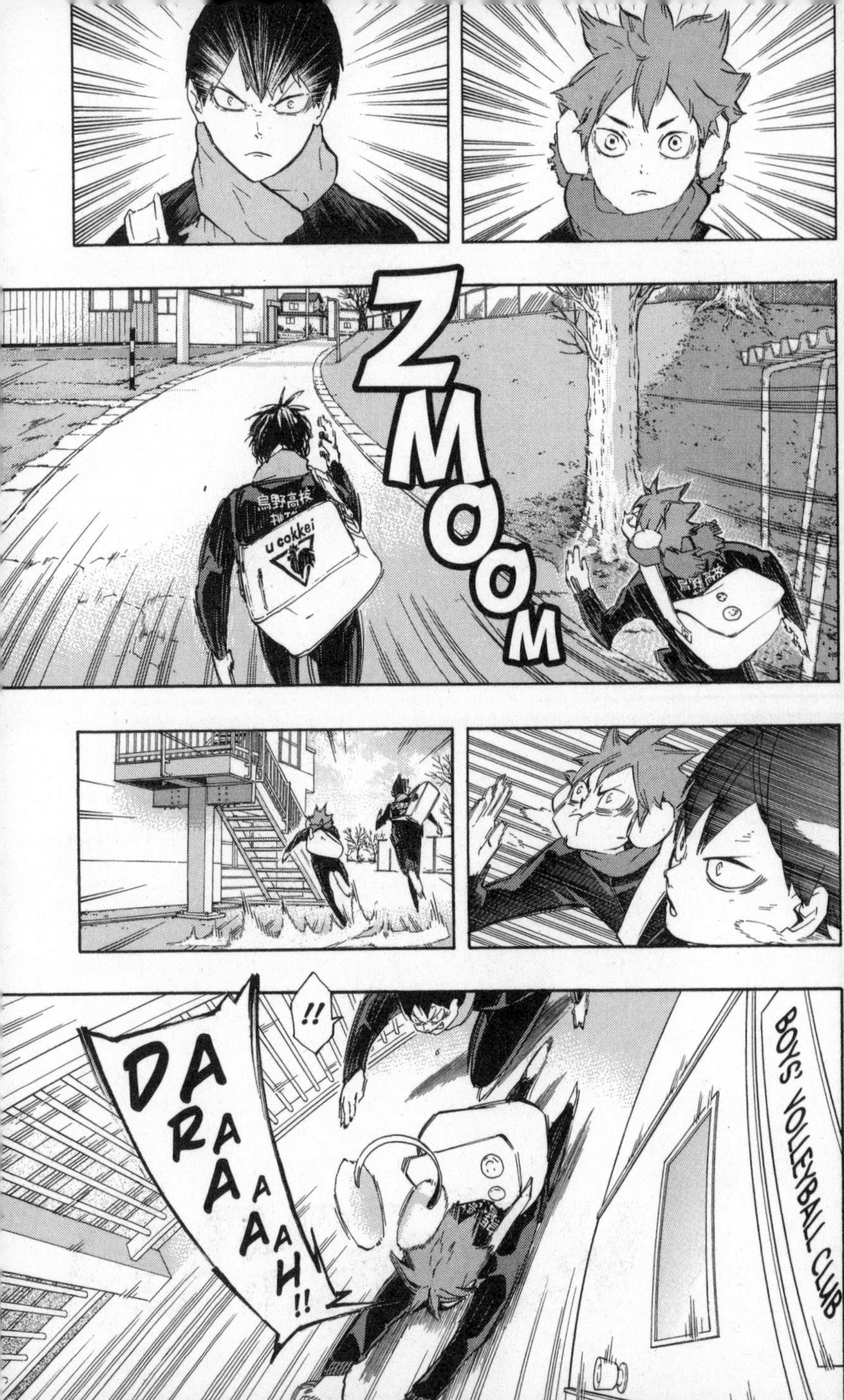
ZMOOM
烏野高校
BOYS' VOLLEYBALL CLUB
!!
DARAAAAAH!!

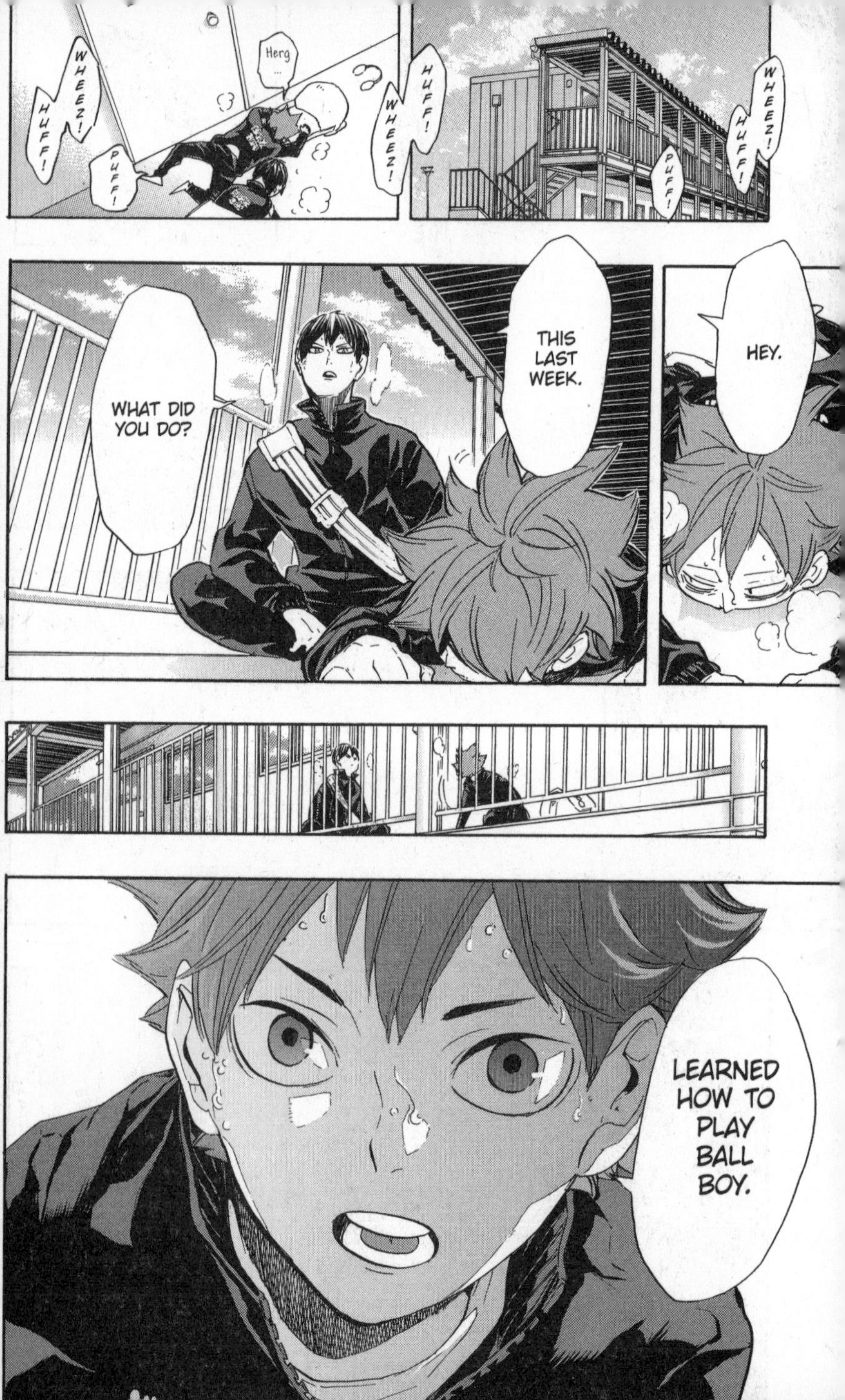
WHEEZ!
HUFF!
PUFF!
HUFF!
WHEEZ!
Herg ...
WHEEZ!
HUFF!
PUFF!
HEY.
THIS LAST WEEK.
WHAT DID YOU DO?
LEARNED HOW TO PLAY BALL BOY.

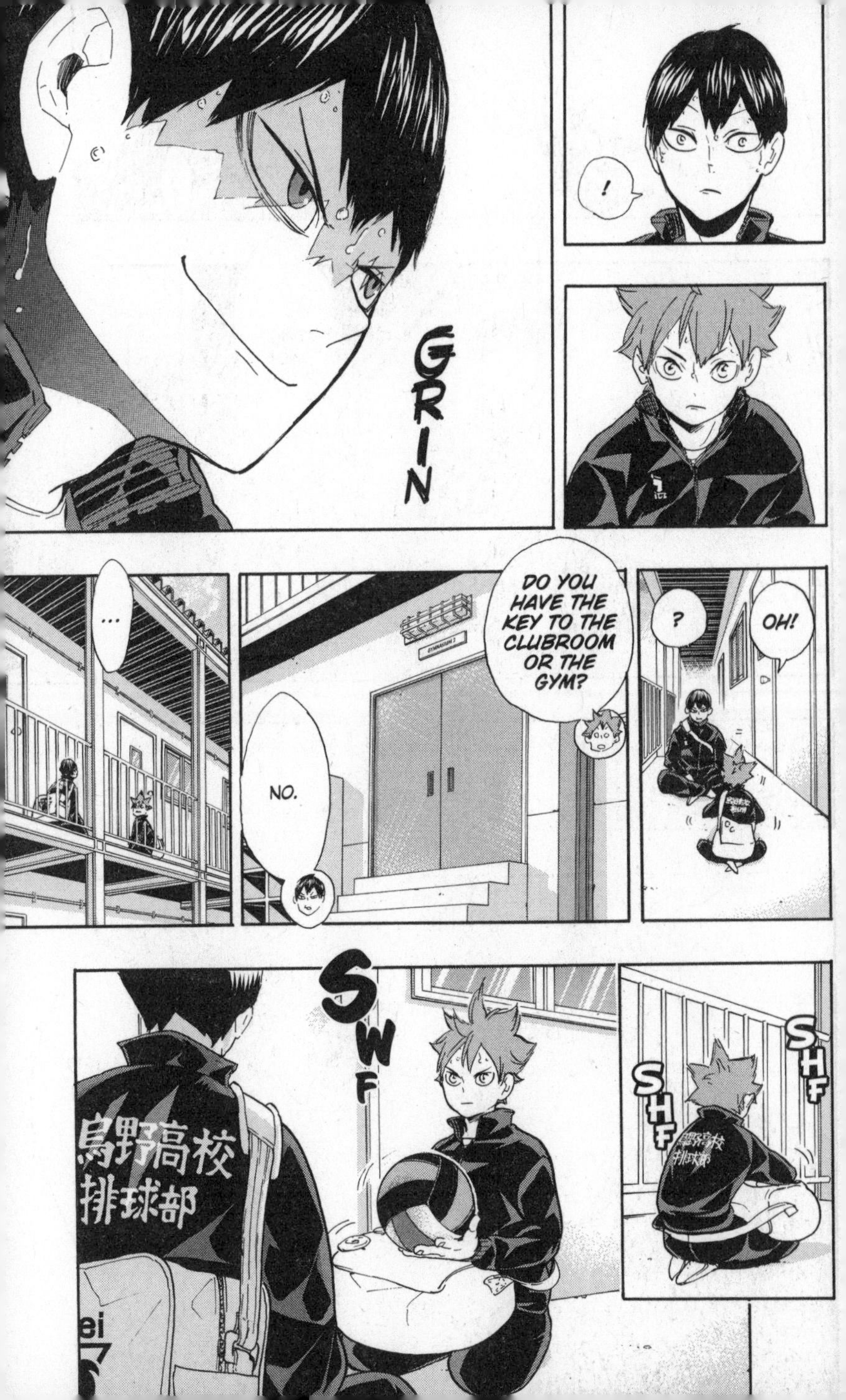
!
GRIN
OH!
?
DO YOU HAVE THE KEY TO THE CLUBROOM OR THE GYM?
NO.
...
SHF
SHF
SWF
烏野高校
排球部

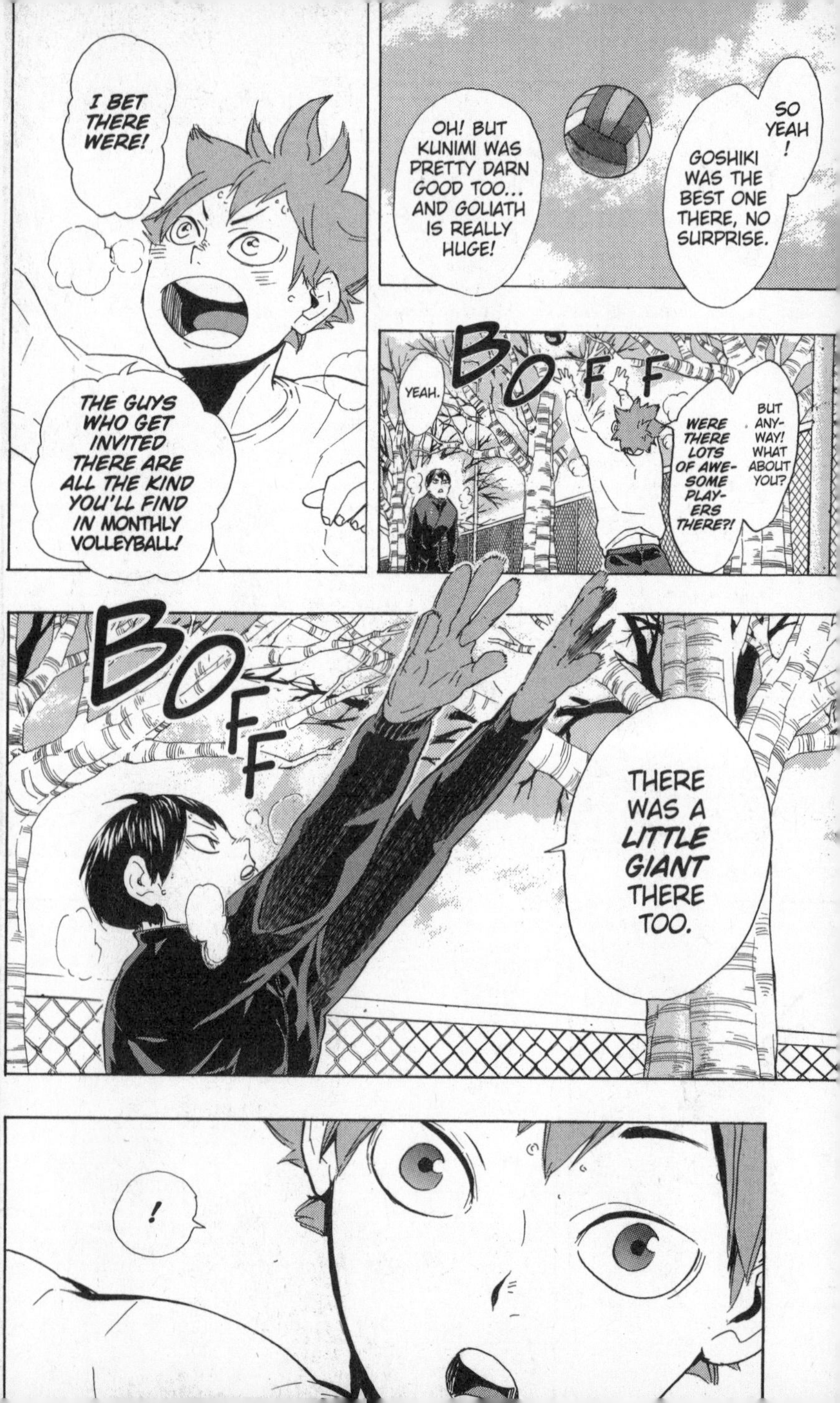
SO YEAH! GOSHIKI WAS THE BEST ONE THERE, NO SURPRISE.
OH! BUT KUNIMI WAS PRETTY DARN GOOD TOO... AND GOLIATH IS REALLY HUGE!
BUT ANYWAY! WHAT ABOUT YOU?
WERE THERE LOTS OF AWESOME PLAYERS THERE?!
BOFF
YEAH.
I BET THERE WERE!
THE GUYS WHO GET INVITED THERE ARE ALL THE KIND YOU'LL FIND IN MONTHLY VOLLEYBALL!
THERE WAS A *LITTLE GIANT* THERE TOO.
BOFF
!

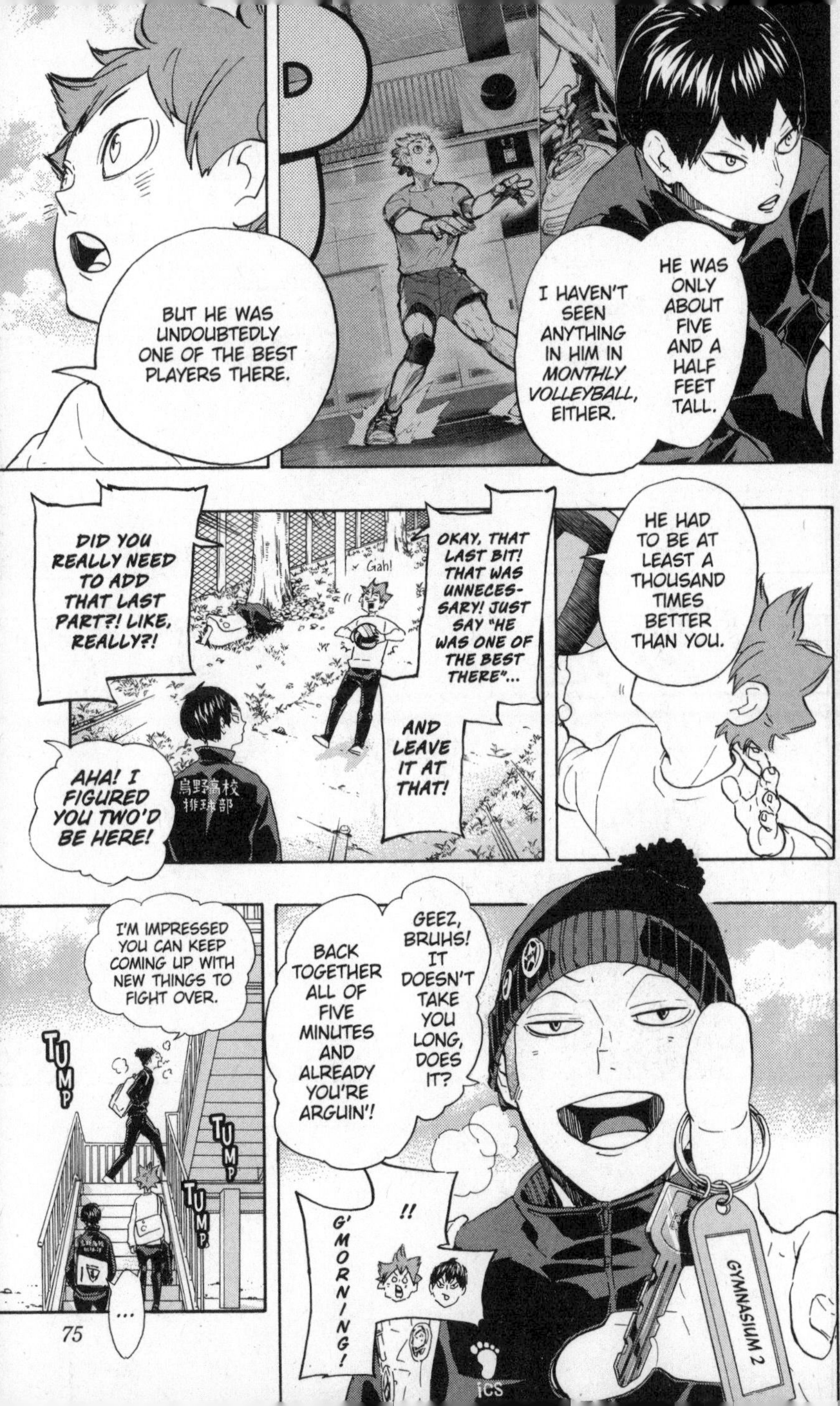
HE WAS ONLY ABOUT FIVE AND A HALF FEET TALL.
I HAVEN'T SEEN ANYTHING IN HIM IN *MONTHLY VOLLEYBALL*, EITHER.
BUT HE WAS UNDOUBTEDLY ONE OF THE BEST PLAYERS THERE.
HE HAD TO BE AT LEAST A THOUSAND TIMES BETTER THAN YOU.
OKAY, THAT LAST BIT! THAT WAS UNNECES-SARY! JUST SAY "HE WAS ONE OF THE BEST THERE"...
AND LEAVE IT AT THAT!
Gah!
DID YOU REALLY NEED TO ADD THAT LAST PART?! LIKE, REALLY?!
AHA! I FIGURED YOU TWO'D BE HERE!
烏野高校
排球部
GEEZ, BRUHS! IT DOESN'T TAKE YOU LONG, DOES IT?
BACK TOGETHER ALL OF FIVE MINUTES AND ALREADY YOU'RE ARGUIN'!
!!
G'MORNING!
GYMNASIUM 2
I'M IMPRESSED YOU CAN KEEP COMING UP WITH NEW THINGS TO FIGHT OVER.
TUMP
TUMP
TUMP
...

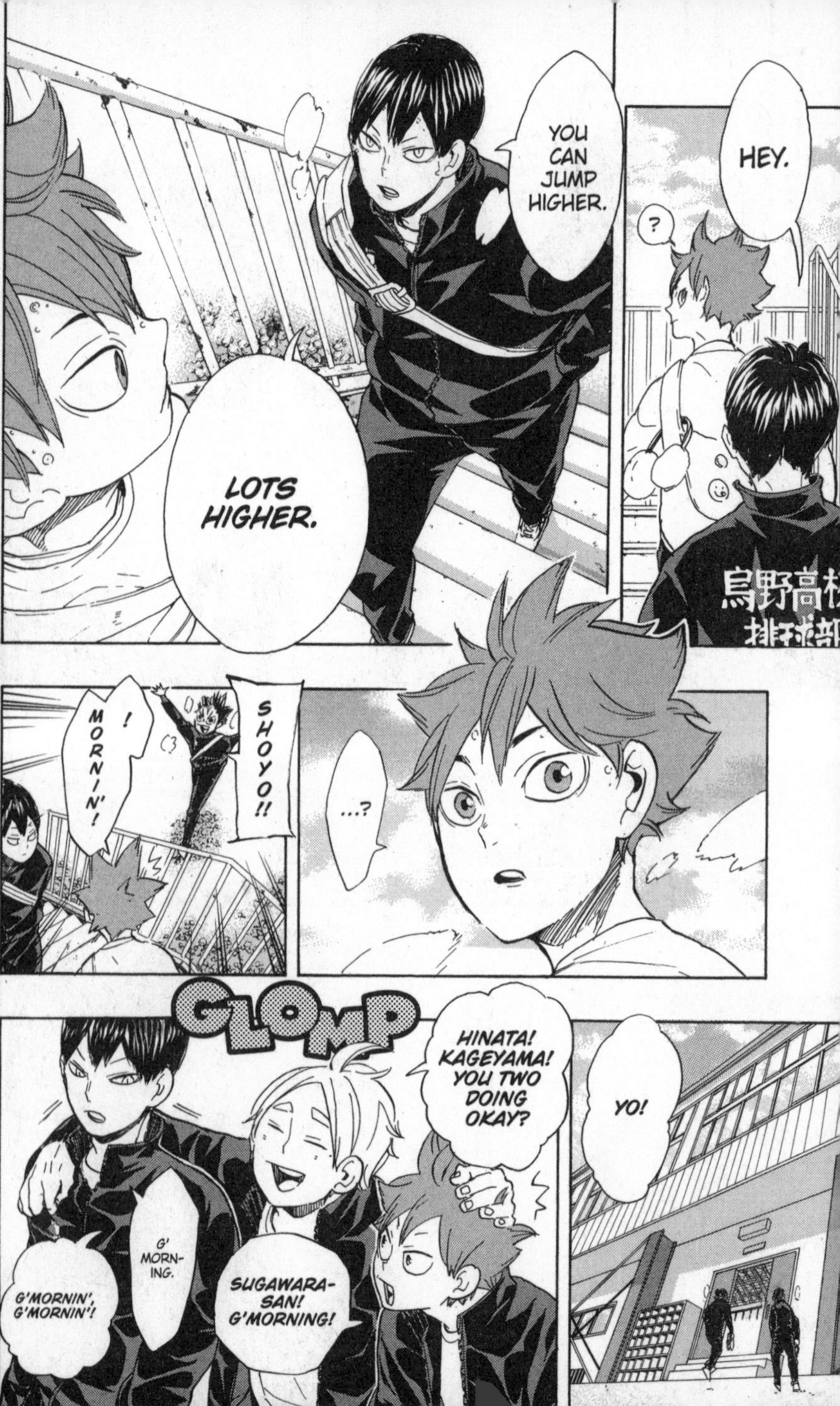
HEY.
?
YOU CAN JUMP HIGHER.
LOTS HIGHER.
...?
SHOYO!!
!
MORNIN'!
YO!
GLOMP
HINATA! KAGEYAMA! YOU TWO DOING OKAY?
SUGAWARA-SAN! G'MORNING!
G' MORN-ING.
G'MORNIN', G'MORNIN'!

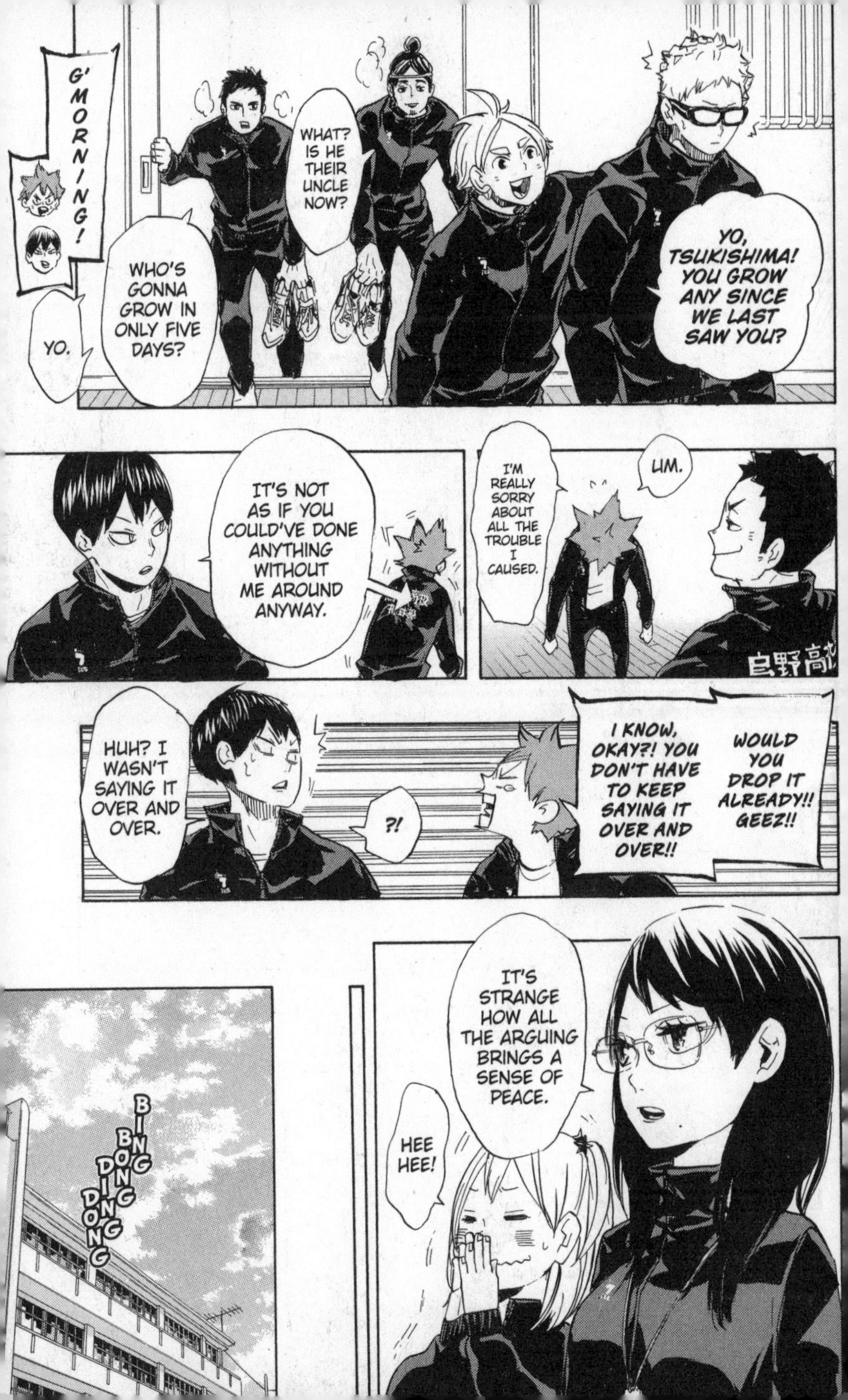
YO, TSUKISHIMA! YOU GROW ANY SINCE WE LAST SAW YOU?
WHAT? IS HE THEIR UNCLE NOW?
WHO'S GONNA GROW IN ONLY FIVE DAYS?
YO.
G'MORNING!
UM.
I'M REALLY SORRY ABOUT ALL THE TROUBLE I CAUSED.
IT'S NOT AS IF YOU COULD'VE DONE ANYTHING WITHOUT ME AROUND ANYWAY.
WOULD YOU DROP IT ALREADY!! GEEZ!!
I KNOW, OKAY?! YOU DON'T HAVE TO KEEP SAYING IT OVER AND OVER!!
?!
HUH? I WASN'T SAYING IT OVER AND OVER.
IT'S STRANGE HOW ALL THE ARGUING BRINGS A SENSE OF PEACE.
HEE HEE!
BING BONG DING DONG

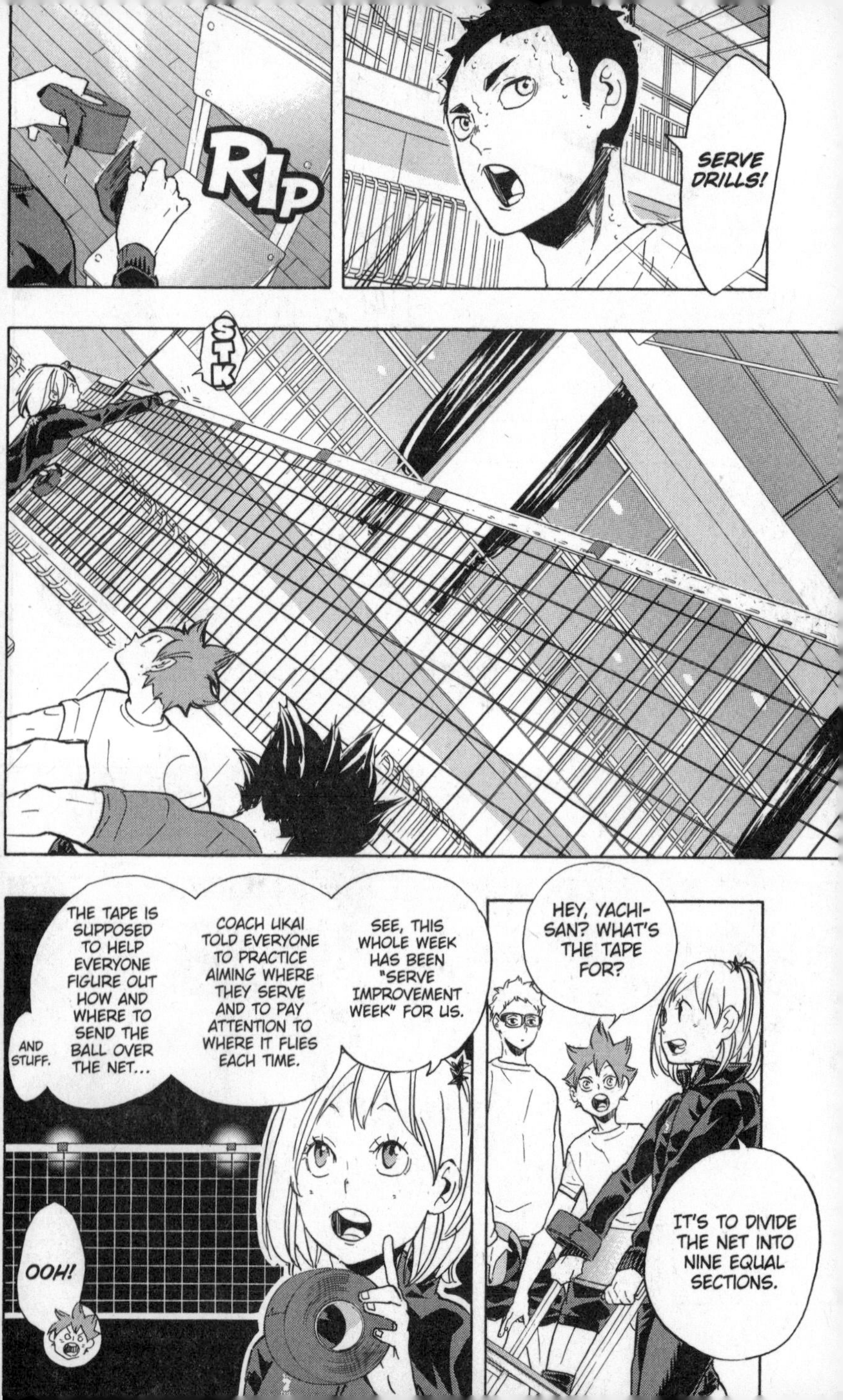
SERVE DRILLS!
RIP
STK
HEY, YACHI-SAN? WHAT'S THE TAPE FOR?
IT'S TO DIVIDE THE NET INTO NINE EQUAL SECTIONS.
SEE, THIS WHOLE WEEK HAS BEEN "SERVE IMPROVEMENT WEEK" FOR US.
COACH UKAI TOLD EVERYONE TO PRACTICE AIMING WHERE THEY SERVE AND TO PAY ATTENTION TO WHERE IT FLIES EACH TIME.
THE TAPE IS SUPPOSED TO HELP EVERYONE FIGURE OUT HOW AND WHERE TO SEND THE BALL OVER THE NET...
AND STUFF.
OOH!

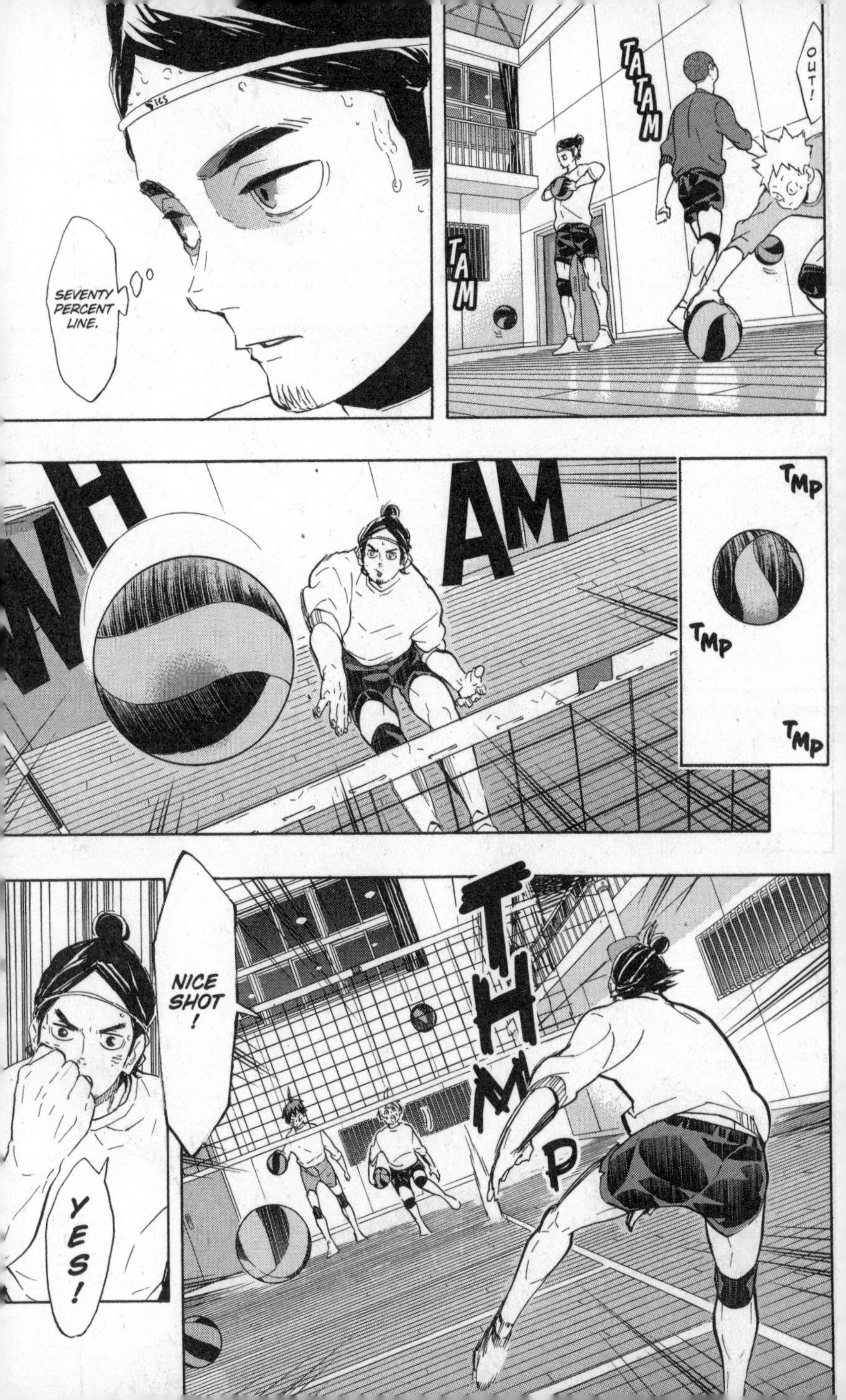
TATAM
OUT!
TAM
SEVENTY PERCENT LINE.
TMP
TMP
TMP
WHAM
THMP
NICE SHOT!
YES!

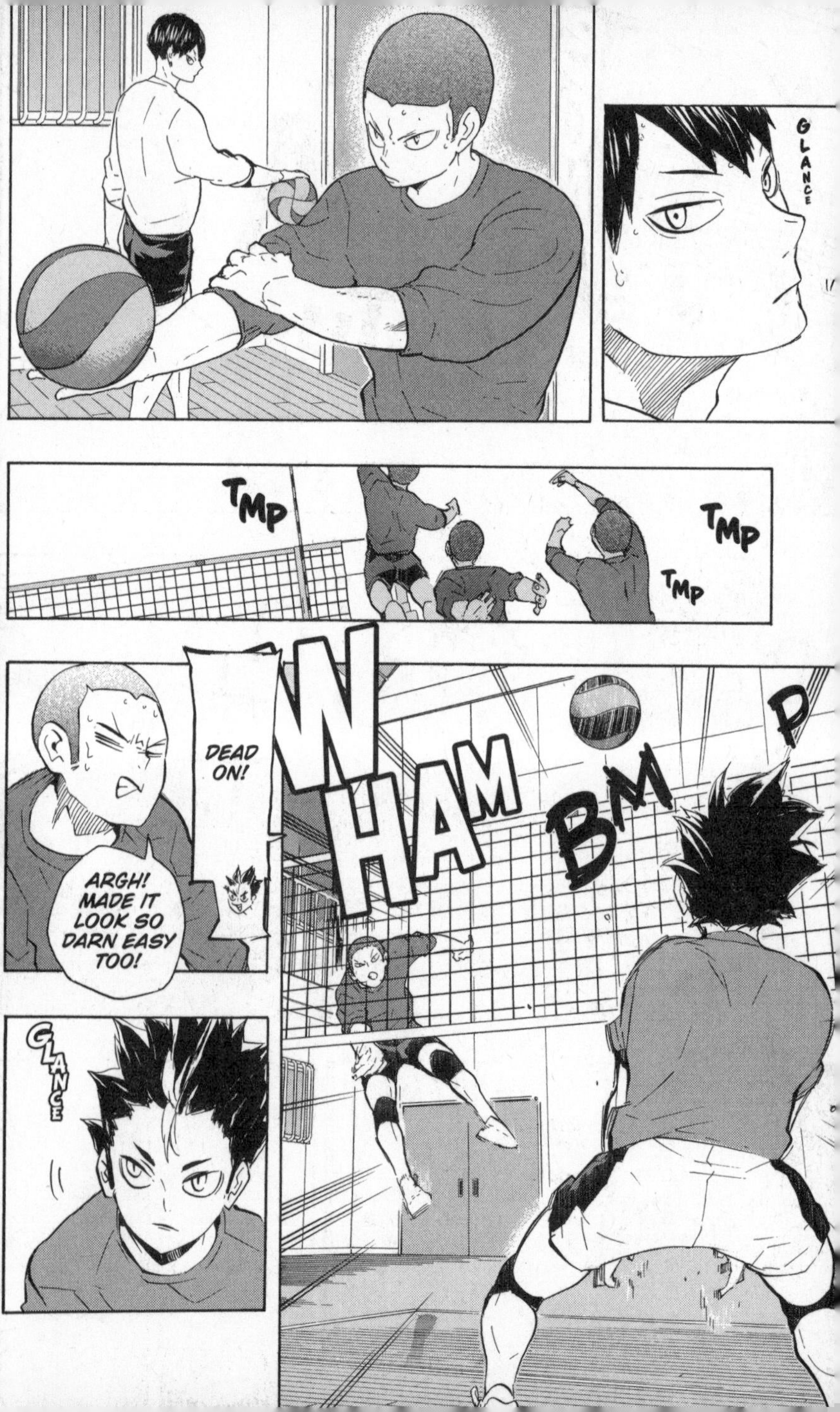
GLANCE
TMP
TMP
TMP
WHAM
BMP
DEAD ON!
ARGH! MADE IT LOOK SO DARN EASY TOO!
GLANCE

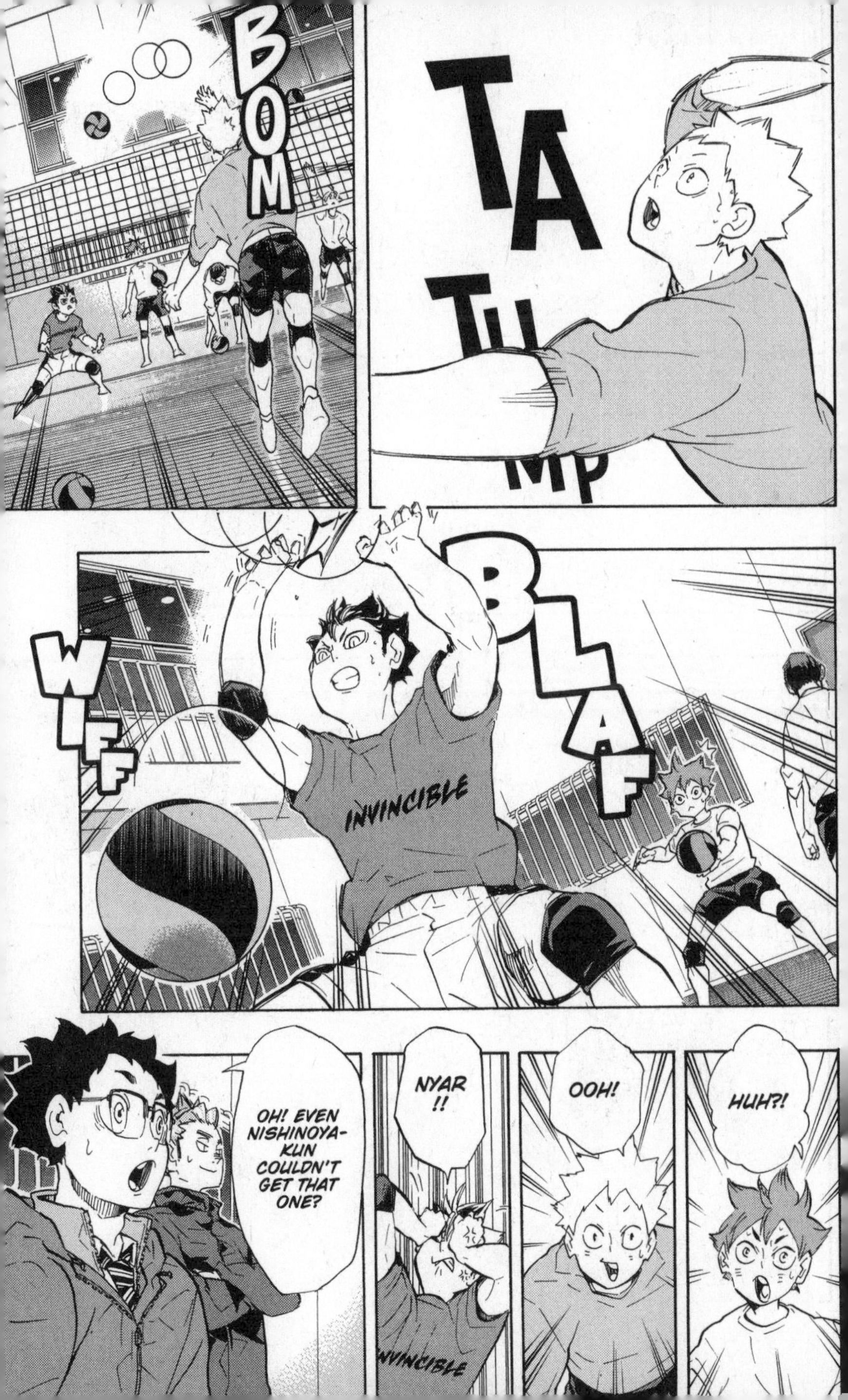
TA
TU
MP
BOM
BLAF
WIFF
INVINCIBLE
HUH?!
OOH!
NYAR !!
INVINCIBLE
OH! EVEN NISHINOYA-KUN COULDN'T GET THAT ONE?

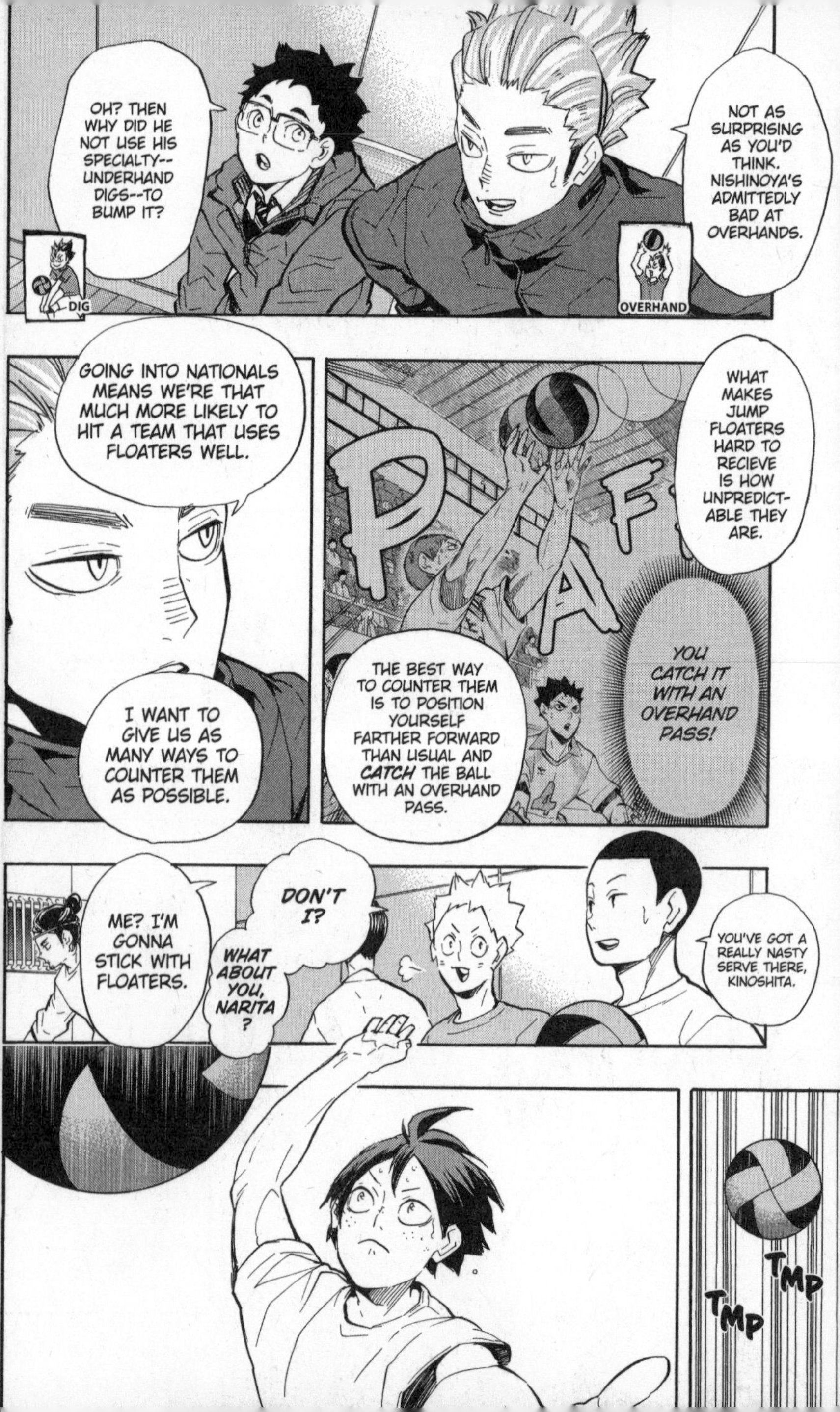
NOT AS SURPRISING AS YOU'D THINK. NISHINOYA'S ADMITTEDLY BAD AT OVERHANDS.
OVERHAND
OH? THEN WHY DID HE NOT USE HIS SPECIALTY--UNDERHAND DIGS--TO BUMP IT?
DIG
WHAT MAKES JUMP FLOATERS HARD TO RECIEVE IS HOW UNPREDICTABLE THEY ARE.
PAF
YOU CATCH IT WITH AN OVERHAND PASS!
THE BEST WAY TO COUNTER THEM IS TO POSITION YOURSELF FARTHER FORWARD THAN USUAL AND CATCH THE BALL WITH AN OVERHAND PASS.
GOING INTO NATIONALS MEANS WE'RE THAT MUCH MORE LIKELY TO HIT A TEAM THAT USES FLOATERS WELL.
I WANT TO GIVE US AS MANY WAYS TO COUNTER THEM AS POSSIBLE.
YOU'VE GOT A REALLY NASTY SERVE THERE, KINOSHITA.
DON'T I?
WHAT ABOUT YOU, NARITA?
ME? I'M GONNA STICK WITH FLOATERS.
TMP TMP

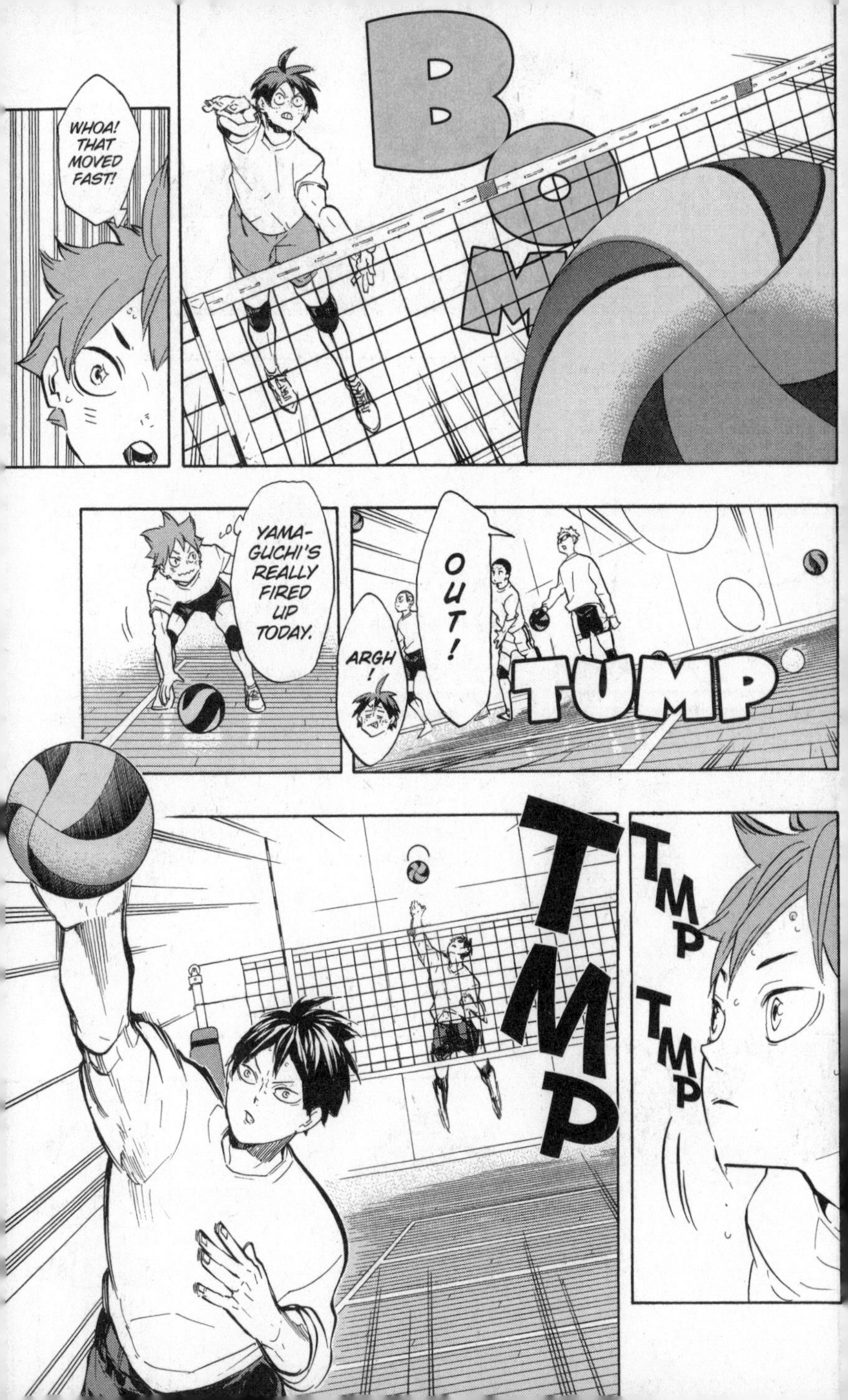
BOOM
WHOA! THAT MOVED FAST!
OUT!
ARGH!
TUMP
YAMAGUCHI'S REALLY FIRED UP TODAY.
TMP
TMP
TMP

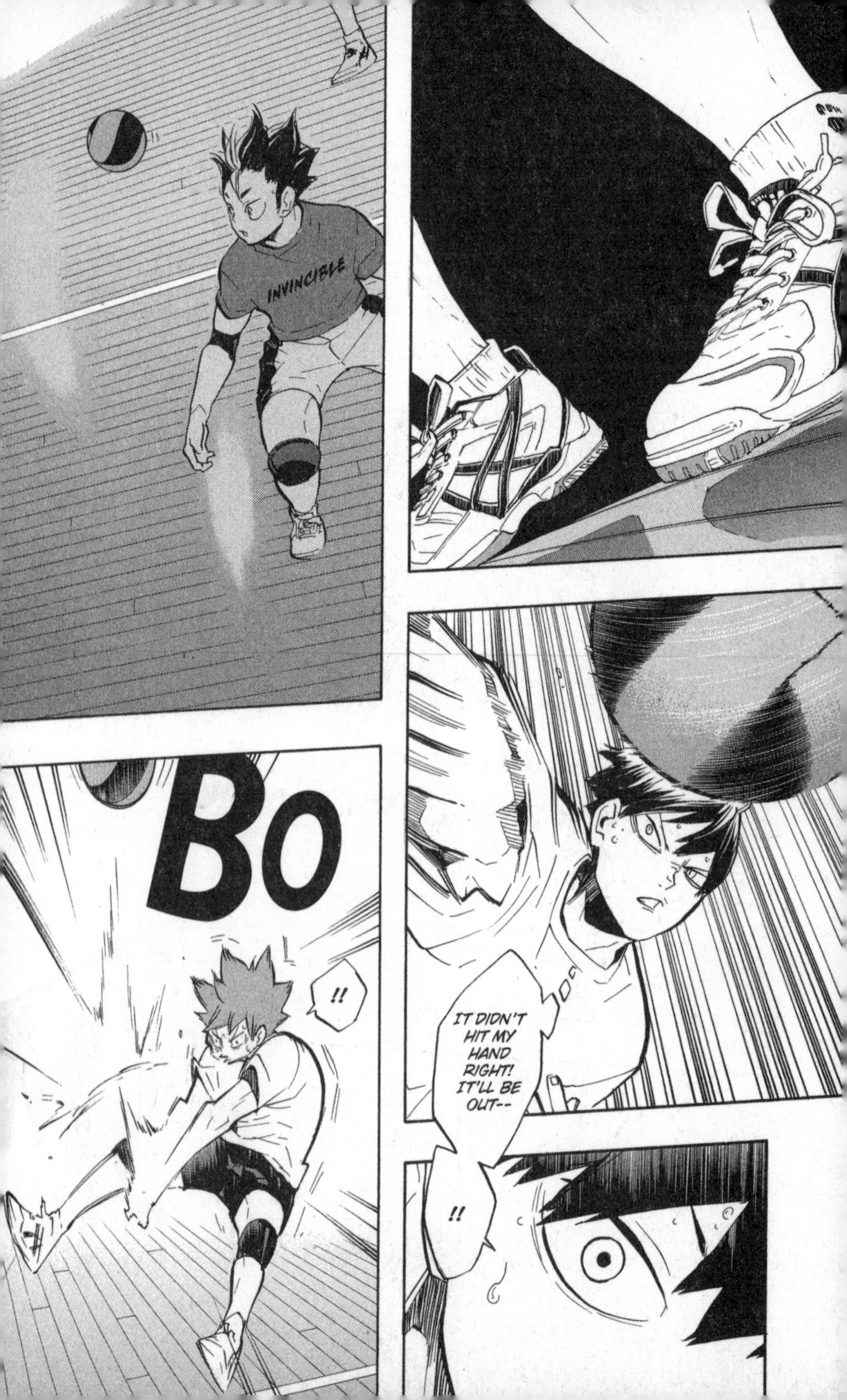
INVINCIBLE
IT DIDN'T HIT MY HAND RIGHT! IT'LL BE OUT--
!!
BO
!!

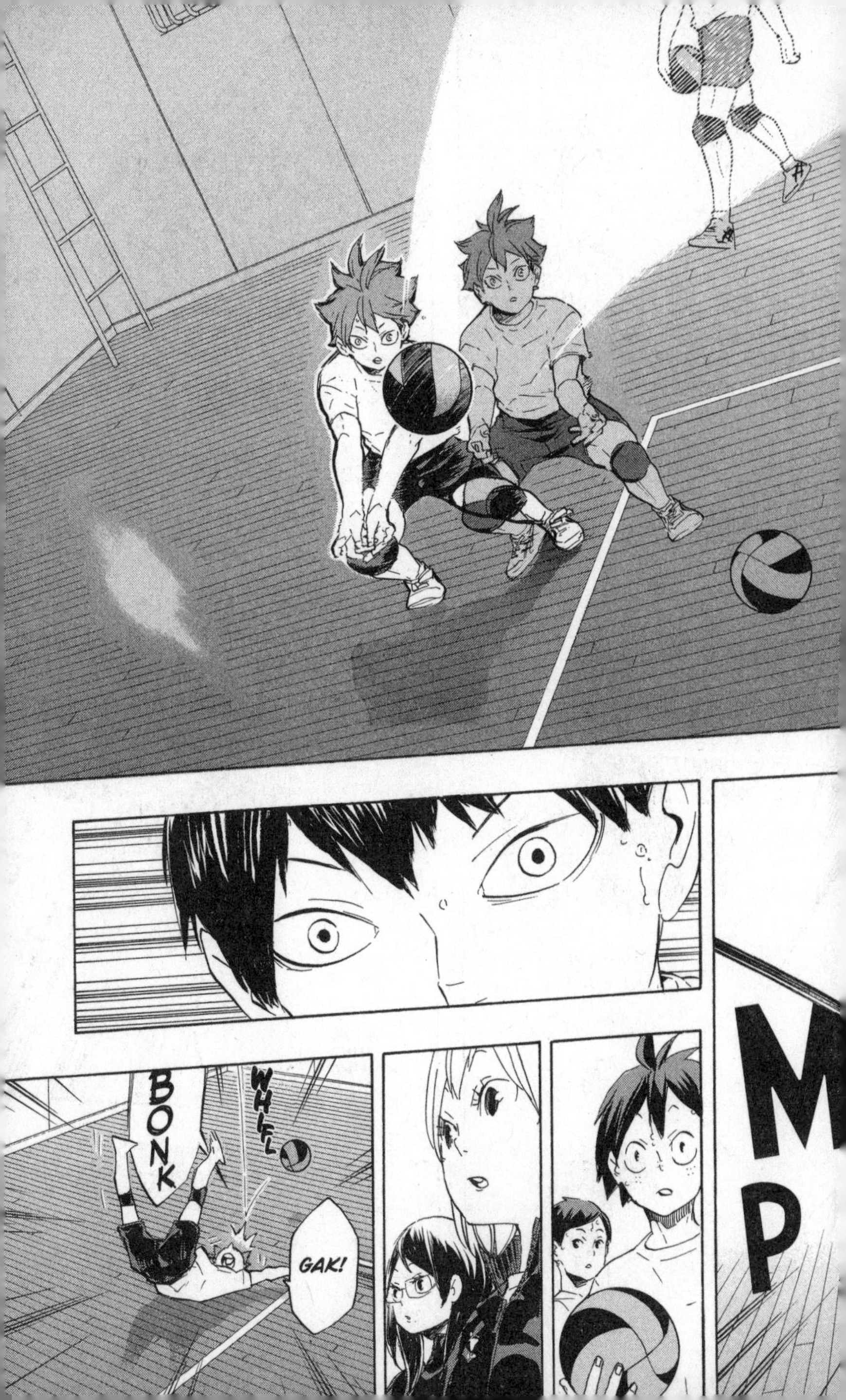
M
P
BONK
WHIFL
GAK!

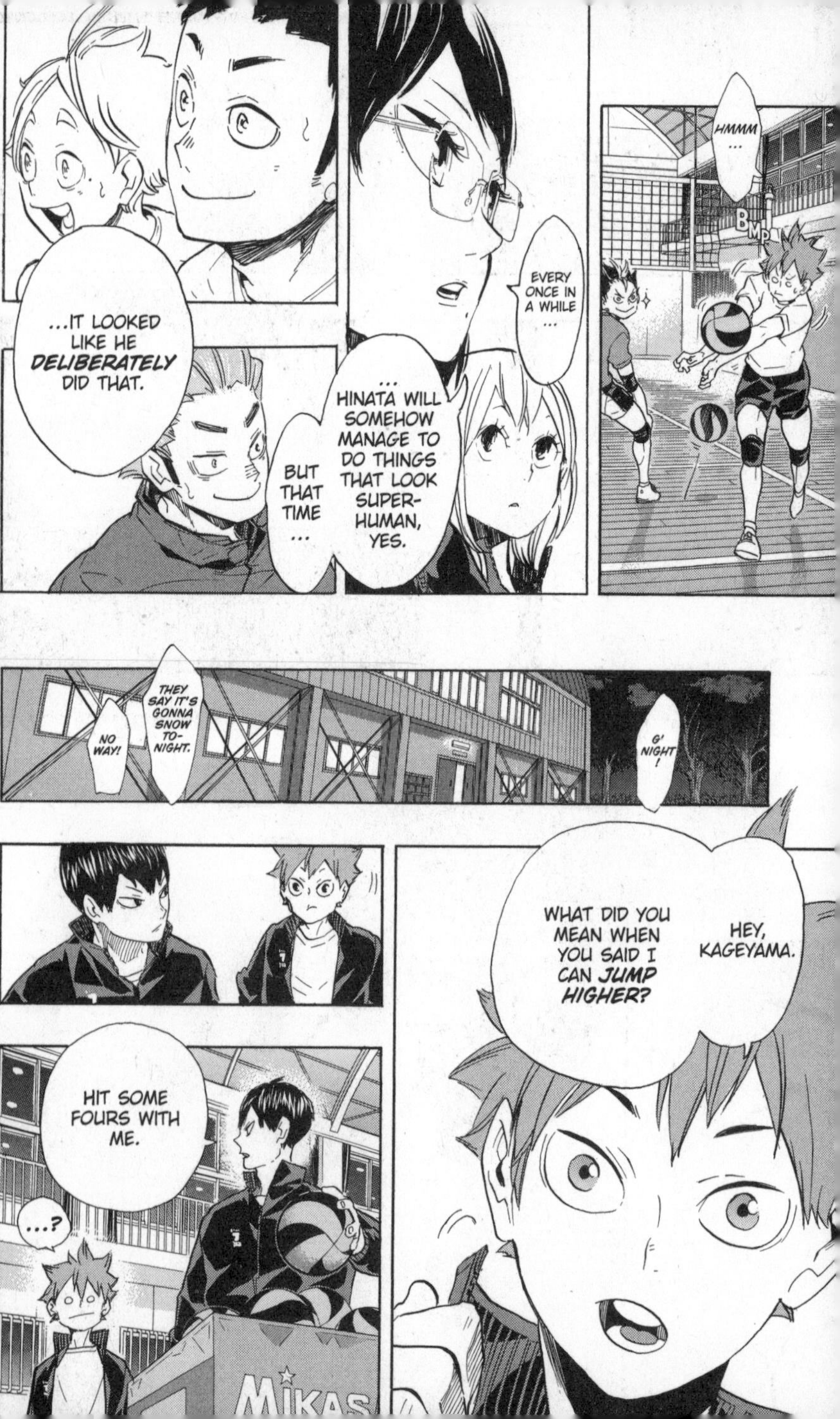
HMMM ...
BMP
EVERY ONCE IN A WHILE ...
... HINATA WILL SOMEHOW MANAGE TO DO THINGS THAT LOOK SUPER-HUMAN, YES.
BUT THAT TIME ...
...IT LOOKED LIKE HE **DELIBERATELY** DID THAT.
G' NIGHT!
THEY SAY IT'S GONNA SNOW TO-NIGHT.
NO WAY!
HEY, KAGEYAMA.
WHAT DID YOU MEAN WHEN YOU SAID I CAN **JUMP HIGHER?**
HIT SOME FOURS WITH ME.
...?
MIKAS

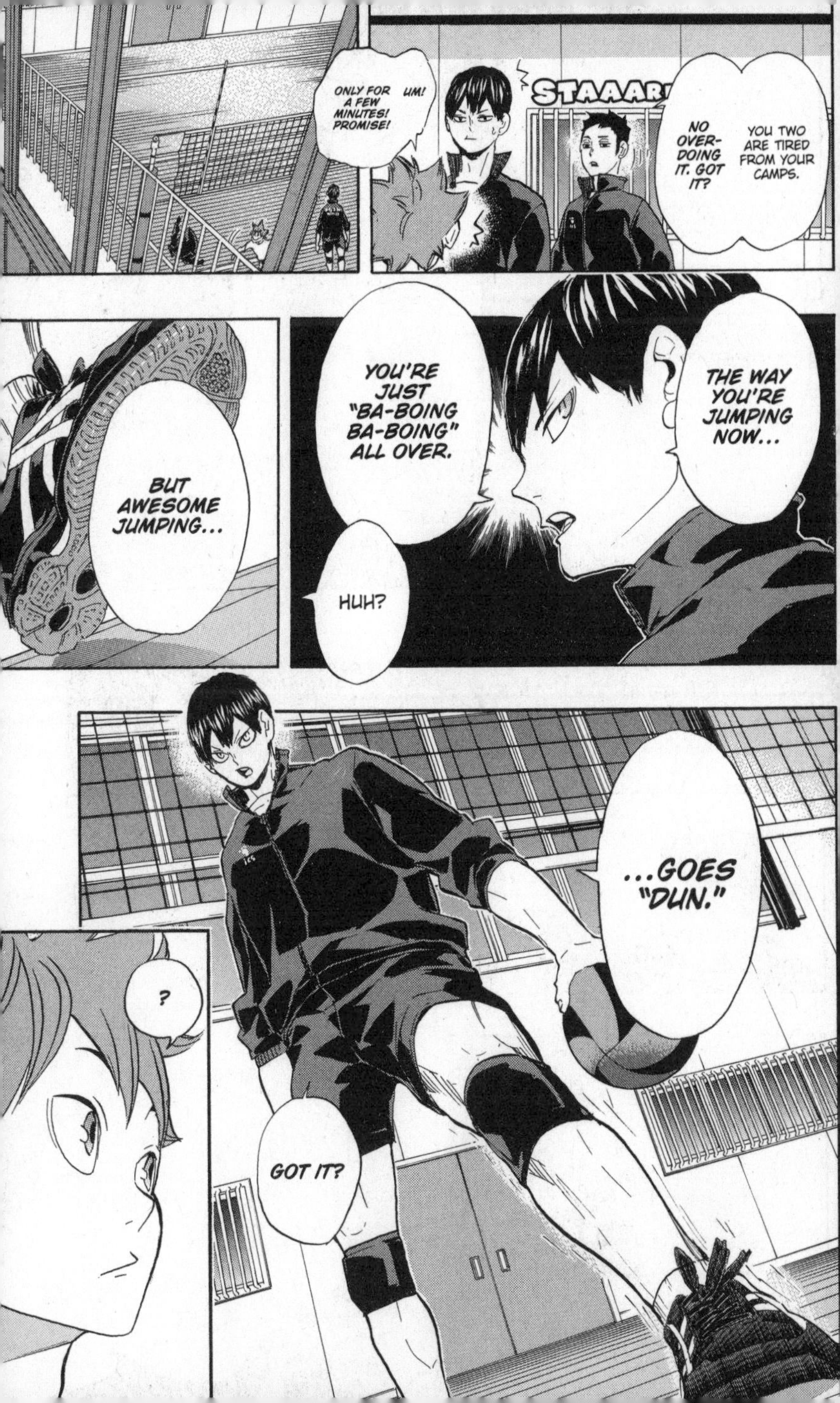
YOU TWO ARE TIRED FROM YOUR CAMPS.
NO OVER-DOING IT. GOT IT?
STAAAR
UM!
ONLY FOR A FEW MINUTES! PROMISE!
THE WAY YOU'RE JUMPING NOW...
YOU'RE JUST "BA-BOING BA-BOING" ALL OVER.
HUH?
BUT AWESOME JUMPING...
...GOES "DUN."
GOT IT?
?

HERO INTERVIEW IN PASSING

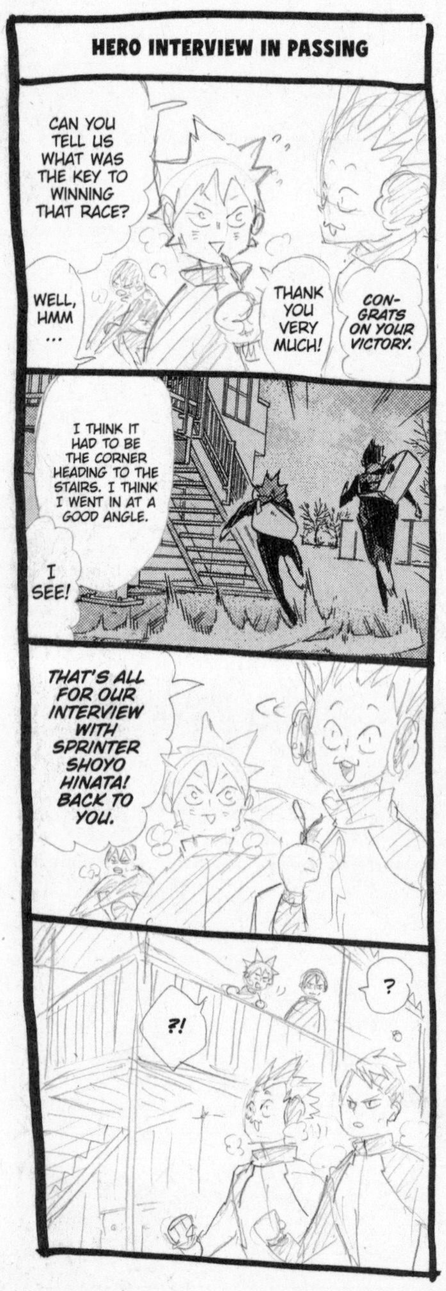
CON-GRATS ON YOUR VICTORY.
THANK YOU VERY MUCH!
CAN YOU TELL US WHAT WAS THE KEY TO WINNING THAT RACE?
WELL, HMM ...
I THINK IT HAD TO BE THE CORNER HEADING TO THE STAIRS. I THINK I WENT IN AT A GOOD ANGLE.
I SEE!
THAT'S ALL FOR OUR INTERVIEW WITH SPRINTER SHOYO HINATA! BACK TO YOU.
?
?!

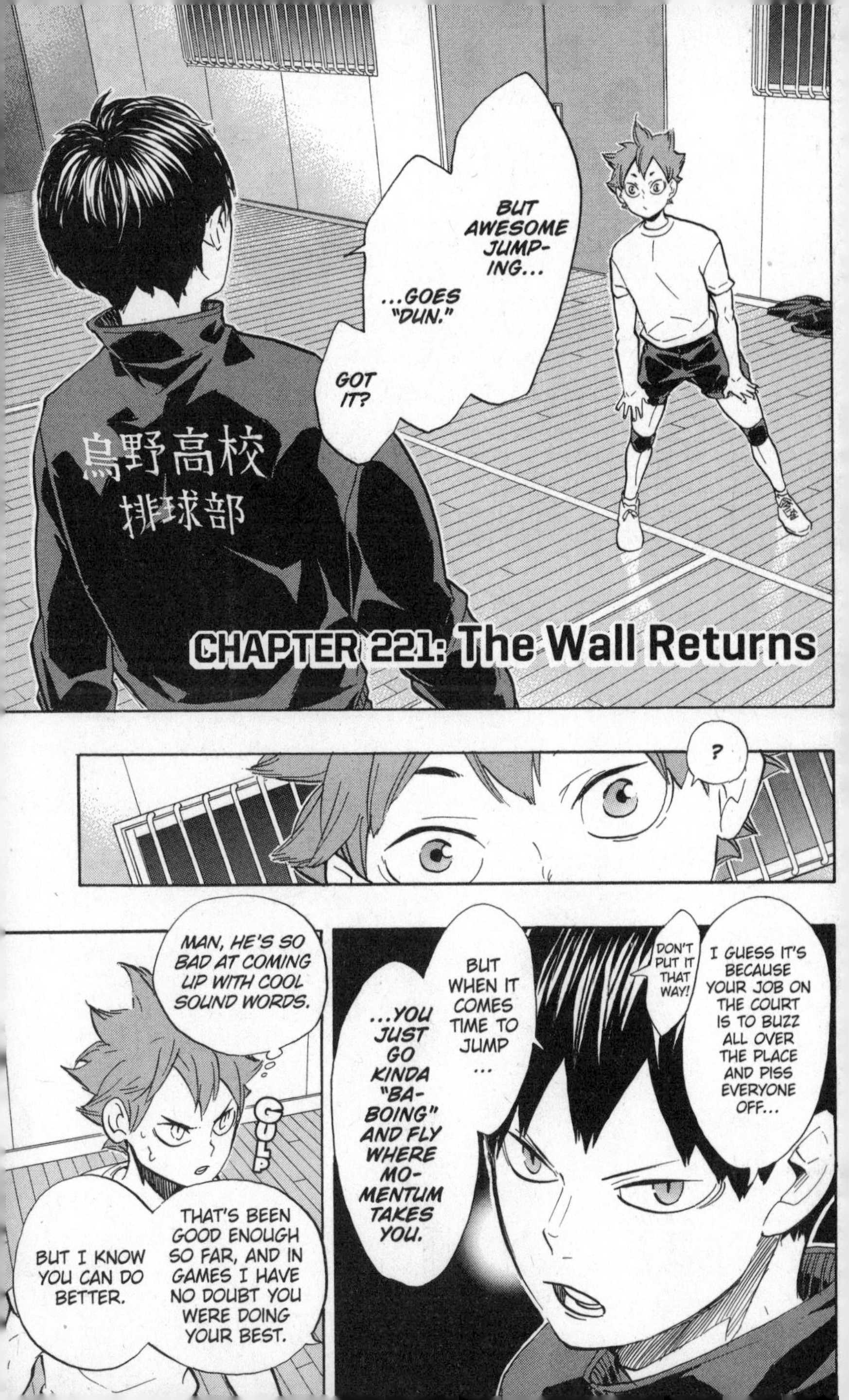
BUT AWESOME JUMPING...
...GOES "DUN."
GOT IT?
烏野高校
排球部
CHAPTER 221: The Wall Returns
?
I GUESS IT'S BECAUSE YOUR JOB ON THE COURT IS TO BUZZ ALL OVER THE PLACE AND PISS EVERYONE OFF...
DON'T PUT IT THAT WAY!
BUT WHEN IT COMES TIME TO JUMP...
...YOU JUST GO KINDA "BA-BOING" AND FLY WHERE MOMENTUM TAKES YOU.
MAN, HE'S SO BAD AT COMING UP WITH COOL SOUND WORDS.
GULP
THAT'S BEEN GOOD ENOUGH SO FAR, AND IN GAMES I HAVE NO DOUBT YOU WERE DOING YOUR BEST.
BUT I KNOW YOU CAN DO BETTER.

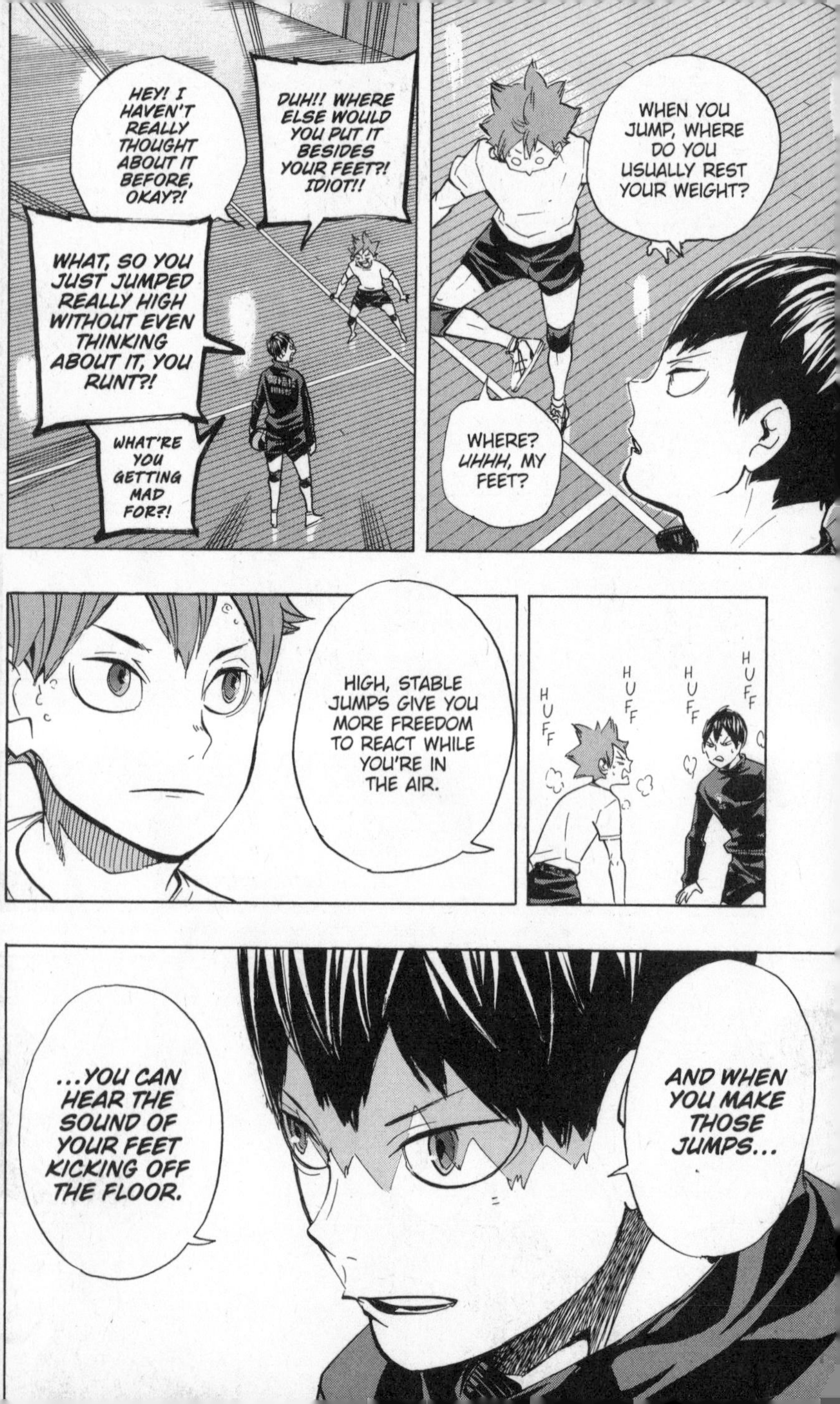
WHEN YOU JUMP, WHERE DO YOU USUALLY REST YOUR WEIGHT?
WHERE? UHHH, MY FEET?
DUH!! WHERE ELSE WOULD YOU PUT IT BESIDES YOUR FEET?! IDIOT!!
HEY! I HAVEN'T REALLY THOUGHT ABOUT IT BEFORE, OKAY?!
WHAT, SO YOU JUST JUMPED REALLY HIGH WITHOUT EVEN THINKING ABOUT IT, YOU RUNT?!
WHAT'RE YOU GETTING MAD FOR?!
HUFF
HUFF
HUFF
HUFF
HIGH, STABLE JUMPS GIVE YOU MORE FREEDOM TO REACT WHILE YOU'RE IN THE AIR.
AND WHEN YOU MAKE THOSE JUMPS...
...YOU CAN HEAR THE SOUND OF YOUR FEET KICKING OFF THE FLOOR.

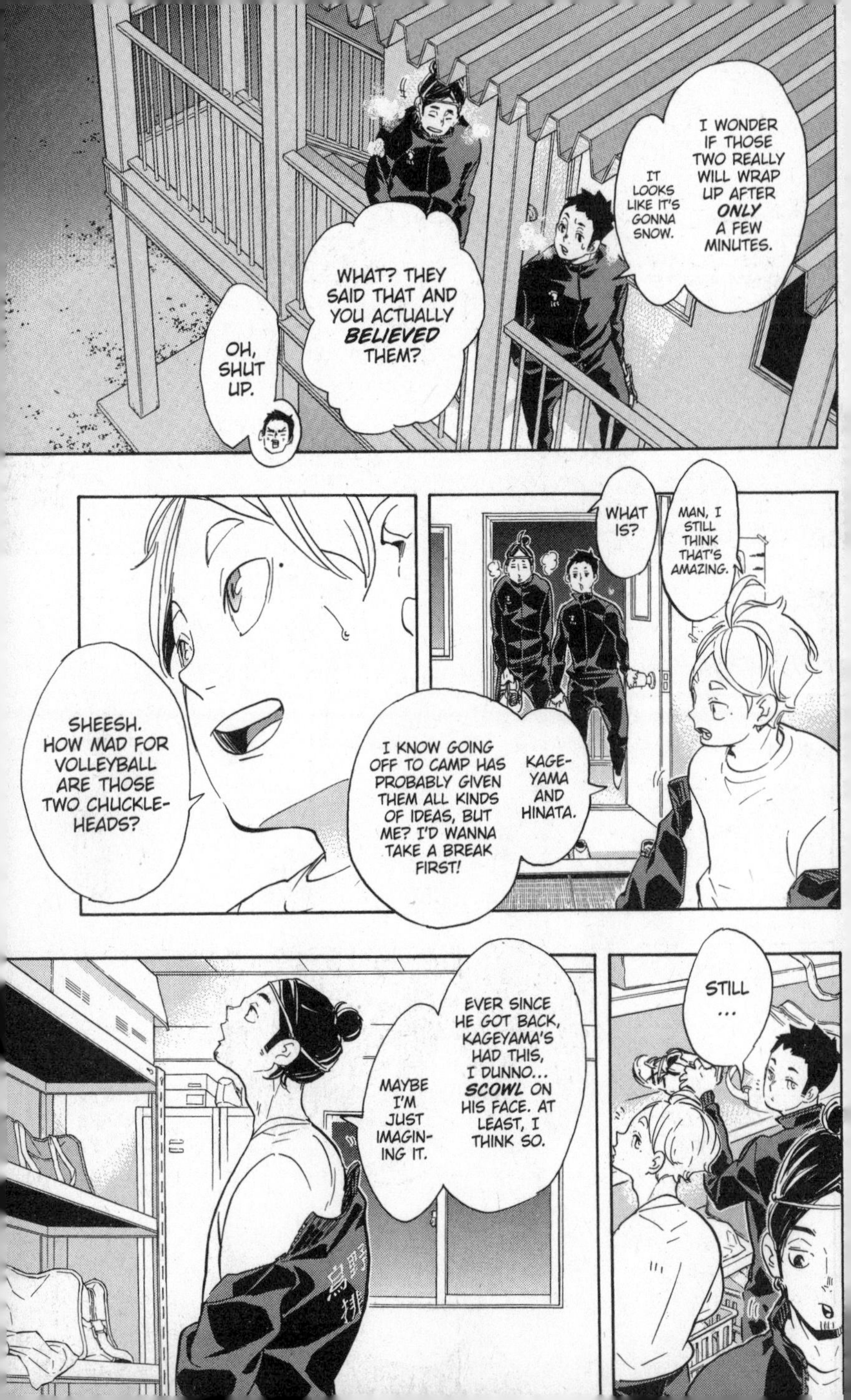
I WONDER IF THOSE TWO REALLY WILL WRAP UP AFTER ONLY A FEW MINUTES.
IT LOOKS LIKE IT'S GONNA SNOW.
WHAT? THEY SAID THAT AND YOU ACTUALLY BELIEVED THEM?
OH, SHUT UP.
MAN, I STILL THINK THAT'S AMAZING.
WHAT IS?
KAGE-YAMA AND HINATA.
I KNOW GOING OFF TO CAMP HAS PROBABLY GIVEN THEM ALL KINDS OF IDEAS, BUT ME? I'D WANNA TAKE A BREAK FIRST!
SHEESH. HOW MAD FOR VOLLEYBALL ARE THOSE TWO CHUCKLE-HEADS?
STILL ...
EVER SINCE HE GOT BACK, KAGEYAMA'S HAD THIS, I DUNNO... SCOWL ON HIS FACE. AT LEAST, I THINK SO.
MAYBE I'M JUST IMAGIN-ING IT.

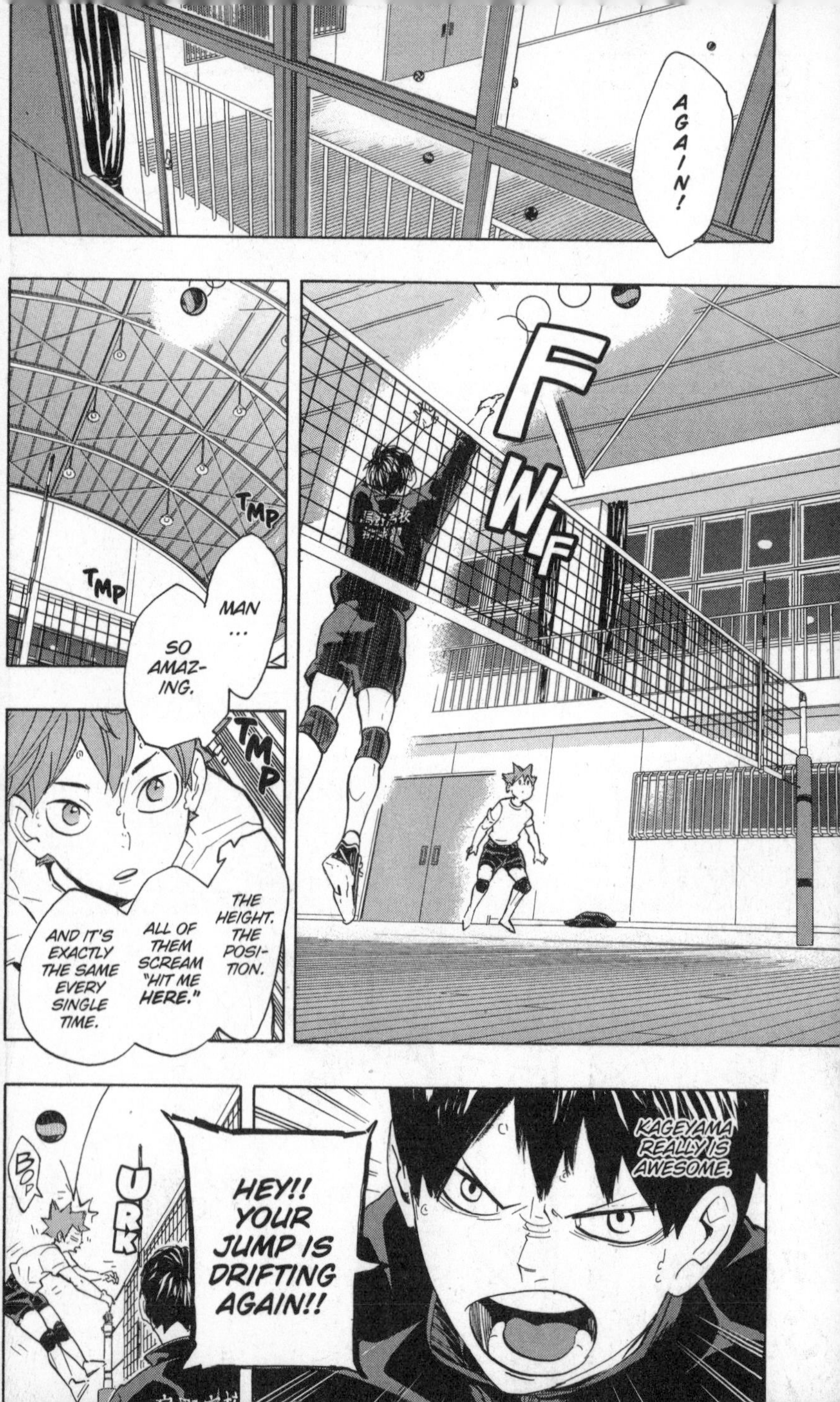
AGAIN!
FWIF
TMP
TMP
MAN...
SO AMAZING.
TMP
THE HEIGHT. THE POSITION.
ALL OF THEM SCREAM "HIT ME HERE."
AND IT'S EXACTLY THE SAME EVERY SINGLE TIME.
KAGEYAMA REALLY IS AWESOME.
HEY!! YOUR JUMP IS DRIFTING AGAIN!!
URK
BOP

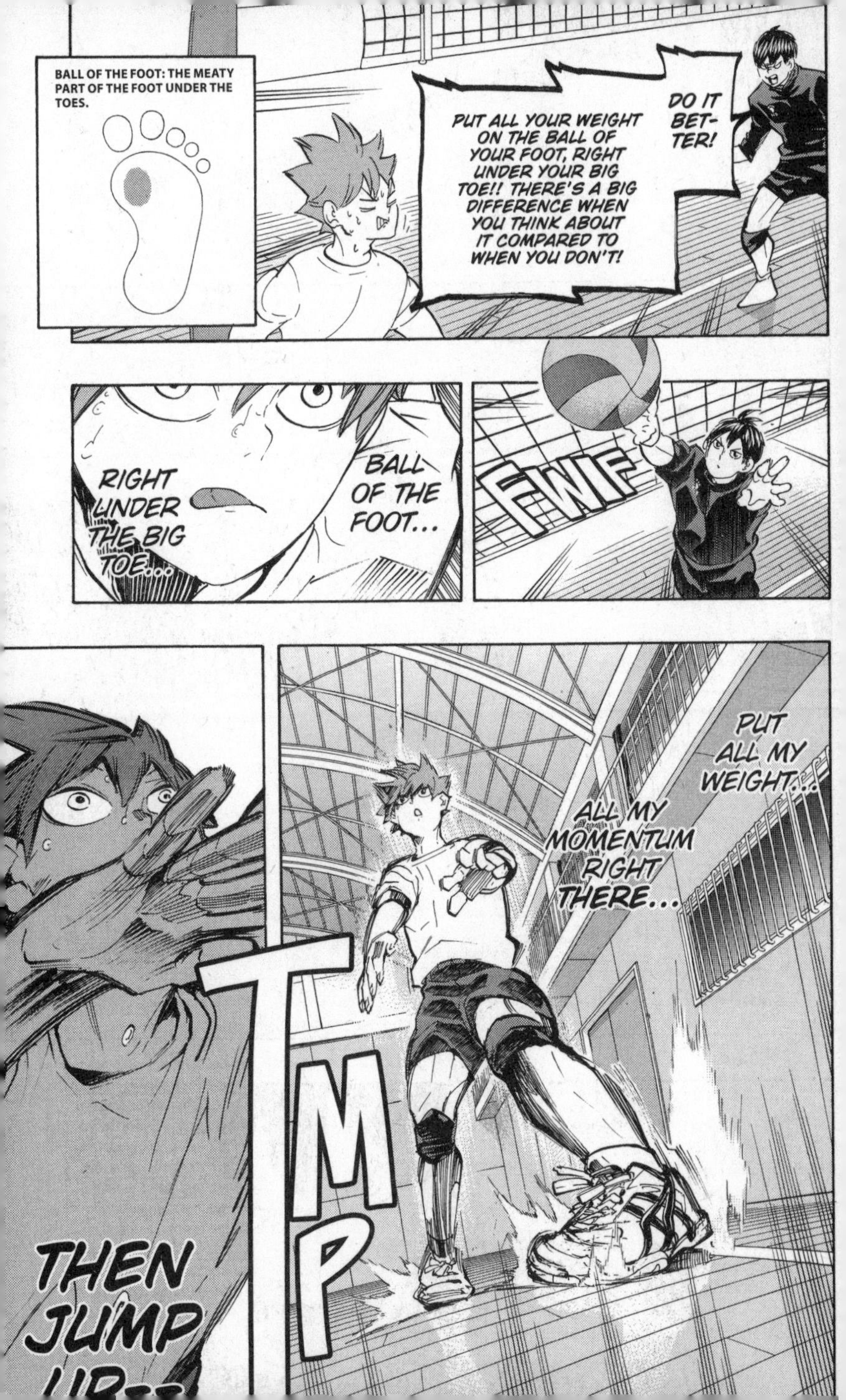
DO IT BETTER!
PUT ALL YOUR WEIGHT ON THE BALL OF YOUR FOOT, RIGHT UNDER YOUR BIG TOE!! THERE'S A BIG DIFFERENCE WHEN YOU THINK ABOUT IT COMPARED TO WHEN YOU DON'T!
BALL OF THE FOOT: THE MEATY PART OF THE FOOT UNDER THE TOES.
FWIP
BALL OF THE FOOT...
RIGHT UNDER THE BIG TOE...
PUT ALL MY WEIGHT...
ALL MY MOMENTUM RIGHT THERE...
TMP
THEN JUMP

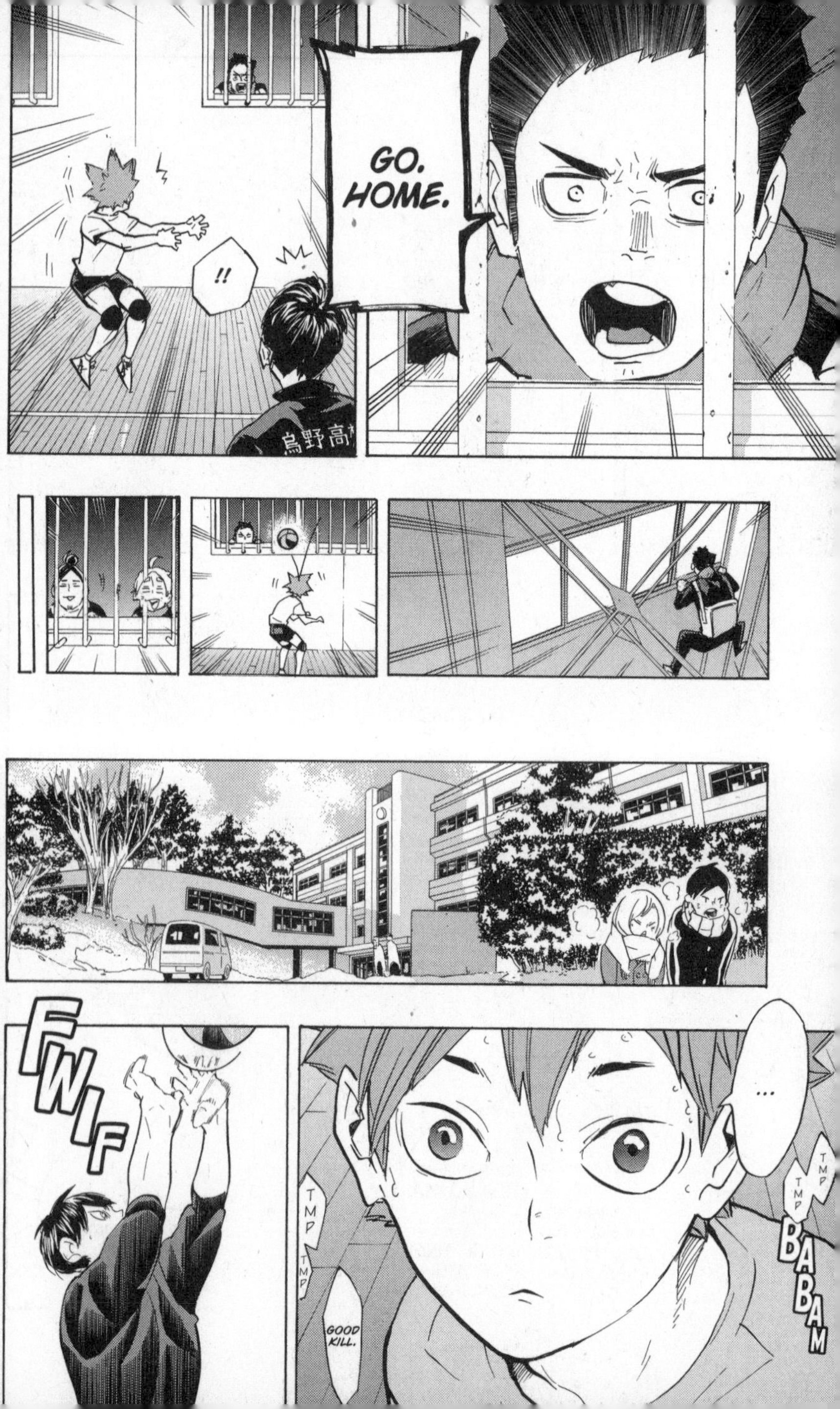
GO. HOME.
!!
...
TMP TMP
BABAM
TMP TMP
GOOD KILL.
FWIF

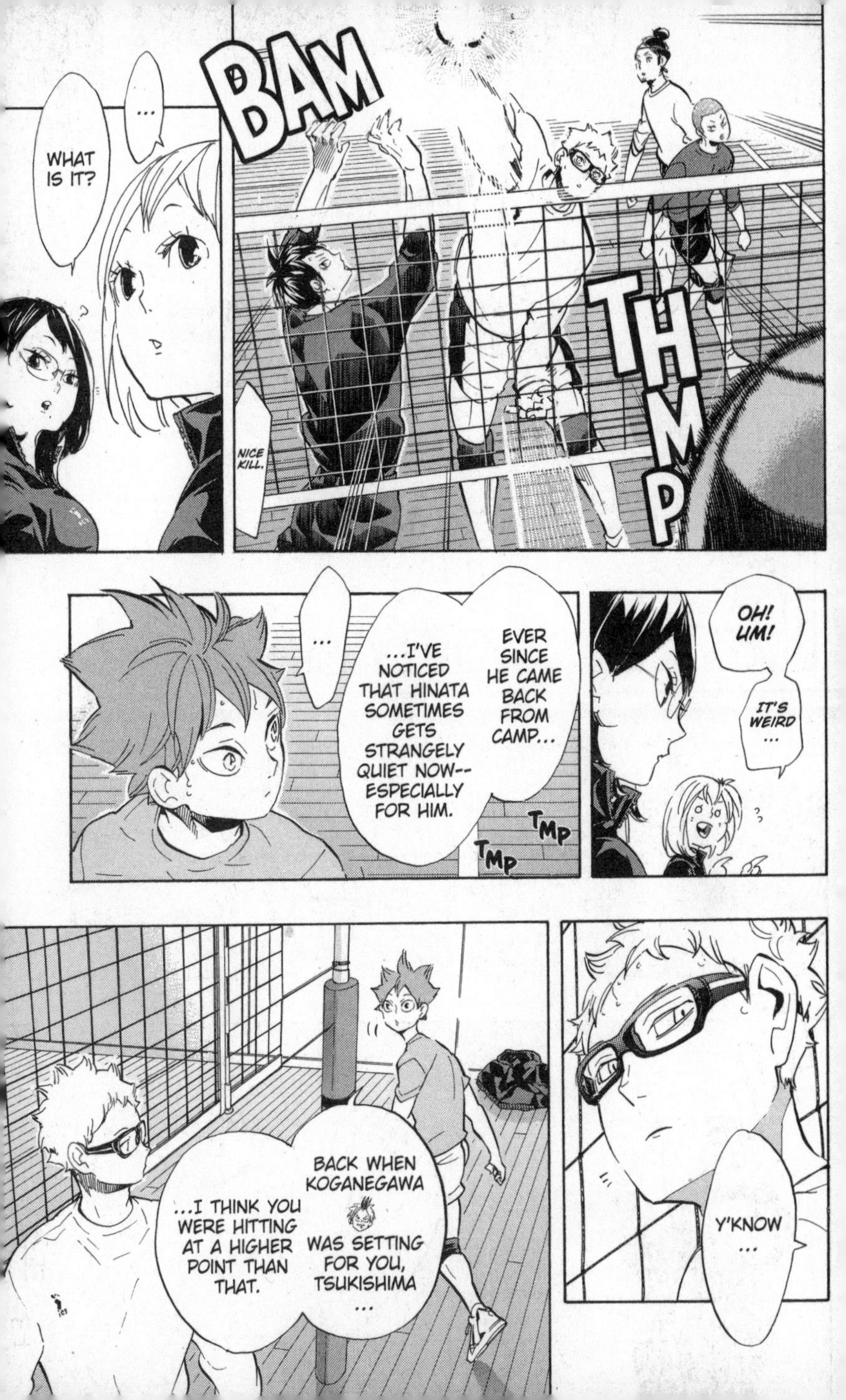
BAM
THUMP
NICE KILL.
...
WHAT IS IT?
OH! UM!
IT'S WEIRD ...
EVER SINCE HE CAME BACK FROM CAMP...
...I'VE NOTICED THAT HINATA SOMETIMES GETS STRANGELY QUIET NOW--ESPECIALLY FOR HIM.
...
TMP
TMP
Y'KNOW ...
BACK WHEN KOGANEGAWA WAS SETTING FOR YOU, TSUKISHIMA ...
...I THINK YOU WERE HITTING AT A HIGHER POINT THAN THAT.

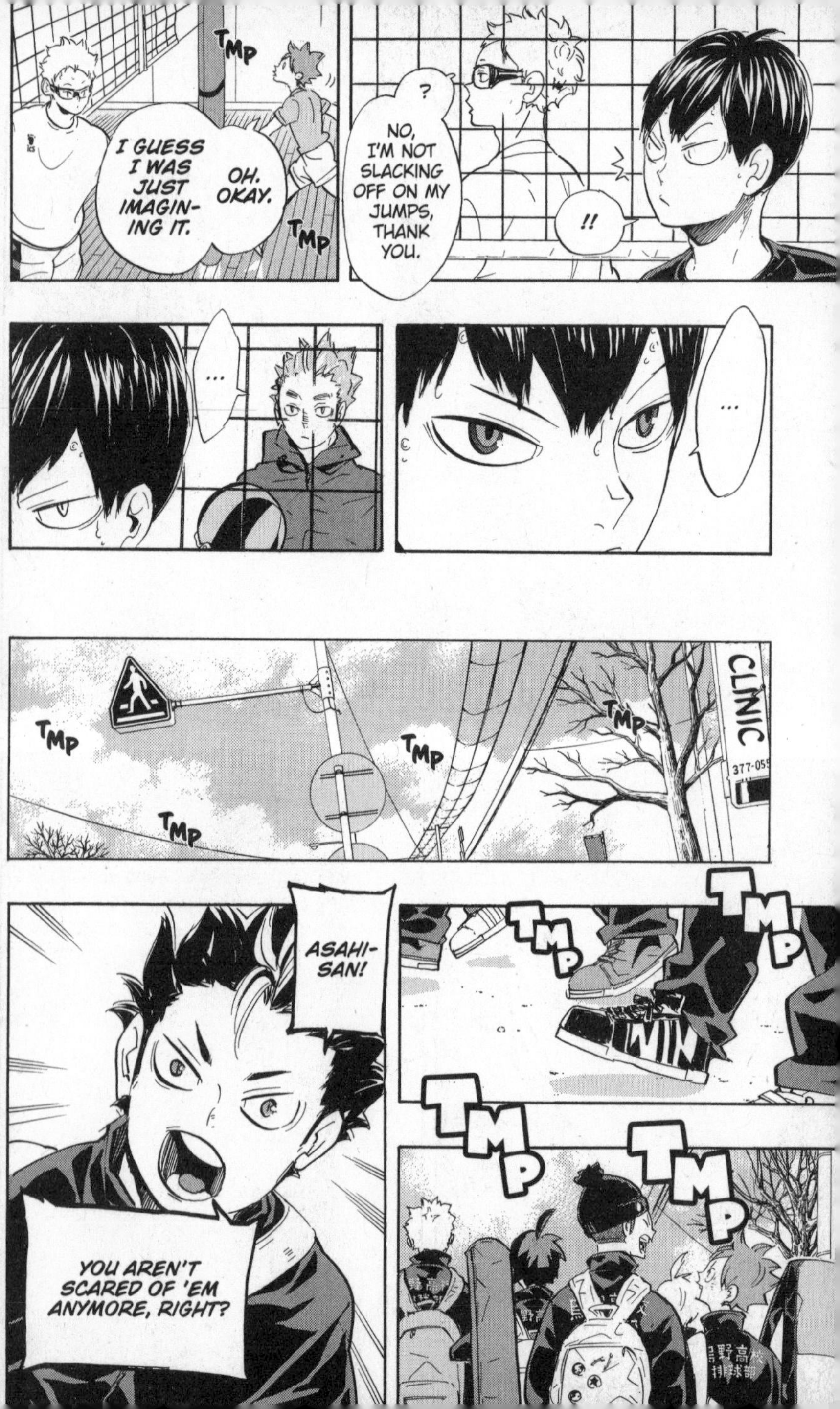
?
NO, I'M NOT SLACKING OFF ON MY JUMPS, THANK YOU.
!!
TMP
I GUESS I WAS JUST IMAGINING IT.
OH. OKAY.
TMP
...
...
CLINIC
377-055
TMP
TMP
TMP
TMP
TMP
TMP
WIN
TMP
TMP
ASAHI-SAN!
YOU AREN'T SCARED OF 'EM ANYMORE, RIGHT?

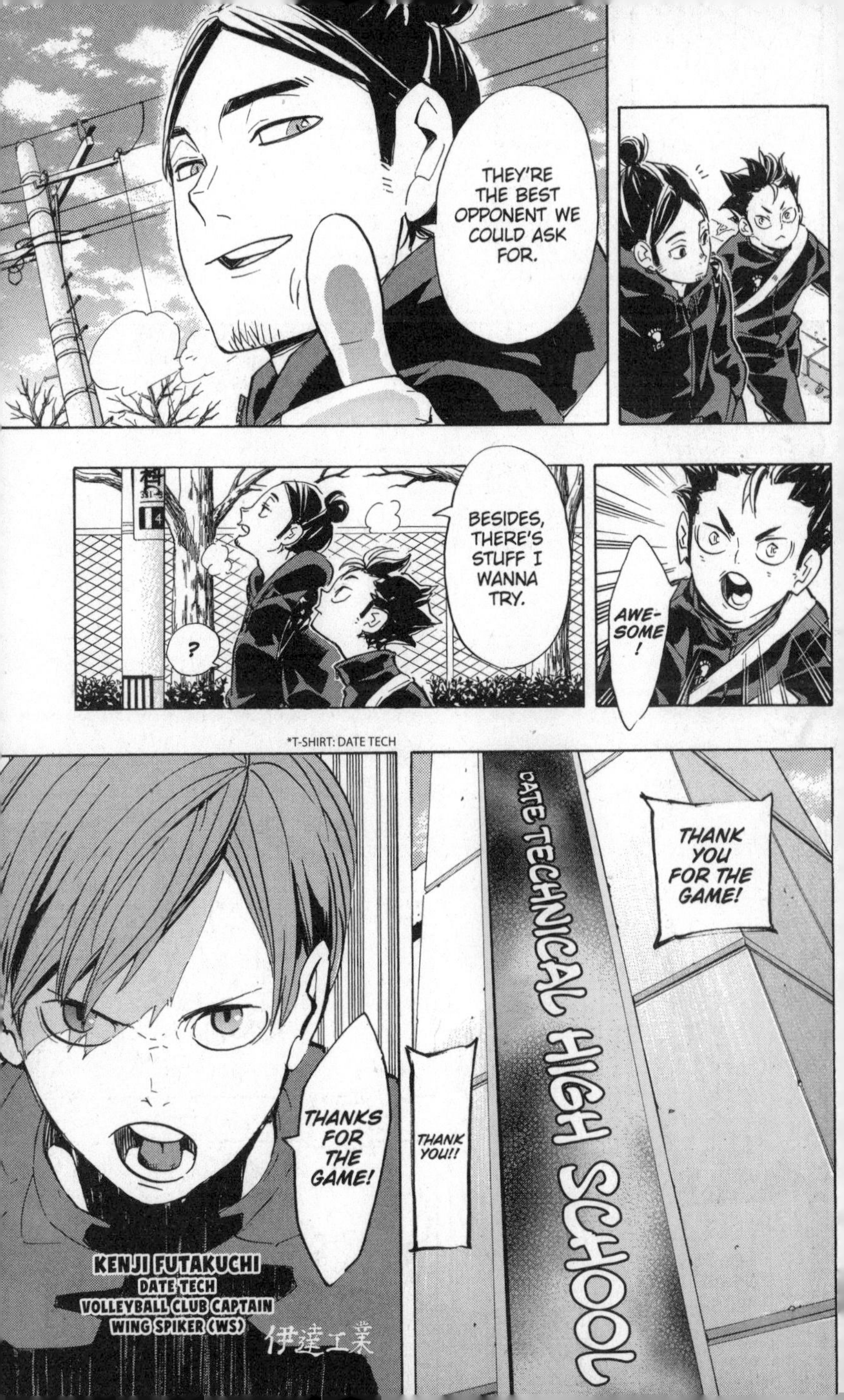
THEY'RE THE BEST OPPONENT WE COULD ASK FOR.
AWE-SOME!
BESIDES, THERE'S STUFF I WANNA TRY.
?
*T-SHIRT: DATE TECH
THANK YOU FOR THE GAME!
DATE TECHNICAL HIGH SCHOOL
THANK YOU!!
THANKS FOR THE GAME!
KENJI FUTAKUCHI
DATE TECH
VOLLEYBALL CLUB CAPTAIN
WING SPIKER (WS)
伊達工業

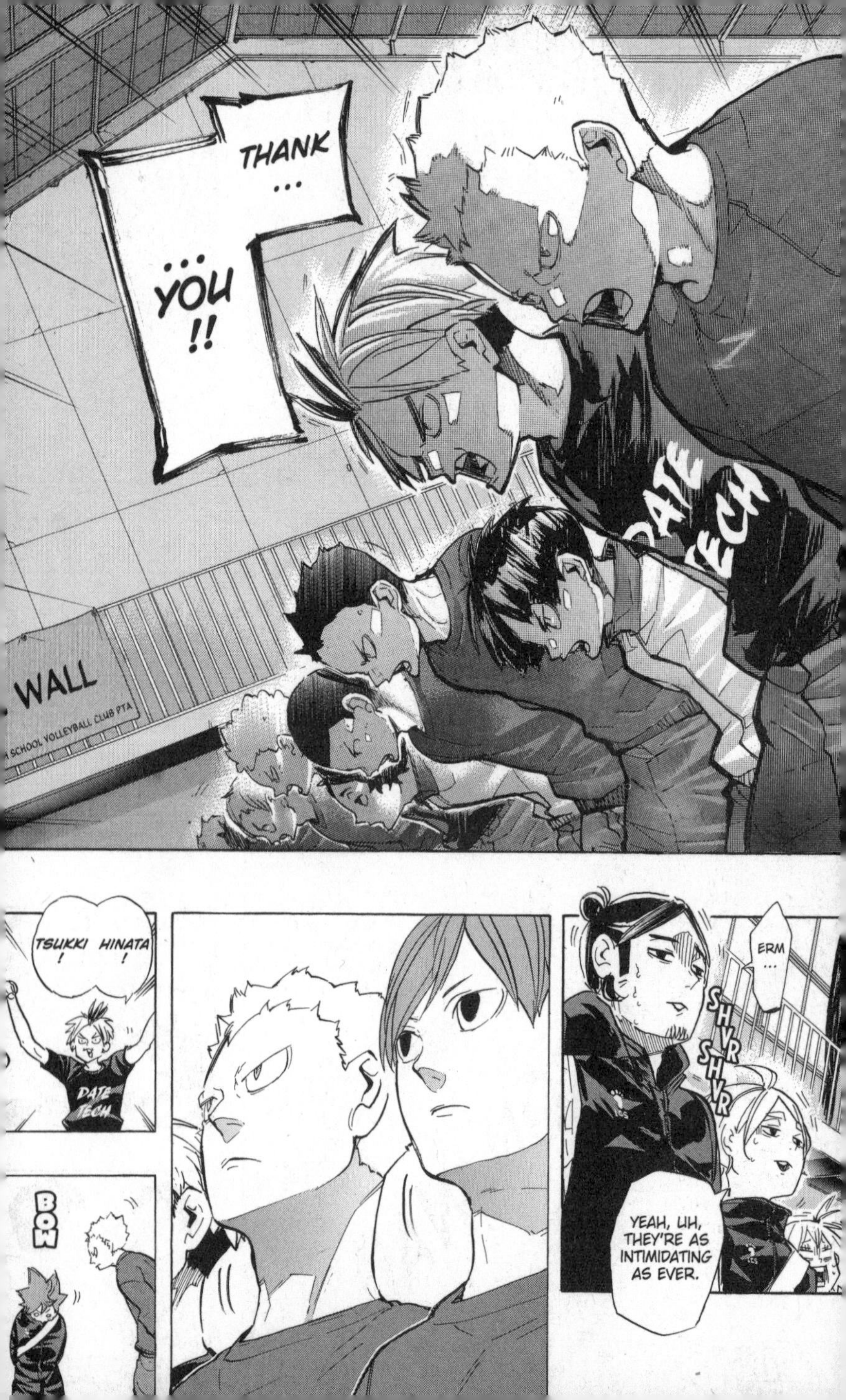
THANK ...
... YOU !!
WALL
SCHOOL VOLLEYBALL CLUB PTA
DATE TECH
ERM ...
SHVR SHVR
YEAH, UH, THEY'RE AS INTIMIDATING AS EVER.
TSUKKI! HINATA!
DATE TECH
BOW

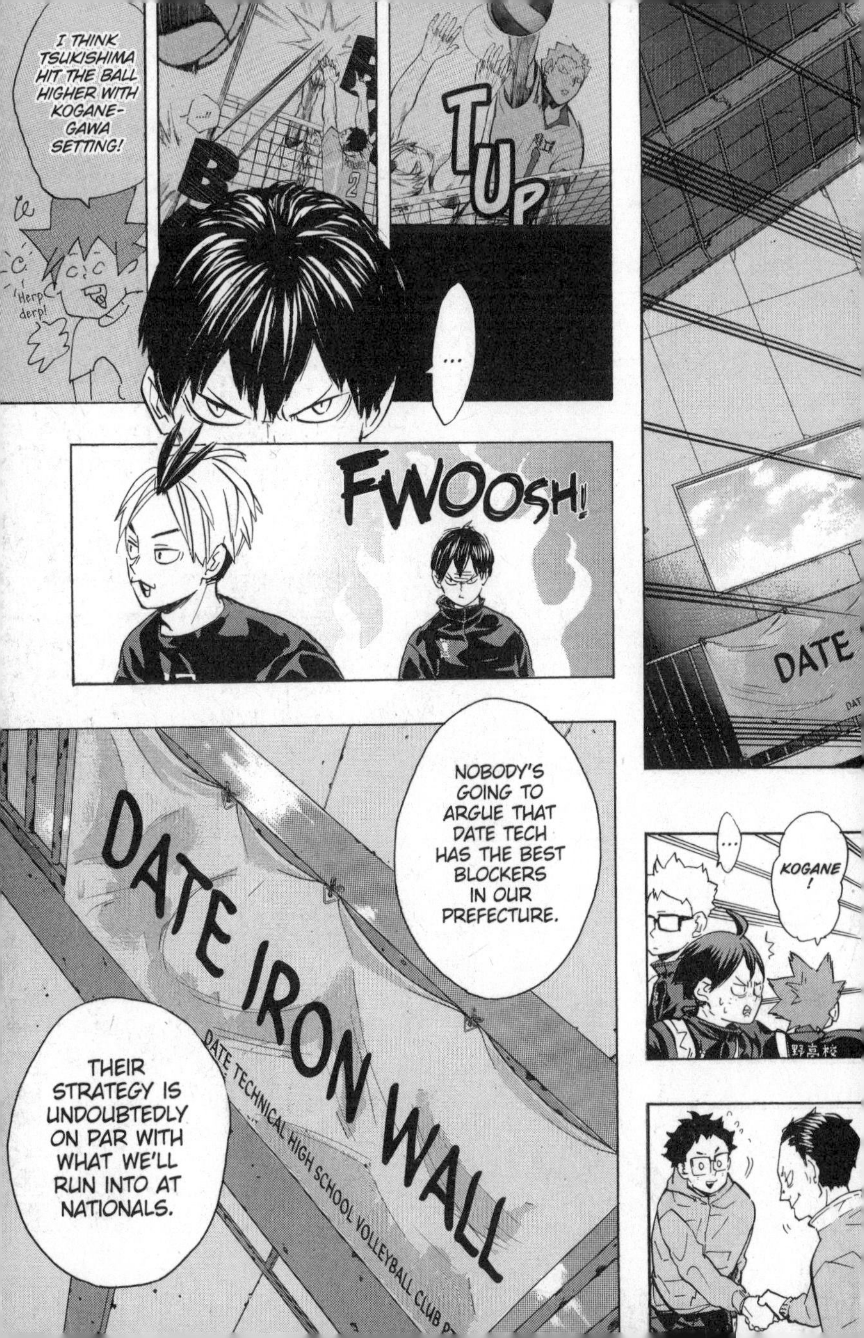
DATE
TUP
...!?
B
B
I THINK TSUKISHIMA HIT THE BALL HIGHER WITH KOGANEGAWA SETTING!
Herp derp!
...
FWOOSH!
KOGANE!
...
NOBODY'S GOING TO ARGUE THAT DATE TECH HAS THE BEST BLOCKERS IN OUR PREFECTURE.
DATE IRON WALL
DATE TECHNICAL HIGH SCHOOL VOLLEYBALL CLUB
THEIR STRATEGY IS UNDOUBTEDLY ON PAR WITH WHAT WE'LL RUN INTO AT NATIONALS.

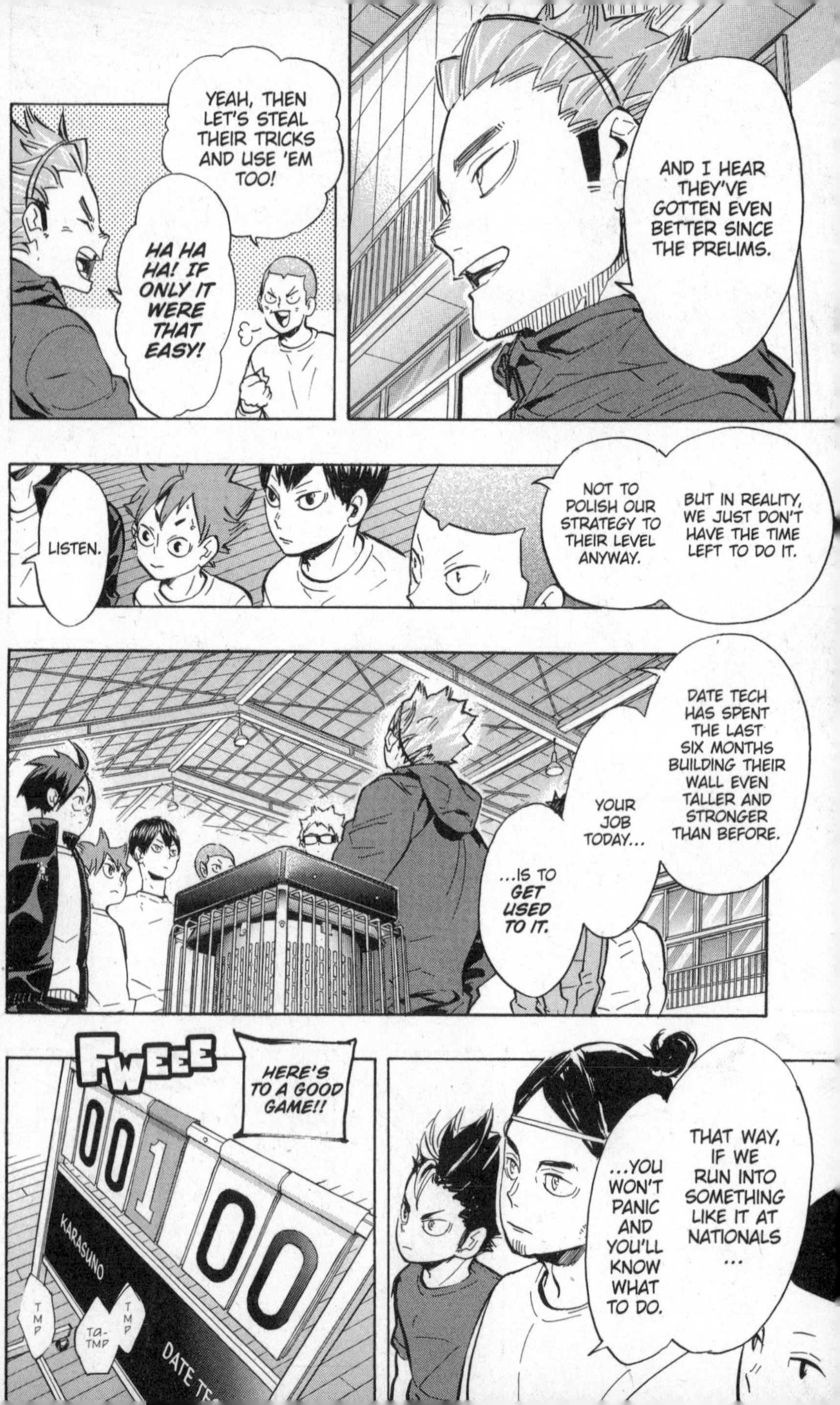
AND I HEAR THEY'VE GOTTEN EVEN BETTER SINCE THE PRELIMS.
YEAH, THEN LET'S STEAL THEIR TRICKS AND USE 'EM TOO!
HA HA HA! IF ONLY IT WERE THAT EASY!
BUT IN REALITY, WE JUST DON'T HAVE THE TIME LEFT TO DO IT.
NOT TO POLISH OUR STRATEGY TO THEIR LEVEL ANYWAY.
LISTEN.
DATE TECH HAS SPENT THE LAST SIX MONTHS BUILDING THEIR WALL EVEN TALLER AND STRONGER THAN BEFORE.
YOUR JOB TODAY...
...IS TO GET USED TO IT.
THAT WAY, IF WE RUN INTO SOMETHING LIKE IT AT NATIONALS ...
...YOU WON'T PANIC AND YOU'LL KNOW WHAT TO DO.
FWEEE
HERE'S TO A GOOD GAME!!
00 1 00
KARASUNO
TMP
Ta-TMP
TMP

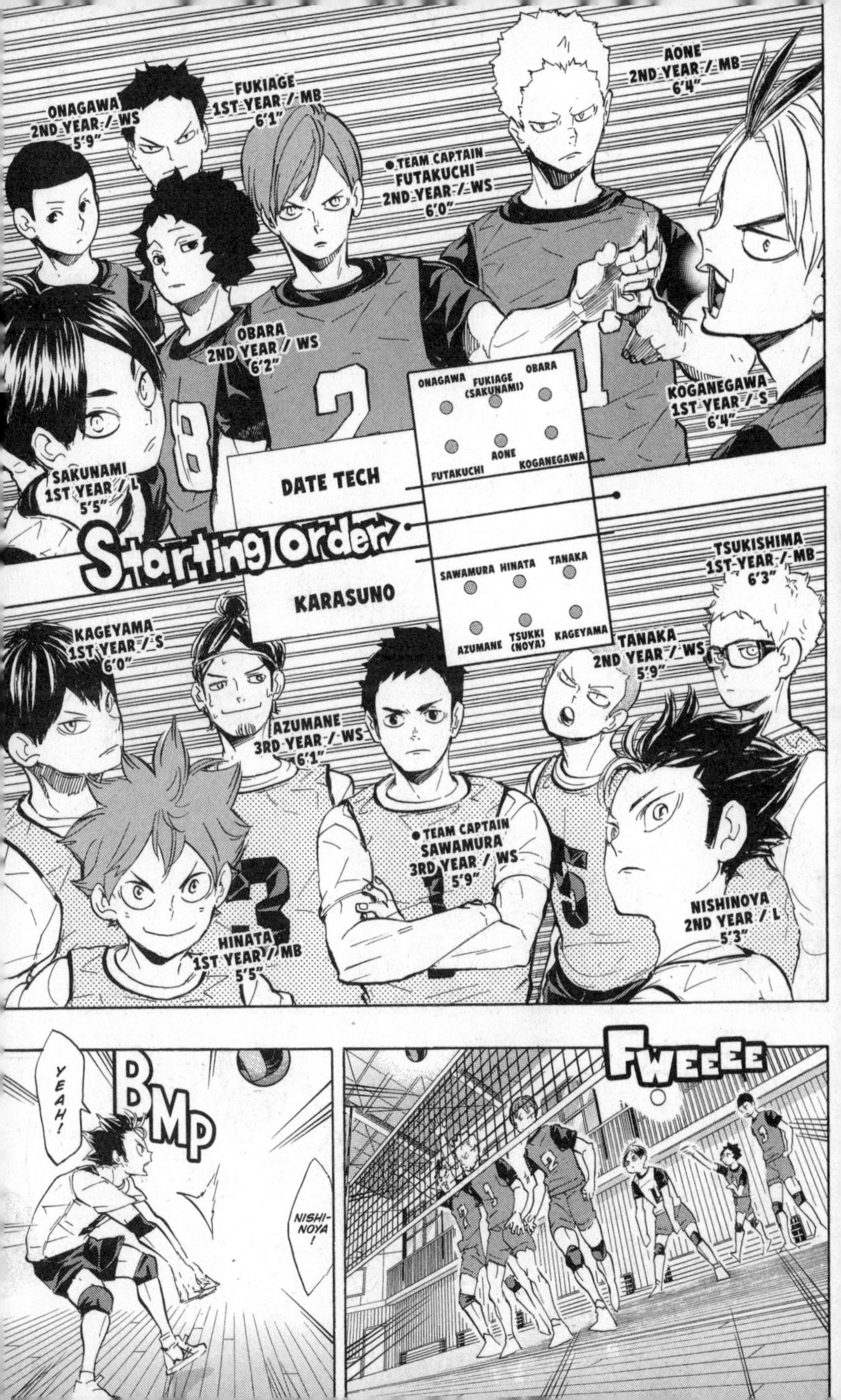
AONE
2ND YEAR / MB
6'4"
FUKIAGE
1ST YEAR / MB
6'1"
ONAGAWA
2ND YEAR / WS
5'9"
● TEAM CAPTAIN
FUTAKUCHI
2ND YEAR / WS
6'0"
KOGANEGAWA
1ST YEAR / S
6'4"
OBARA
2ND YEAR / WS
6'2"
SAKUNAMI
1ST YEAR / L
5'5"
DATE TECH
ONAGAWA FUKIAGE (SAKUNAMI) OBARA
FUTAKUCHI AONE KOGANEGAWA
Starting Order
KARASUNO
SAWAMURA HINATA TANAKA
AZUMANE TSUKKI (NOYA) KAGEYAMA
TSUKISHIMA
1ST YEAR / MB
6'3"
TANAKA
2ND YEAR / WS
5'9"
KAGEYAMA
1ST YEAR / S
6'0"
AZUMANE
3RD YEAR / WS
6'1"
NISHINOYA
2ND YEAR / L
5'3"
● TEAM CAPTAIN
SAWAMURA
3RD YEAR / WS
5'9"
HINATA
1ST YEAR / MB
5'5"
FWEEEE
BMP
YEAH!
NISHI-NOYA!

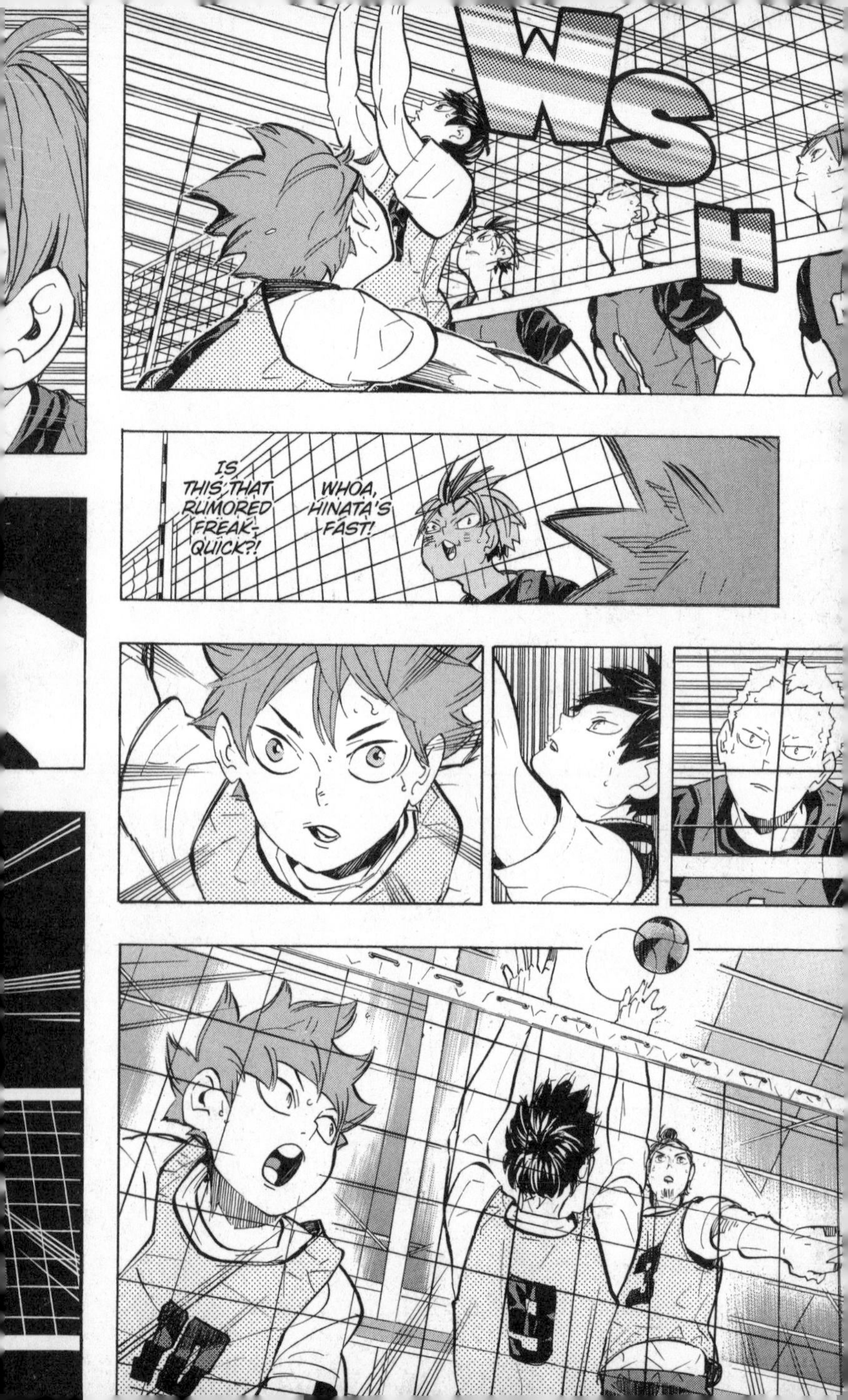
WSH
WHOA, HINATA'S FAST!
IS THIS THAT RUMORED FREAK-QUICK?!

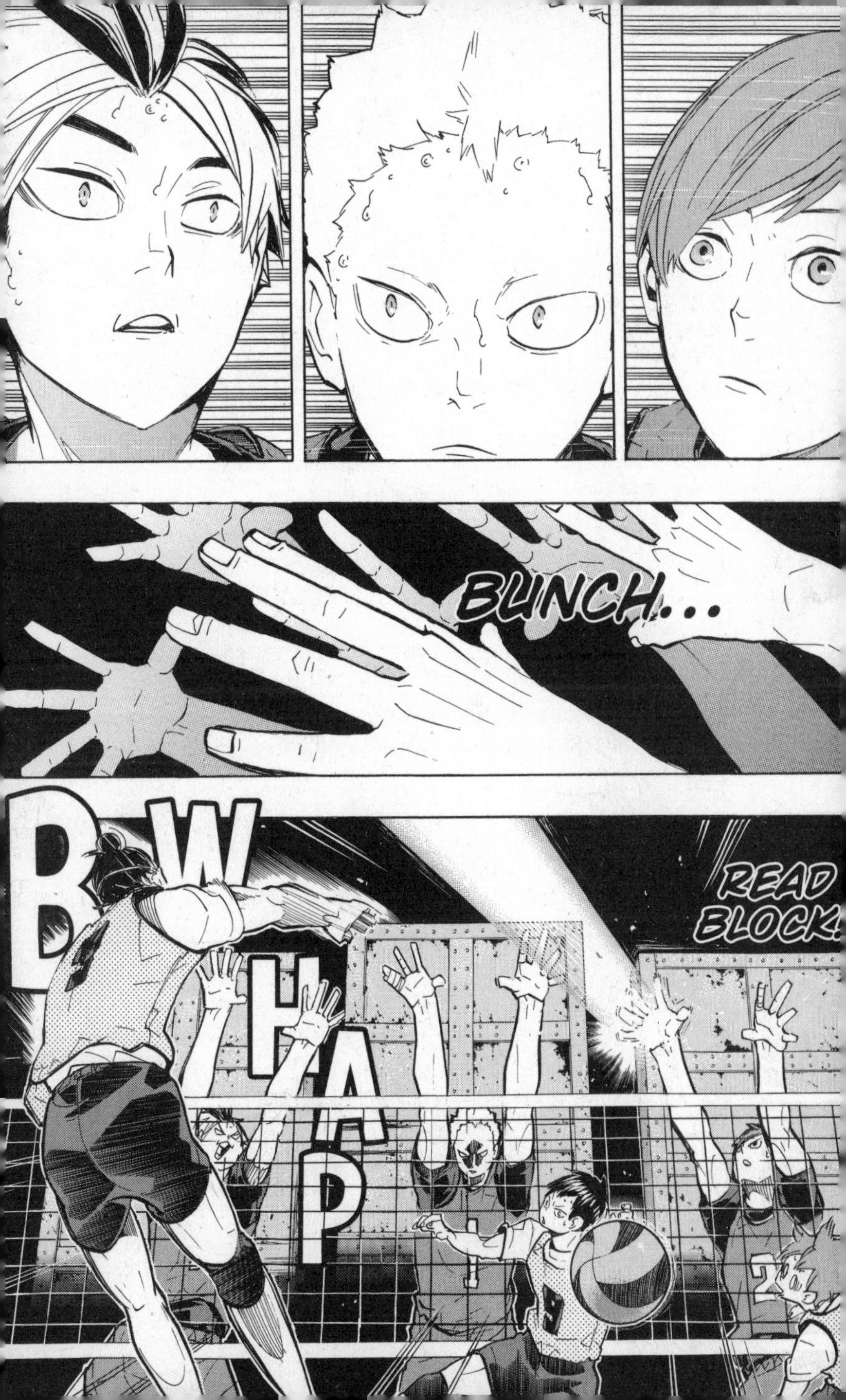
BUNCH...
READ BLOCK!
BWHAP

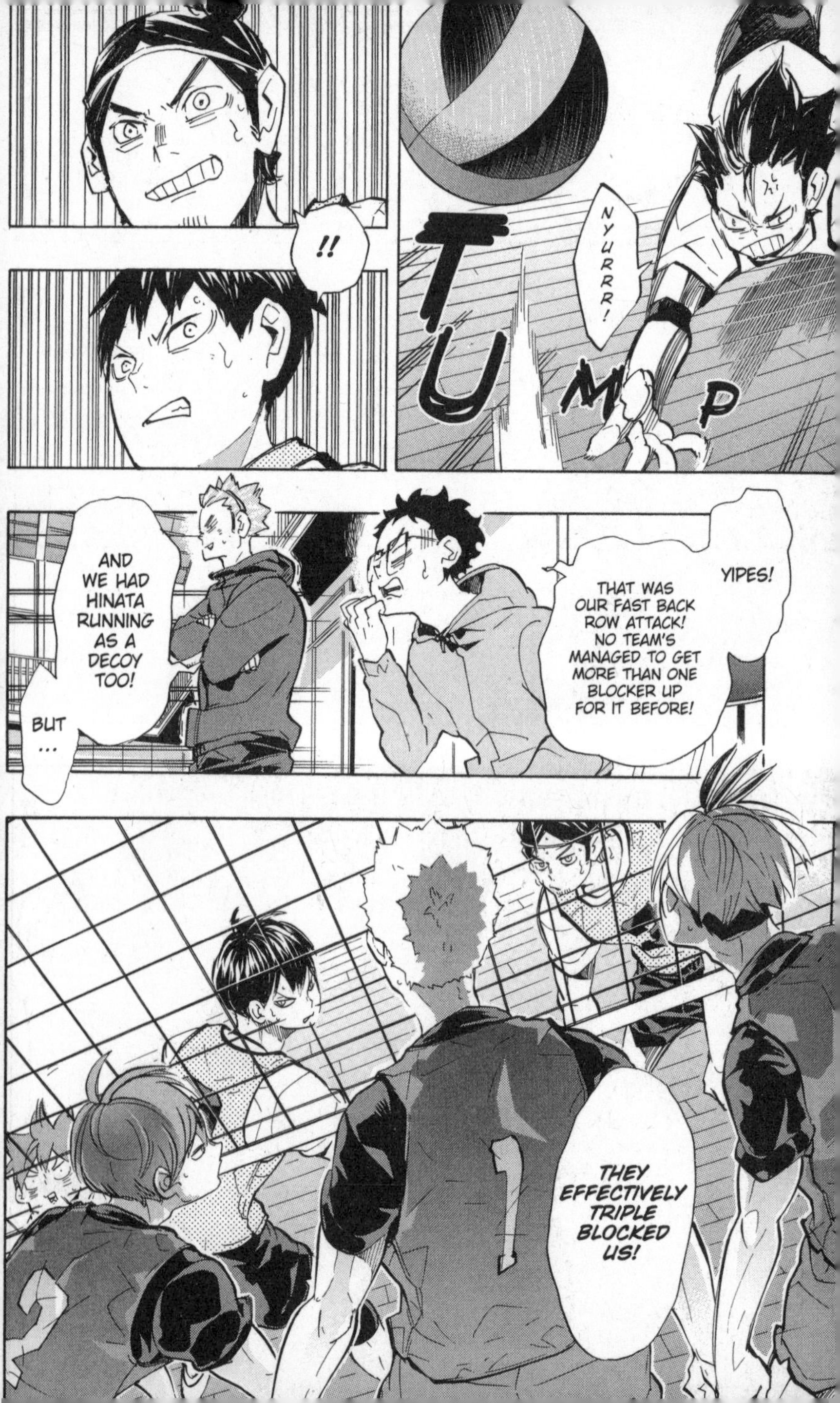
NYURRR!
TUMP
!!
YIPES!
THAT WAS OUR FAST BACK ROW ATTACK! NO TEAM'S MANAGED TO GET MORE THAN ONE BLOCKER UP FOR IT BEFORE!
AND WE HAD HINATA RUNNING AS A DECOY TOO!
BUT ...
THEY EFFECTIVELY TRIPLE BLOCKED US!

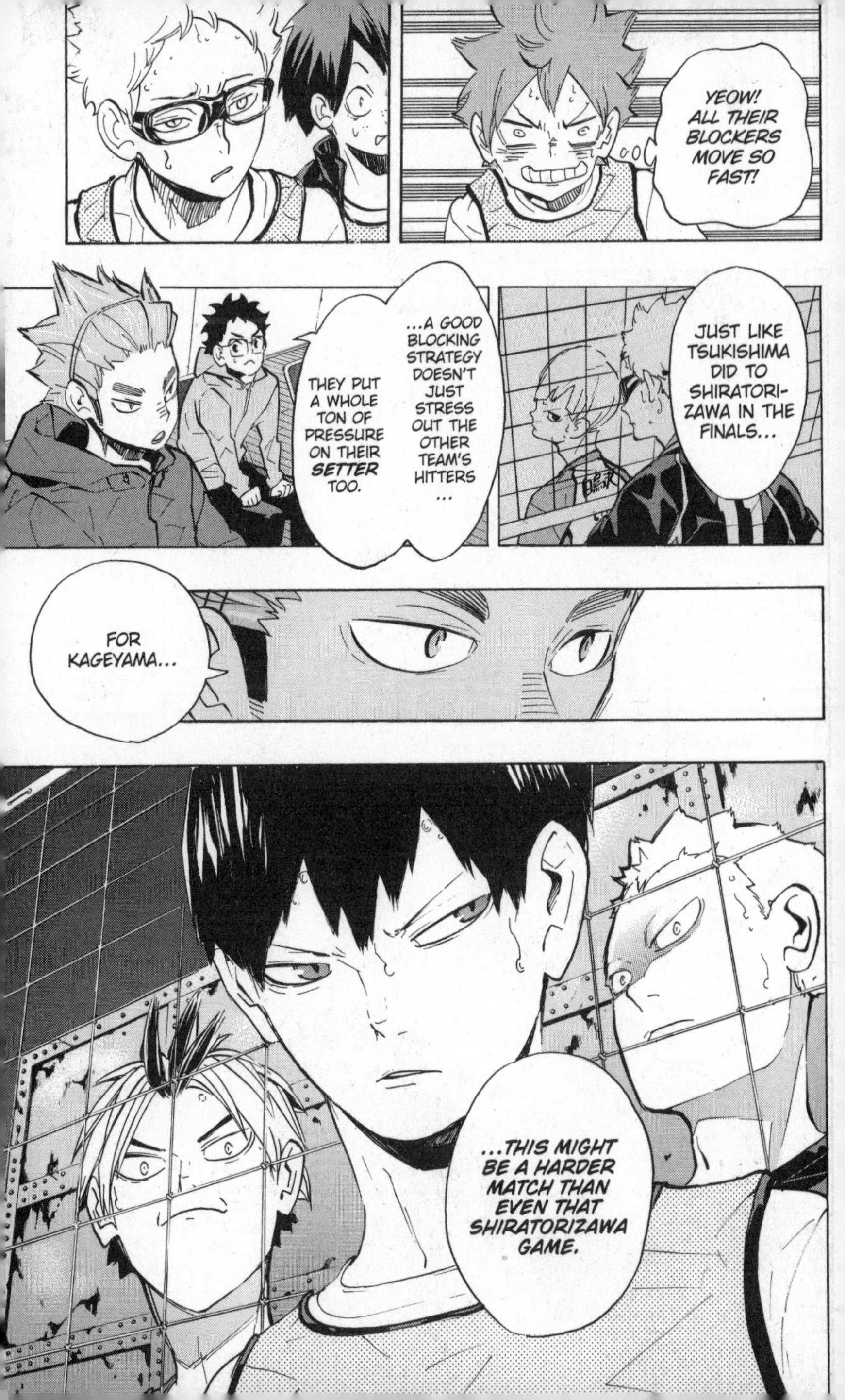
YEOW! ALL THEIR BLOCKERS MOVE SO FAST!
JUST LIKE TSUKISHIMA DID TO SHIRATORI-ZAWA IN THE FINALS...
...A GOOD BLOCKING STRATEGY DOESN'T JUST STRESS OUT THE OTHER TEAM'S HITTERS...
THEY PUT A WHOLE TON OF PRESSURE ON THEIR SETTER TOO.
FOR KAGEYAMA...
...THIS MIGHT BE A HARDER MATCH THAN EVEN THAT SHIRATORIZAWA GAME.

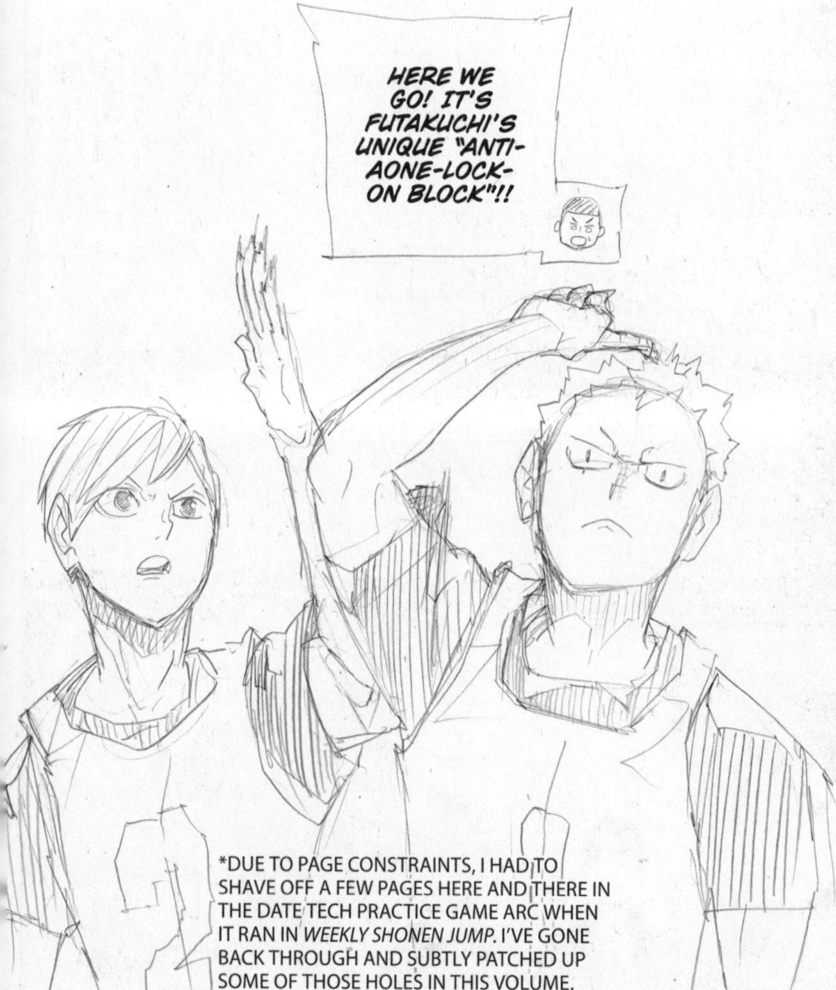
HERE WE GO! IT'S FUTAKUCHI'S UNIQUE "ANTI-AONE-LOCK-ON BLOCK"!!

*DUE TO PAGE CONSTRAINTS, I HAD TO SHAVE OFF A FEW PAGES HERE AND THERE IN THE DATE TECH PRACTICE GAME ARC WHEN IT RAN IN *WEEKLY SHONEN JUMP*. I'VE GONE BACK THROUGH AND SUBTLY PATCHED UP SOME OF THOSE HOLES IN THIS VOLUME.

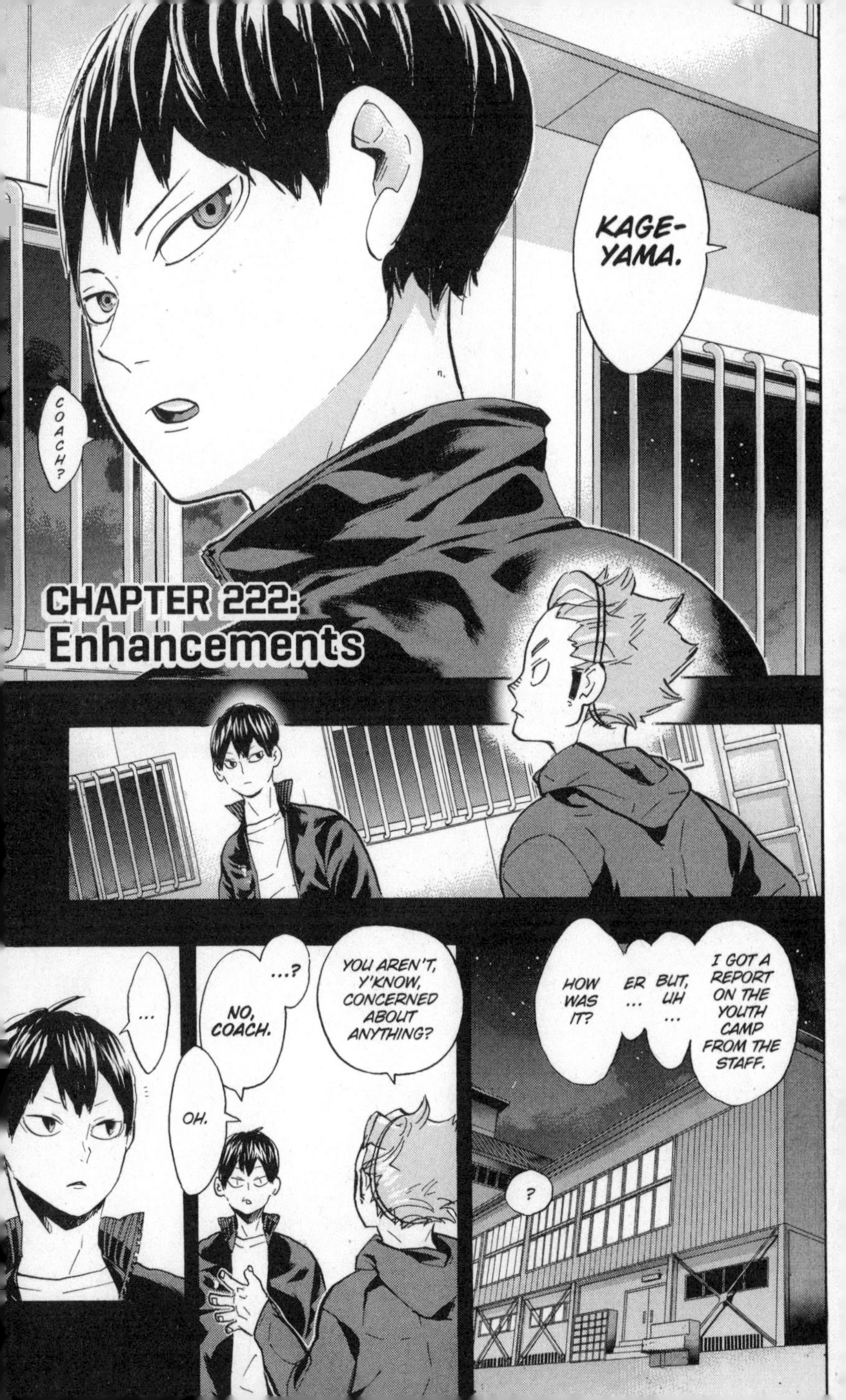
KAGE-YAMA.
COACH?
CHAPTER 222:
Enhancements
I GOT A REPORT ON THE YOUTH CAMP FROM THE STAFF.
BUT, UH...
ER...
HOW WAS IT?
?
YOU AREN'T, Y'KNOW, CONCERNED ABOUT ANYTHING?
...?
NO, COACH.
OH.
...

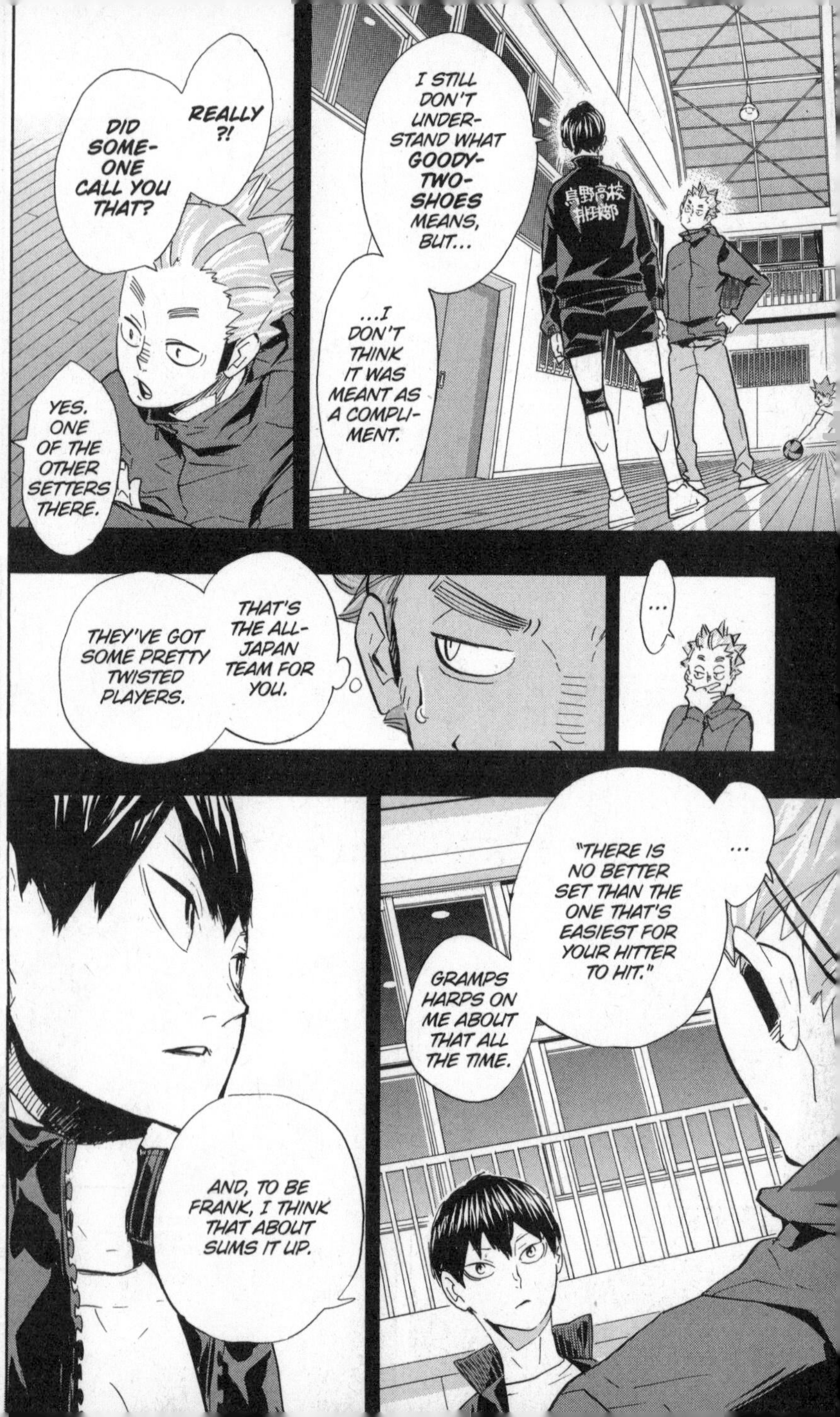
I STILL DON'T UNDERSTAND WHAT GOODY-TWO-SHOES MEANS, BUT...
...I DON'T THINK IT WAS MEANT AS A COMPLIMENT.
REALLY ?!
DID SOMEONE CALL YOU THAT?
YES. ONE OF THE OTHER SETTERS THERE.
...
THAT'S THE ALL-JAPAN TEAM FOR YOU.
THEY'VE GOT SOME PRETTY TWISTED PLAYERS.
...
"THERE IS NO BETTER SET THAN THE ONE THAT'S EASIEST FOR YOUR HITTER TO HIT."
GRAMPS HARPS ON ME ABOUT THAT ALL THE TIME.
AND, TO BE FRANK, I THINK THAT ABOUT SUMS IT UP.

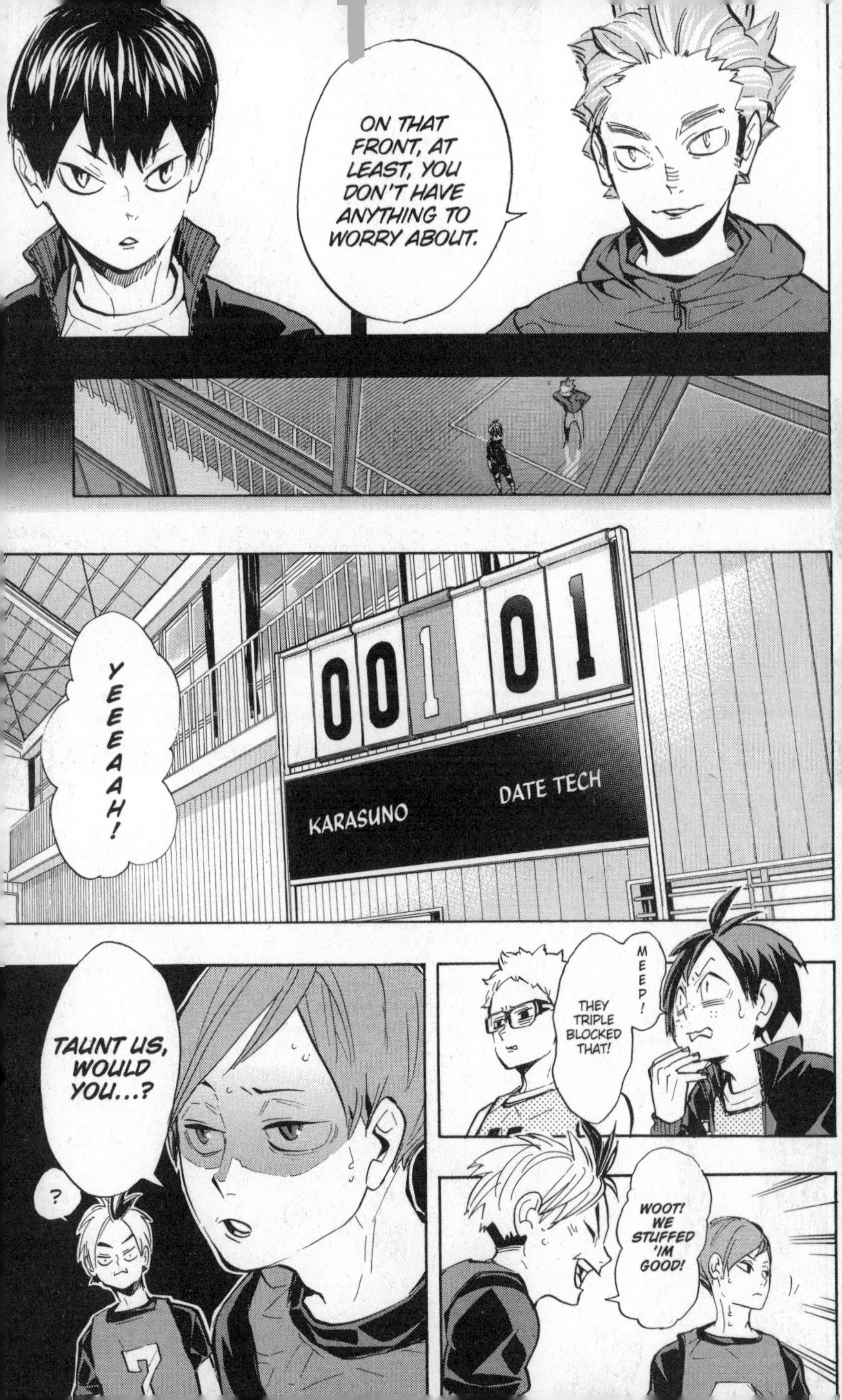
ON THAT FRONT, AT LEAST, YOU DON'T HAVE ANYTHING TO WORRY ABOUT.
001 01
DATE TECH
KARASUNO
YEEEEAAH!
MEEP!
THEY TRIPLE BLOCKED THAT!
WOOT! WE STUFFED 'IM GOOD!
TAUNT US, WOULD YOU...?
?

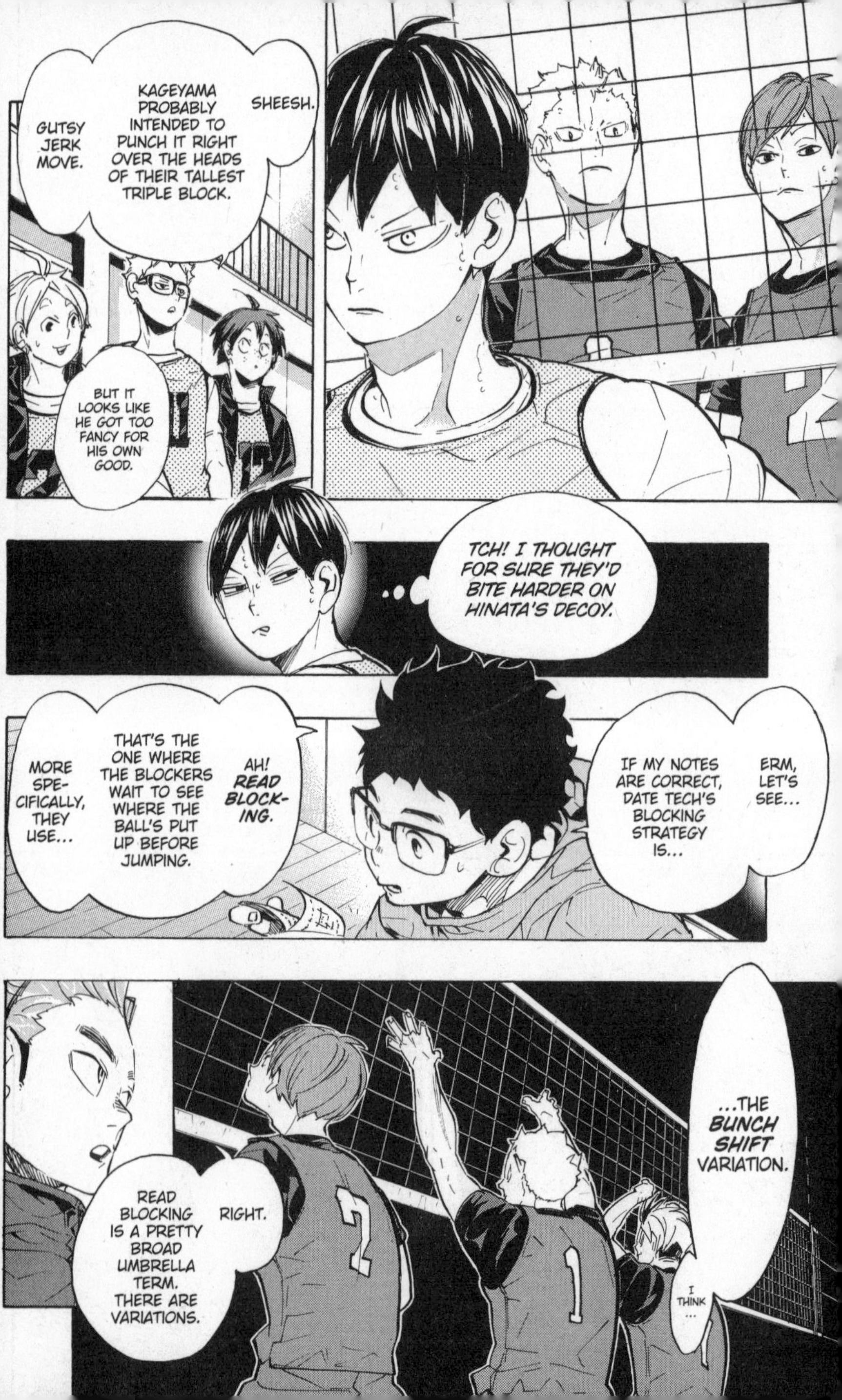
SHEESH.
KAGEYAMA PROBABLY INTENDED TO PUNCH IT RIGHT OVER THE HEADS OF THEIR TALLEST TRIPLE BLOCK.
GUTSY JERK MOVE.
BUT IT LOOKS LIKE HE GOT TOO FANCY FOR HIS OWN GOOD.
TCH! I THOUGHT FOR SURE THEY'D BITE HARDER ON HINATA'S DECOY.
ERM, LET'S SEE...
IF MY NOTES ARE CORRECT, DATE TECH'S BLOCKING STRATEGY IS...
AH! *READ BLOCKING*.
THAT'S THE ONE WHERE THE BLOCKERS WAIT TO SEE WHERE THE BALL'S PUT UP BEFORE JUMPING.
MORE SPECIFICALLY, THEY USE...
...THE *BUNCH SHIFT* VARIATION.
I THINK...
RIGHT.
READ BLOCKING IS A PRETTY BROAD UMBRELLA TERM. THERE ARE VARIATIONS.

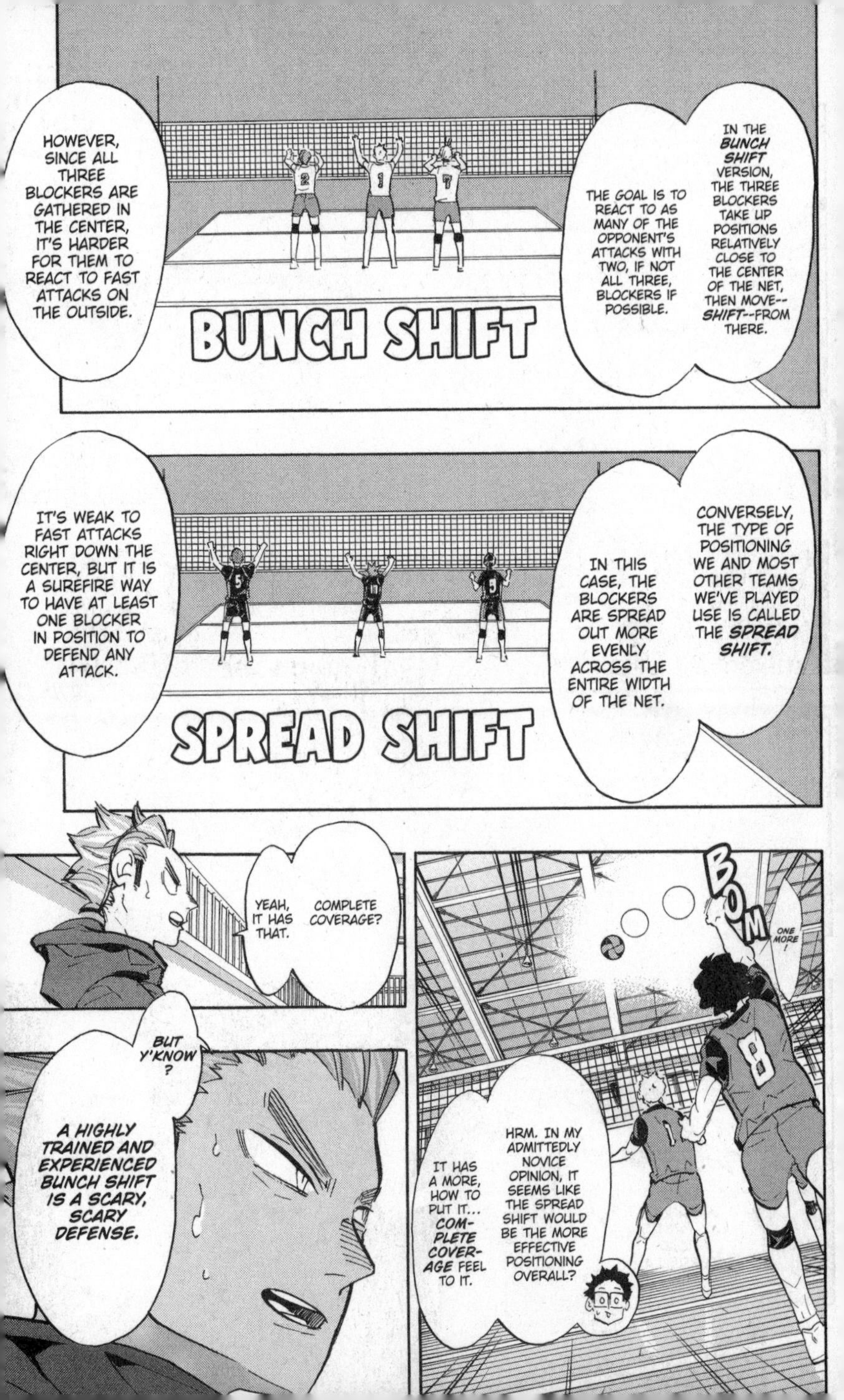
IN THE BUNCH SHIFT VERSION, THE THREE BLOCKERS TAKE UP POSITIONS RELATIVELY CLOSE TO THE CENTER OF THE NET, THEN MOVE--SHIFT--FROM THERE.
THE GOAL IS TO REACT TO AS MANY OF THE OPPONENT'S ATTACKS WITH TWO, IF NOT ALL THREE, BLOCKERS IF POSSIBLE.
BUNCH SHIFT
HOWEVER, SINCE ALL THREE BLOCKERS ARE GATHERED IN THE CENTER, IT'S HARDER FOR THEM TO REACT TO FAST ATTACKS ON THE OUTSIDE.
CONVERSELY, THE TYPE OF POSITIONING WE AND MOST OTHER TEAMS WE'VE PLAYED USE IS CALLED THE SPREAD SHIFT.
IN THIS CASE, THE BLOCKERS ARE SPREAD OUT MORE EVENLY ACROSS THE ENTIRE WIDTH OF THE NET.
SPREAD SHIFT
IT'S WEAK TO FAST ATTACKS RIGHT DOWN THE CENTER, BUT IT IS A SUREFIRE WAY TO HAVE AT LEAST ONE BLOCKER IN POSITION TO DEFEND ANY ATTACK.
BOM
ONE MORE!
HRM. IN MY ADMITTEDLY NOVICE OPINION, IT SEEMS LIKE THE SPREAD SHIFT WOULD BE THE MORE EFFECTIVE POSITIONING OVERALL?
IT HAS A MORE, HOW TO PUT IT... COMPLETE COVERAGE FEEL TO IT.
COMPLETE COVERAGE?
YEAH, IT HAS THAT.
BUT Y'KNOW?
A HIGHLY TRAINED AND EXPERIENCED BUNCH SHIFT IS A SCARY, SCARY DEFENSE.

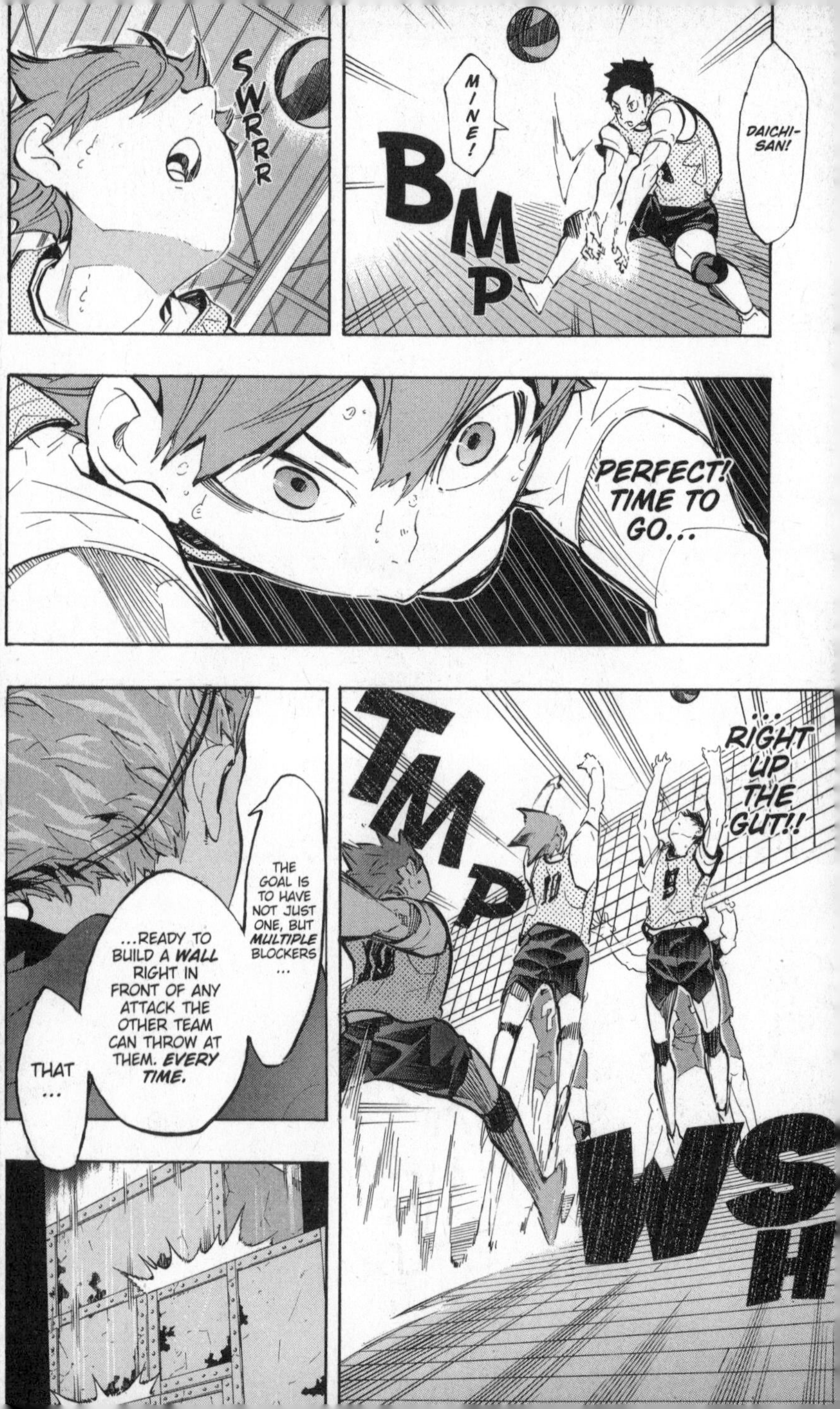
DAICHI-SAN!
MINE!
BMP
SWRRR
PERFECT! TIME TO GO...
TMP
...RIGHT UP THE GUT!!
WSH
THE GOAL IS TO HAVE NOT JUST ONE, BUT MULTIPLE BLOCKERS ...
...READY TO BUILD A WALL RIGHT IN FRONT OF ANY ATTACK THE OTHER TEAM CAN THROW AT THEM. EVERY TIME.
THAT ...

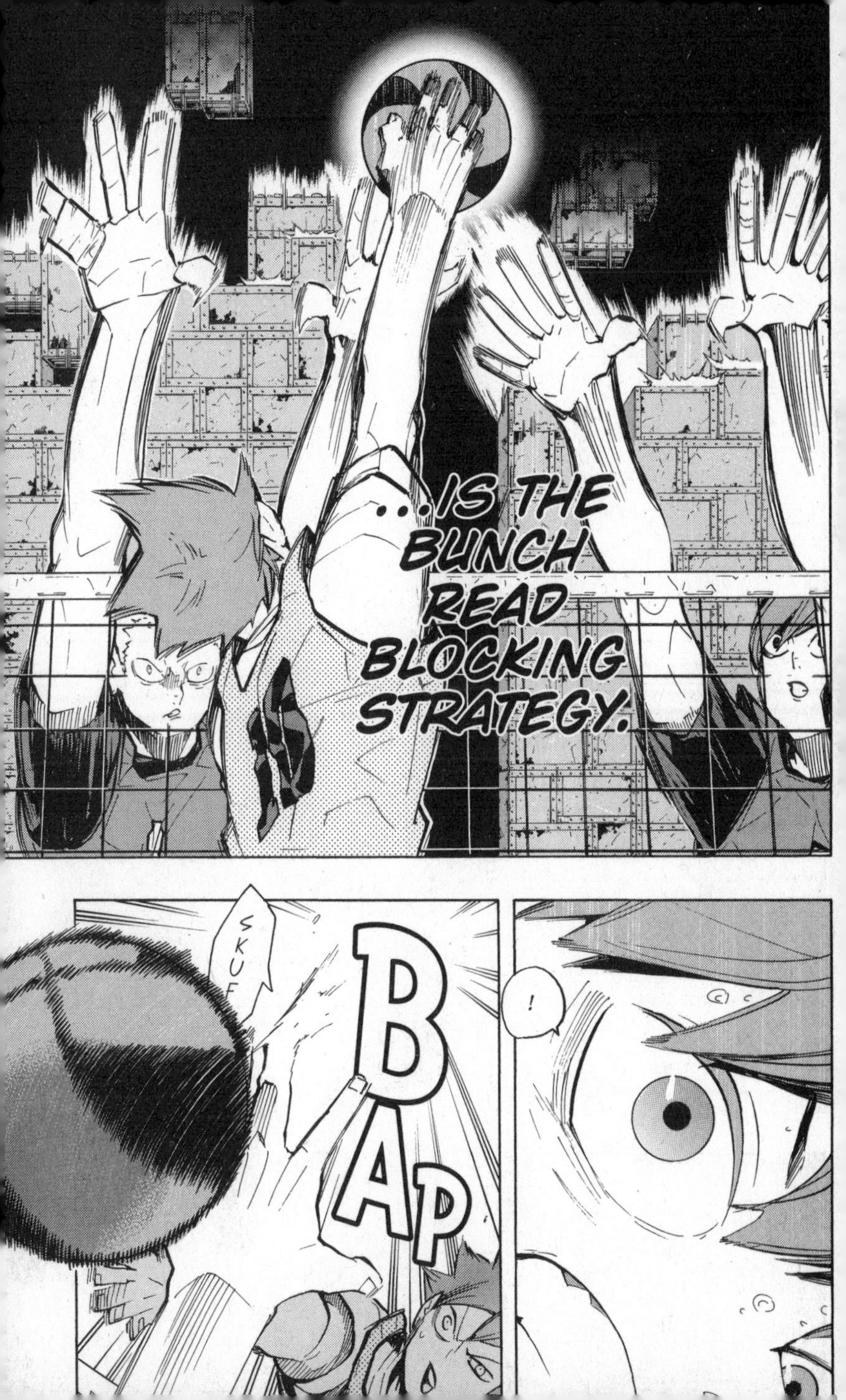
...IS THE BUNCH READ BLOCKING STRATEGY.
!
SKUF
BAP

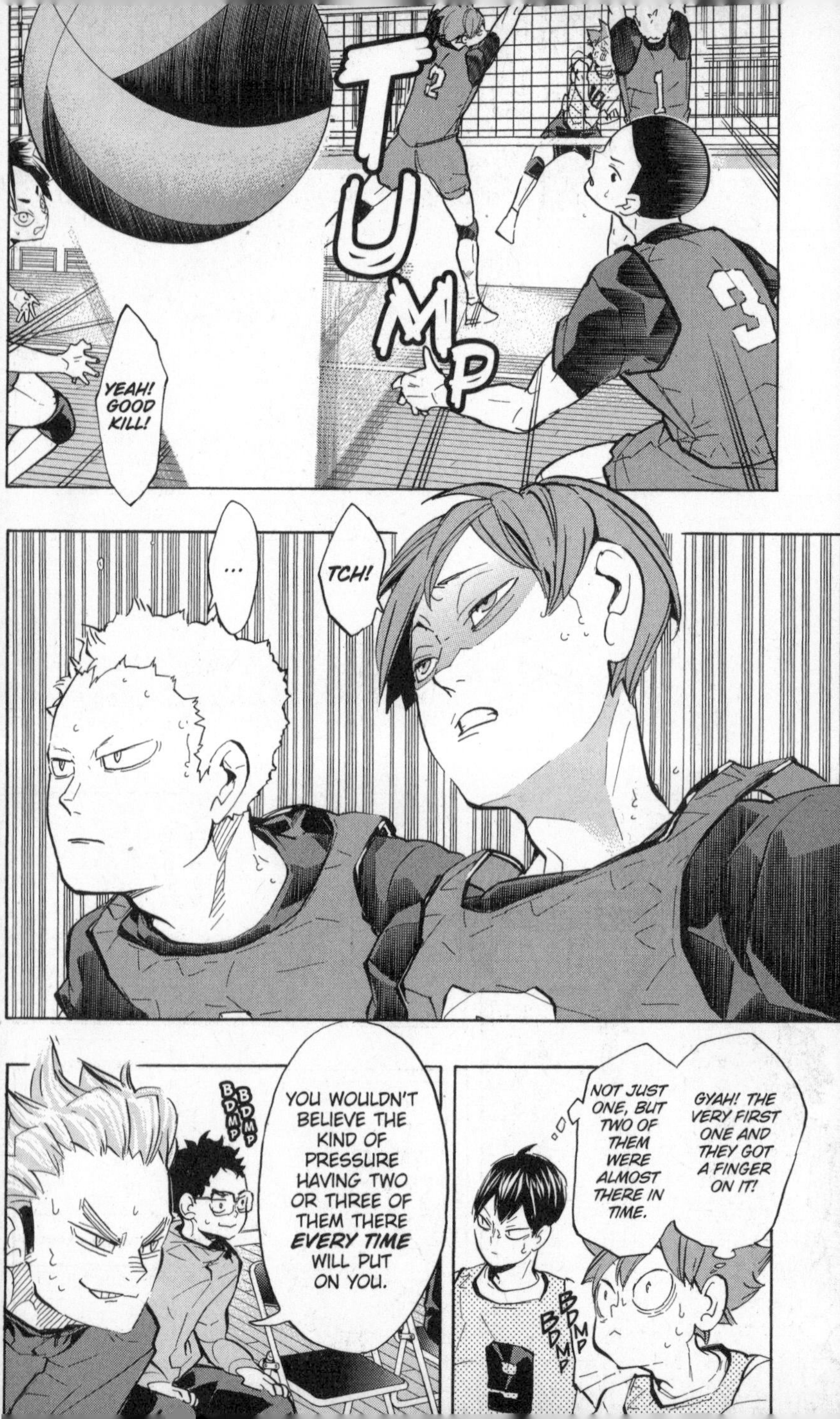
TUMP
YEAH! GOOD KILL!
TCH!
...
GYAH! THE VERY FIRST ONE AND THEY GOT A FINGER ON IT!
NOT JUST ONE, BUT TWO OF THEM WERE ALMOST THERE IN TIME.
BDMP BDMP
YOU WOULDN'T BELIEVE THE KIND OF PRESSURE HAVING TWO OR THREE OF THEM THERE **EVERY TIME** WILL PUT ON YOU.
BDMP BDMP

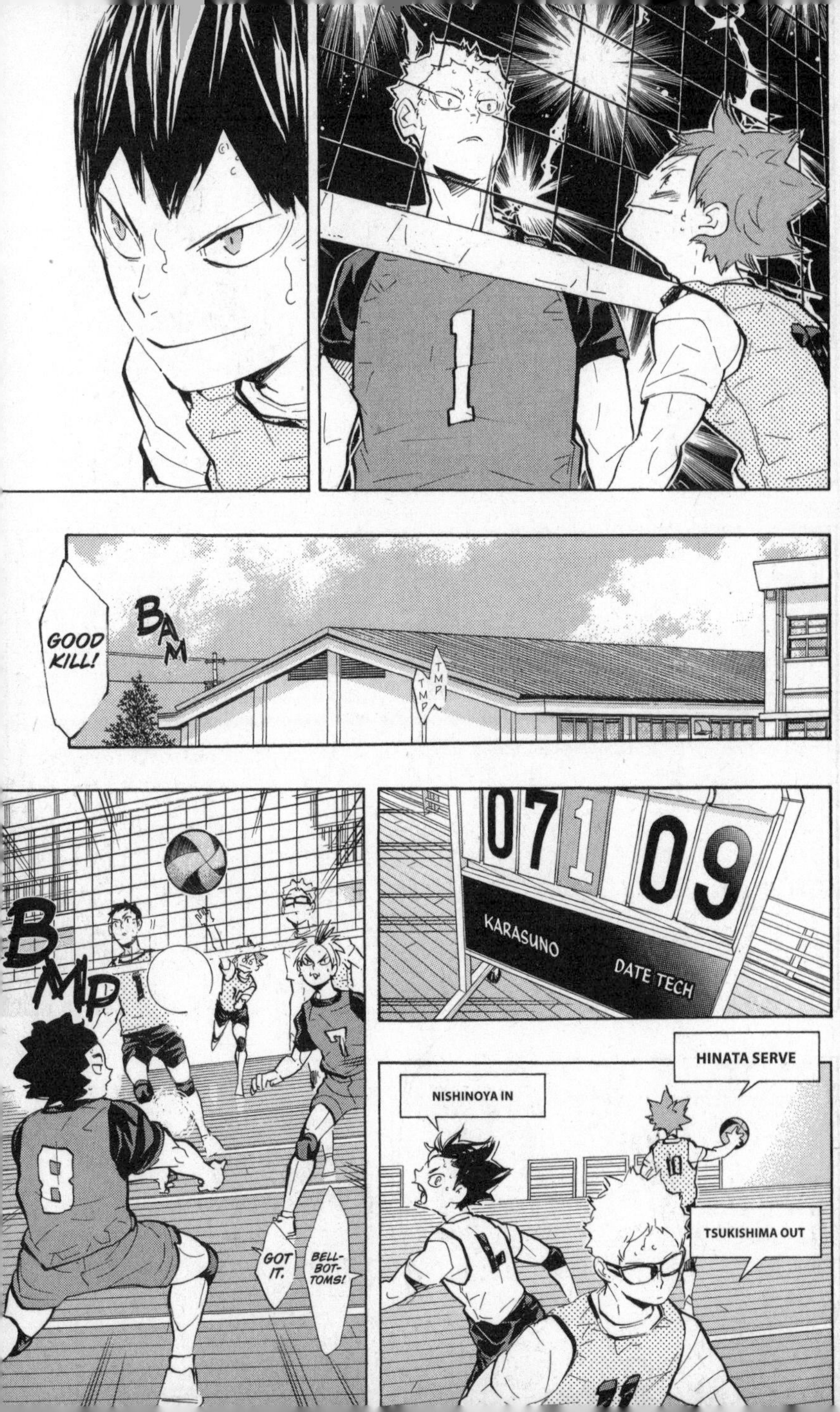
GOOD KILL!
BAM
TMP TMP
07
1
09
KARASUNO
DATE TECH
HINATA SERVE
NISHINOYA IN
TSUKISHIMA OUT
BUMP
GOT IT.
BELL-BOTTOMS!

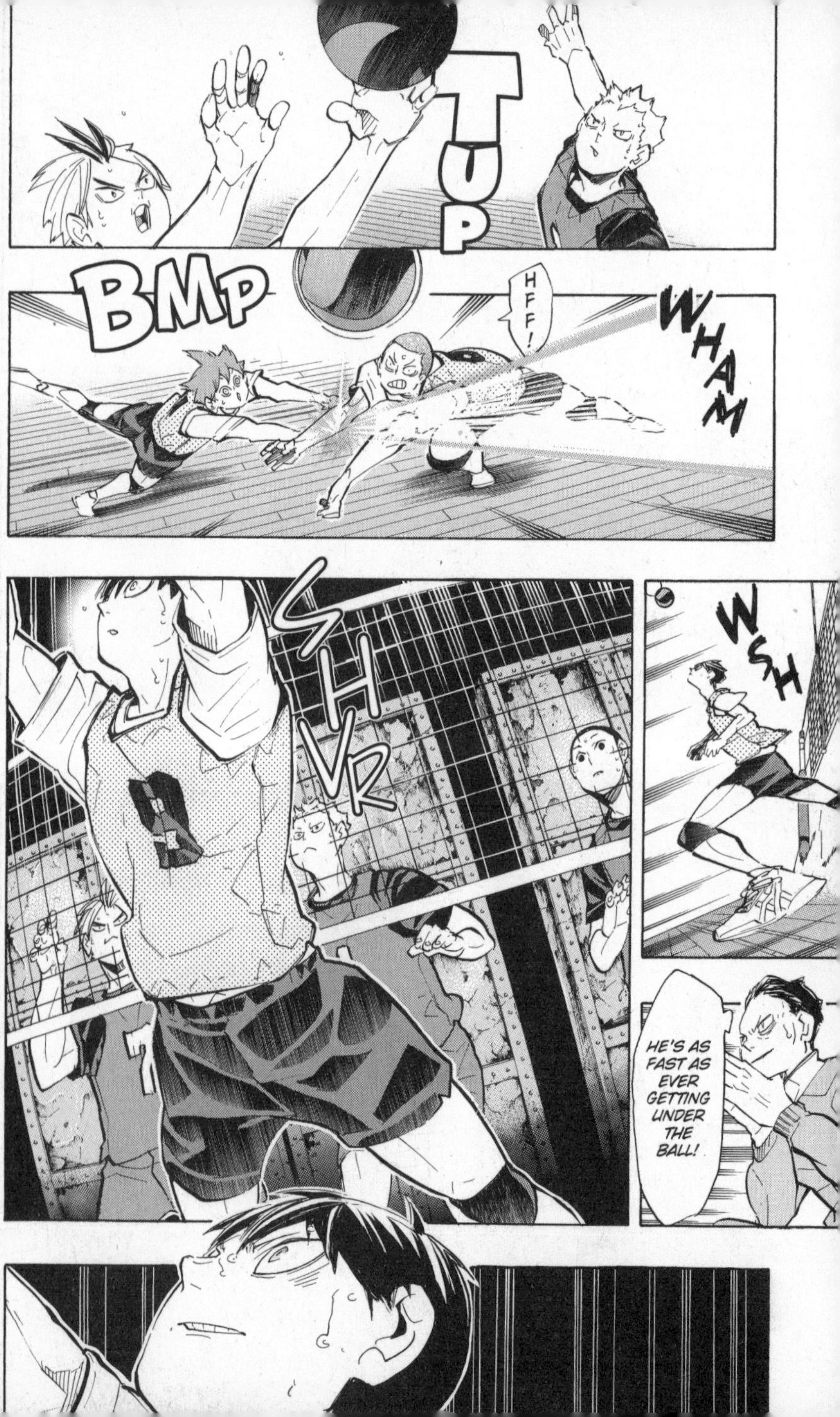
TUP
BMP
WHAM
HFF!
WSH
SHVR
HE'S AS FAST AS EVER GETTING UNDER THE BALL!

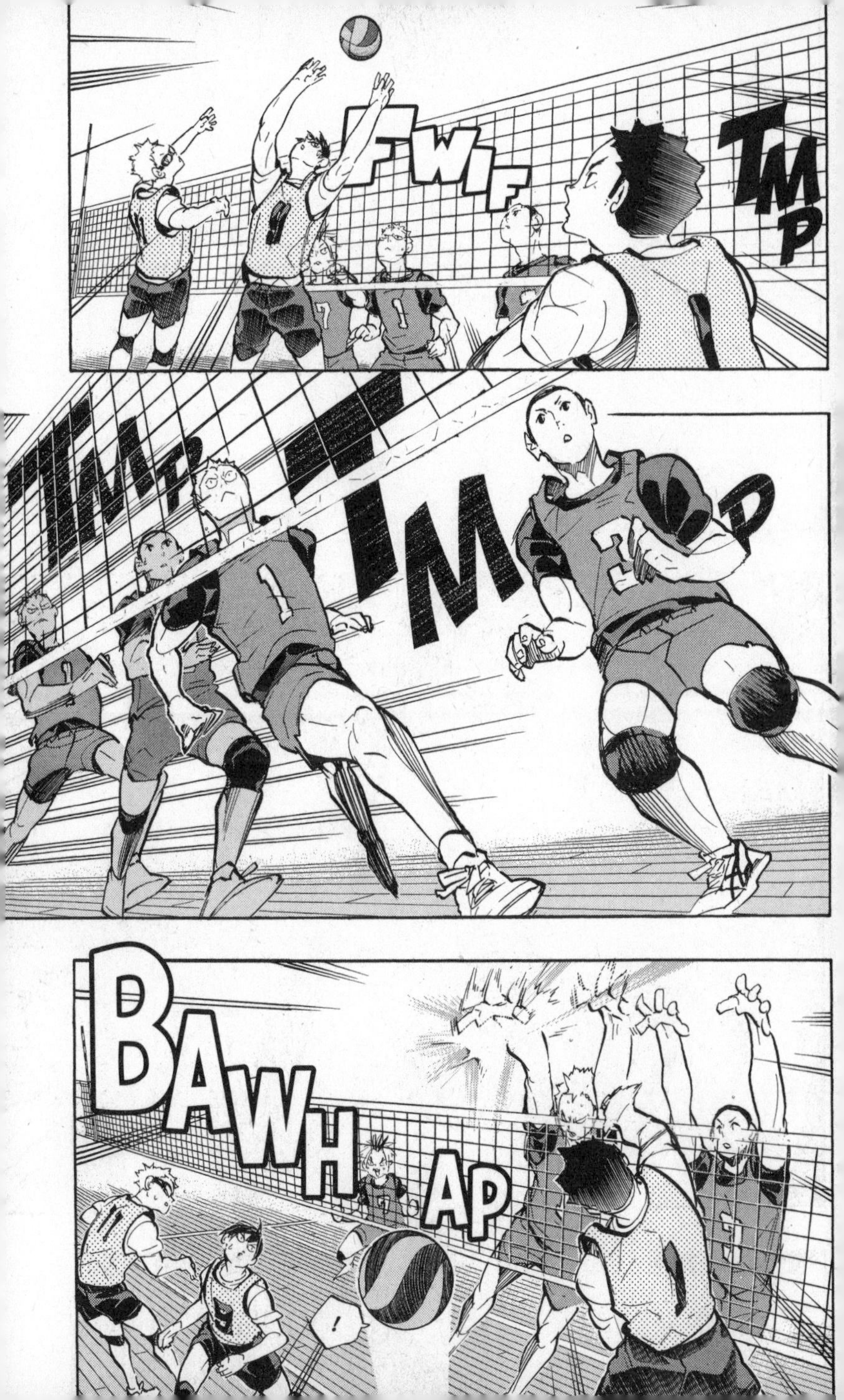
TMP
FWIF
TMP
TMP
TMP
BAWHAP
!

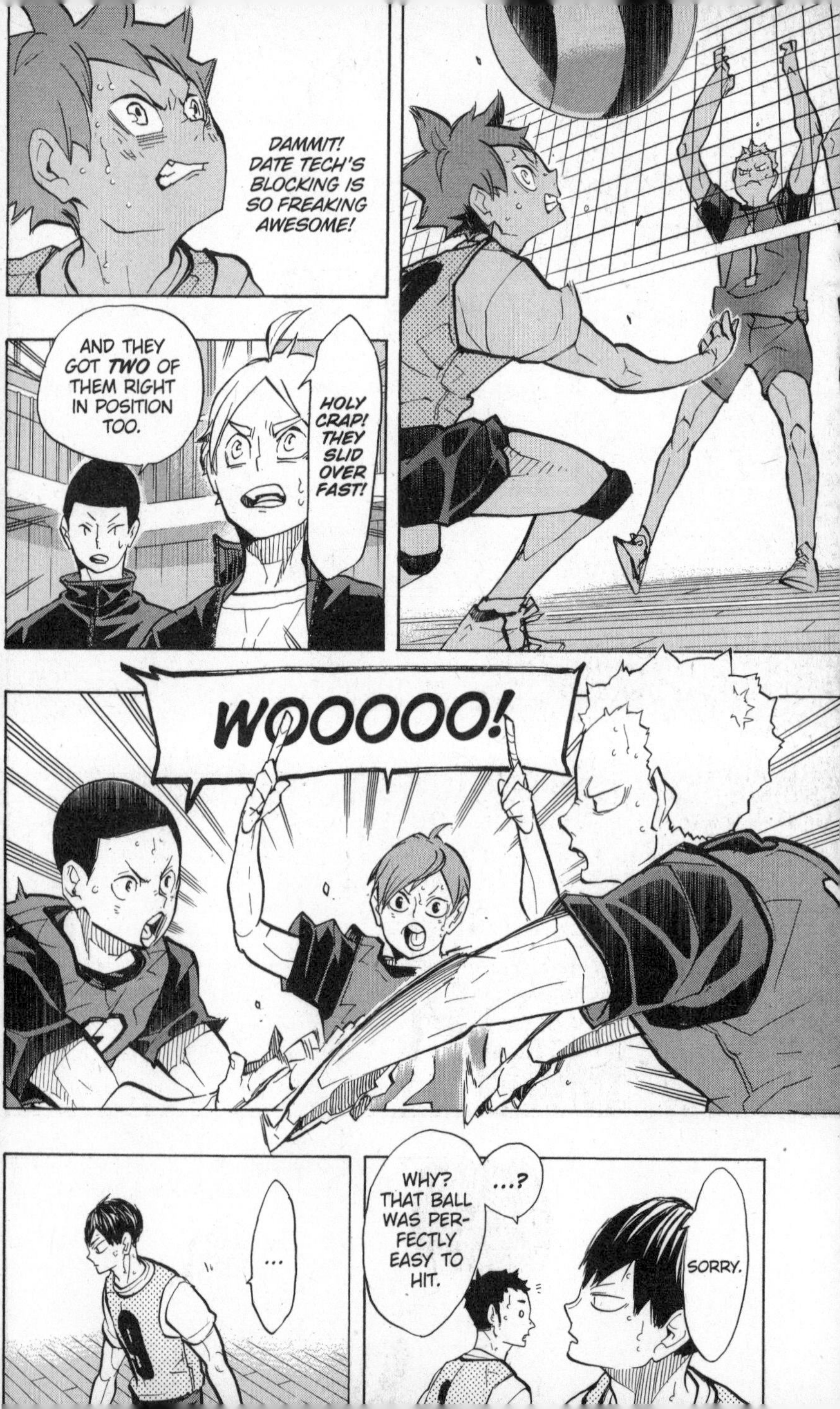
DAMMIT! DATE TECH'S BLOCKING IS SO FREAKING AWESOME!
HOLY CRAP! THEY SLID OVER FAST!
AND THEY GOT TWO OF THEM RIGHT IN POSITION TOO.
WOOOOO!
SORRY.
...?
WHY? THAT BALL WAS PER-FECTLY EASY TO HIT.
...

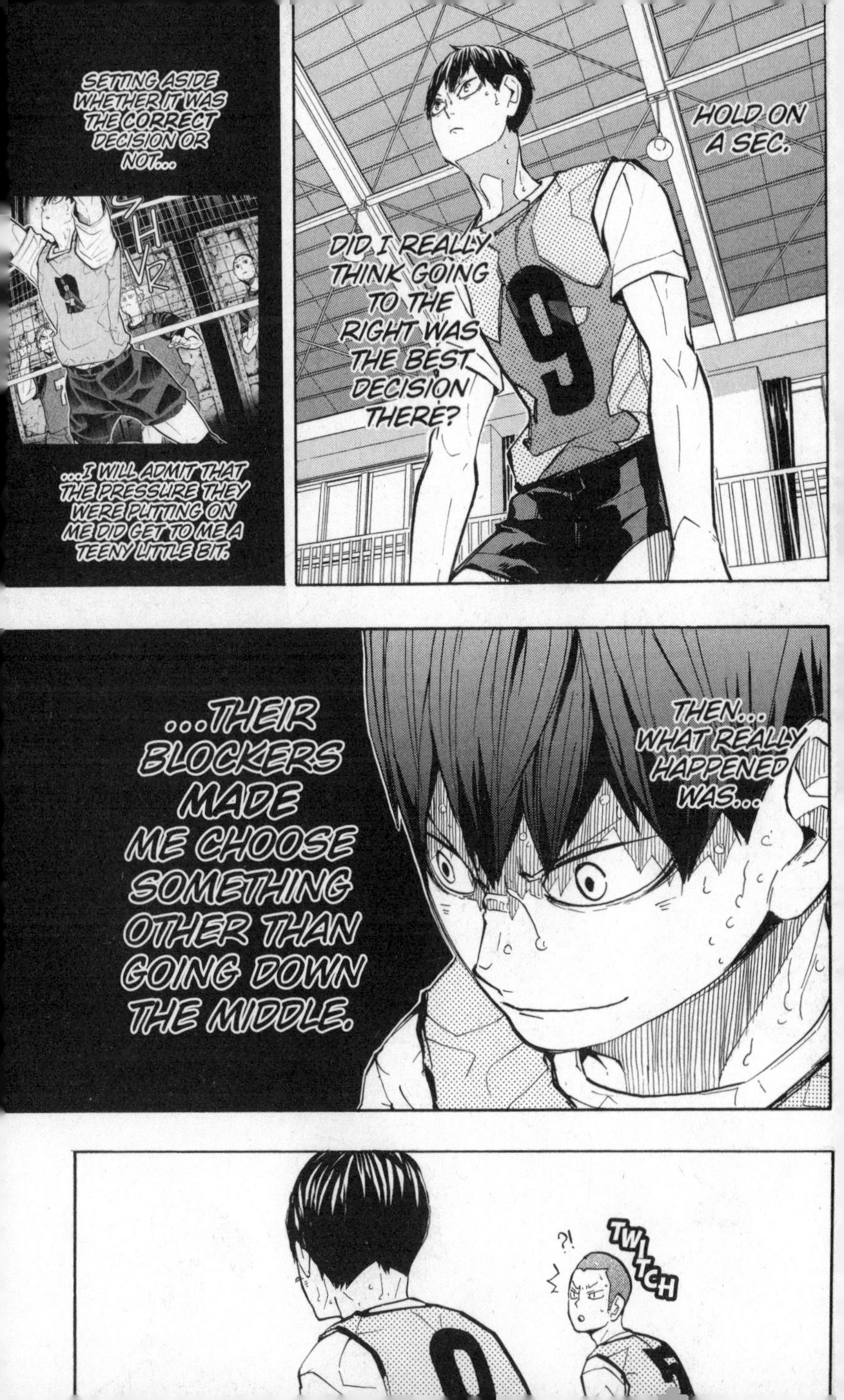
HOLD ON A SEC.
DID I REALLY THINK GOING TO THE RIGHT WAS THE BEST DECISION THERE?
SETTING ASIDE WHETHER IT WAS THE CORRECT DECISION OR NOT...
...I WILL ADMIT THAT THE PRESSURE THEY WERE PUTTING ON ME DID GET TO ME A TEENY LITTLE BIT.
THEN... WHAT REALLY HAPPENED WAS...
...THEIR BLOCKERS MADE ME CHOOSE SOMETHING OTHER THAN GOING DOWN THE MIDDLE.
?!
TWITCH

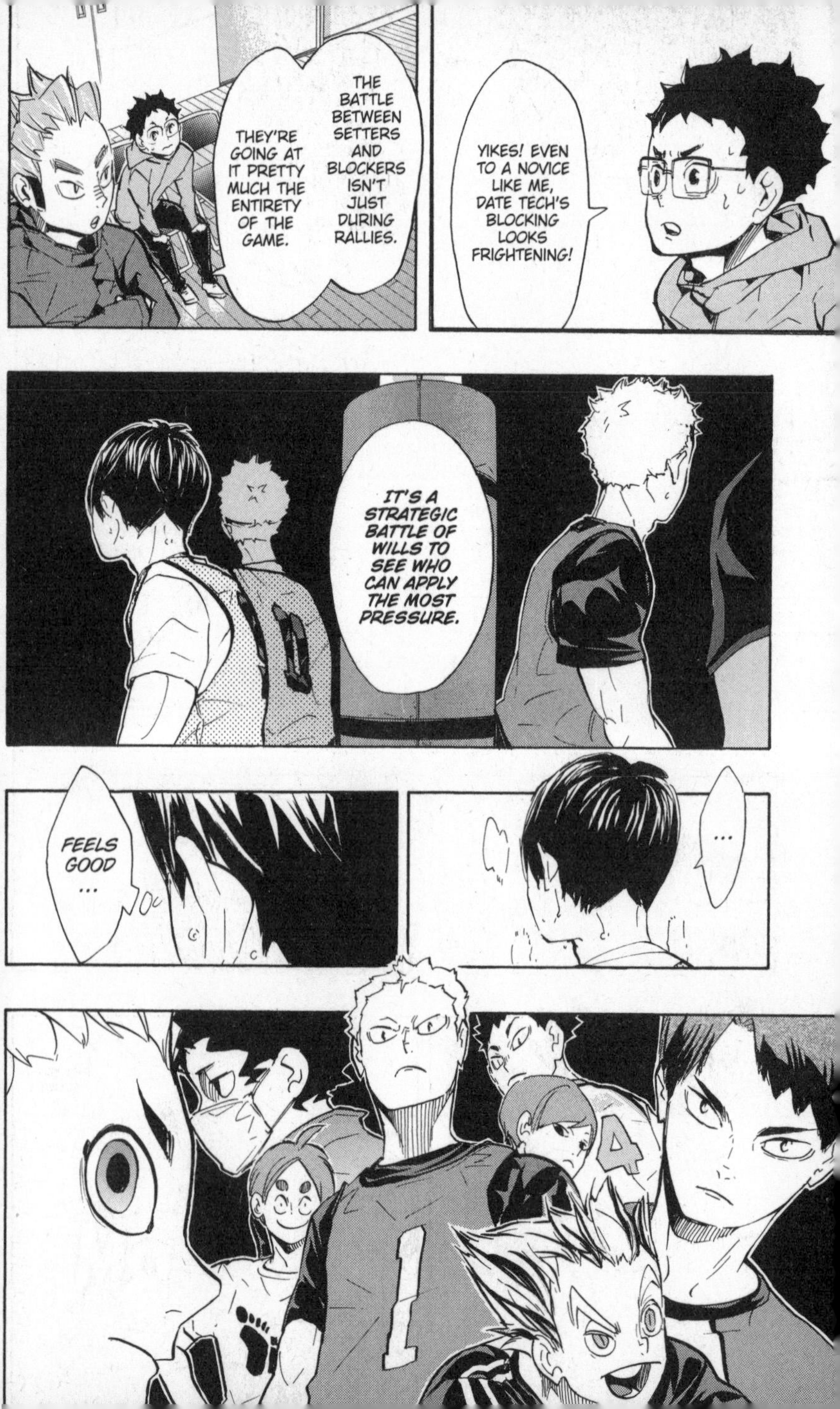
YIKES! EVEN TO A NOVICE LIKE ME, DATE TECH'S BLOCKING LOOKS FRIGHTENING!
THE BATTLE BETWEEN SETTERS AND BLOCKERS ISN'T JUST DURING RALLIES.
THEY'RE GOING AT IT PRETTY MUCH THE ENTIRETY OF THE GAME.
IT'S A STRATEGIC BATTLE OF WILLS TO SEE WHO CAN APPLY THE MOST PRESSURE.
...
FEELS GOOD ...

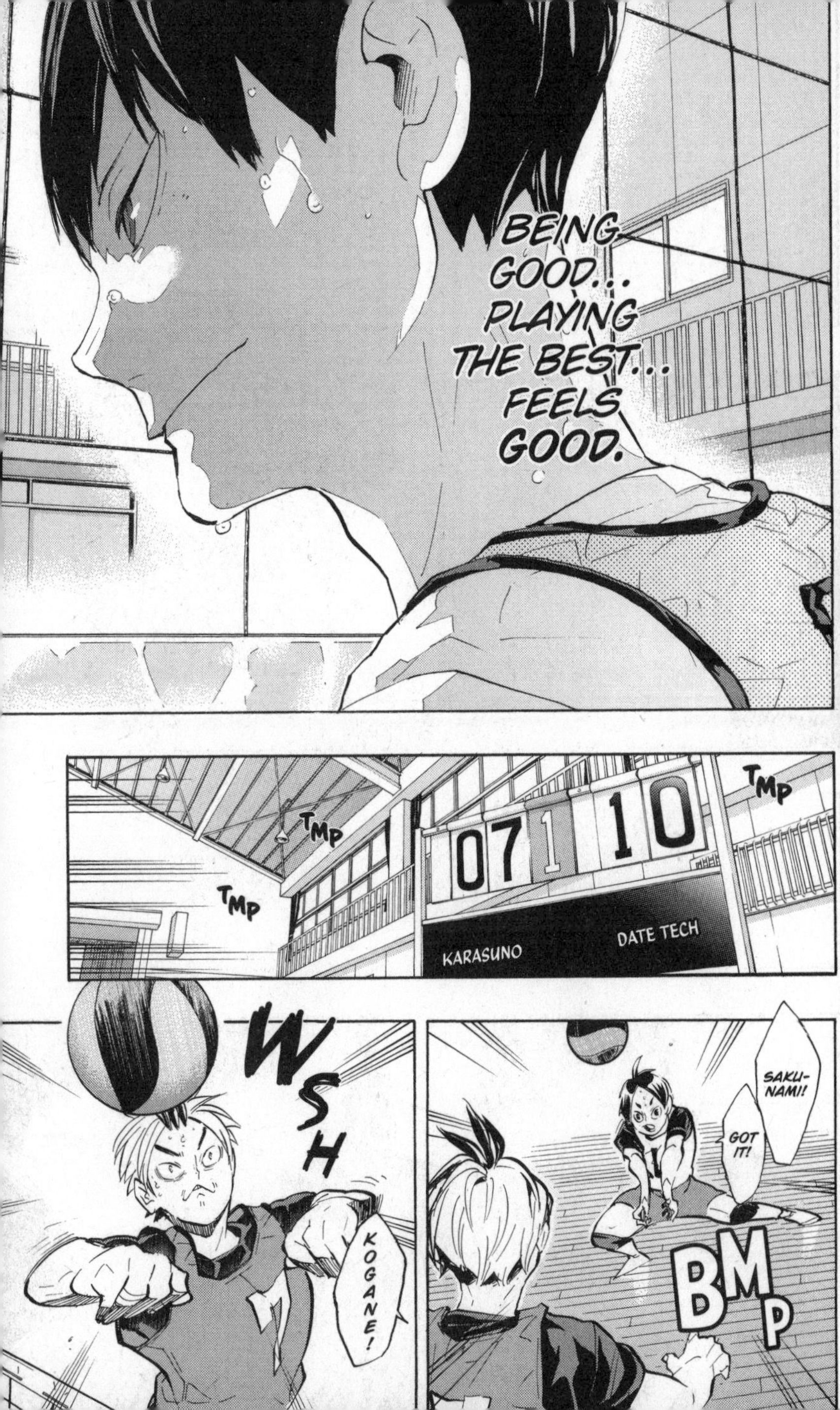
BEING GOOD... PLAYING THE BEST... FEELS GOOD.
TMP
TMP
TMP
07
1
10
KARASUNO
DATE TECH
SAKU-NAMI!
GOT IT!
BMP
WSH
KOGANE!

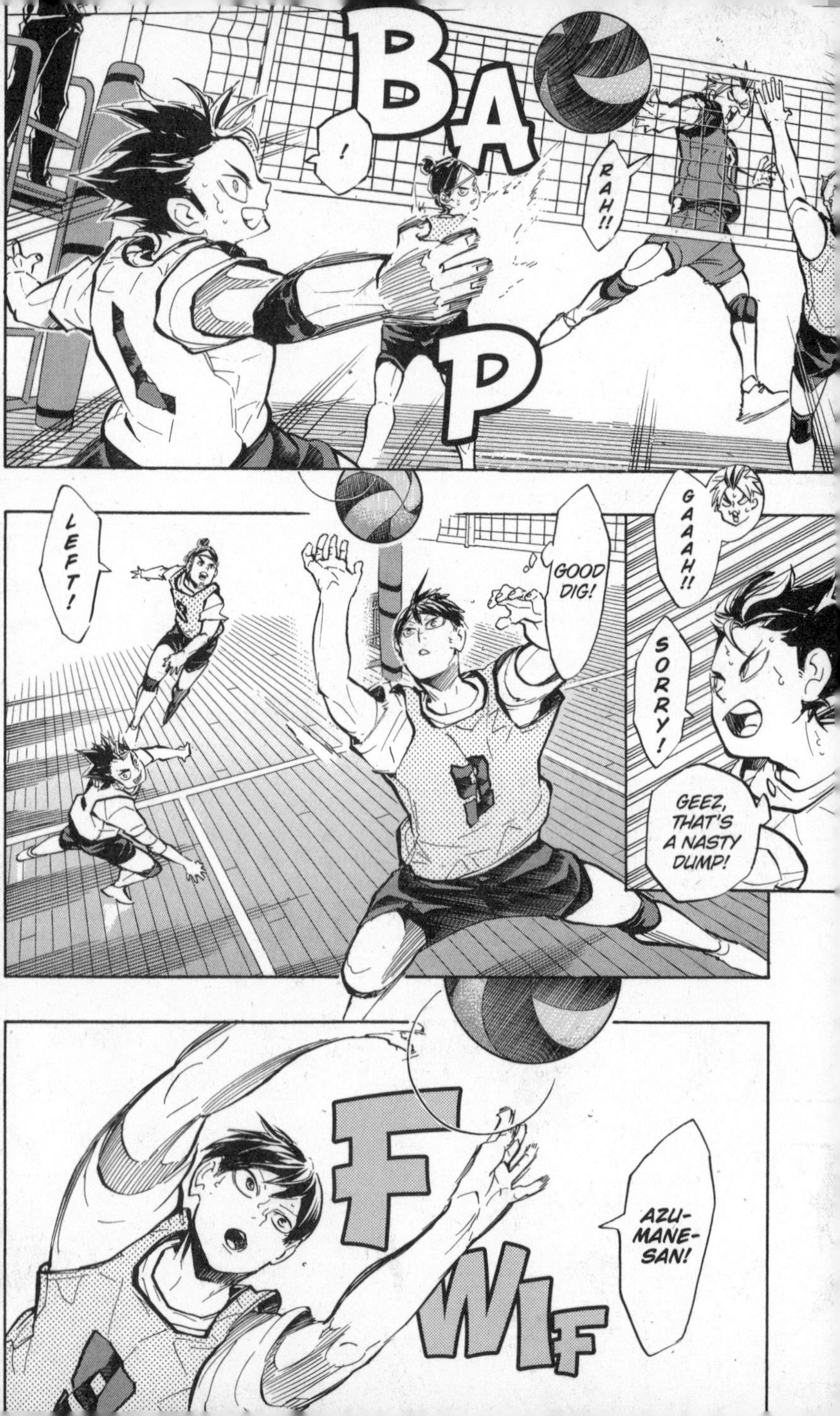
RAH!!
BAP
!
GAAAH!!
SORRY!
GEEZ, THAT'S A NASTY DUMP!
GOOD DIG!
LEFT!
AZU-MANE-SAN!
FWIF

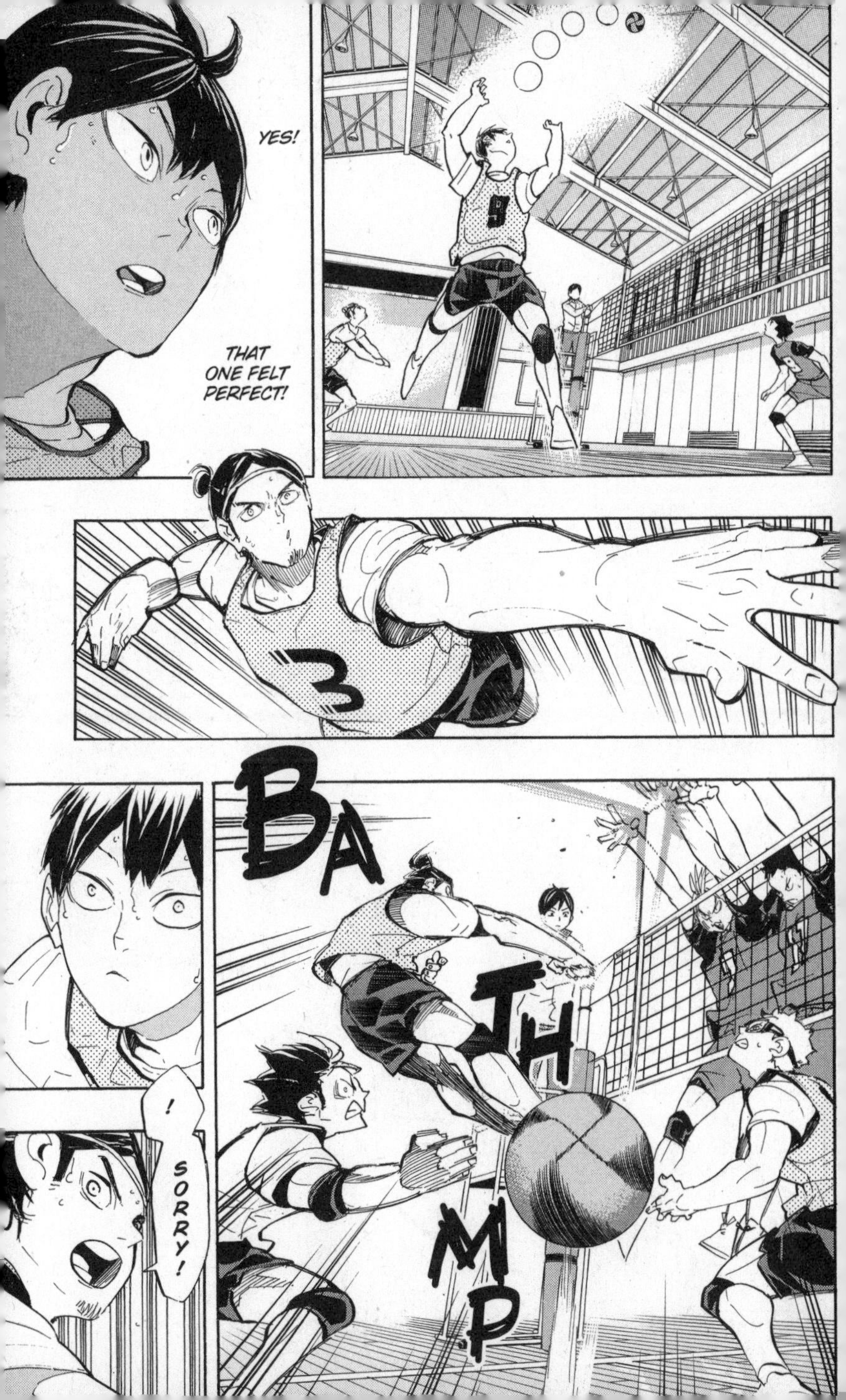
YES!
THAT ONE FELT PERFECT!
BATHMP
!
SORRY!

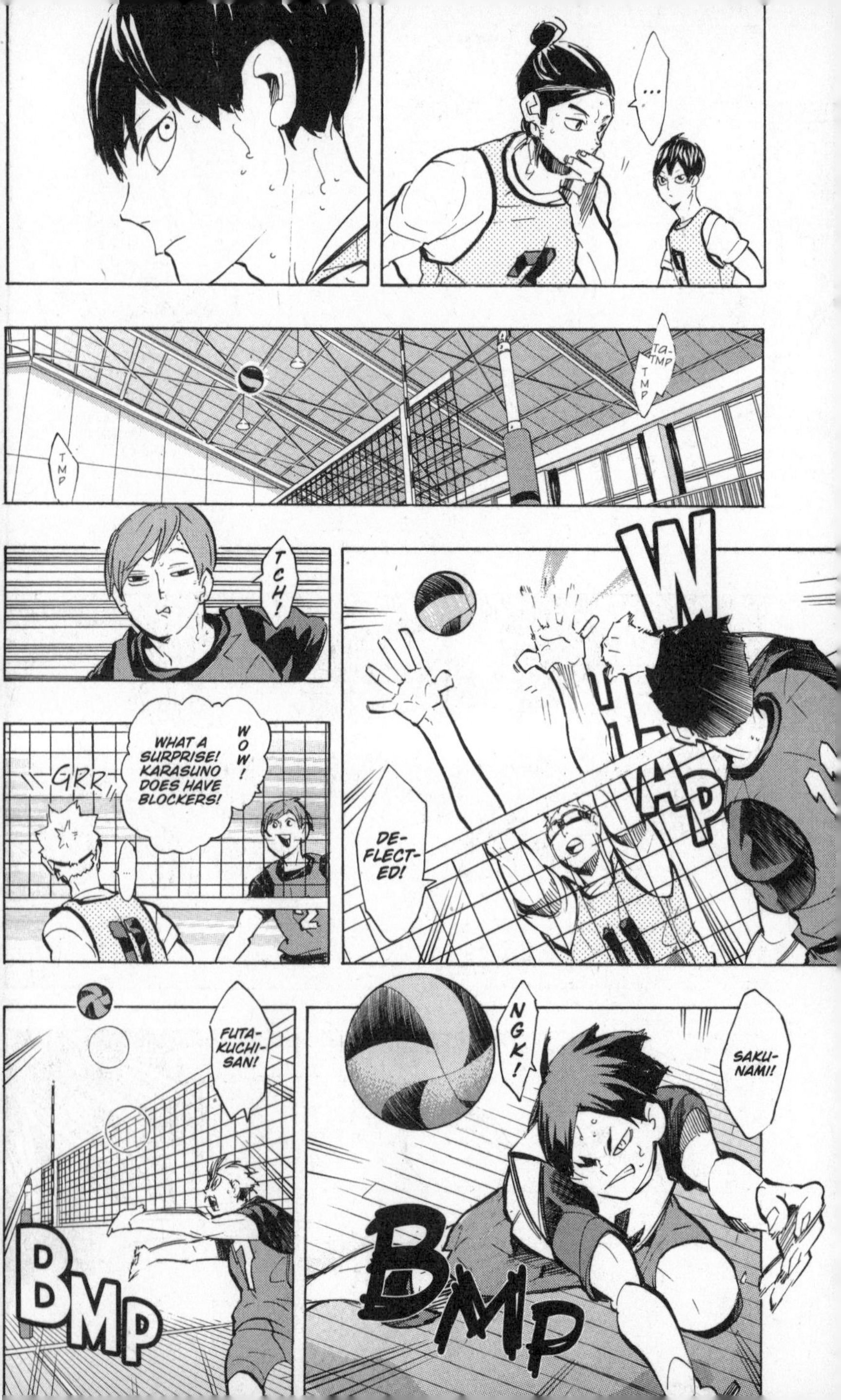
...
TA-TMP
TMP
TMP
WHAP
DE-FLECTED!
TCH!
WOW!
WHAT A SURPRISE! KARASUNO DOES HAVE BLOCKERS!
GRR
...
SAKU-NAMI!
NGK!
BMP
FUTA-KUCHI-SAN!
BMP

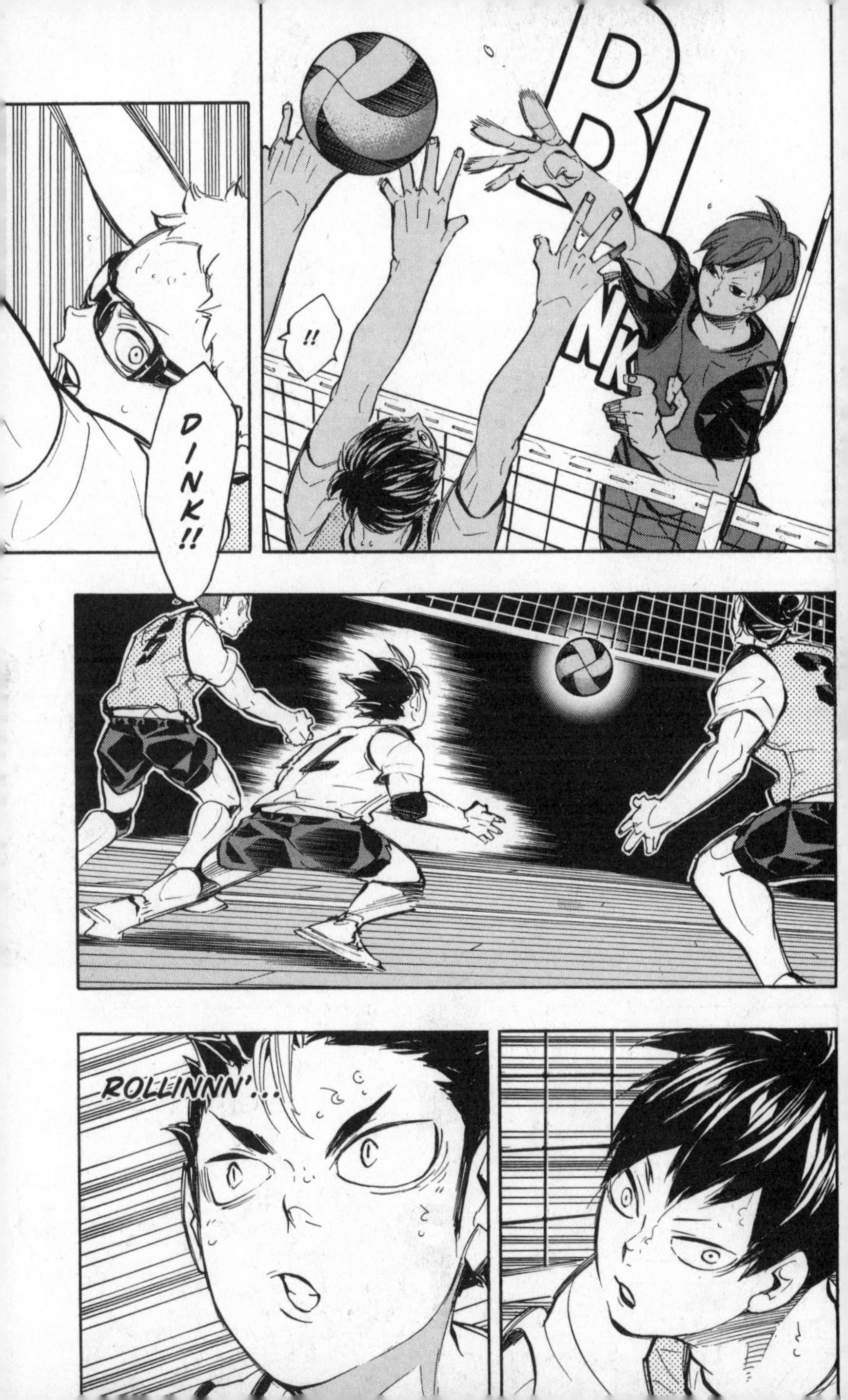
!!
DINK!!
ROLLINNN'...

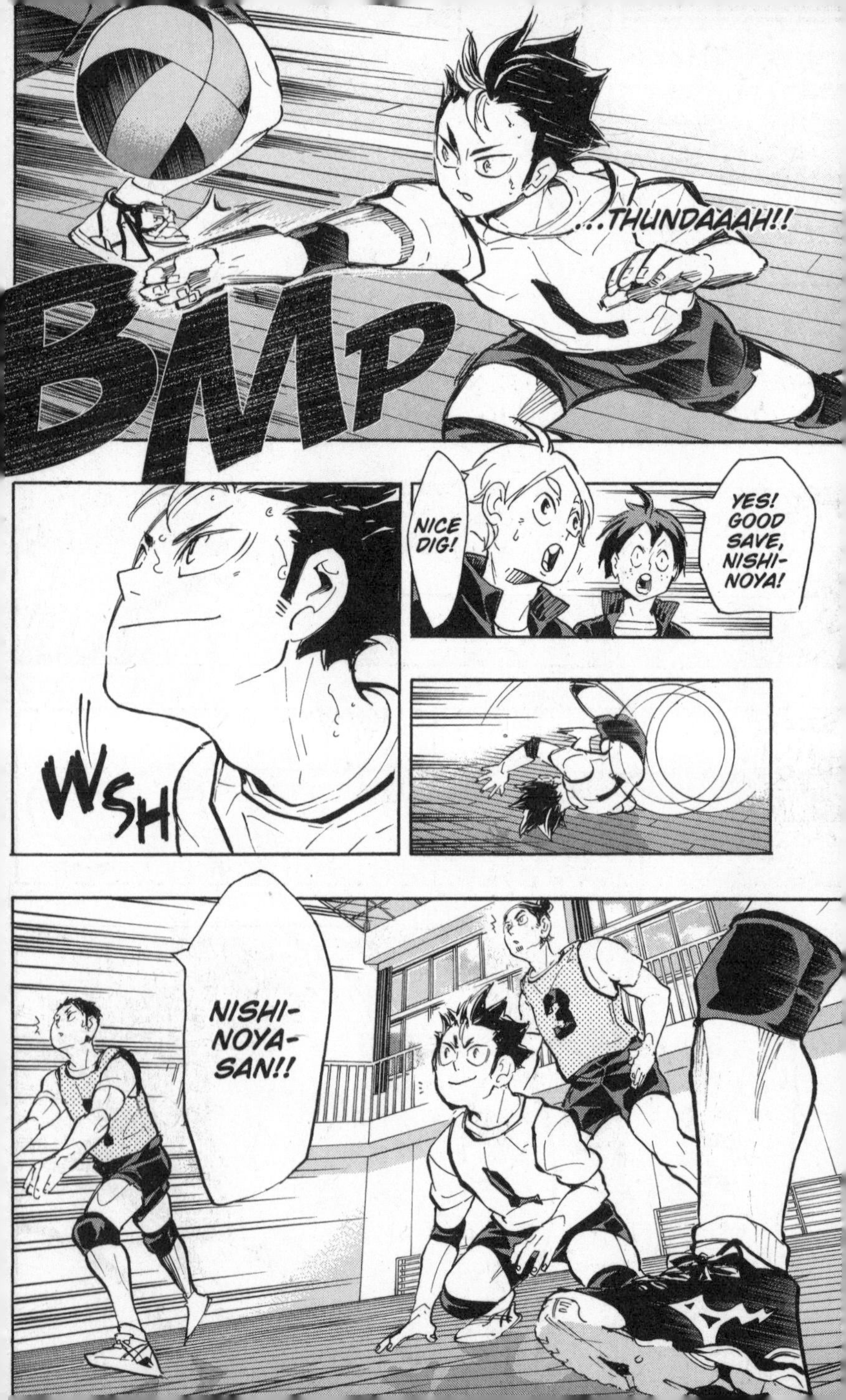
...THUNDAAAH!!
BMP
YES! GOOD SAVE, NISHI-NOYA!
NICE DIG!
WSH
NISHI-NOYA-SAN!!

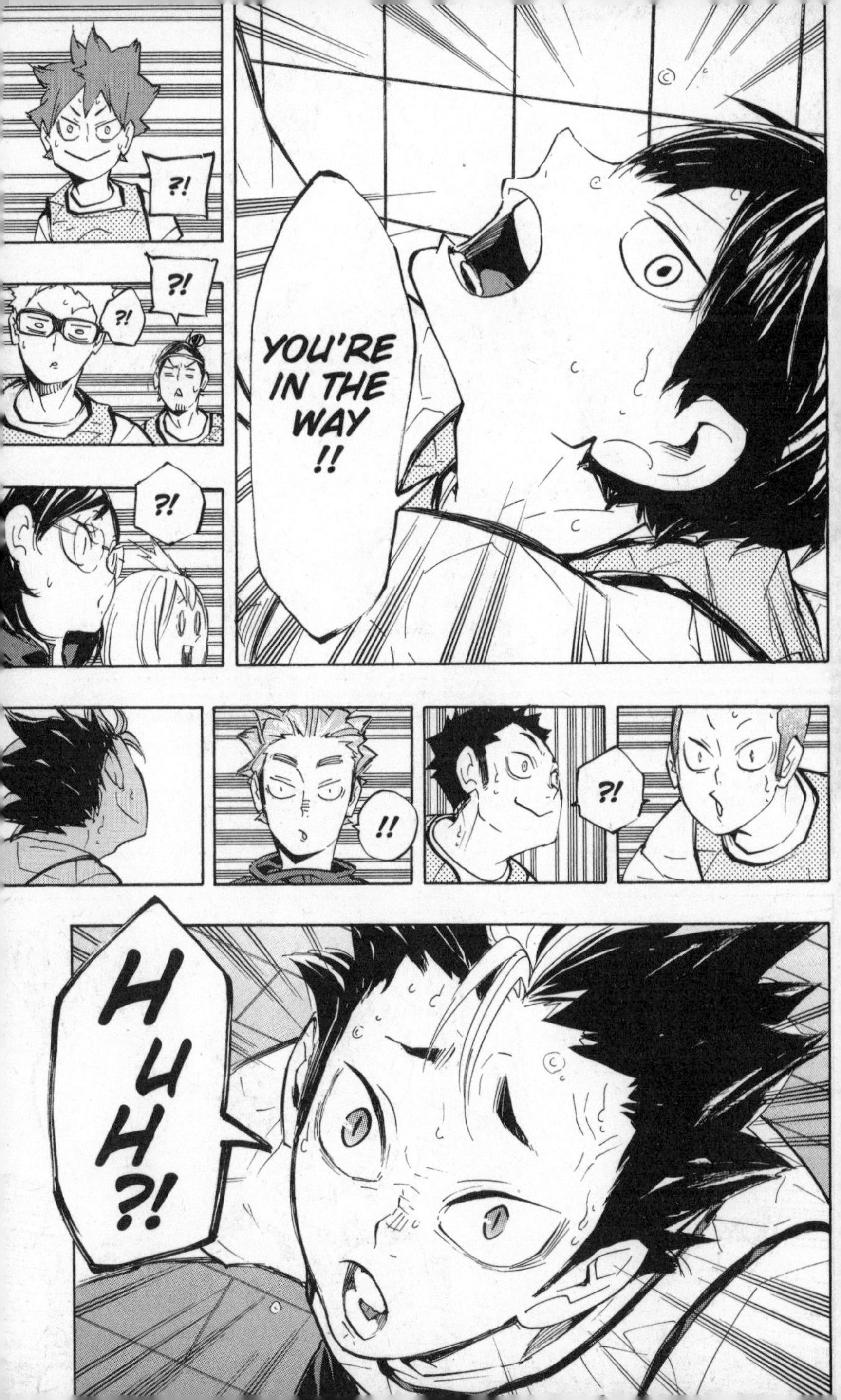
YOU'RE IN THE WAY!!
?!
?!
?!
?!
?!
!!
HUH?!

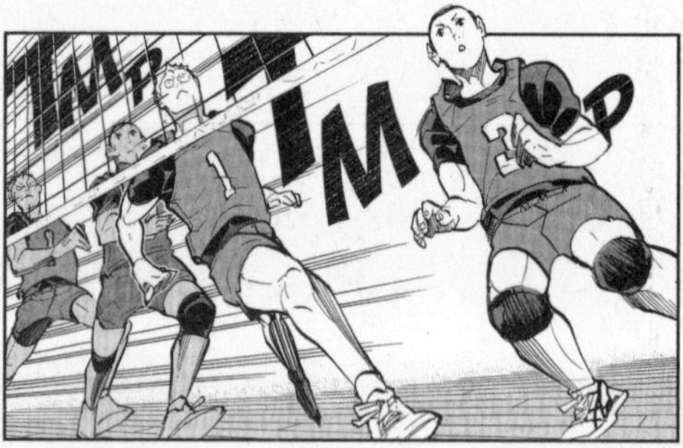
THUMP
THUMP
FOLLOW THIS...

↓

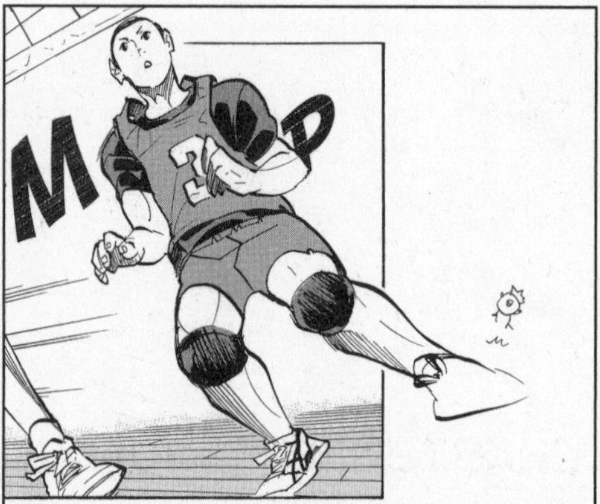
THUMP
...AND IT LOOKS LIKE THIS!

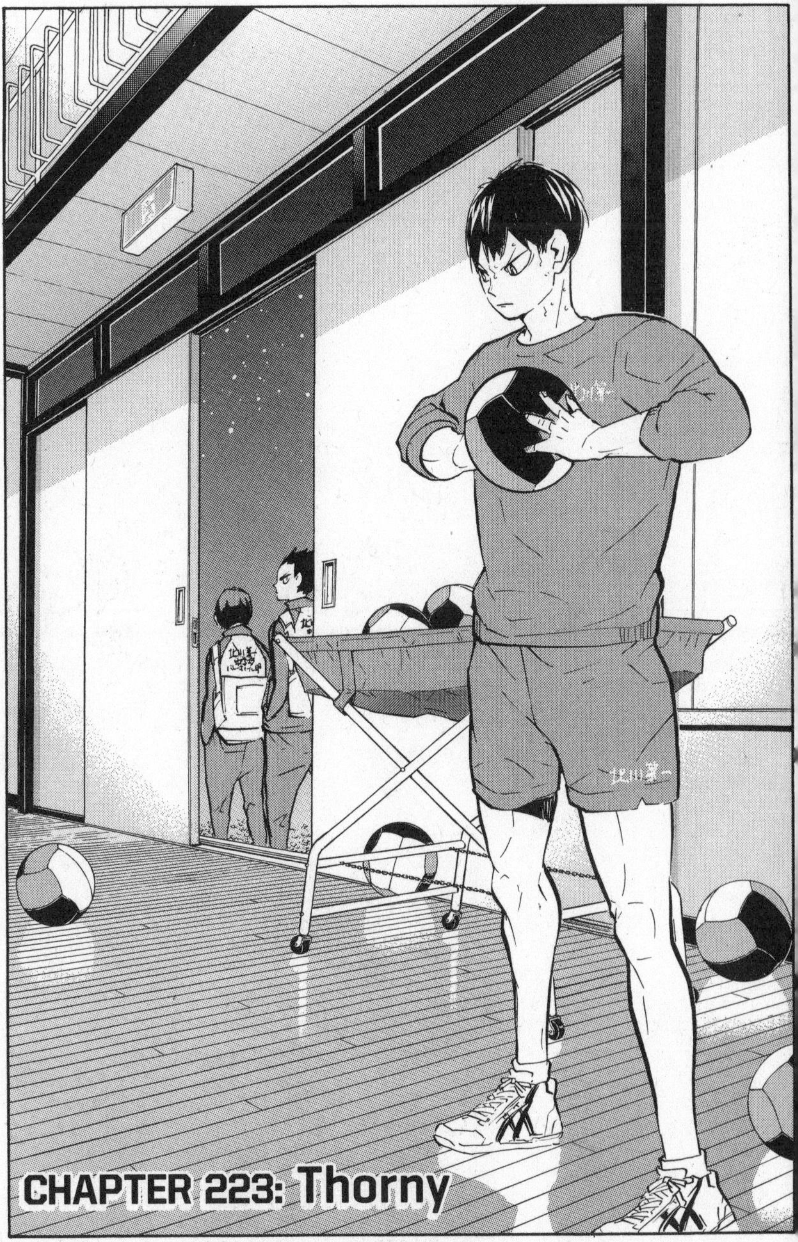
CHAPTER 223: Thorny

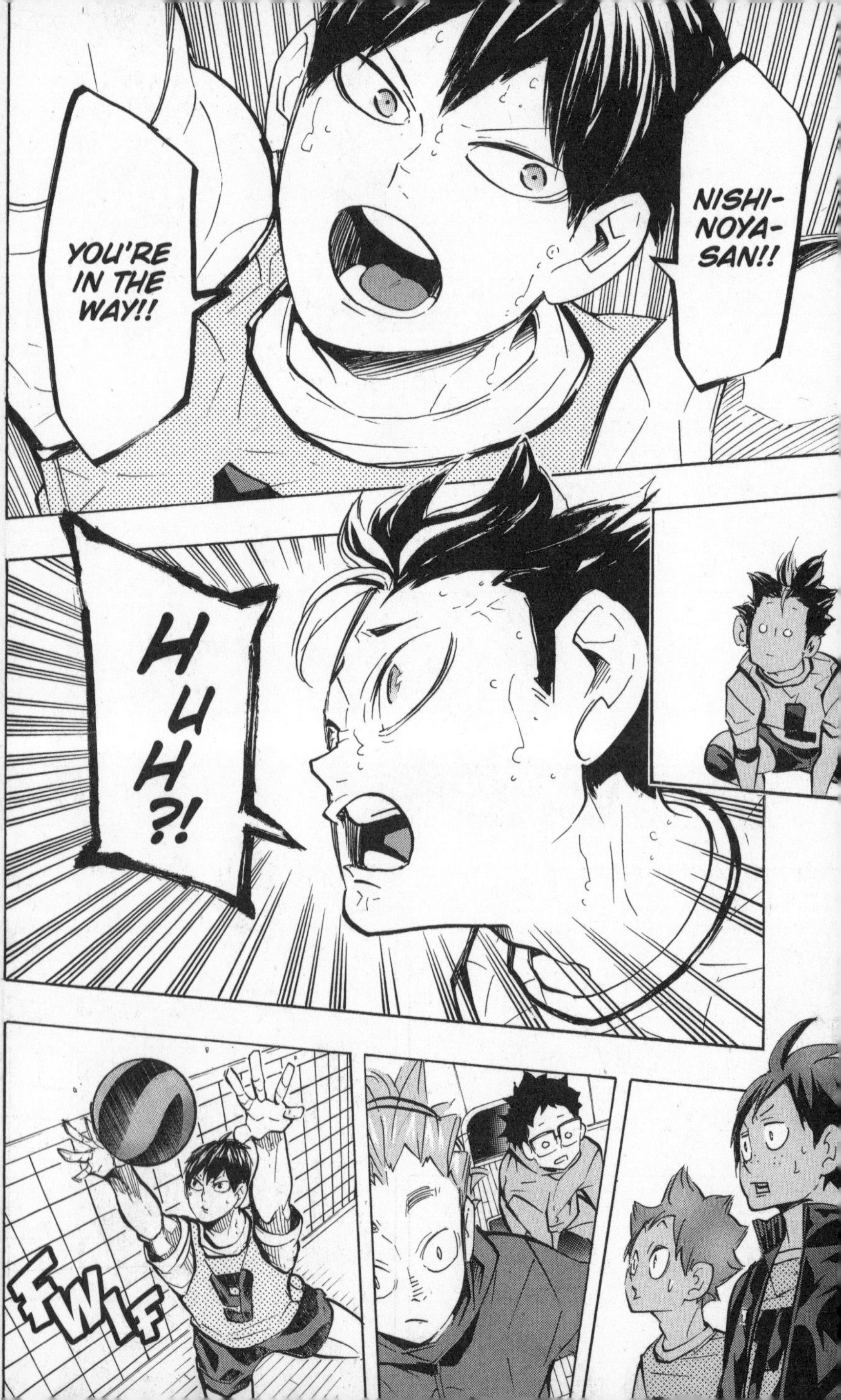
NISHI-NOYA-SAN!!
YOU'RE IN THE WAY!!
HUH?!
FWIP

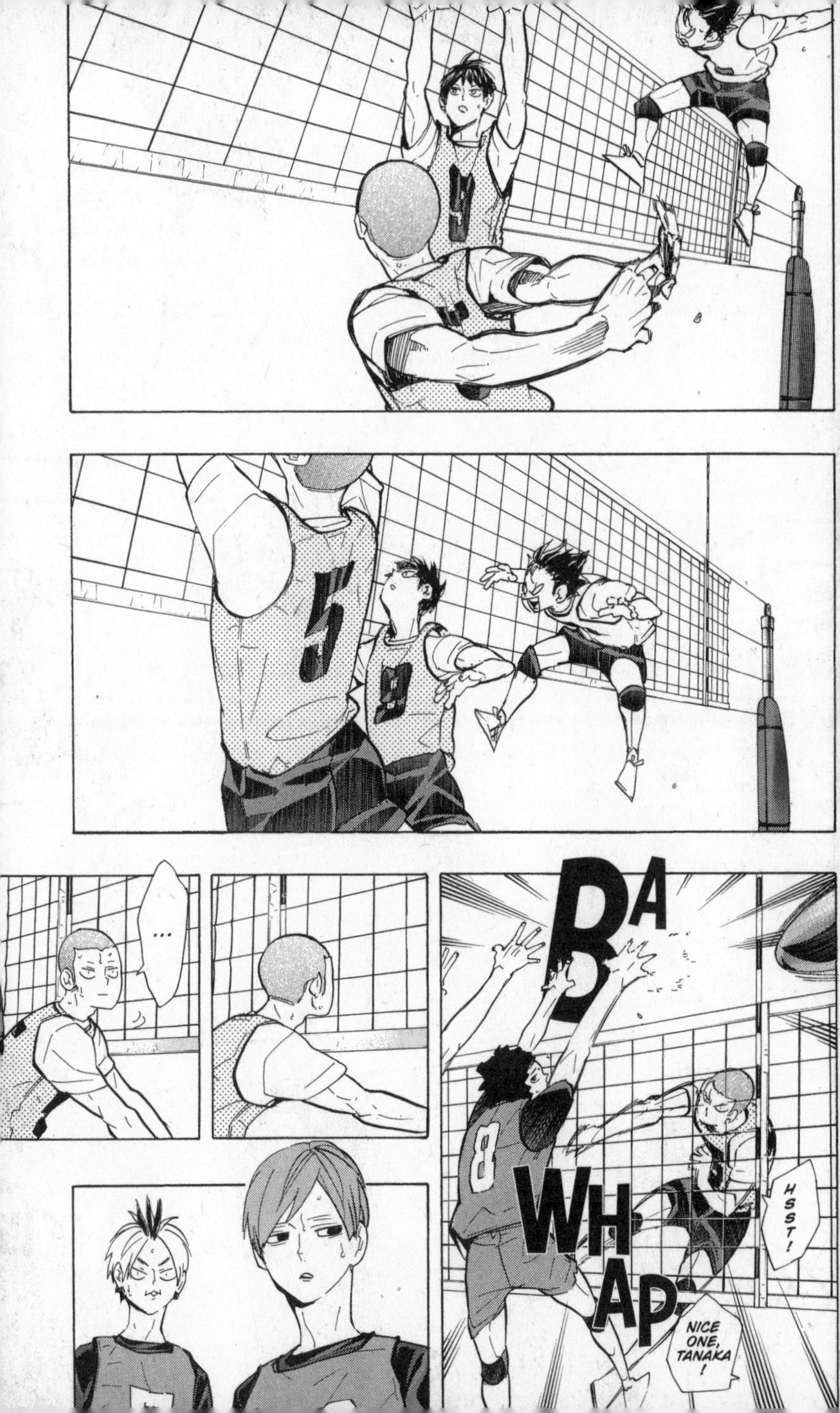
BA
WHAP
HSST!
NICE ONE, TANAKA!
...

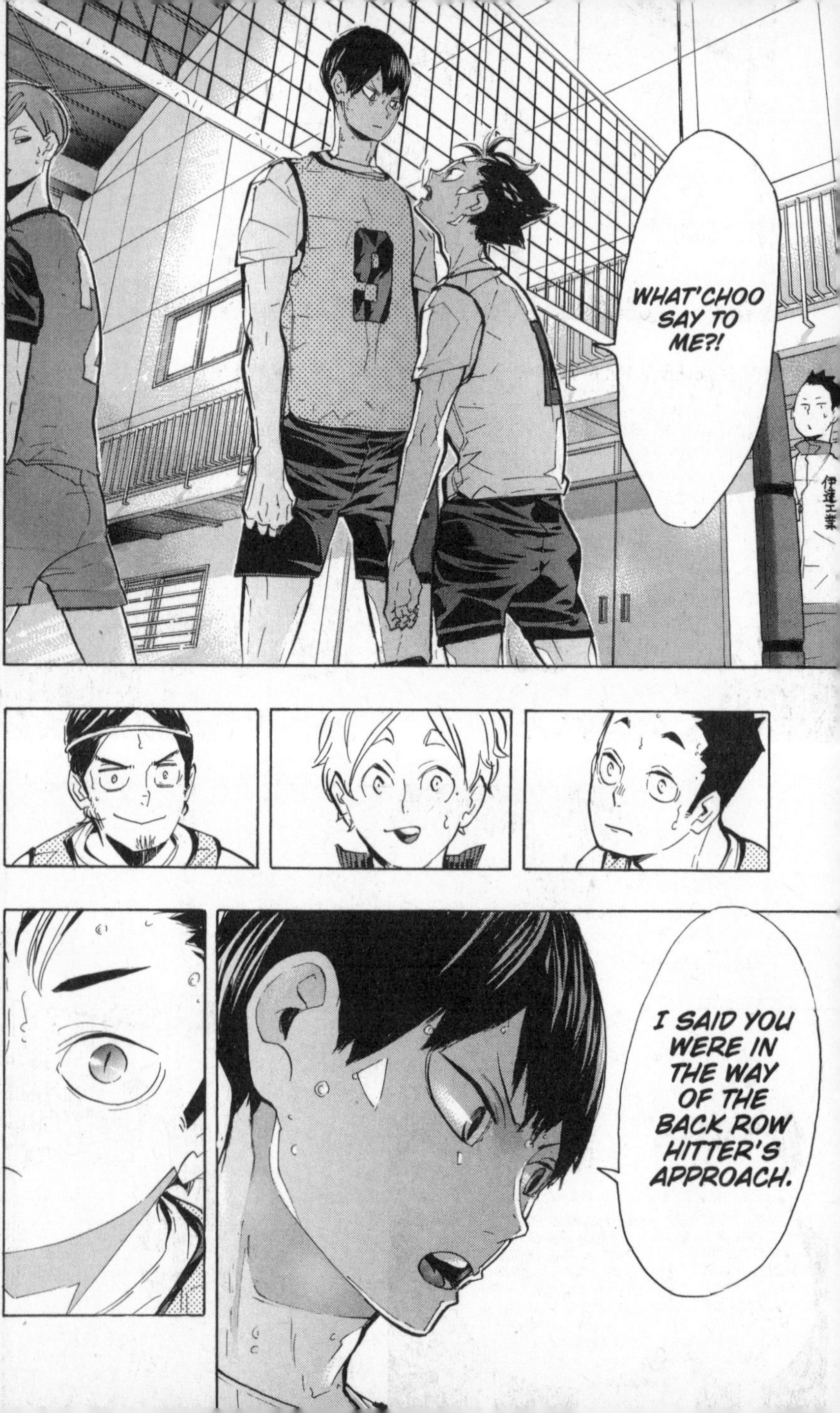
WHAT'CHOO SAY TO ME?!
伊達工業
I SAID YOU WERE IN THE WAY OF THE BACK ROW HITTER'S APPROACH.

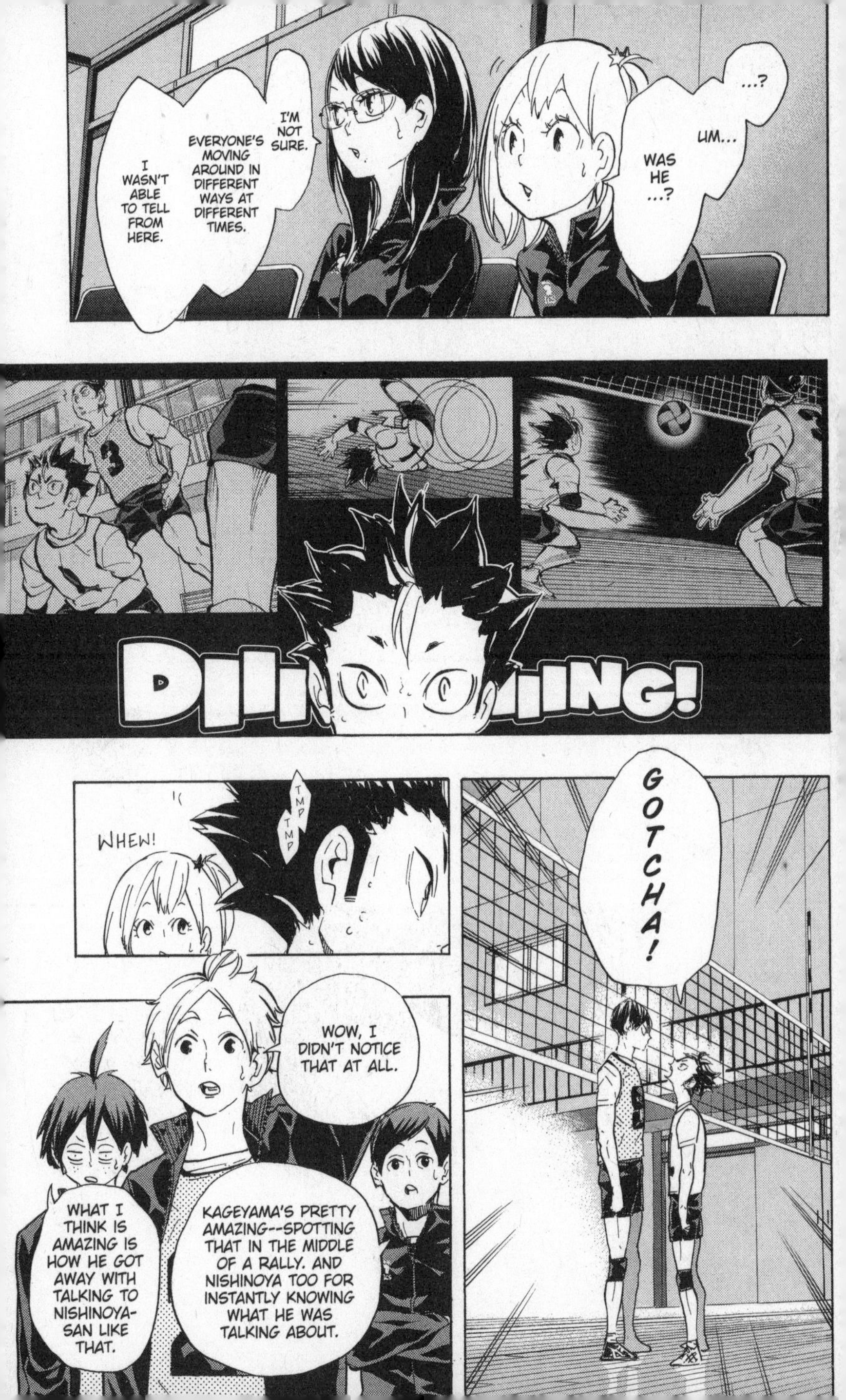
...?
UM...
WAS HE ...?
I'M NOT SURE.
EVERYONE'S MOVING AROUND IN DIFFERENT WAYS AT DIFFERENT TIMES.
I WASN'T ABLE TO TELL FROM HERE.
DIII IIING!
GOTCHA!
TMP TMP
WHEW!
WOW, I DIDN'T NOTICE THAT AT ALL.
KAGEYAMA'S PRETTY AMAZING--SPOTTING THAT IN THE MIDDLE OF A RALLY. AND NISHINOYA TOO FOR INSTANTLY KNOWING WHAT HE WAS TALKING ABOUT.
WHAT I THINK IS AMAZING IS HOW HE GOT AWAY WITH TALKING TO NISHINOYA-SAN LIKE THAT.

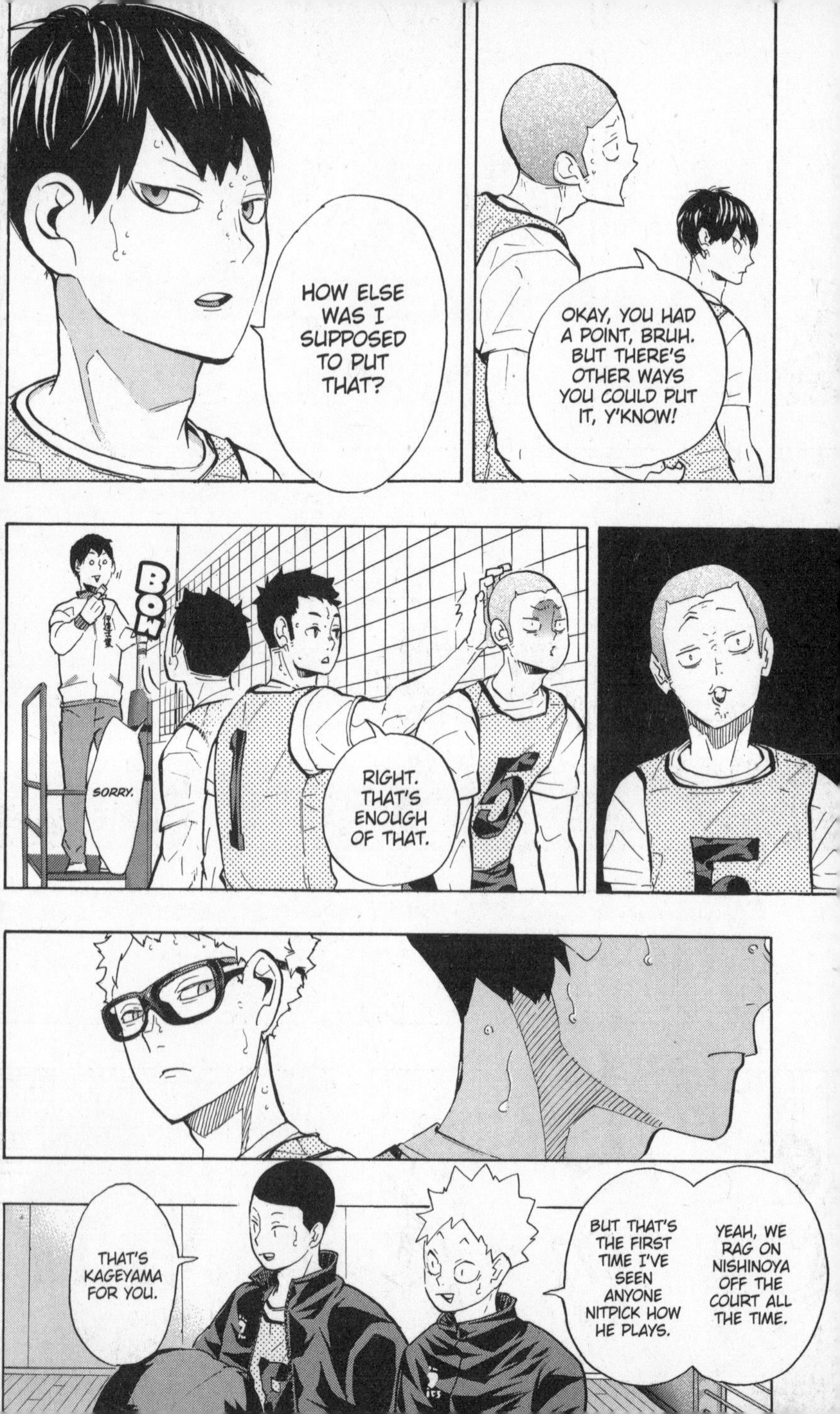
OKAY, YOU HAD A POINT, BRUH. BUT THERE'S OTHER WAYS YOU COULD PUT IT, Y'KNOW!
HOW ELSE WAS I SUPPOSED TO PUT THAT?
BOW
RIGHT. THAT'S ENOUGH OF THAT.
SORRY.
YEAH, WE RAG ON NISHINOYA OFF THE COURT ALL THE TIME.
BUT THAT'S THE FIRST TIME I'VE SEEN ANYONE NITPICK HOW HE PLAYS.
THAT'S KAGEYAMA FOR YOU.

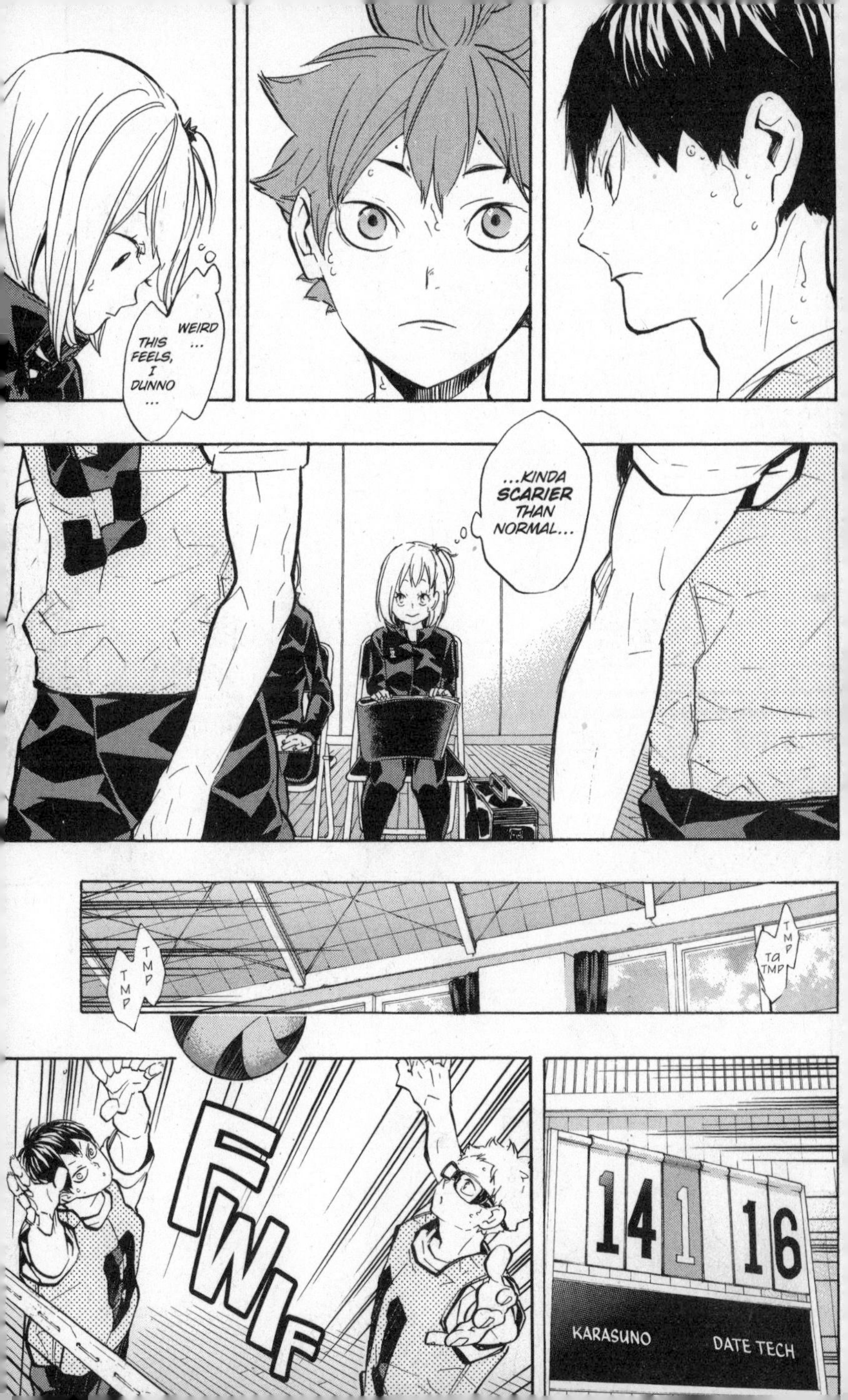
THIS FEELS, I DUNNO... WEIRD...
...KINDA SCARIER THAN NORMAL...
TMP Ta TMP
TMP TMP
14 1 16
KARASUNO
DATE TECH
FWIF

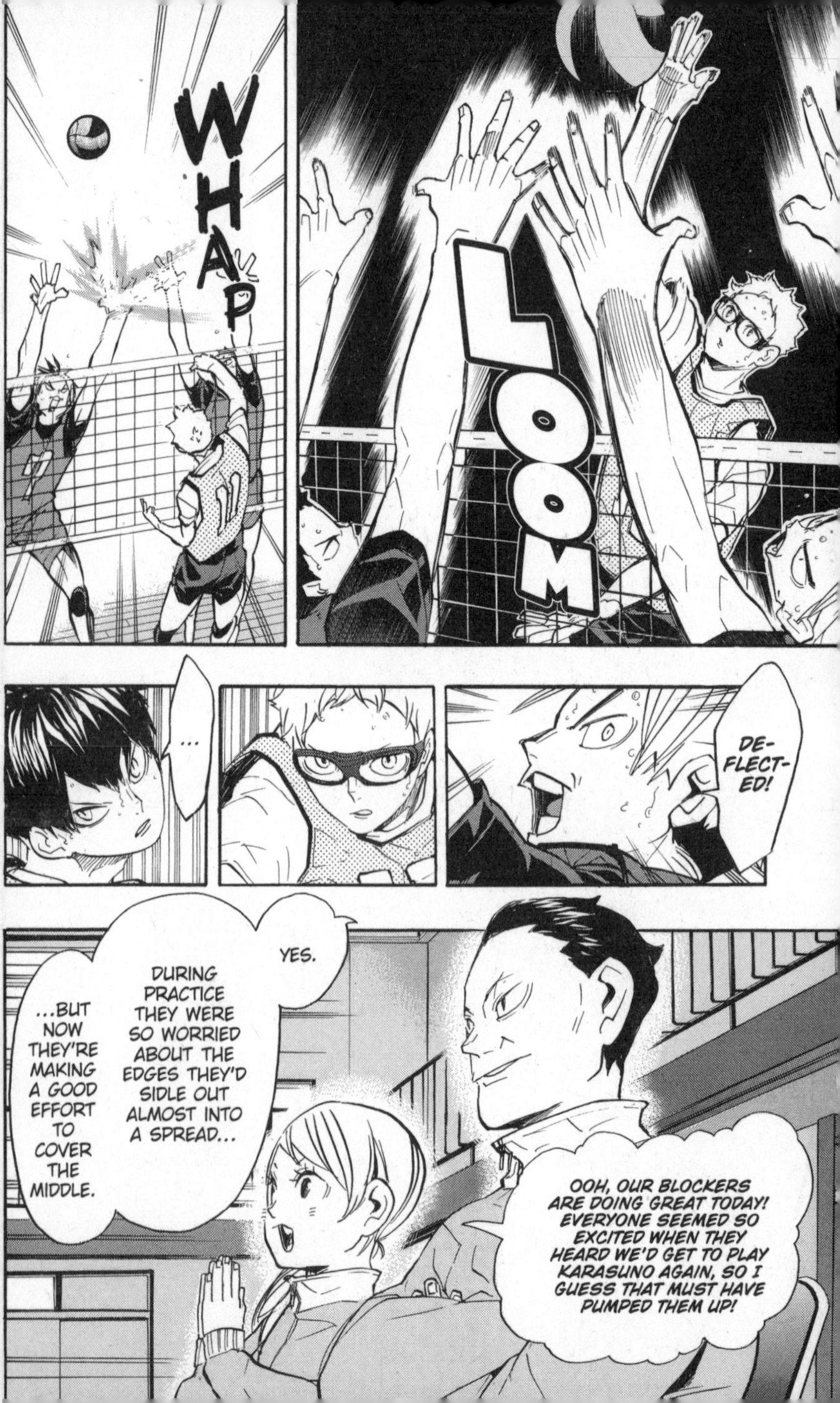
LOOM
WHAP
DE-FLECT-ED!
...
OOH, OUR BLOCKERS ARE DOING GREAT TODAY! EVERYONE SEEMED SO EXCITED WHEN THEY HEARD WE'D GET TO PLAY KARASUNO AGAIN, SO I GUESS THAT MUST HAVE PUMPED THEM UP!
YES.
DURING PRACTICE THEY WERE SO WORRIED ABOUT THE EDGES THEY'D SIDLE OUT ALMOST INTO A SPREAD...
...BUT NOW THEY'RE MAKING A GOOD EFFORT TO COVER THE MIDDLE.

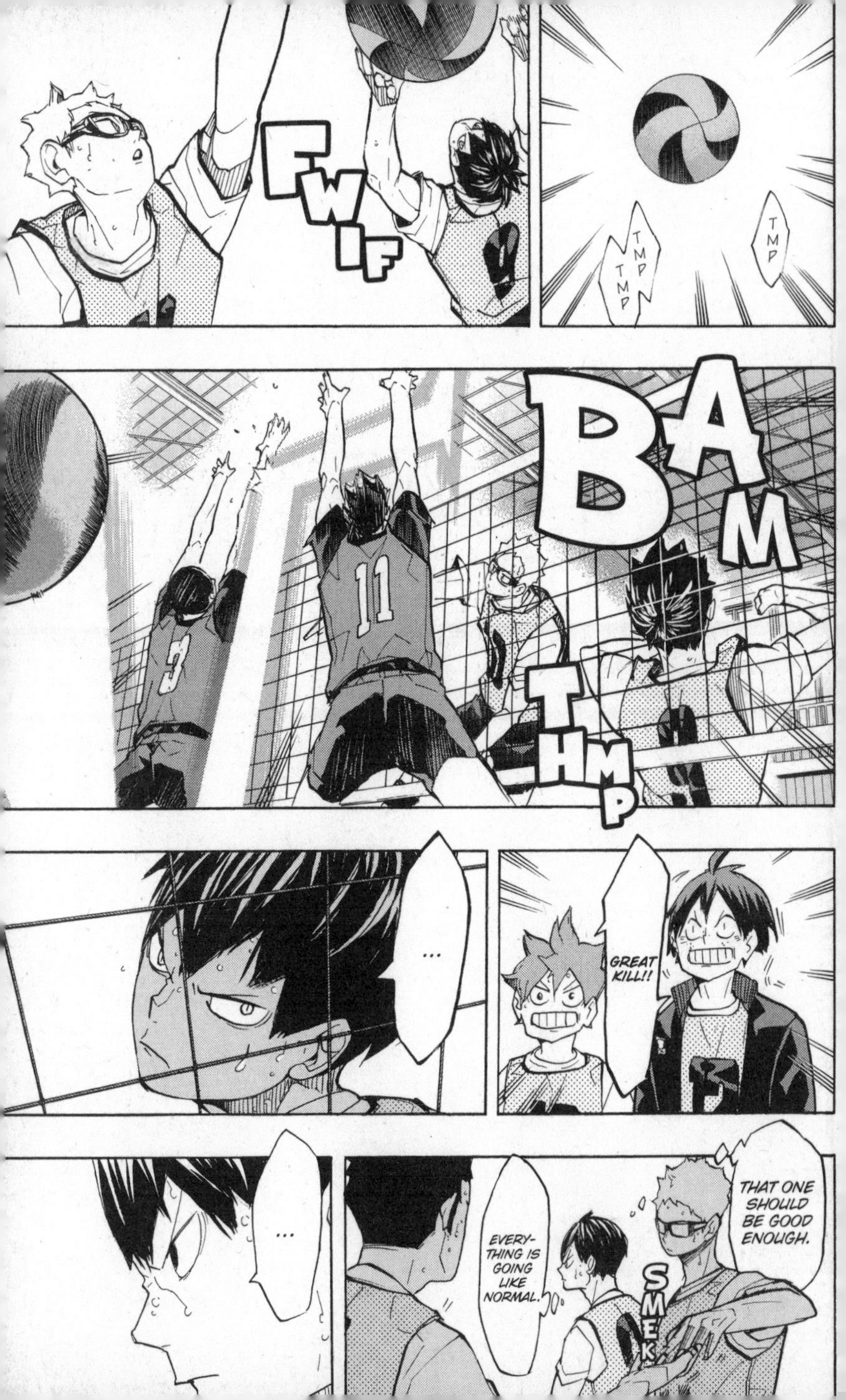
TMP
TMP TMP
FWIF
BAM
THMP
GREAT KILL!!
...
THAT ONE SHOULD BE GOOD ENOUGH.
SMEK
EVERY-THING IS GOING LIKE NORMAL.
...

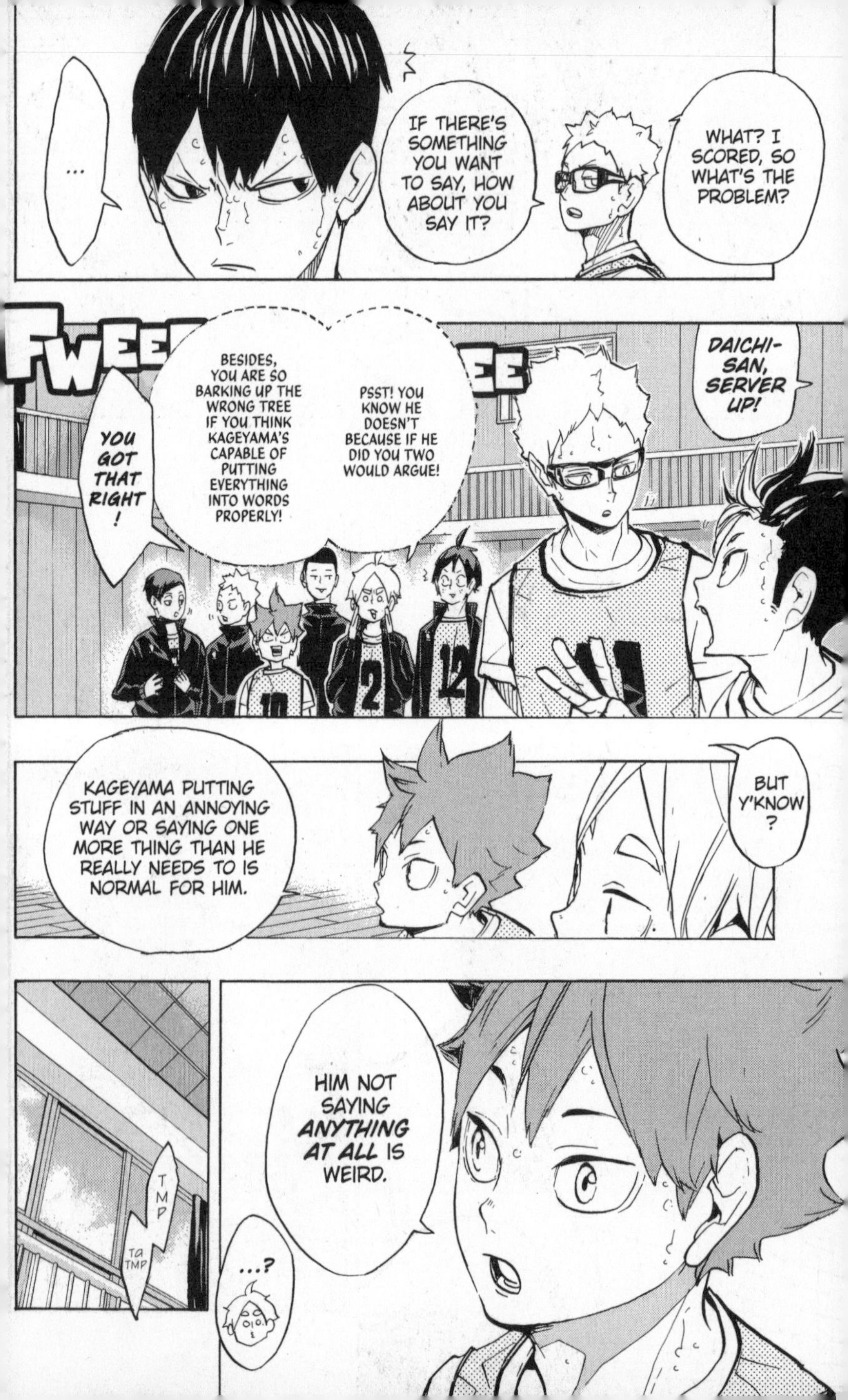
WHAT? I SCORED, SO WHAT'S THE PROBLEM?
IF THERE'S SOMETHING YOU WANT TO SAY, HOW ABOUT YOU SAY IT?
...
DAICHI-SAN, SERVER UP!
FWEEEEE
PSST! YOU KNOW HE DOESN'T BECAUSE IF HE DID YOU TWO WOULD ARGUE!
BESIDES, YOU ARE SO BARKING UP THE WRONG TREE IF YOU THINK KAGEYAMA'S CAPABLE OF PUTTING EVERYTHING INTO WORDS PROPERLY!
YOU GOT THAT RIGHT!
BUT Y'KNOW?
KAGEYAMA PUTTING STUFF IN AN ANNOYING WAY OR SAYING ONE MORE THING THAN HE REALLY NEEDS TO IS NORMAL FOR HIM.
HIM NOT SAYING ANYTHING AT ALL IS WEIRD.
...?
TMP
TA TMP

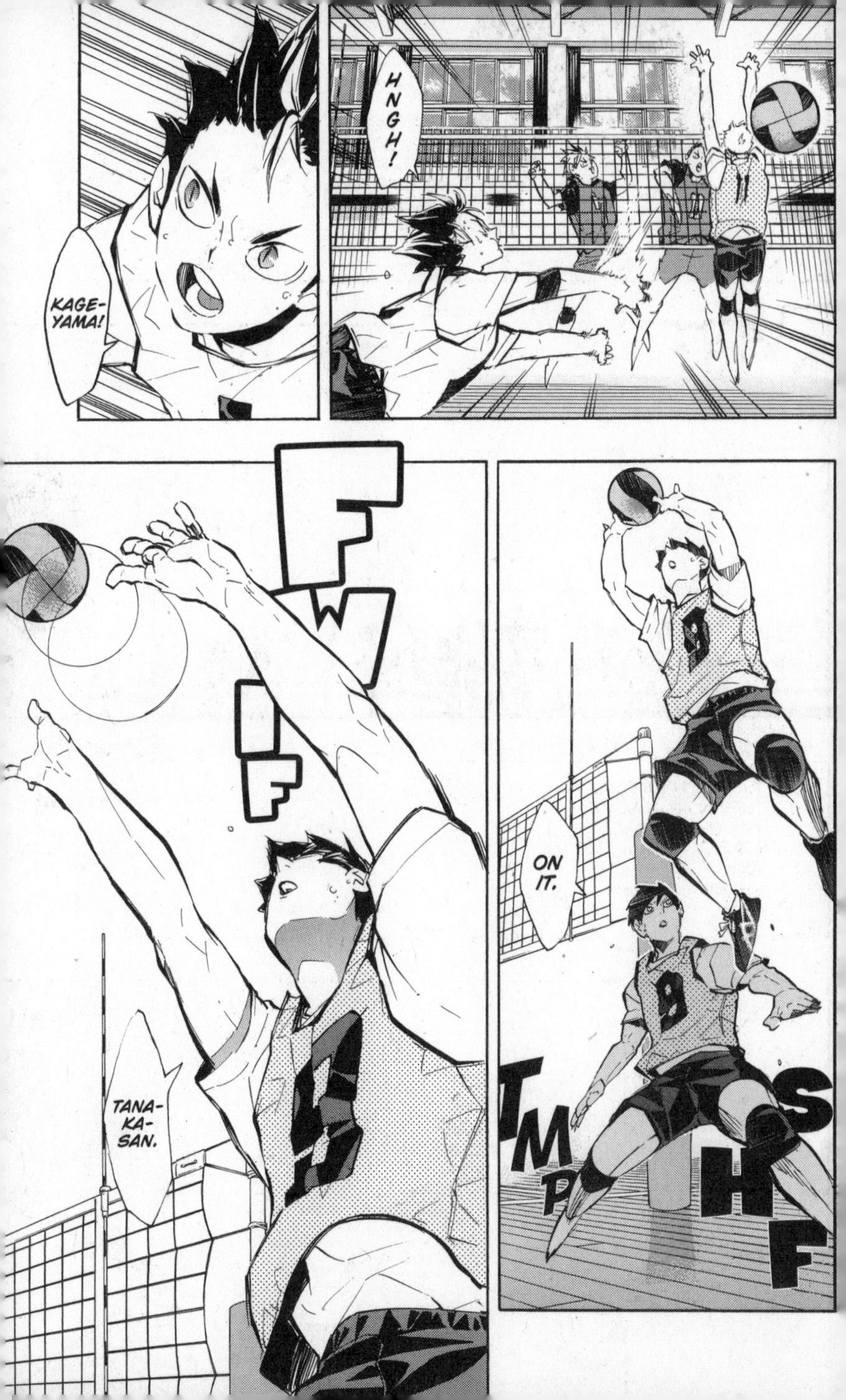
HNGH!
KAGE-YAMA!
ON IT.
TMP
SHHF
FWHF
TANA-KA-SAN.

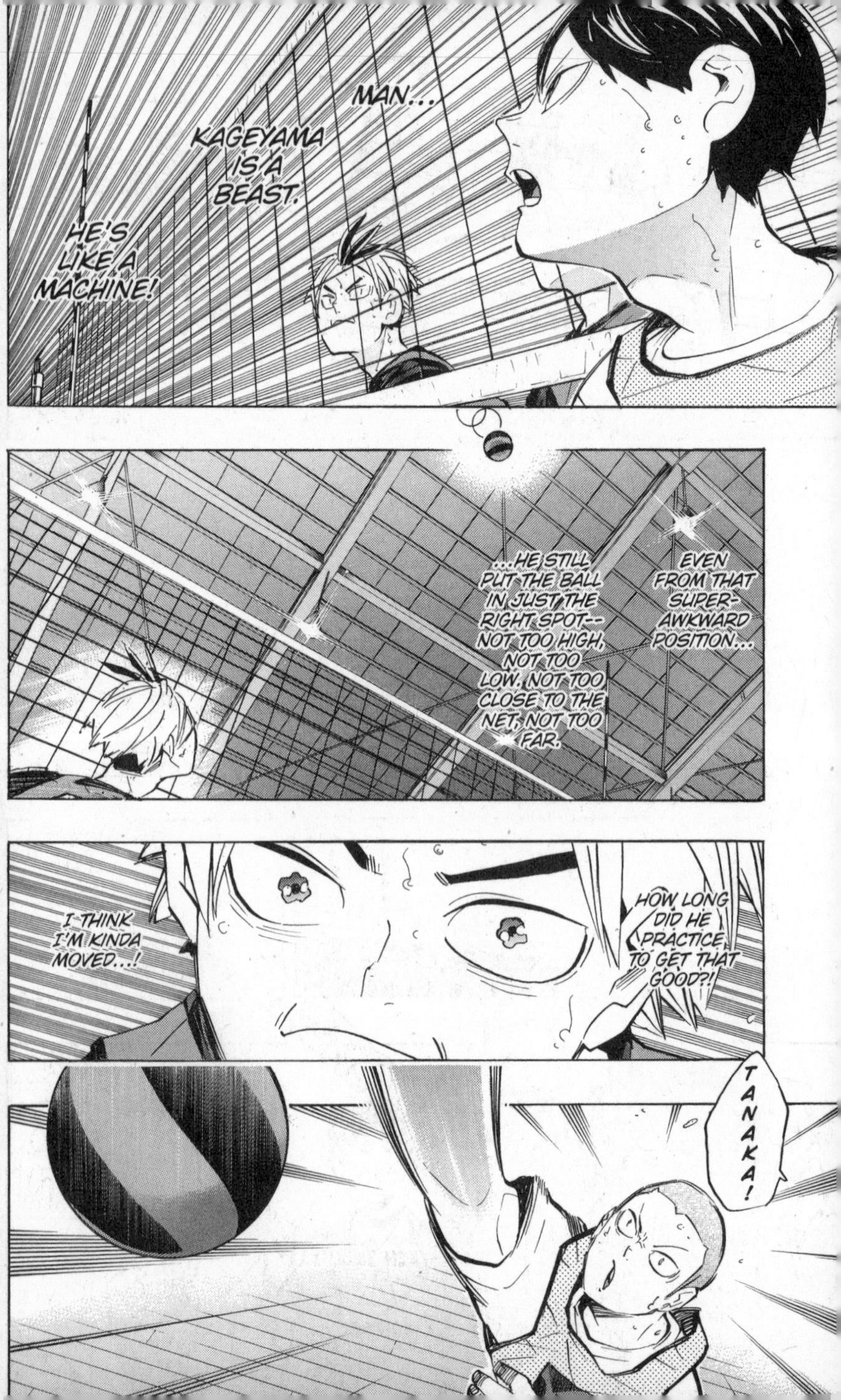
MAN...
KAGEYAMA IS A BEAST.
HE'S LIKE A MACHINE!
EVEN FROM THAT SUPER-AWKWARD POSITION...
...HE STILL PUT THE BALL IN JUST THE RIGHT SPOT-- NOT TOO HIGH, NOT TOO LOW. NOT TOO CLOSE TO THE NET, NOT TOO FAR.
HOW LONG DID HE PRACTICE TO GET THAT GOOD?!
I-THINK I'M KINDA MOVED...!
TANAKA!

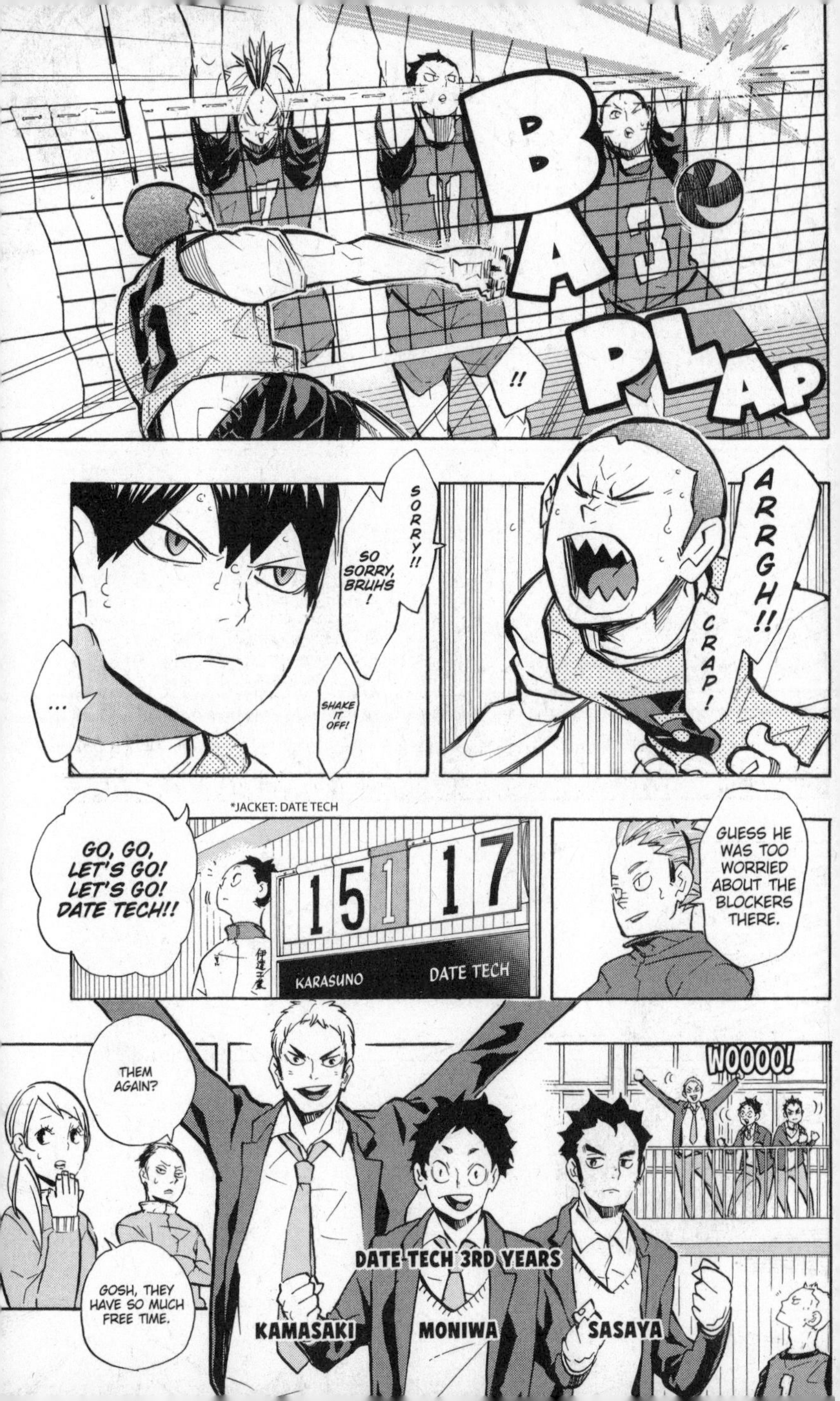
BA
PLAP
!!
ARRGH!!
CRAP!
SORRY!!
SO SORRY, BRUHS!
SHAKE IT OFF!
...
GUESS HE WAS TOO WORRIED ABOUT THE BLOCKERS THERE.
*JACKET: DATE TECH
15 1 1 7
KARASUNO
DATE TECH
GO, GO, LET'S GO! LET'S GO! DATE TECH!!
WOOOO!
DATE TECH 3RD YEARS
SASAYA
MONIWA
KAMASAKI
THEM AGAIN?
GOSH, THEY HAVE SO MUCH FREE TIME.

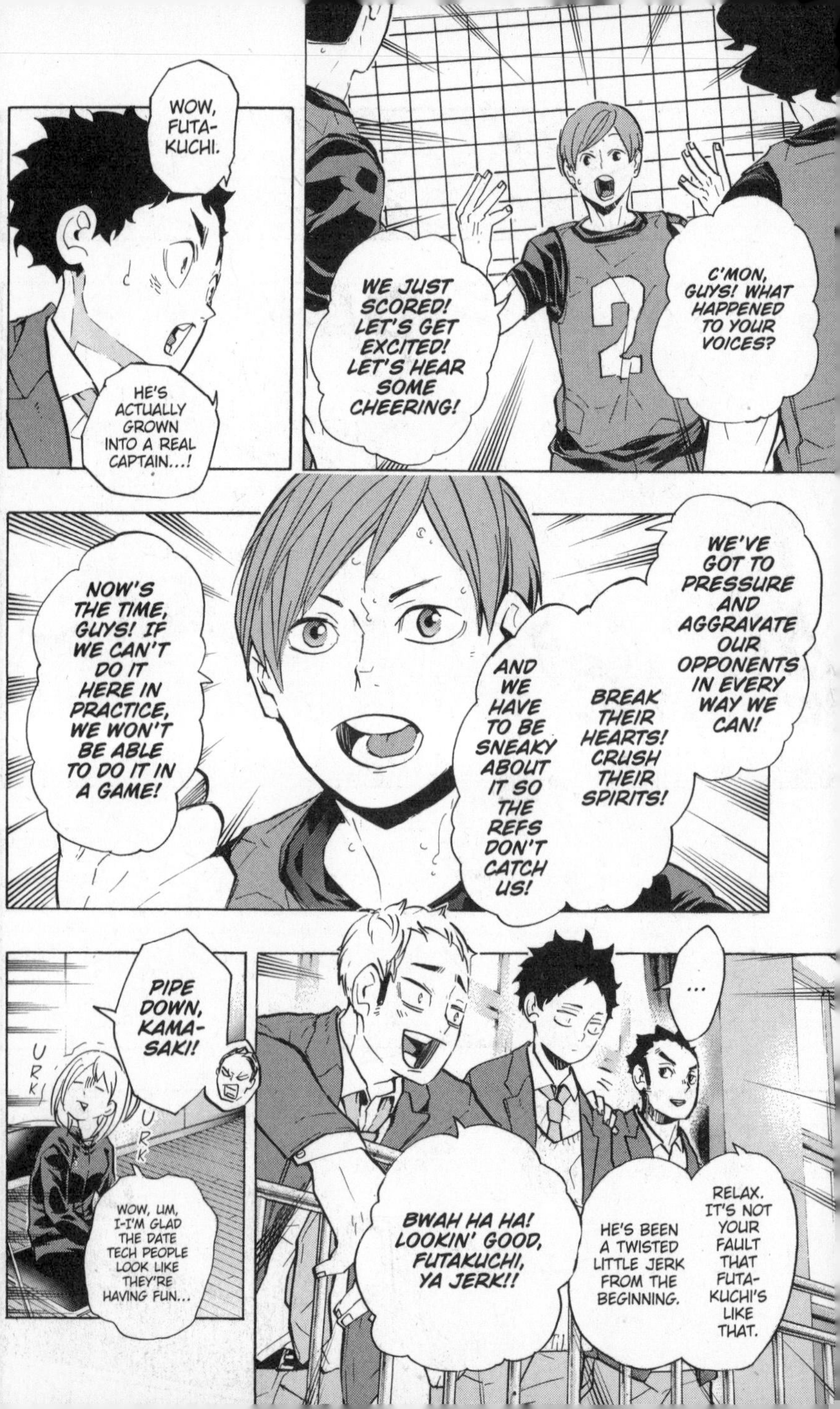
C'MON, GUYS! WHAT HAPPENED TO YOUR VOICES?
WE JUST SCORED! LET'S GET EXCITED! LET'S HEAR SOME CHEERING!
WOW, FUTA-KUCHI.
HE'S ACTUALLY GROWN INTO A REAL CAPTAIN...!
WE'VE GOT TO PRESSURE AND AGGRAVATE OUR OPPONENTS IN EVERY WAY WE CAN!
BREAK THEIR HEARTS! CRUSH THEIR SPIRITS!
AND WE HAVE TO BE SNEAKY ABOUT IT SO THE REFS DON'T CATCH US!
NOW'S THE TIME, GUYS! IF WE CAN'T DO IT HERE IN PRACTICE, WE WON'T BE ABLE TO DO IT IN A GAME!
...
RELAX. IT'S NOT YOUR FAULT THAT FUTA-KUCHI'S LIKE THAT.
HE'S BEEN A TWISTED LITTLE JERK FROM THE BEGINNING.
BWAH HA HA! LOOKIN' GOOD, FUTAKUCHI, YA JERK!!
PIPE DOWN, KAMA-SAKI!
URK
URK
WOW, UM, I-I'M GLAD THE DATE TECH PEOPLE LOOK LIKE THEY'RE HAVING FUN...

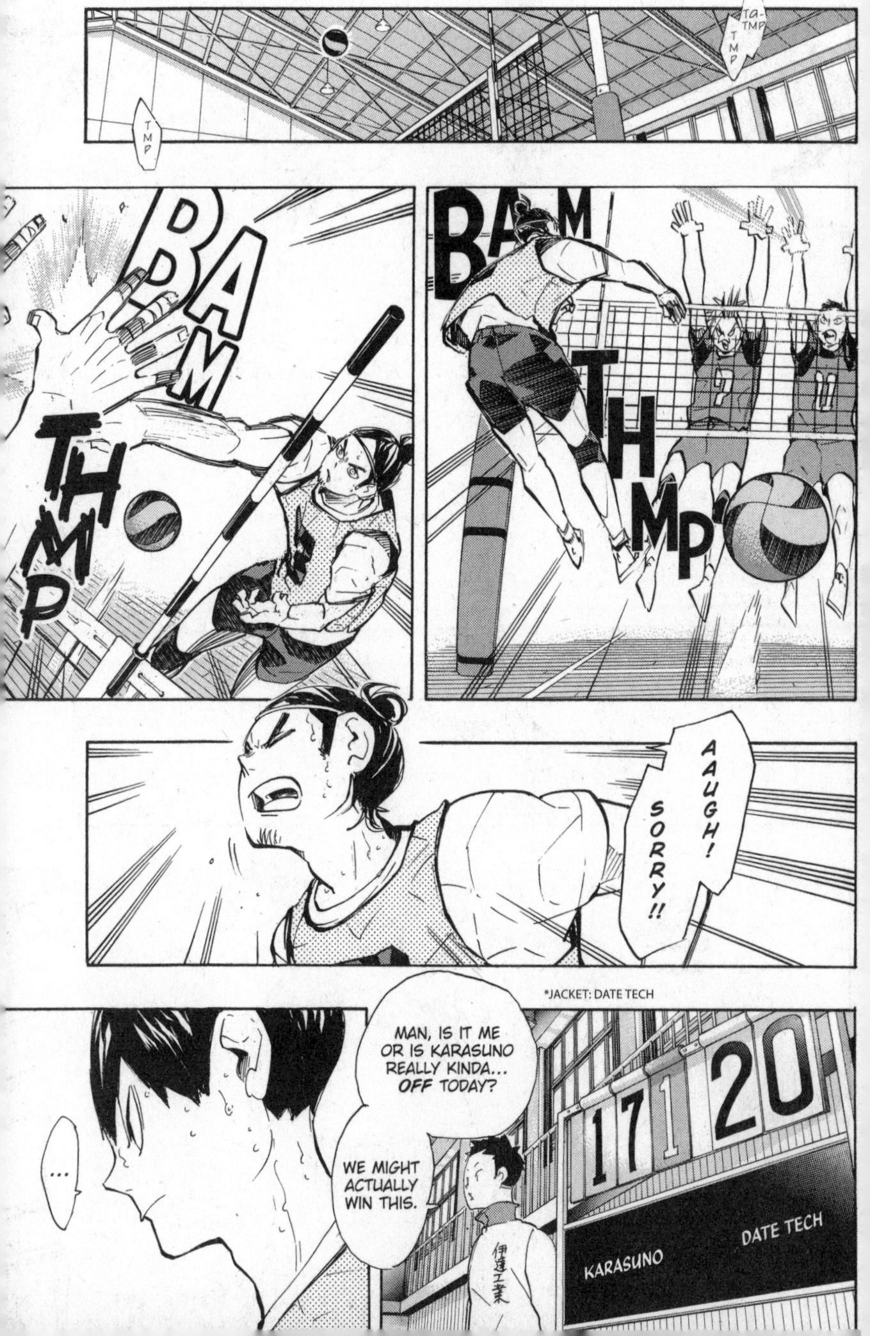
Ta-TMP
TMP
TMP
BAM
THMP
BAM
THMP
AAUGH! SORRY!!
*JACKET: DATE TECH
20
1
17
DATE TECH
KARASUNO
MAN, IS IT ME OR IS KARASUNO REALLY KINDA... OFF TODAY?
WE MIGHT ACTUALLY WIN THIS.
伊達工業
...

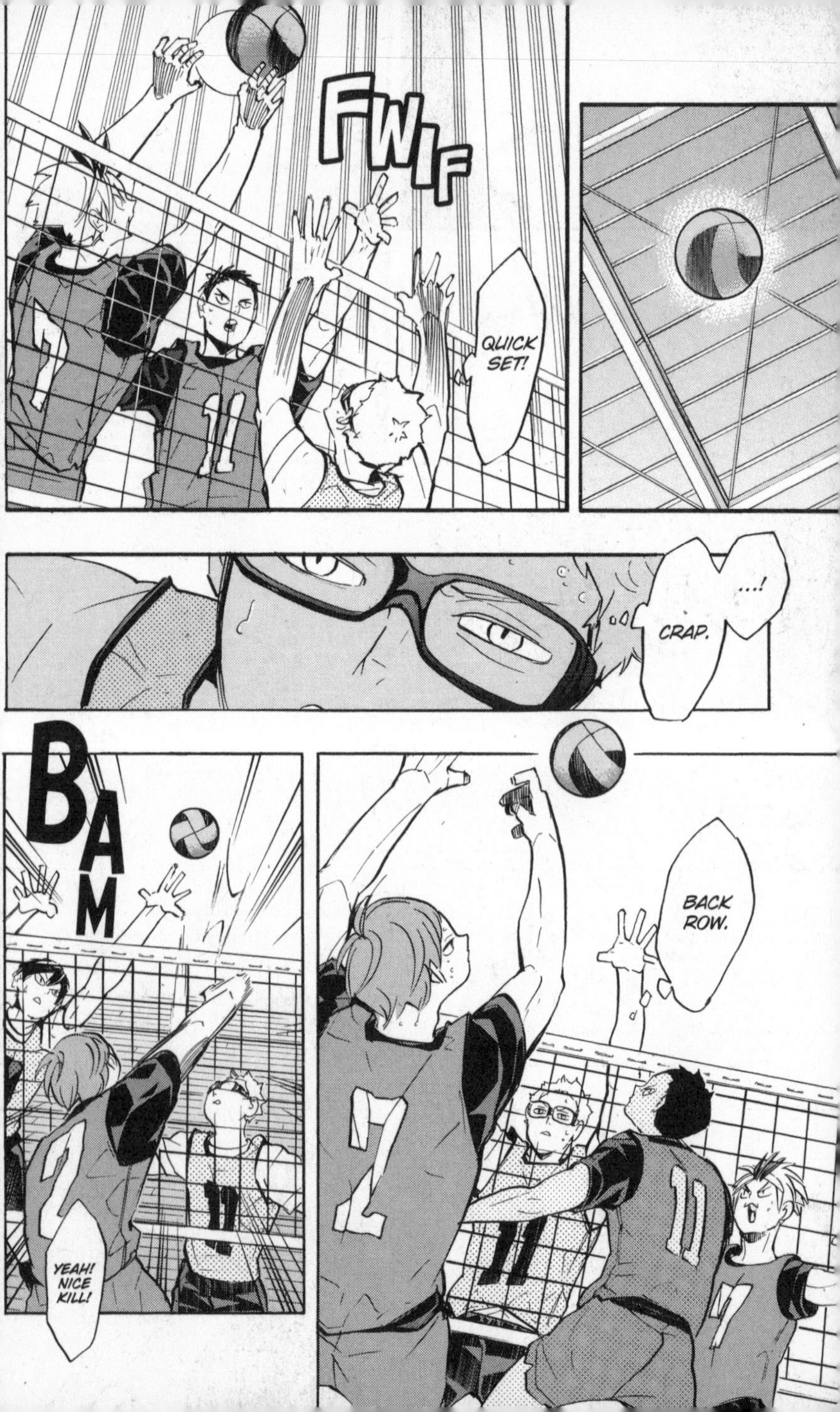
FWIF
QUICK SET!
...!
CRAP.
BACK ROW.
BAM
YEAH! NICE KILL!

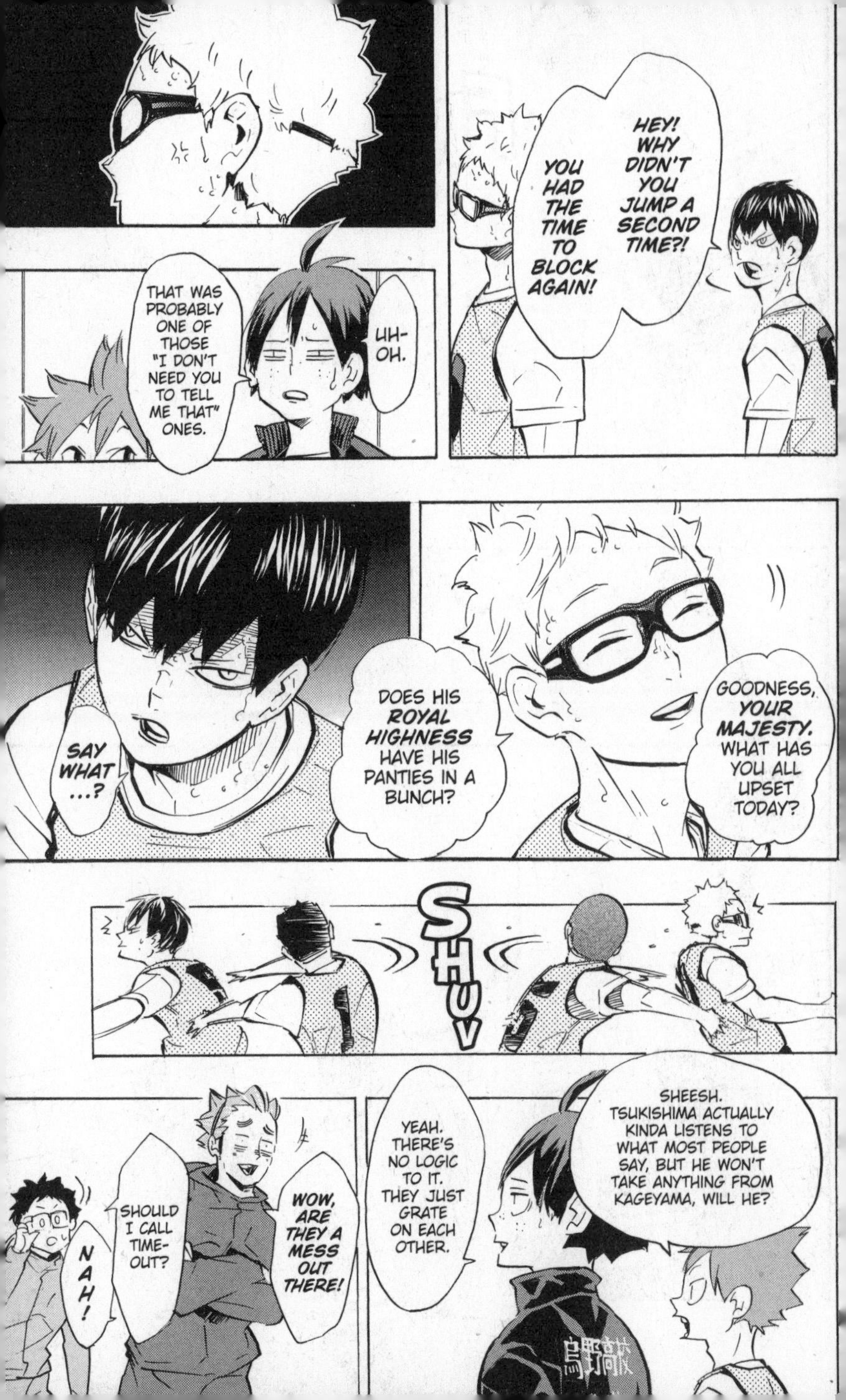
HEY! WHY DIDN'T YOU JUMP A SECOND TIME?!
YOU HAD THE TIME TO BLOCK AGAIN!
UH-OH.
THAT WAS PROBABLY ONE OF THOSE "I DON'T NEED YOU TO TELL ME THAT" ONES.
GOODNESS, YOUR MAJESTY. WHAT HAS YOU ALL UPSET TODAY?
DOES HIS ROYAL HIGHNESS HAVE HIS PANTIES IN A BUNCH?
SAY WHAT ...?
SHUV
SHEESH. TSUKISHIMA ACTUALLY KINDA LISTENS TO WHAT MOST PEOPLE SAY, BUT HE WON'T TAKE ANYTHING FROM KAGEYAMA, WILL HE?
YEAH. THERE'S NO LOGIC TO IT. THEY JUST GRATE ON EACH OTHER.
WOW, ARE THEY A MESS OUT THERE!
SHOULD I CALL TIME-OUT?
NAH!

THEY'RE FINE.

YEAH!

BOM

DAICHI-SAN!

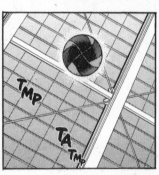

TMP

TA TMP

FWIF

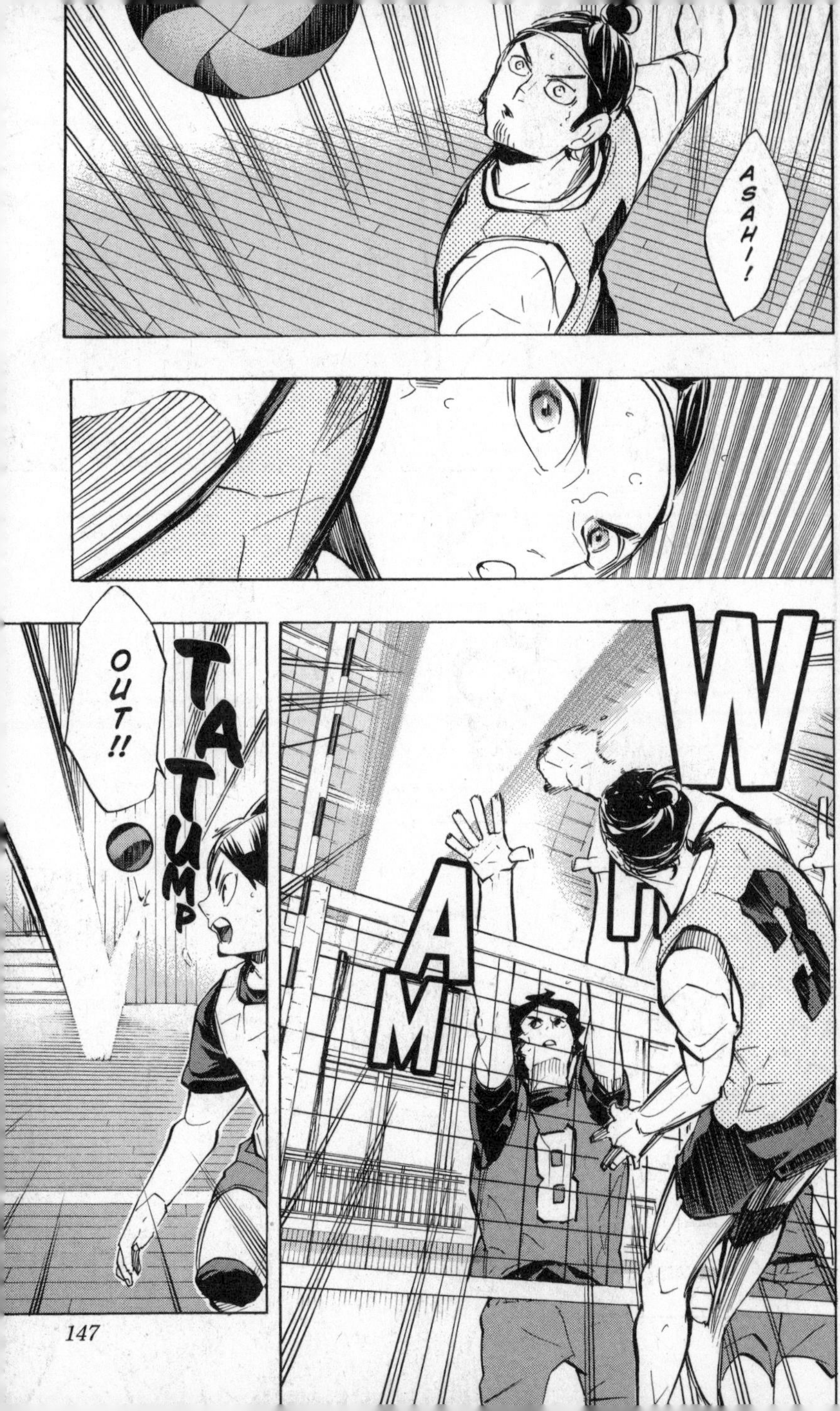
ASAHI!!
WHAM
OUT!!
TATUMP

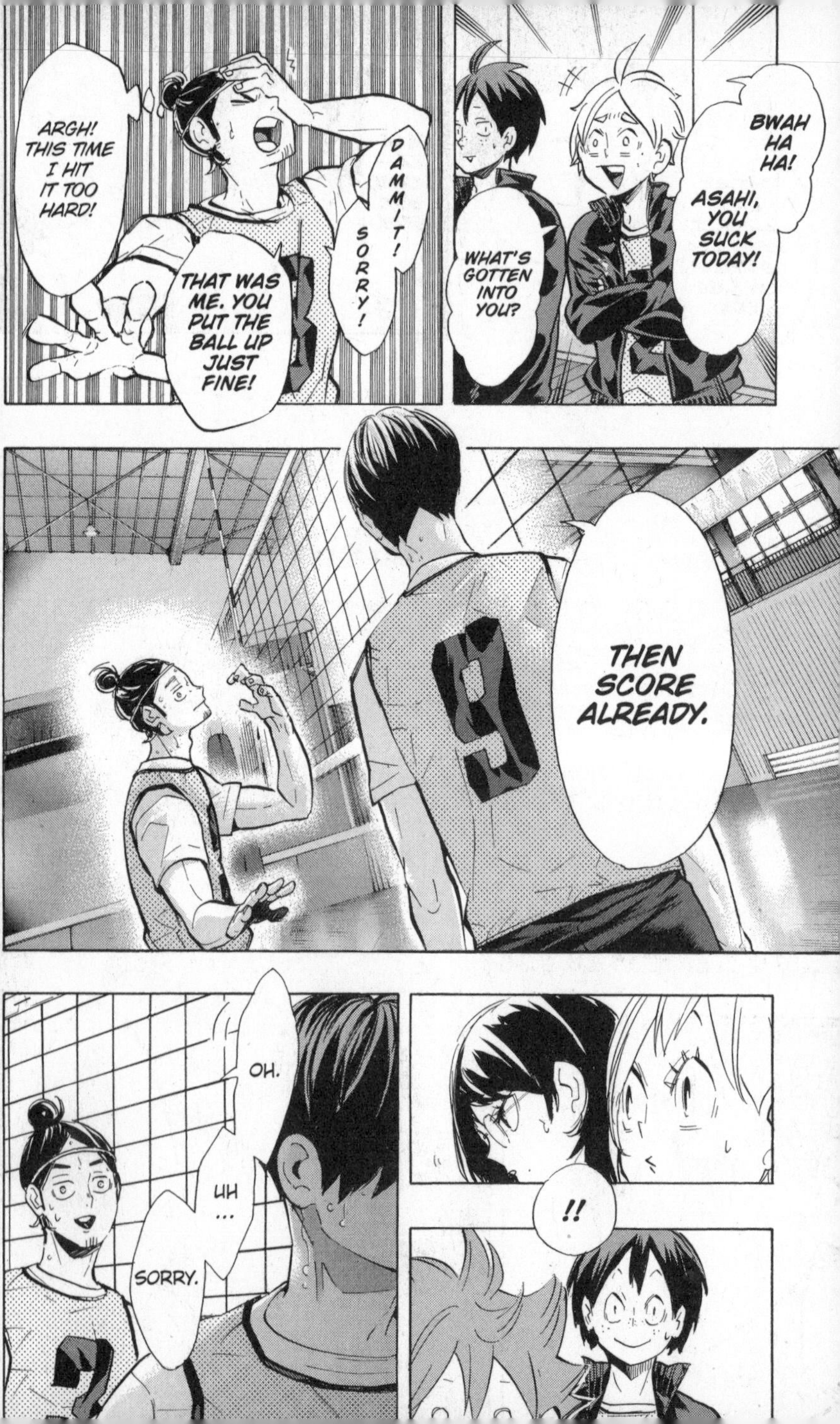
BWAH HA HA!
ASAHI, YOU SUCK TODAY!
WHAT'S GOTTEN INTO YOU?
DAMMIT!
SORRY!
ARGH! THIS TIME I HIT IT TOO HARD!
THAT WAS ME. YOU PUT THE BALL UP JUST FINE!
THEN SCORE ALREADY.
!!
OH.
UH...
SORRY.

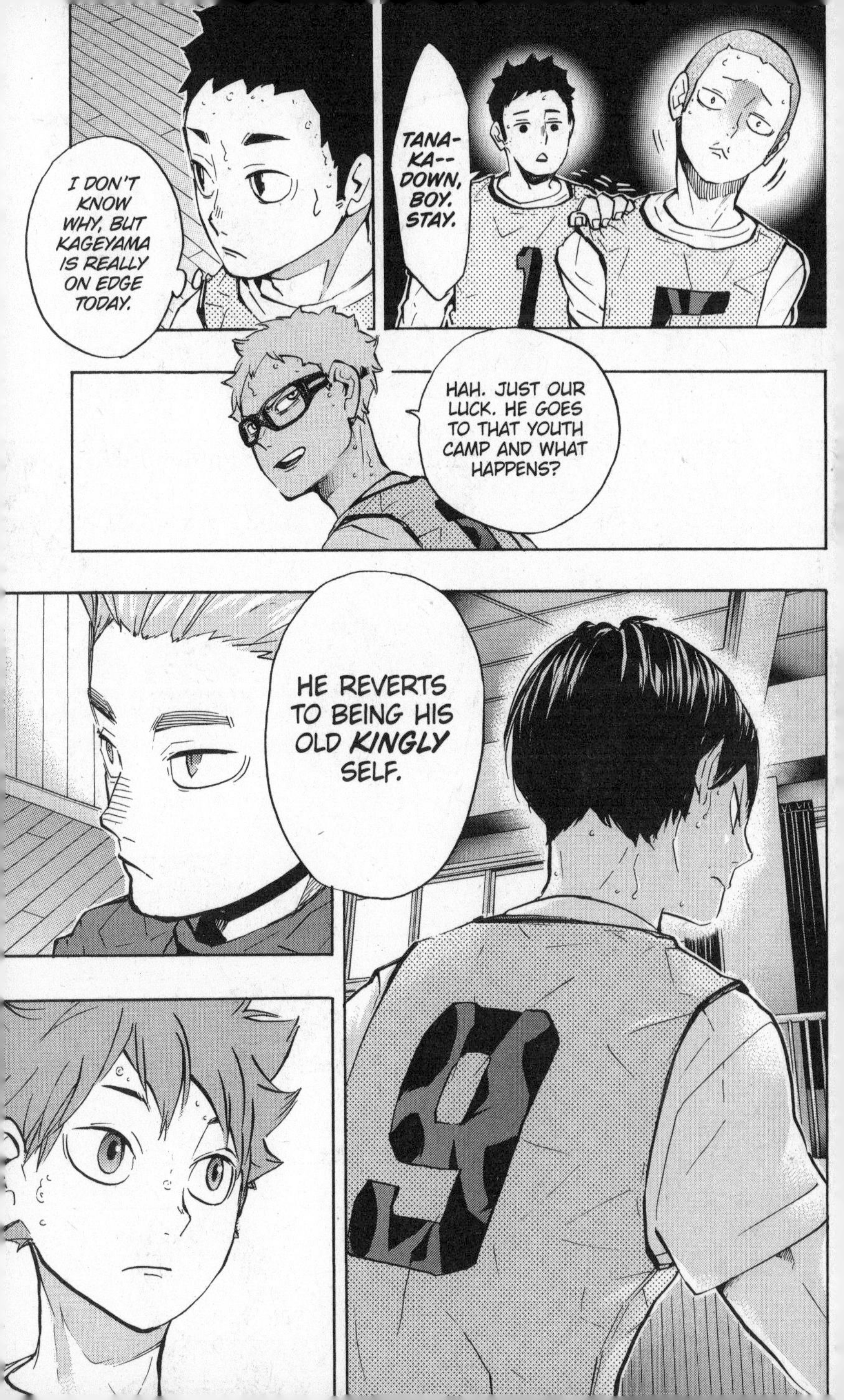
TANAKA-- DOWN, BOY. STAY.
I DON'T KNOW WHY, BUT KAGEYAMA IS REALLY ON EDGE TODAY.
HAH. JUST OUR LUCK. HE GOES TO THAT YOUTH CAMP AND WHAT HAPPENS?
HE REVERTS TO BEING HIS OLD *KINGLY* SELF.

Suddenly, just because!!

TOP 3 BIGGEST EATERS!!	
#1	**YASUSHI KAMASAKI (DATE TECH)**
#2	**DAICHI SAWAMURA (KARASUNO)**
#3	**YU NISHINOYA (KARASUNO)**

I TAKE A DUMP AFTER EVERY MEAL!

THEY'RE GOOD ...ES O. ...RK ...ND ...M--

AH-HEM!

CHAPTER 224

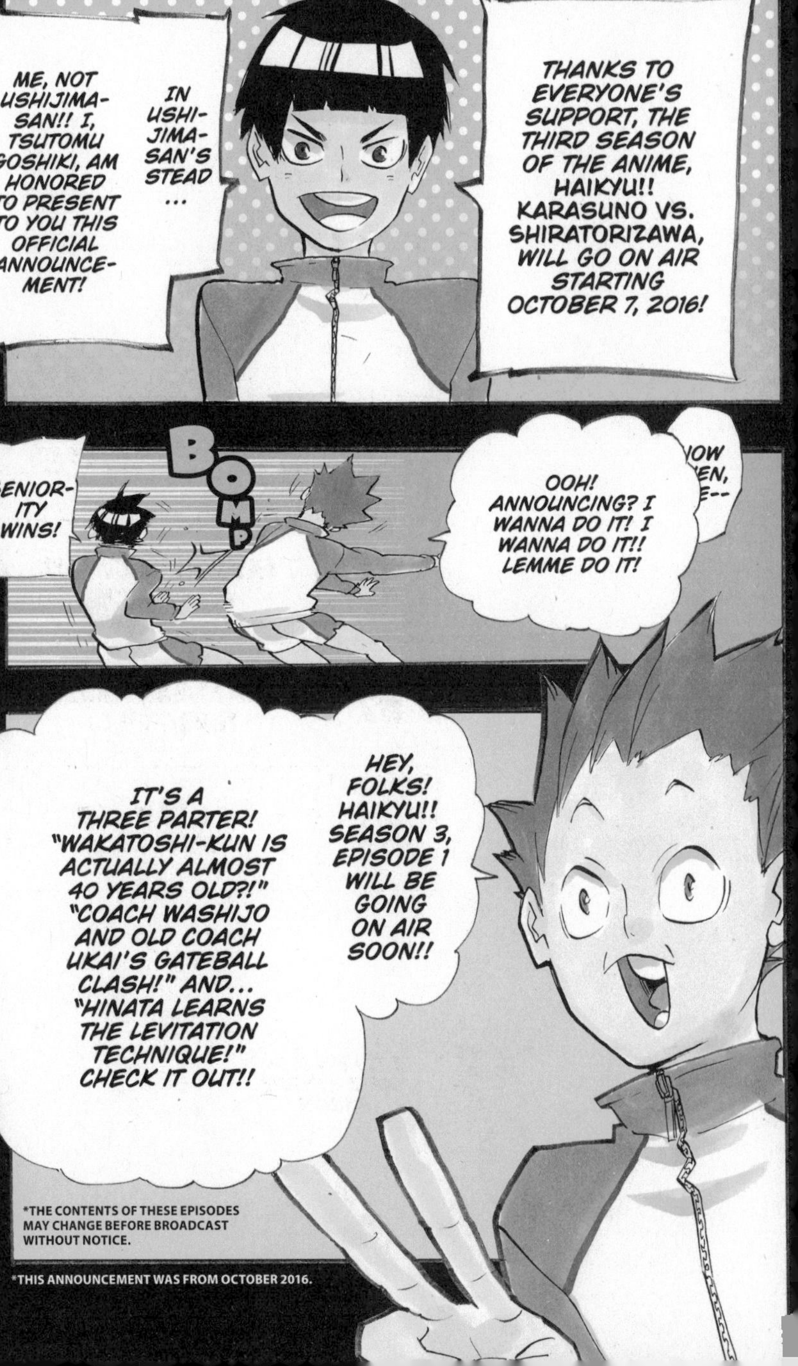
THANKS TO EVERYONE'S SUPPORT, THE THIRD SEASON OF THE ANIME, HAIKYU!! KARASUNO VS. SHIRATORIZAWA, WILL GO ON AIR STARTING OCTOBER 7, 2016!
IN USHIJIMA-SAN'S STEAD...
ME, NOT USHIJIMA-SAN!! I, TSUTOMU GOSHIKI, AM HONORED TO PRESENT TO YOU THIS OFFICIAL ANNOUNCEMENT!
OOH! ANNOUNCING? I WANNA DO IT! I WANNA DO IT!! LEMME DO IT!
BOMP
SENIORITY WINS!
HEY, FOLKS! HAIKYU!! SEASON 3, EPISODE 1 WILL BE GOING ON AIR SOON!!
IT'S A THREE PARTER! "WAKATOSHI-KUN IS ACTUALLY ALMOST 40 YEARS OLD?!" "COACH WASHIJO AND OLD COACH UKAI'S GATEBALL CLASH!" AND... "HINATA LEARNS THE LEVITATION TECHNIQUE!" CHECK IT OUT!!
*THE CONTENTS OF THESE EPISODES MAY CHANGE BEFORE BROADCAST WITHOUT NOTICE.

*THIS ANNOUNCEMENT WAS FROM OCTOBER 2016.

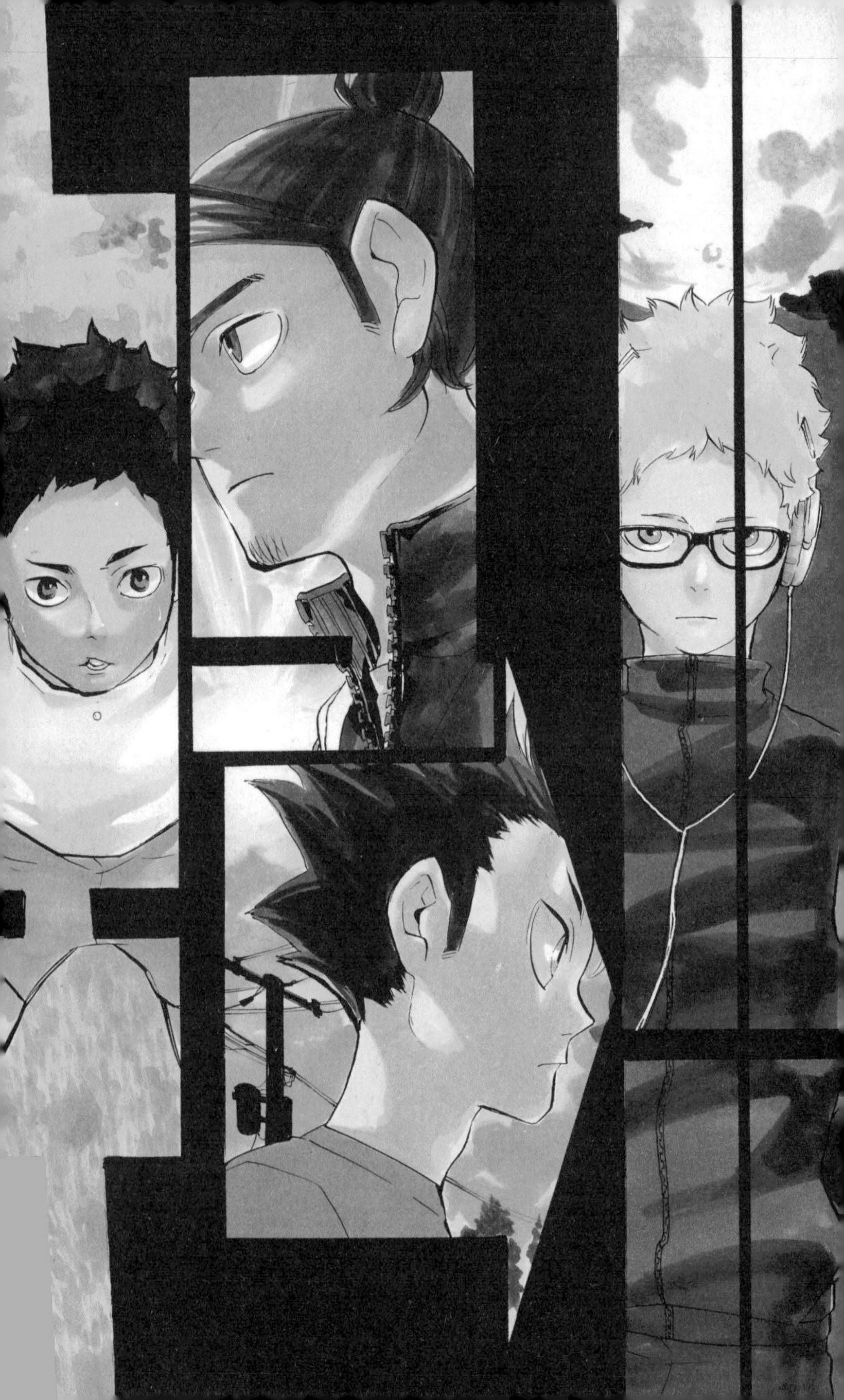

CHAPTER 224: Return of the King

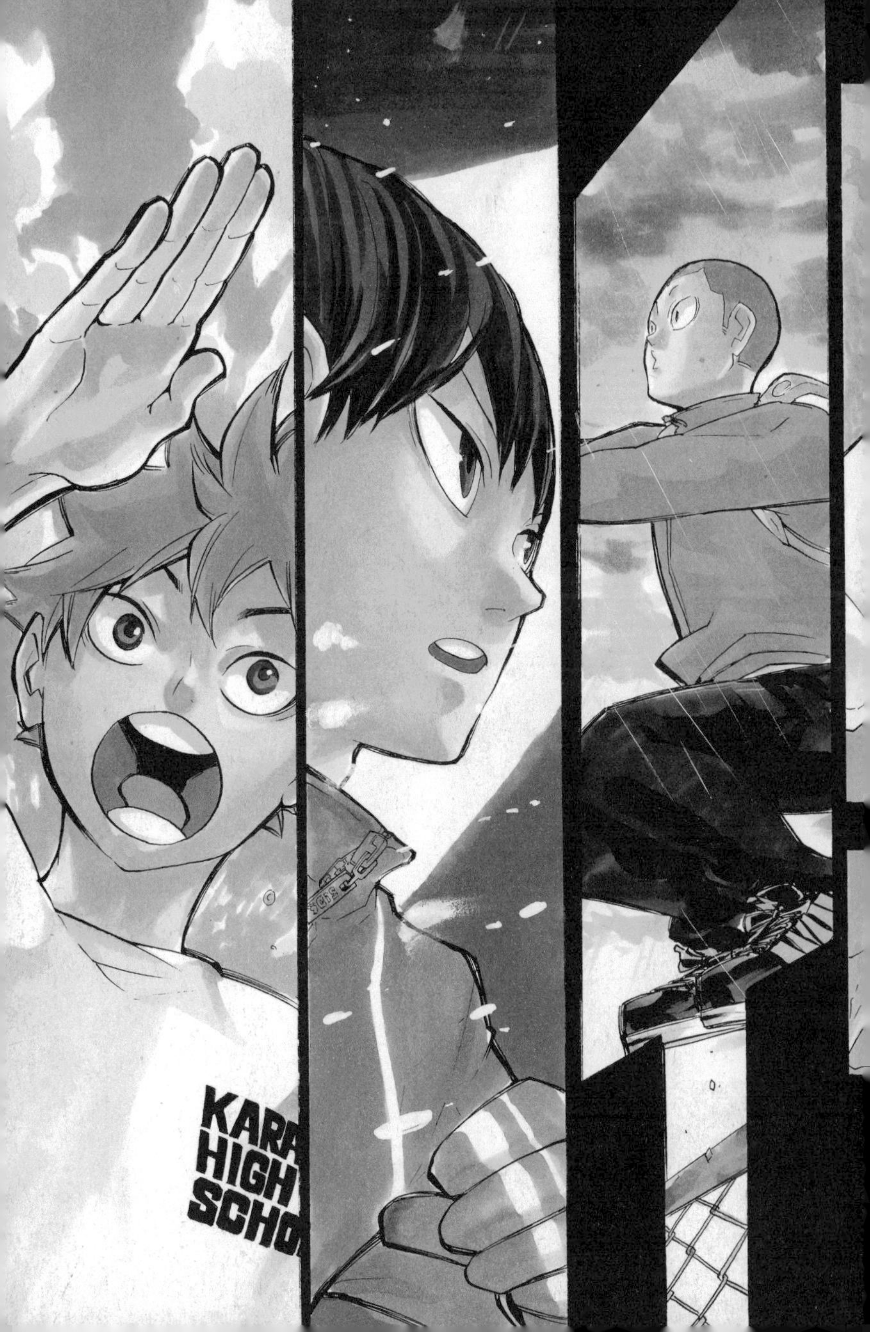
KARA
HIGH
SCHO

HAIKYU!!

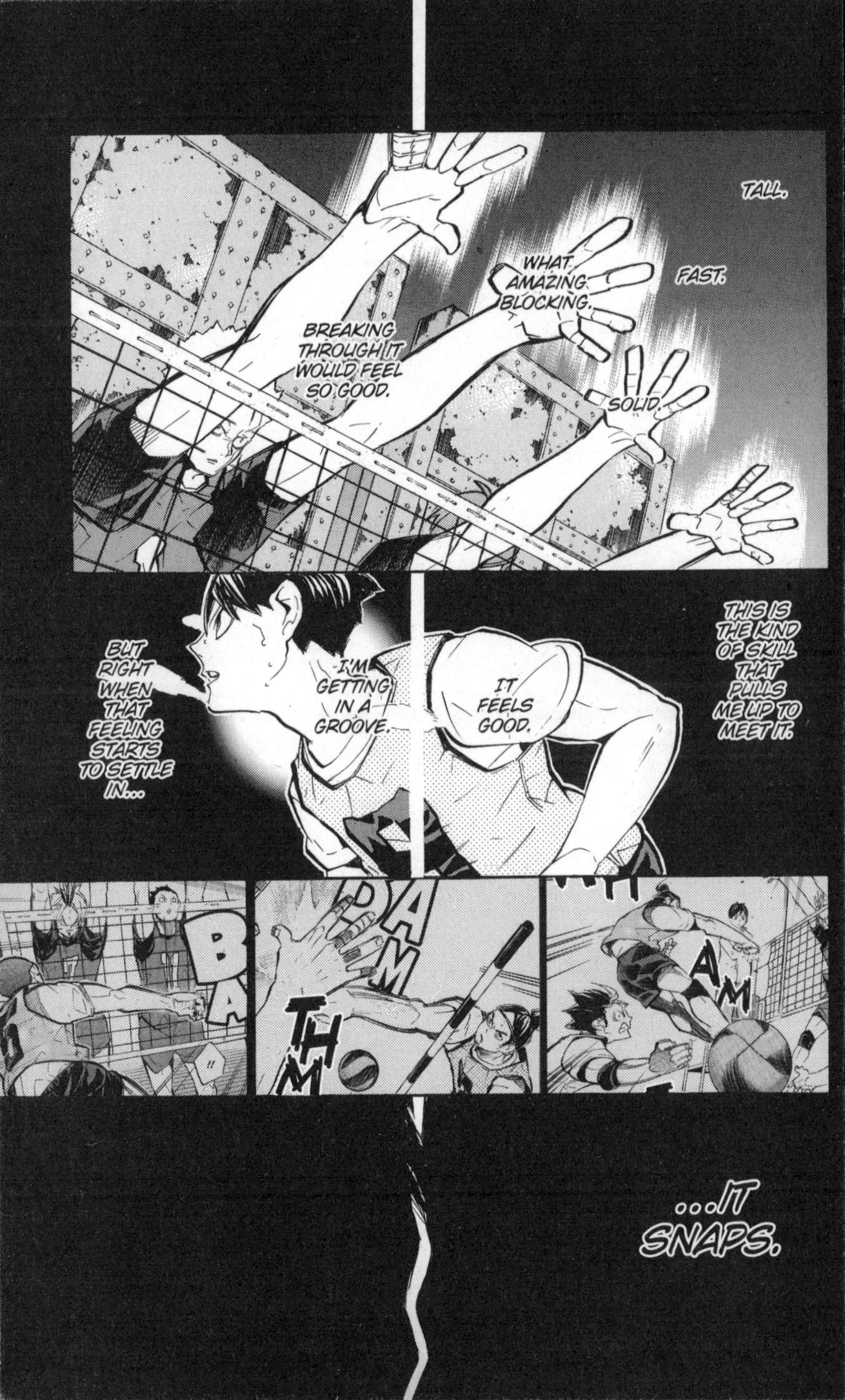
TALL.
FAST.
WHAT AMAZING BLOCKING.
SOLID.
BREAKING THROUGH IT WOULD FEEL SO GOOD.
THIS IS THE KIND OF SKILL THAT PULLS ME UP TO MEET IT.
IT FEELS GOOD.
I'M GETTING IN A GROOVE.
BUT RIGHT WHEN THAT FEELING STARTS TO SETTLE IN...
AM
DAM
THM
BA
...IT SNAPS.

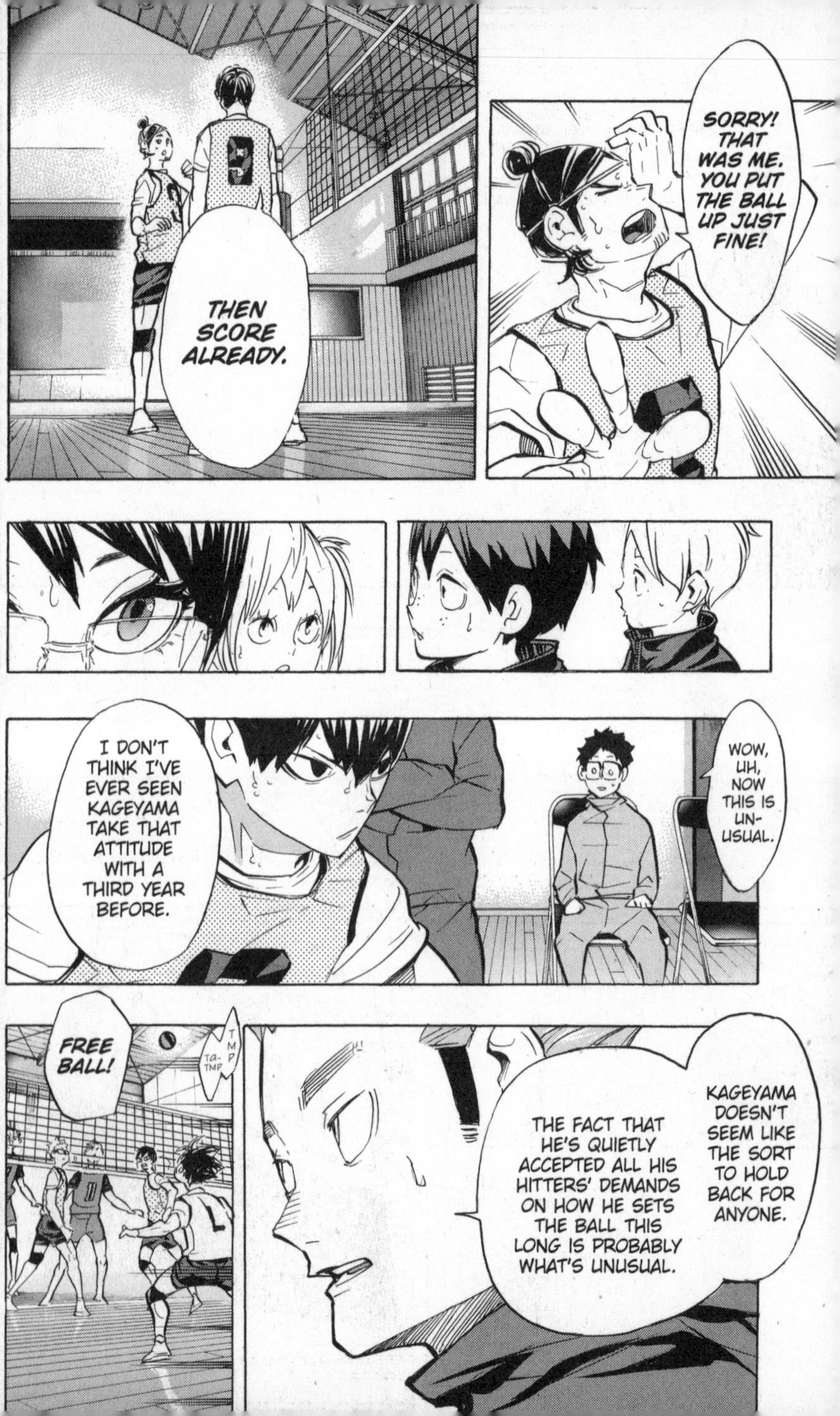
SORRY! THAT WAS ME. YOU PUT THE BALL UP JUST FINE!
THEN SCORE ALREADY.
WOW, UH, NOW THIS IS UNUSUAL.
I DON'T THINK I'VE EVER SEEN KAGEYAMA TAKE THAT ATTITUDE WITH A THIRD YEAR BEFORE.
KAGEYAMA DOESN'T SEEM LIKE THE SORT TO HOLD BACK FOR ANYONE.
THE FACT THAT HE'S QUIETLY ACCEPTED ALL HIS HITTERS' DEMANDS ON HOW HE SETS THE BALL THIS LONG IS PROBABLY WHAT'S UNUSUAL.
TMP
TA-TMP
FREE BALL!

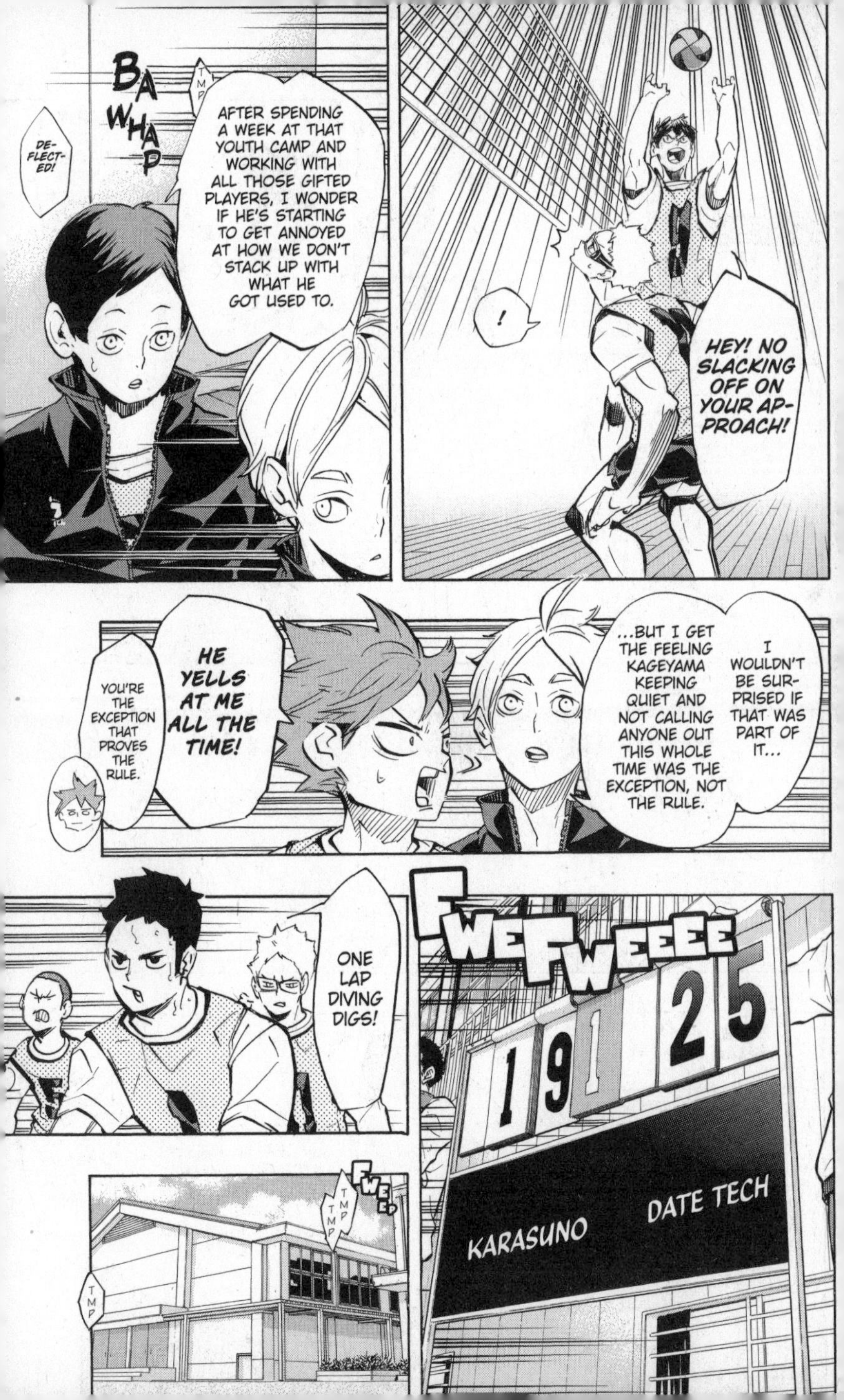
!
HEY! NO SLACKING OFF ON YOUR AP-PROACH!
BAWHAP
DE-FLECTED!
TMP
AFTER SPENDING A WEEK AT THAT YOUTH CAMP AND WORKING WITH ALL THOSE GIFTED PLAYERS, I WONDER IF HE'S STARTING TO GET ANNOYED AT HOW WE DON'T STACK UP WITH WHAT HE GOT USED TO.
I WOULDN'T BE SUR-PRISED IF THAT WAS PART OF IT...
...BUT I GET THE FEELING KAGEYAMA KEEPING QUIET AND NOT CALLING ANYONE OUT THIS WHOLE TIME WAS THE EXCEPTION, NOT THE RULE.
HE YELLS AT ME ALL THE TIME!
YOU'RE THE EXCEPTION THAT PROVES THE RULE.
FWEFWEEEE
19 25
DATE TECH
KARASUNO
ONE LAP DIVING DIGS!
FWEP
TMP TMP
TMP

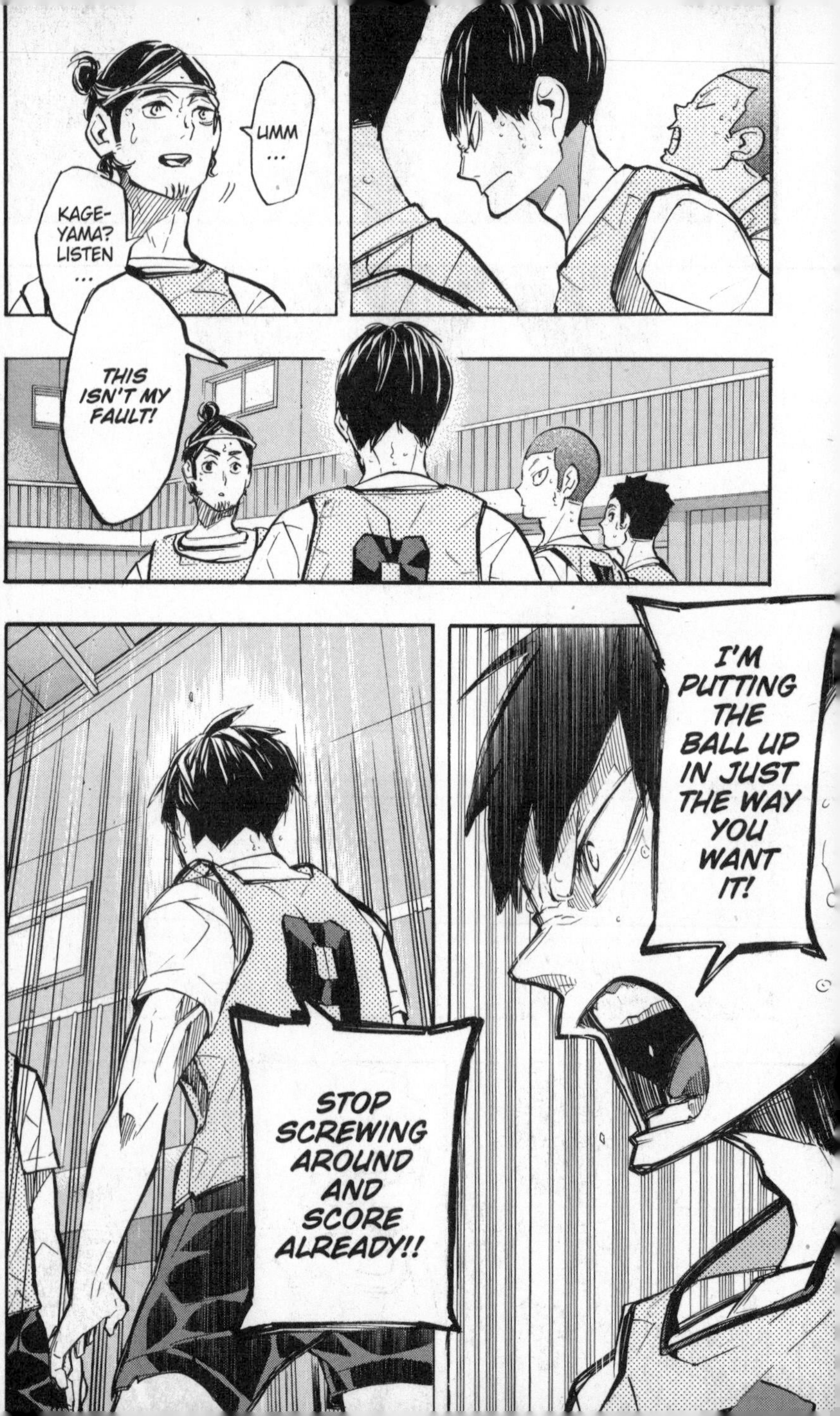
UMM ...
KAGE-YAMA? LISTEN ...
THIS ISN'T MY FAULT!
I'M PUTTING THE BALL UP IN JUST THE WAY YOU WANT IT!
STOP SCREWING AROUND AND SCORE ALREADY!!

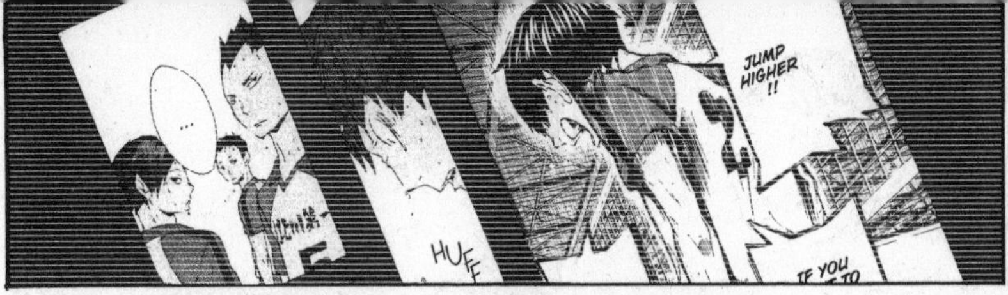
JUMP HIGHER !!
IF YOU
HUFF
...

*JERSEY: KITAGAWA DAIICHI

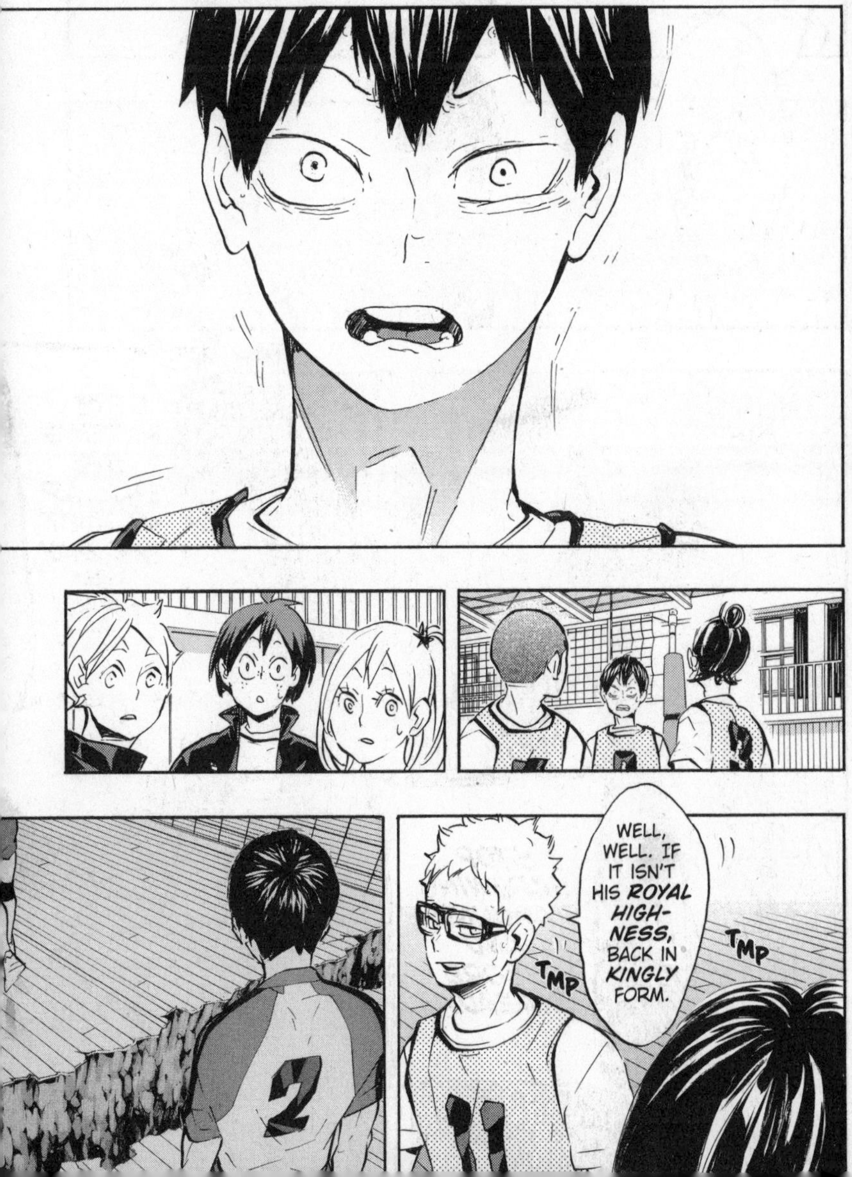
WELL, WELL. IF IT ISN'T HIS *ROYAL HIGH-NESS*, BACK IN *KINGLY* FORM.
TMP
TMP

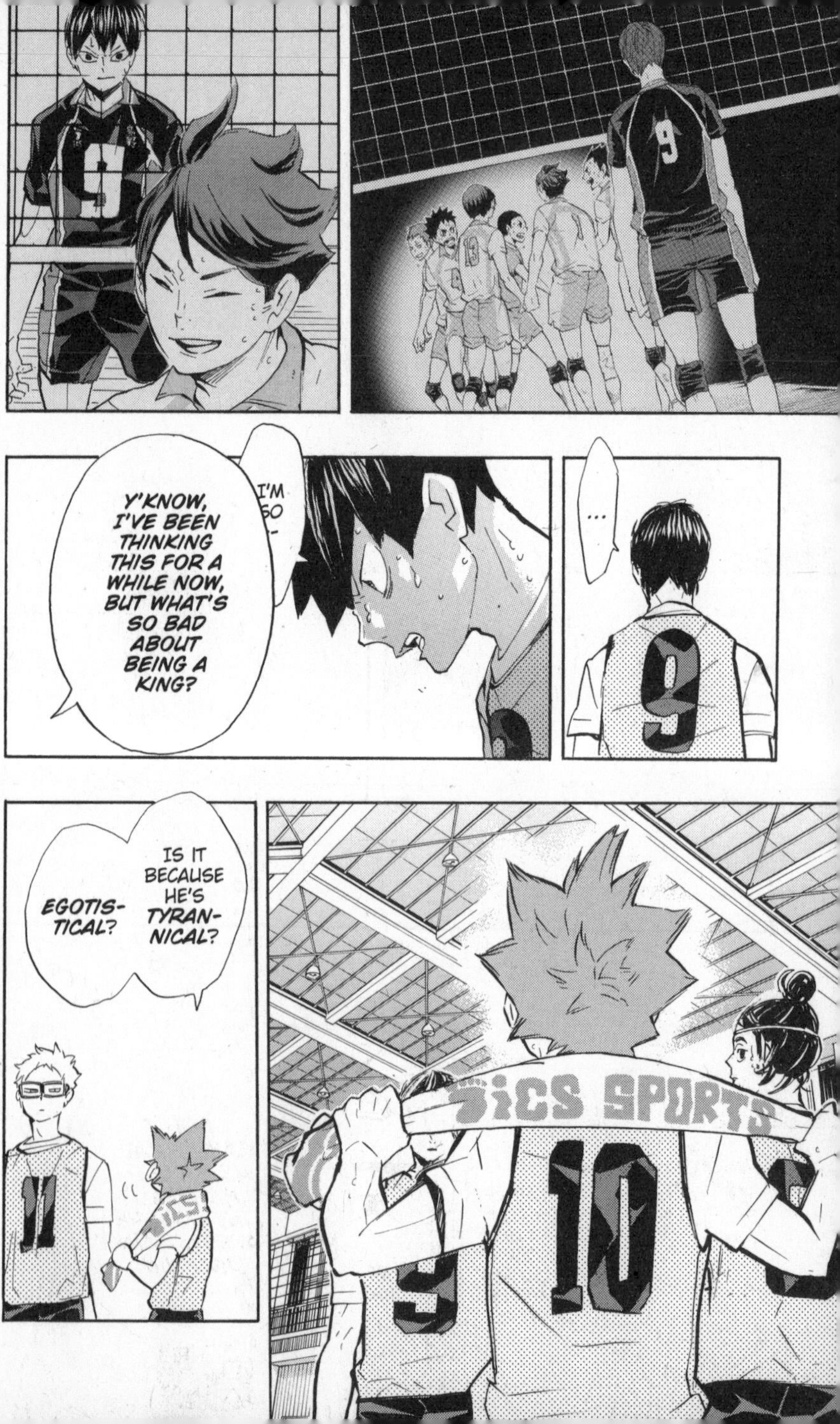
...
I'M SO—
Y'KNOW, I'VE BEEN THINKING THIS FOR A WHILE NOW, BUT WHAT'S SO BAD ABOUT BEING A KING?
IS IT BECAUSE HE'S TYRAN-NICAL?
EGOTIS-TICAL?

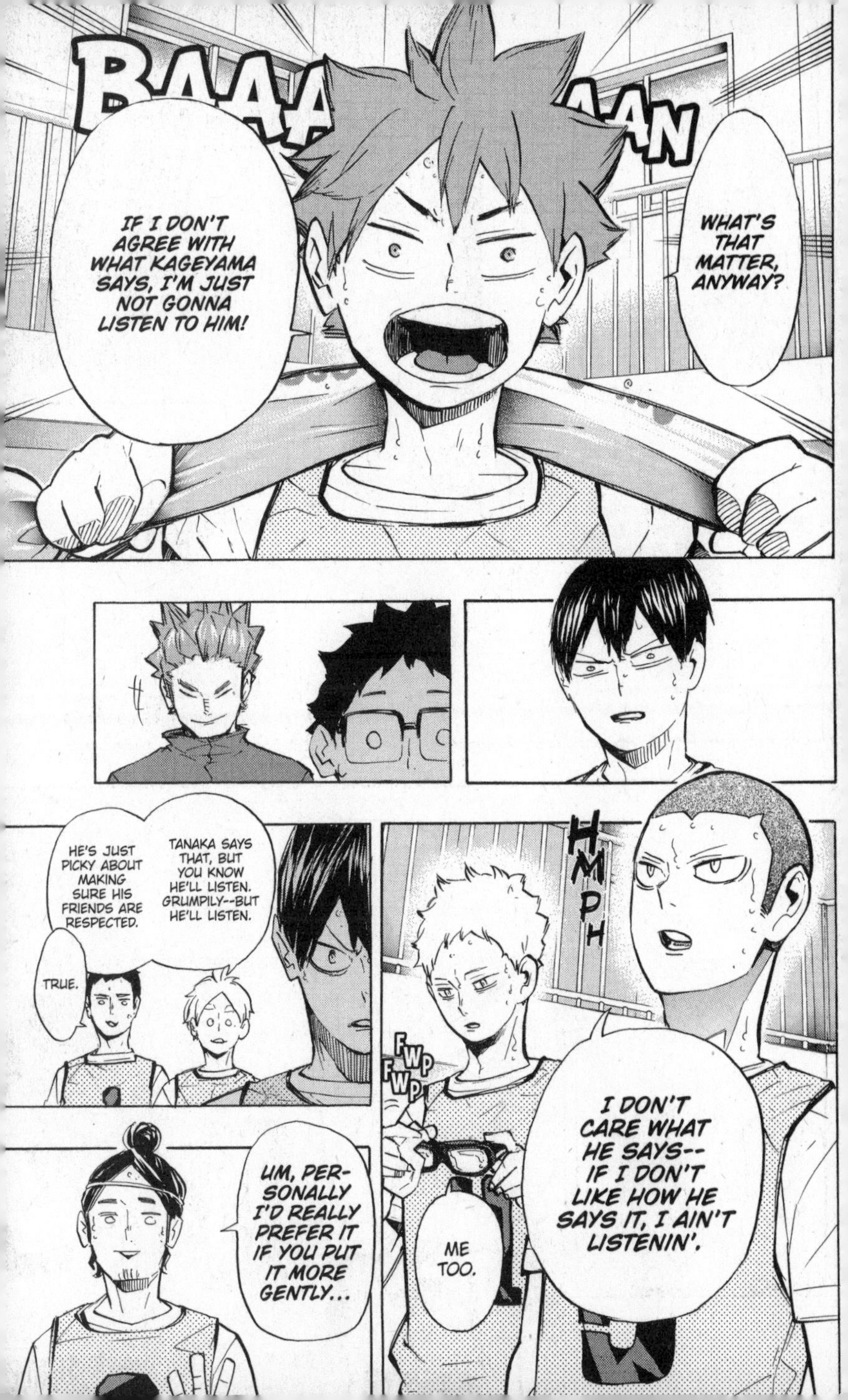
BAAA
AAN
WHAT'S THAT MATTER, ANYWAY?
IF I DON'T AGREE WITH WHAT KAGEYAMA SAYS, I'M JUST NOT GONNA LISTEN TO HIM!
HMPH
I DON'T CARE WHAT HE SAYS-- IF I DON'T LIKE HOW HE SAYS IT, I AIN'T LISTENIN'.
FWP FWP
ME TOO.
TANAKA SAYS THAT, BUT YOU KNOW HE'LL LISTEN. GRUMPILY--BUT HE'LL LISTEN.
HE'S JUST PICKY ABOUT MAKING SURE HIS FRIENDS ARE RESPECTED.
TRUE.
UM, PER-SONALLY I'D REALLY PREFER IT IF YOU PUT IT MORE GENTLY...

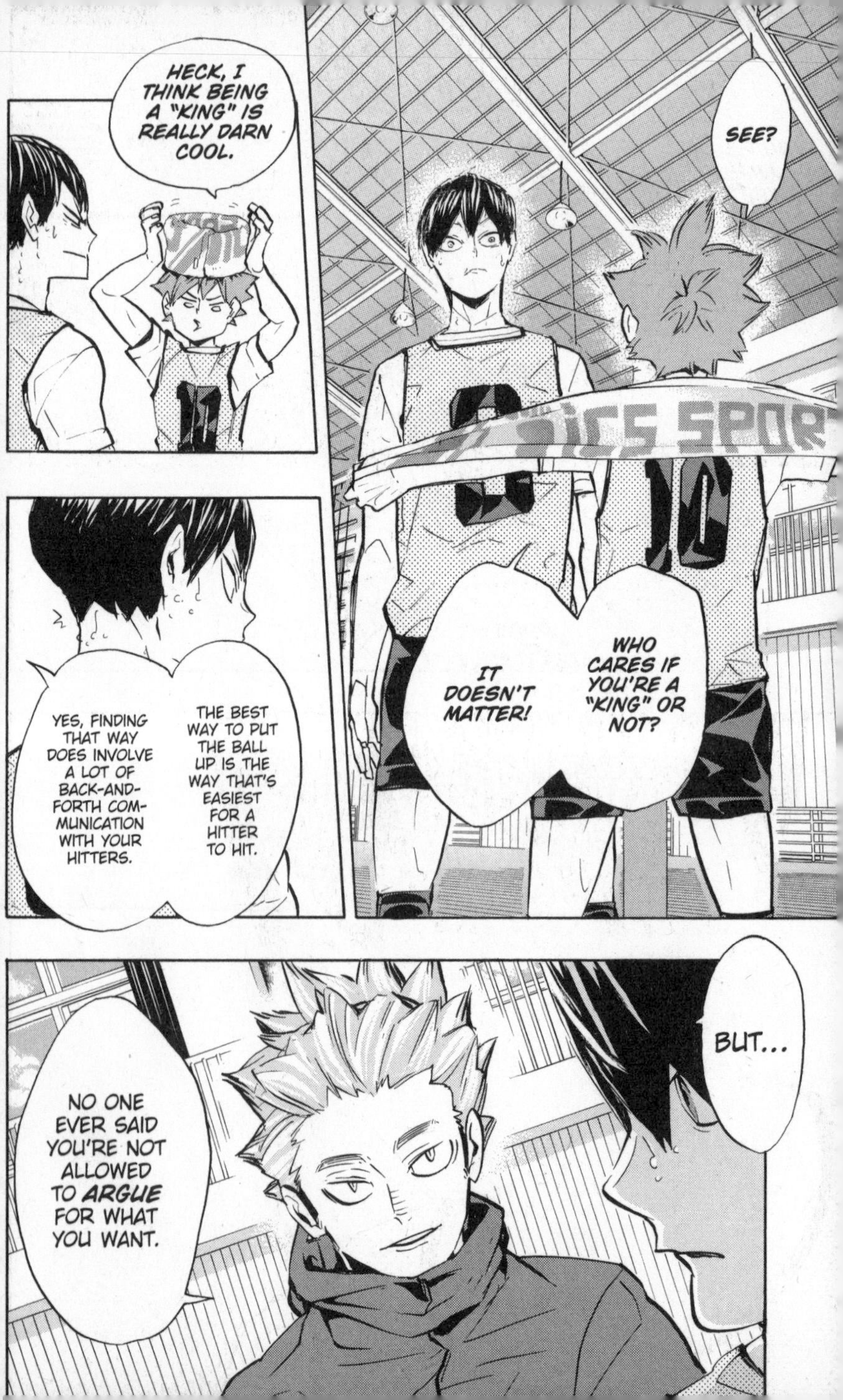
SEE?
WHO CARES IF YOU'RE A "KING" OR NOT?
IT DOESN'T MATTER!
HECK, I THINK BEING A "KING" IS REALLY DARN COOL.
THE BEST WAY TO PUT THE BALL UP IS THE WAY THAT'S EASIEST FOR A HITTER TO HIT.
YES, FINDING THAT WAY DOES INVOLVE A LOT OF BACK-AND-FORTH COM-MUNICATION WITH YOUR HITTERS.
BUT...
NO ONE EVER SAID YOU'RE NOT ALLOWED TO ARGUE FOR WHAT YOU WANT.

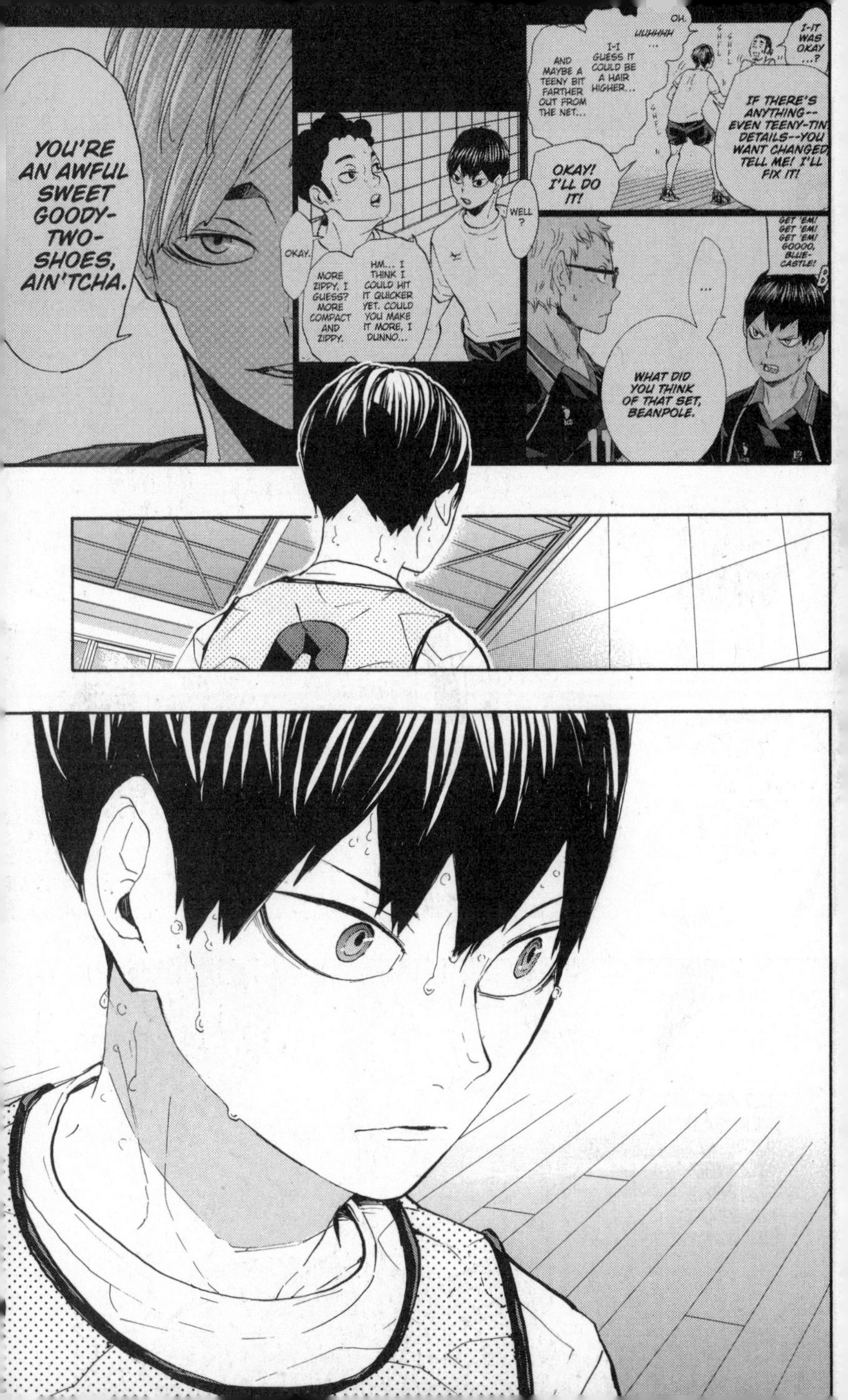
I-IT WAS OKAY...?
OH.
UUHHHH...
SHFL SHFL
I-I GUESS IT COULD BE A HAIR HIGHER...
AND MAYBE A TEENY BIT FARTHER OUT FROM THE NET...
SHFL
IF THERE'S ANYTHING--EVEN TEENY-TIN DETAILS--YOU WANT CHANGED, TELL ME! I'LL FIX IT!
OKAY! I'LL DO IT!
GET 'EM! GET 'EM! GOOOO, BLUE-CASTLE!
...
WHAT DID YOU THINK OF THAT SET, BEANPOLE.
WELL?
OKAY.
HM... I THINK I COULD HIT IT QUICKER YET. COULD YOU MAKE IT MORE, I DUNNO...
MORE ZIPPY, I GUESS? MORE COMPACT AND ZIPPY.
YOU'RE AN AWFUL SWEET GOODY-TWO-SHOES, AIN'TCHA.

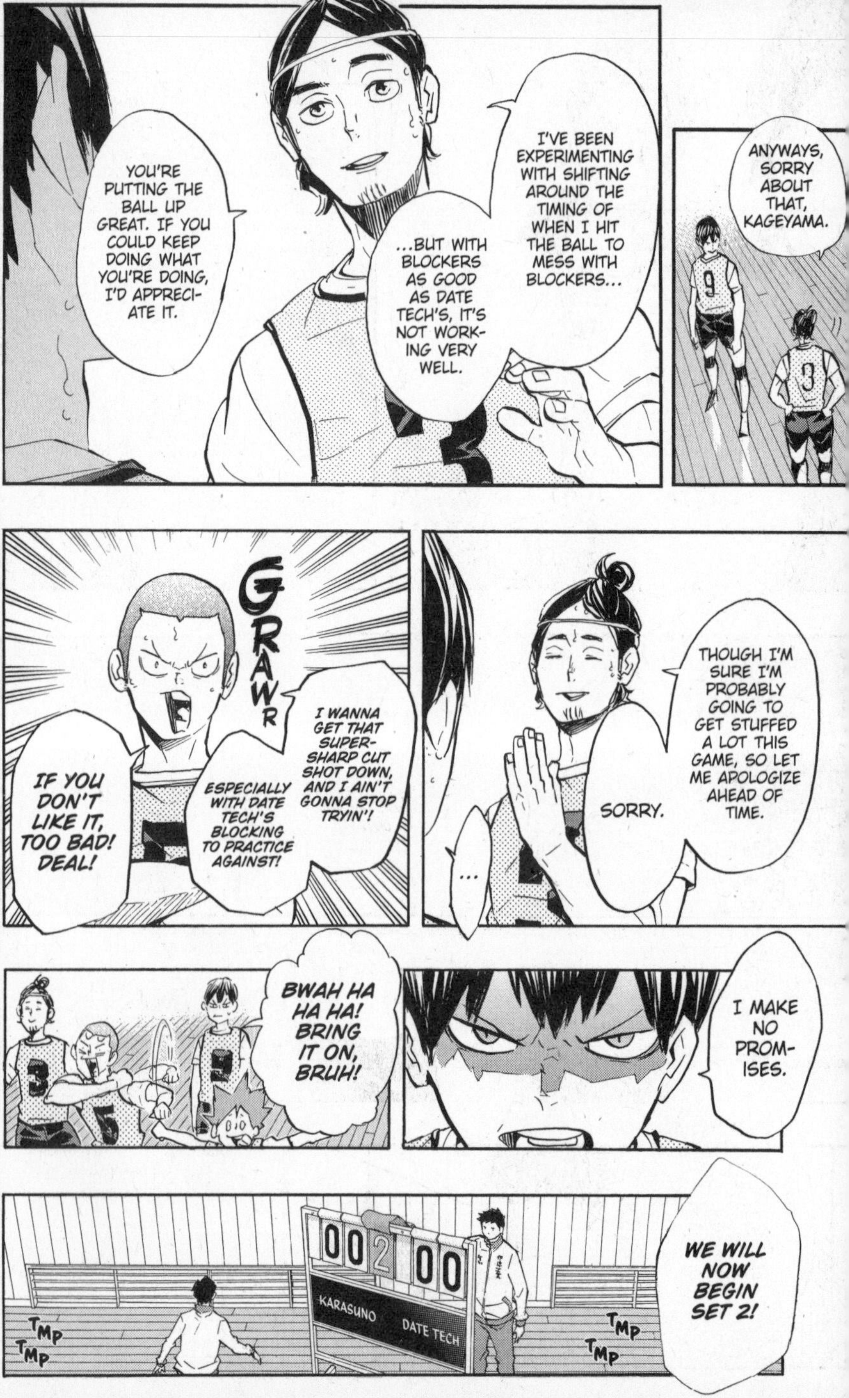
ANYWAYS, SORRY ABOUT THAT, KAGEYAMA.
I'VE BEEN EXPERIMENTING WITH SHIFTING AROUND THE TIMING OF WHEN I HIT THE BALL TO MESS WITH BLOCKERS...
...BUT WITH BLOCKERS AS GOOD AS DATE TECH'S, IT'S NOT WORKING VERY WELL.
YOU'RE PUTTING THE BALL UP GREAT. IF YOU COULD KEEP DOING WHAT YOU'RE DOING, I'D APPRECIATE IT.
THOUGH I'M SURE I'M PROBABLY GOING TO GET STUFFED A LOT THIS GAME, SO LET ME APOLOGIZE AHEAD OF TIME.
SORRY.
...
GRAWR
I WANNA GET THAT SUPER-SHARP CUT SHOT DOWN, AND I AIN'T GONNA STOP TRYIN'!
ESPECIALLY WITH DATE TECH'S BLOCKING TO PRACTICE AGAINST!
IF YOU DON'T LIKE IT, TOO BAD! DEAL!
I MAKE NO PROMISES.
BWAH HA HA HA! BRING IT ON, BRUH!
WE WILL NOW BEGIN SET 2!
TMP TMP
00 2 00
KARASUNO
DATE TECH
TMP TMP

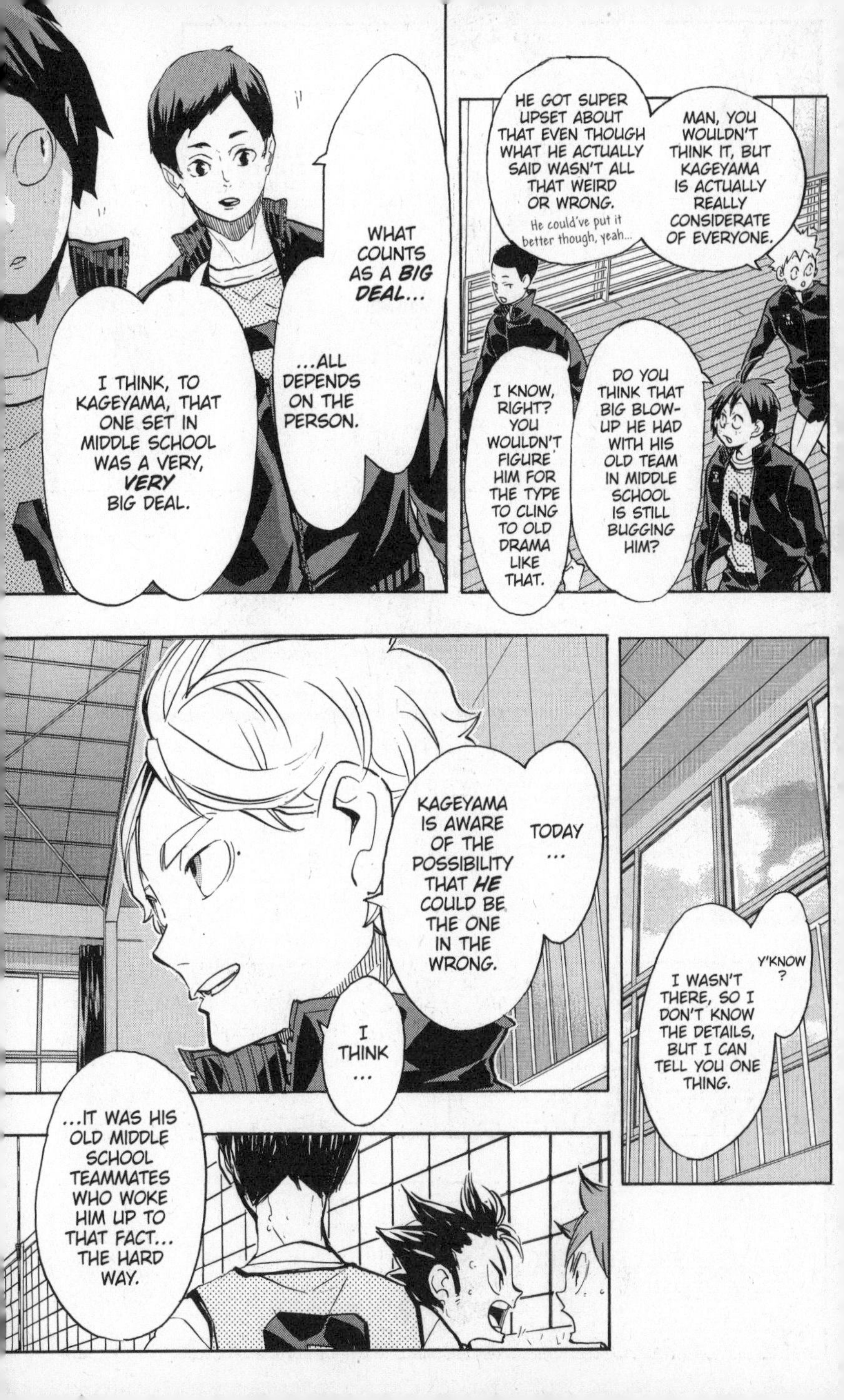
MAN, YOU WOULDN'T THINK IT, BUT KAGEYAMA IS ACTUALLY REALLY CONSIDERATE OF EVERYONE.
HE GOT SUPER UPSET ABOUT THAT EVEN THOUGH WHAT HE ACTUALLY SAID WASN'T ALL THAT WEIRD OR WRONG.
He could've put it better though, yeah...
DO YOU THINK THAT BIG BLOW-UP HE HAD WITH HIS OLD TEAM IN MIDDLE SCHOOL IS STILL BUGGING HIM?
I KNOW, RIGHT? YOU WOULDN'T FIGURE HIM FOR THE TYPE TO CLING TO OLD DRAMA LIKE THAT.
WHAT COUNTS AS A ***BIG DEAL***...
...ALL DEPENDS ON THE PERSON.
I THINK, TO KAGEYAMA, THAT ONE SET IN MIDDLE SCHOOL WAS A VERY, ***VERY*** BIG DEAL.
I WASN'T THERE, SO I DON'T KNOW THE DETAILS, BUT I CAN TELL YOU ONE THING.
Y'KNOW?
TODAY...
KAGEYAMA IS AWARE OF THE POSSIBILITY THAT ***HE*** COULD BE THE ONE IN THE WRONG.
I THINK...
...IT WAS HIS OLD MIDDLE SCHOOL TEAMMATES WHO WOKE HIM UP TO THAT FACT... THE HARD WAY.

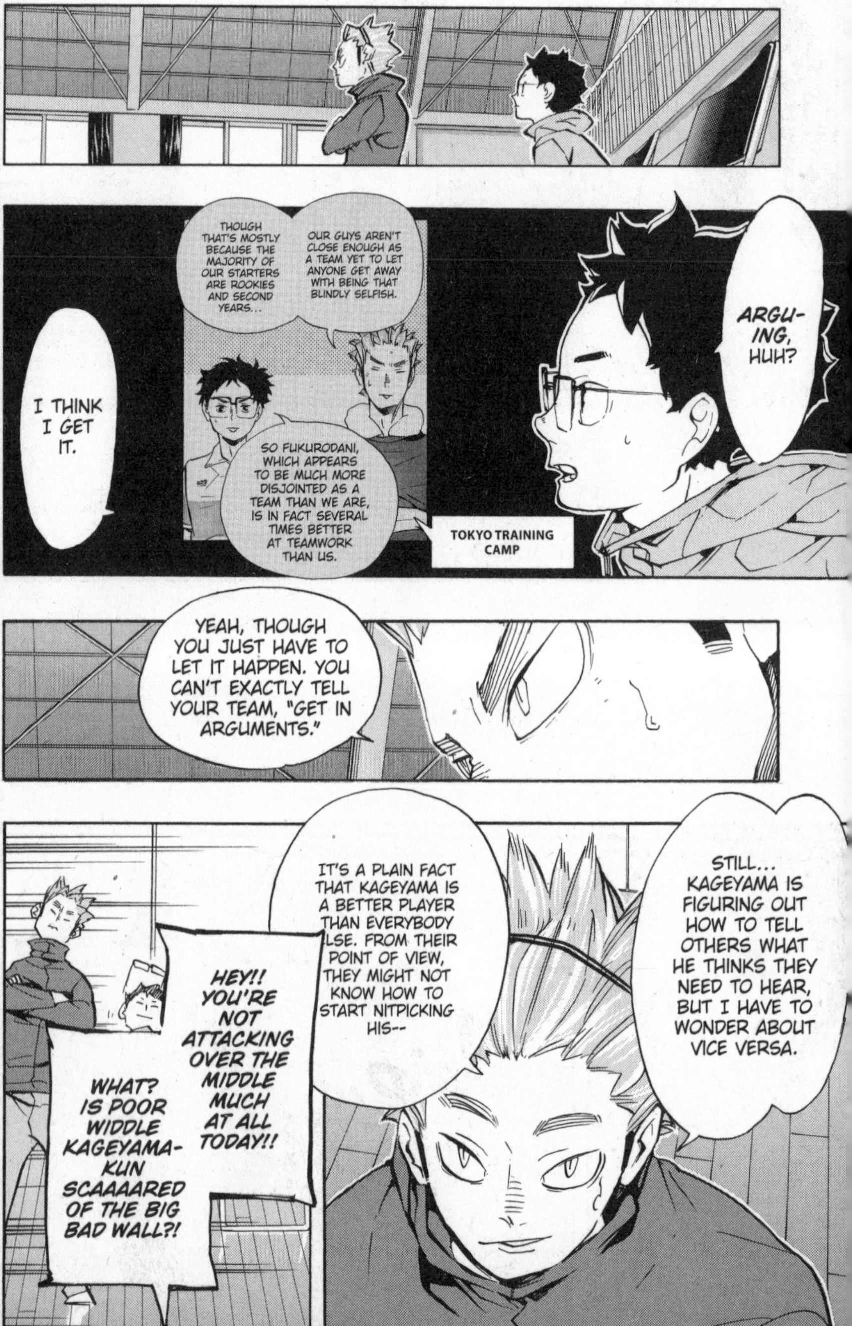
TOKYO TRAINING CAMP
ARGU-ING, HUH?
OUR GUYS AREN'T CLOSE ENOUGH AS A TEAM YET TO LET ANYONE GET AWAY WITH BEING THAT BLINDLY SELFISH.
THOUGH THAT'S MOSTLY BECAUSE THE MAJORITY OF OUR STARTERS ARE ROOKIES AND SECOND YEARS...
SO FUKURODANI, WHICH APPEARS TO BE MUCH MORE DISJOINTED AS A TEAM THAN WE ARE, IS IN FACT SEVERAL TIMES BETTER AT TEAMWORK THAN US.
I THINK I GET IT.
YEAH, THOUGH YOU JUST HAVE TO LET IT HAPPEN. YOU CAN'T EXACTLY TELL YOUR TEAM, "GET IN ARGUMENTS."
STILL... KAGEYAMA IS FIGURING OUT HOW TO TELL OTHERS WHAT HE THINKS THEY NEED TO HEAR, BUT I HAVE TO WONDER ABOUT VICE VERSA.
IT'S A PLAIN FACT THAT KAGEYAMA IS A BETTER PLAYER THAN EVERYBODY ELSE. FROM THEIR POINT OF VIEW, THEY MIGHT NOT KNOW HOW TO START NITPICKING HIS--
HEY!! YOU'RE NOT ATTACKING OVER THE MIDDLE MUCH AT ALL TODAY!!
WHAT? IS POOR WIDDLE KAGEYAMA-KUN SCAAAARED OF THE BIG BAD WALL?!

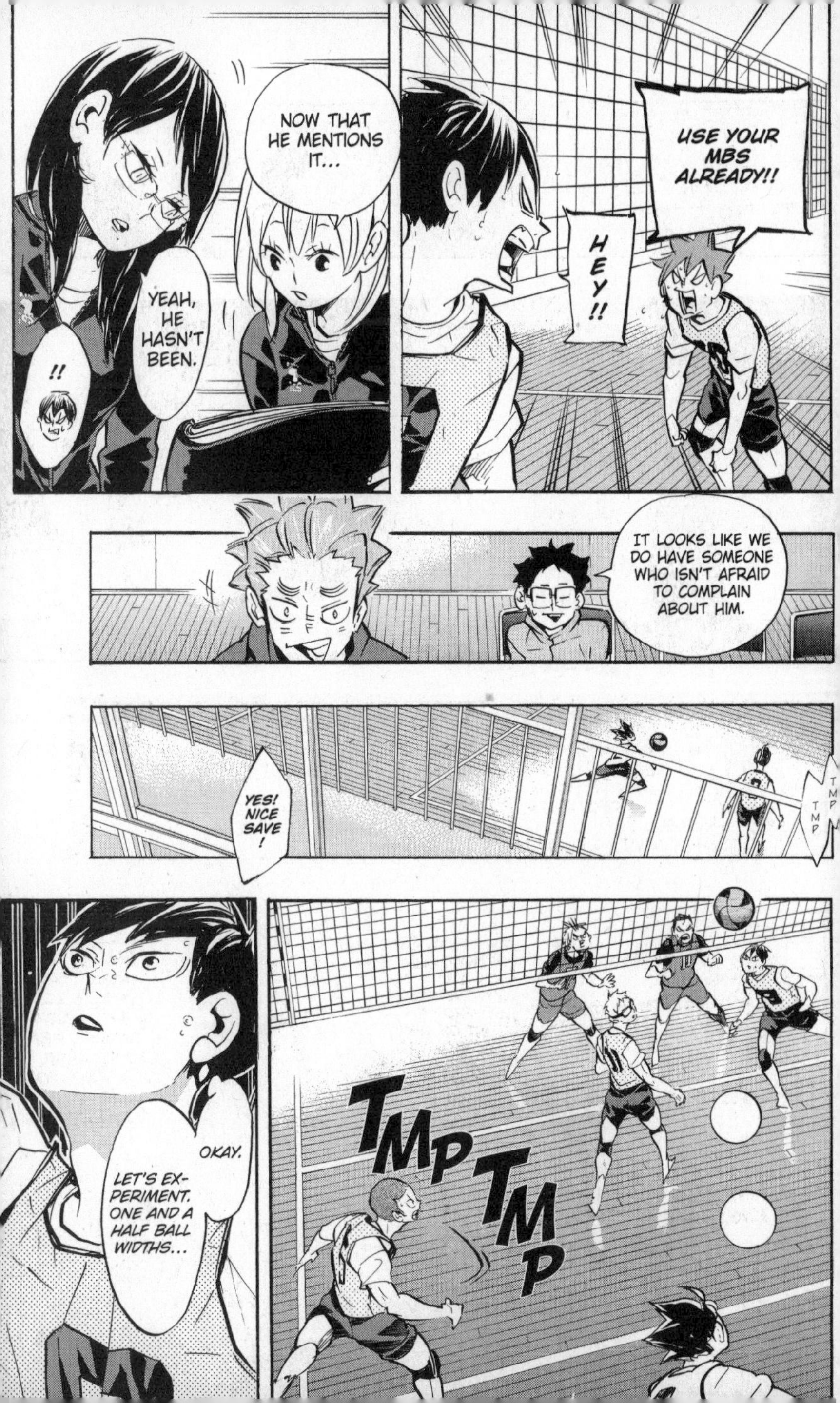
USE YOUR MBS ALREADY!!
HEY!!
NOW THAT HE MENTIONS IT...
YEAH, HE HASN'T BEEN.
!!
IT LOOKS LIKE WE DO HAVE SOMEONE WHO ISN'T AFRAID TO COMPLAIN ABOUT HIM.
TMP TMP
YES! NICE SAVE!
TMP TMP TMP
OKAY.
LET'S EX-PERIMENT. ONE AND A HALF BALL WIDTHS...

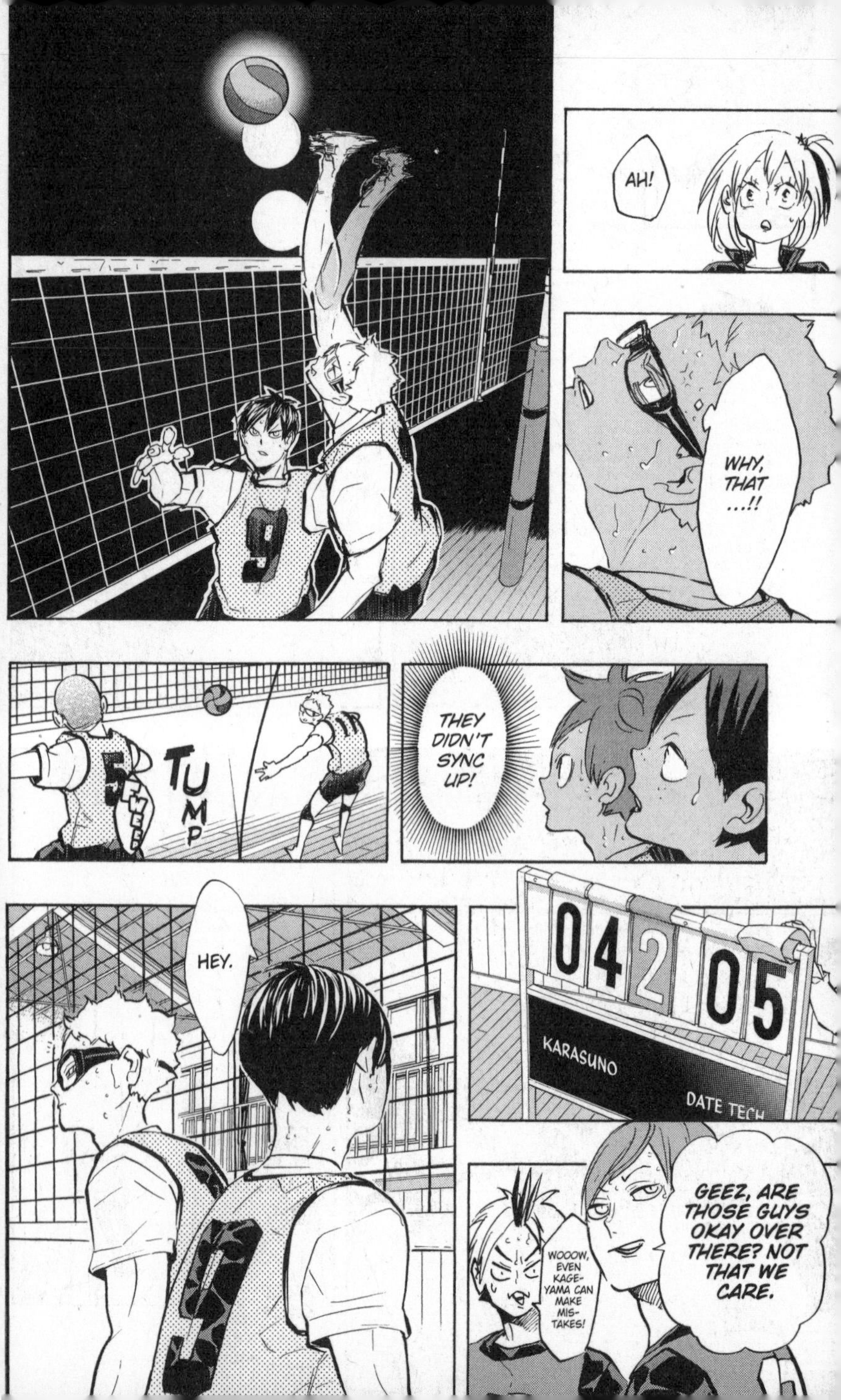
AH!
WHY, THAT ...!!
THEY DIDN'T SYNC UP!
TUMP
FWEEP
04
2
05
KARASUNO
DATE TECH
HEY.
GEEZ, ARE THOSE GUYS OKAY OVER THERE? NOT THAT WE CARE.
WOOOW, EVEN KAGE-YAMA CAN MAKE MIS-TAKES!

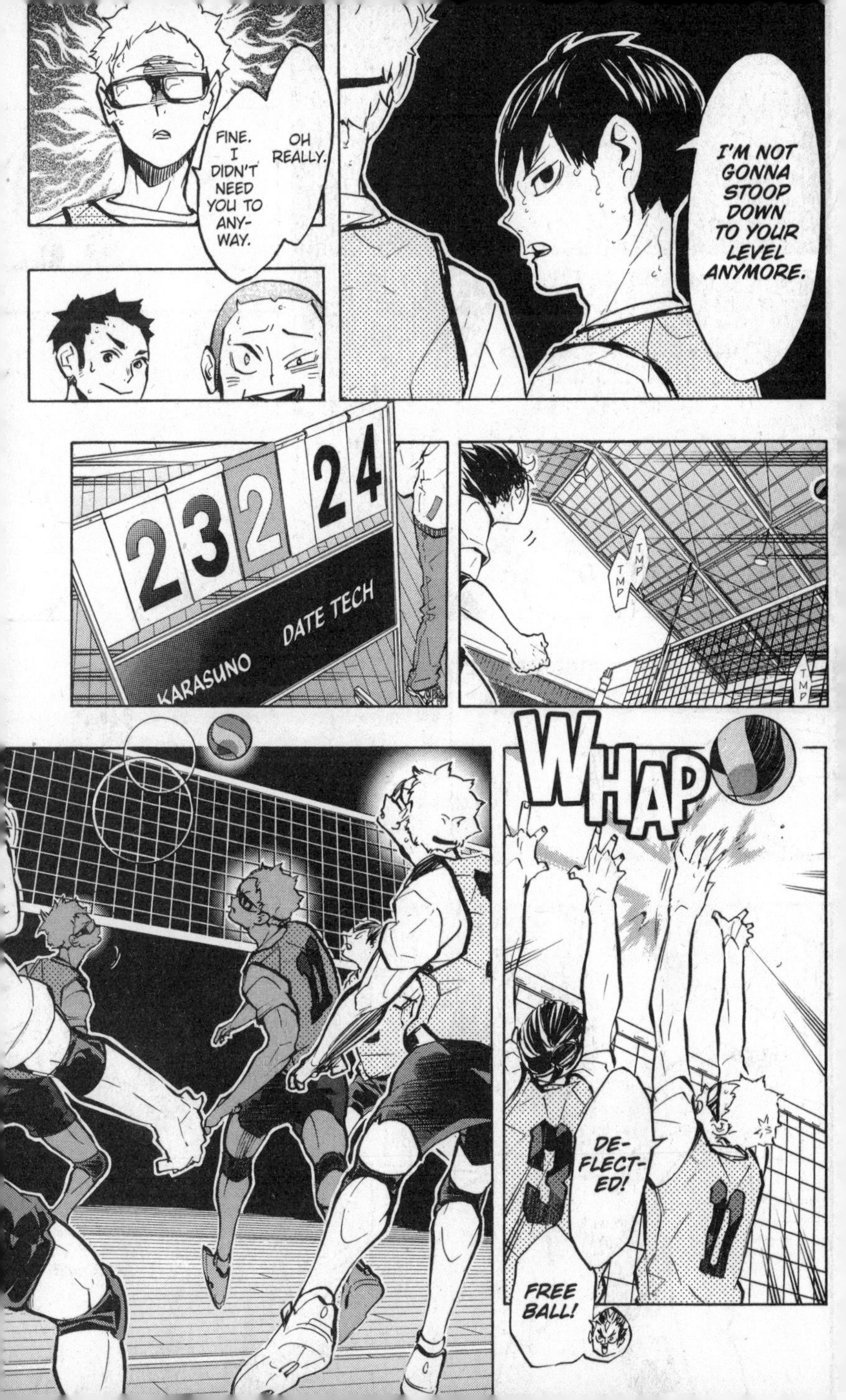
I'M NOT GONNA STOOP DOWN TO YOUR LEVEL ANYMORE.
OH REALLY.
FINE. I DIDN'T NEED YOU TO ANY-WAY.
TMP TMP TMP
23 2 24
KARASUNO
DATE TECH
WHAP
DE-FLECT-ED!
FREE BALL!

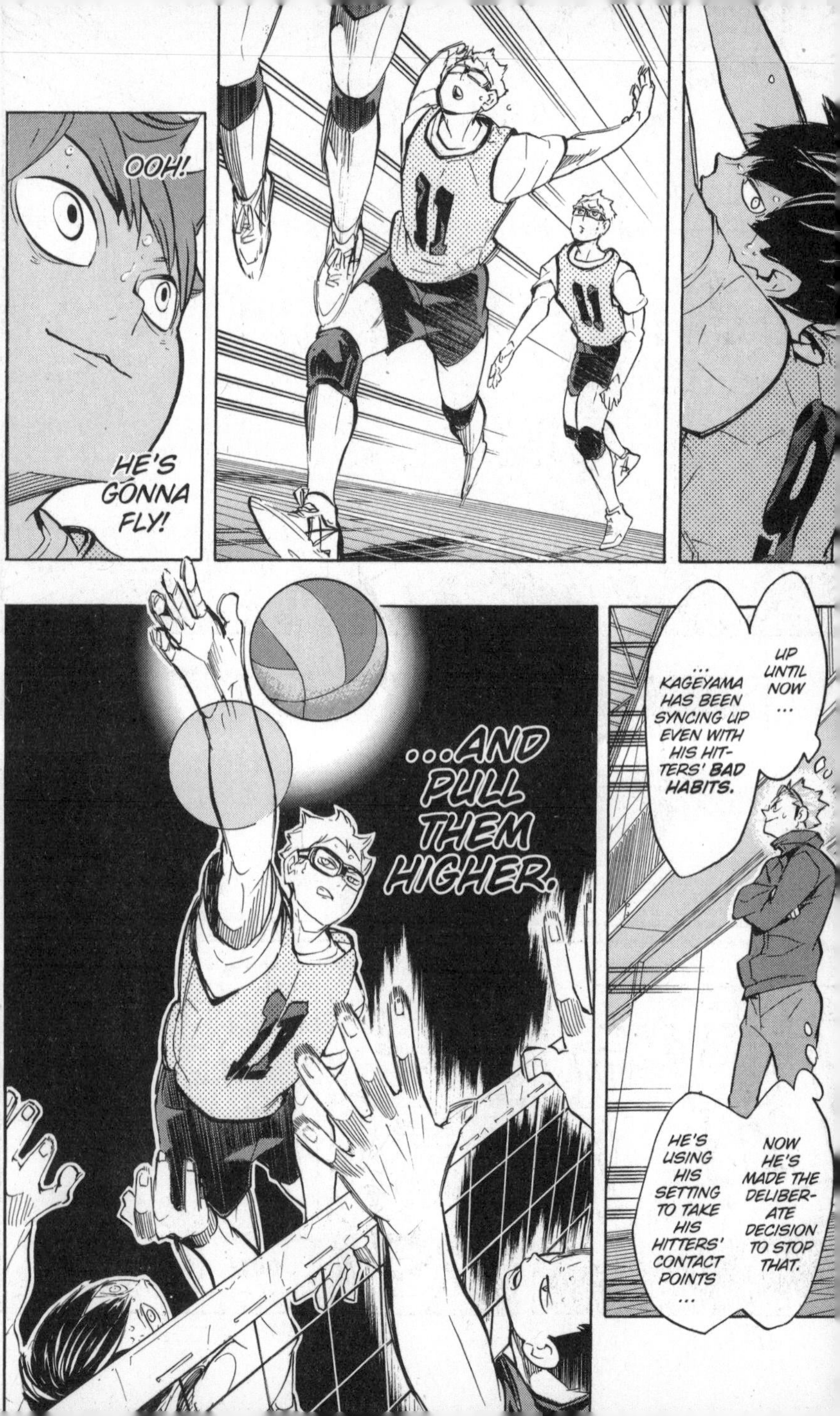
OOH!
HE'S GONNA FLY!
UP UNTIL NOW...
...KAGEYAMA HAS BEEN SYNCING UP EVEN WITH HIS HITTERS' BAD HABITS.
NOW HE'S MADE THE DELIBERATE DECISION TO STOP THAT.
HE'S USING HIS SETTING TO TAKE HIS HITTERS' CONTACT POINTS...
...AND PULL THEM HIGHER.

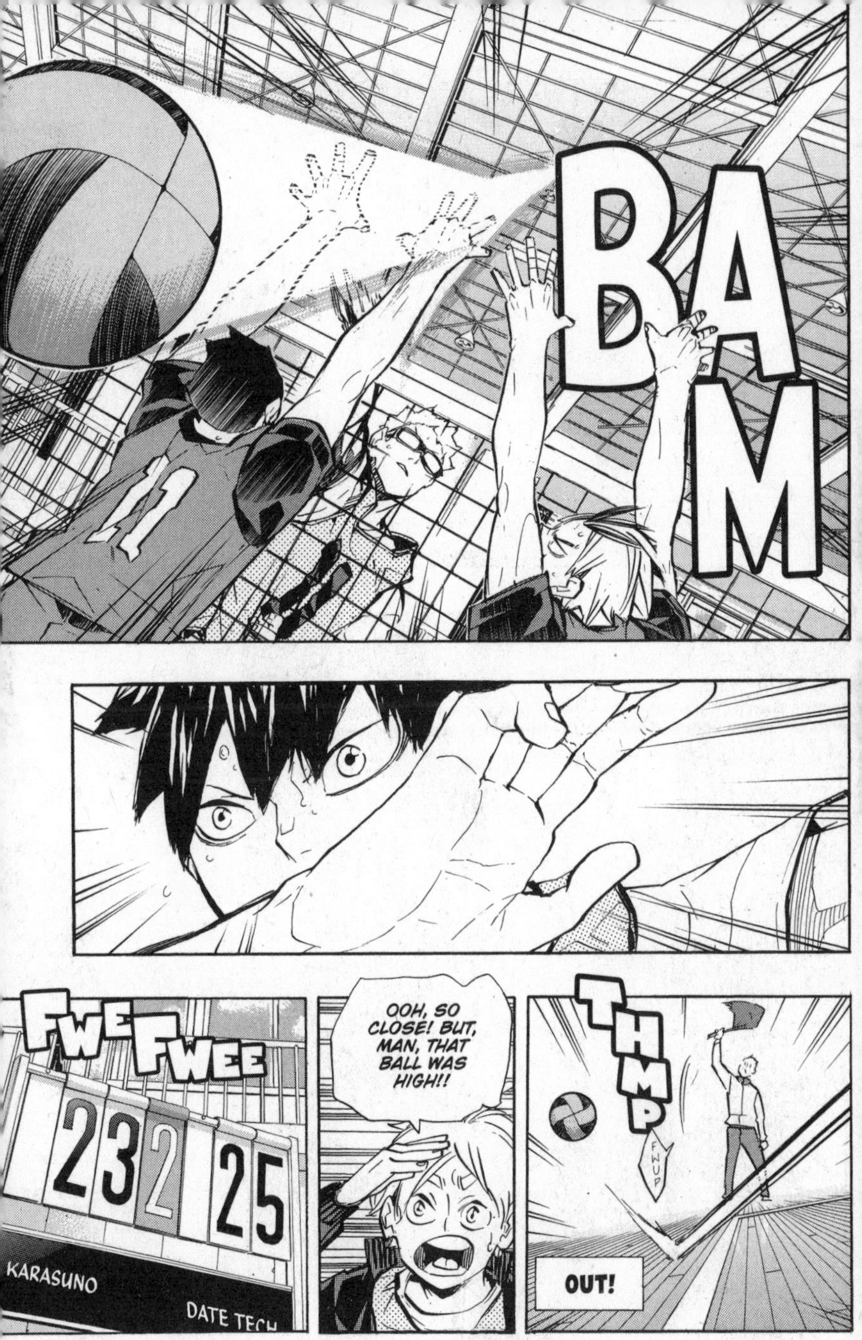
BAM
THMP
FWUP
OUT!
OOH, SO CLOSE! BUT, MAN, THAT BALL WAS HIGH!!
FWEFWEE
KARASUNO
DATE TECH

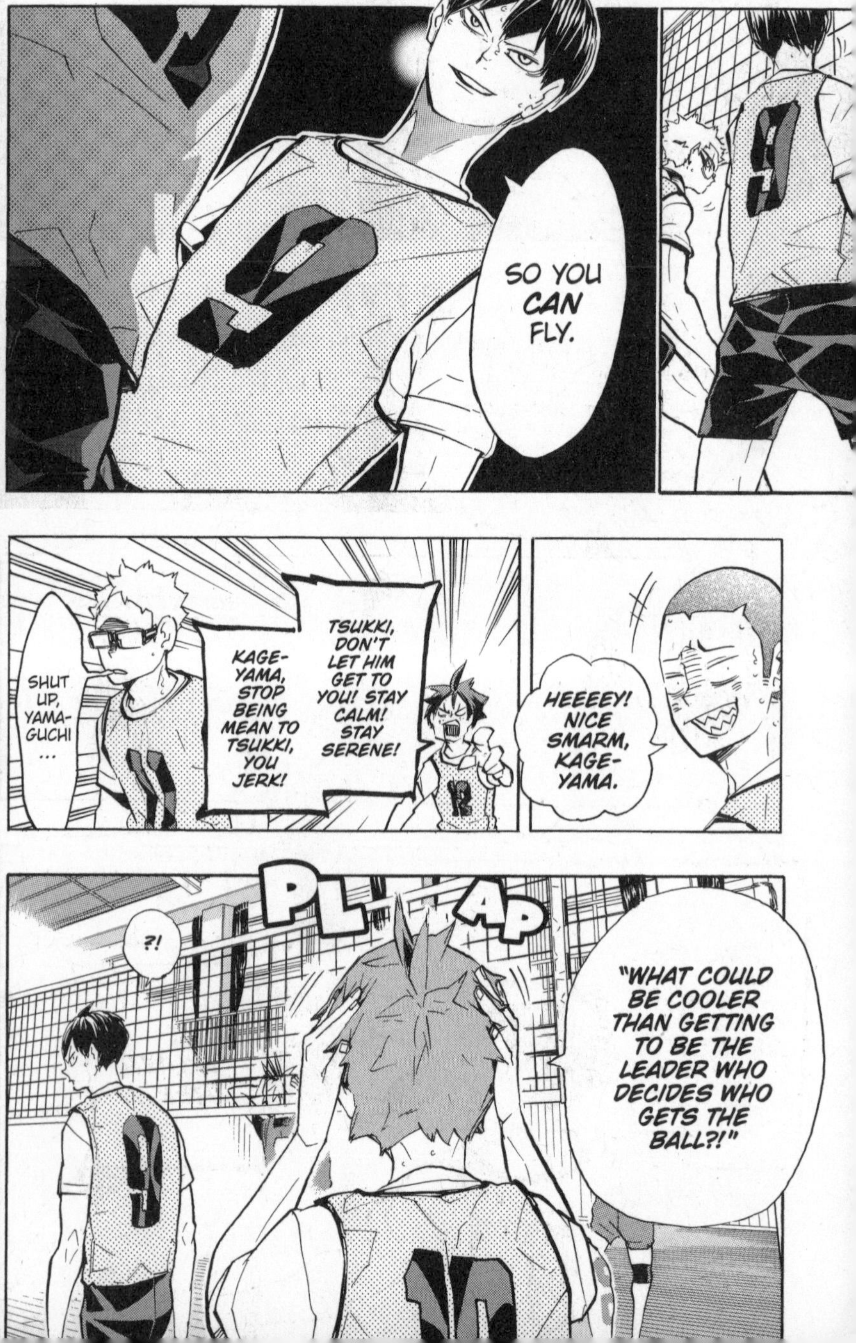
SO YOU CAN FLY.
HEEEEY! NICE SMARM, KAGE-YAMA.
TSUKKI, DON'T LET HIM GET TO YOU! STAY CALM! STAY SERENE!
KAGE-YAMA, STOP BEING MEAN TO TSUKKI, YOU JERK!
SHUT UP, YAMA-GUCHI...
PLAP
"WHAT COULD BE COOLER THAN GETTING TO BE THE LEADER WHO DECIDES WHO GETS THE BALL?!"
?!

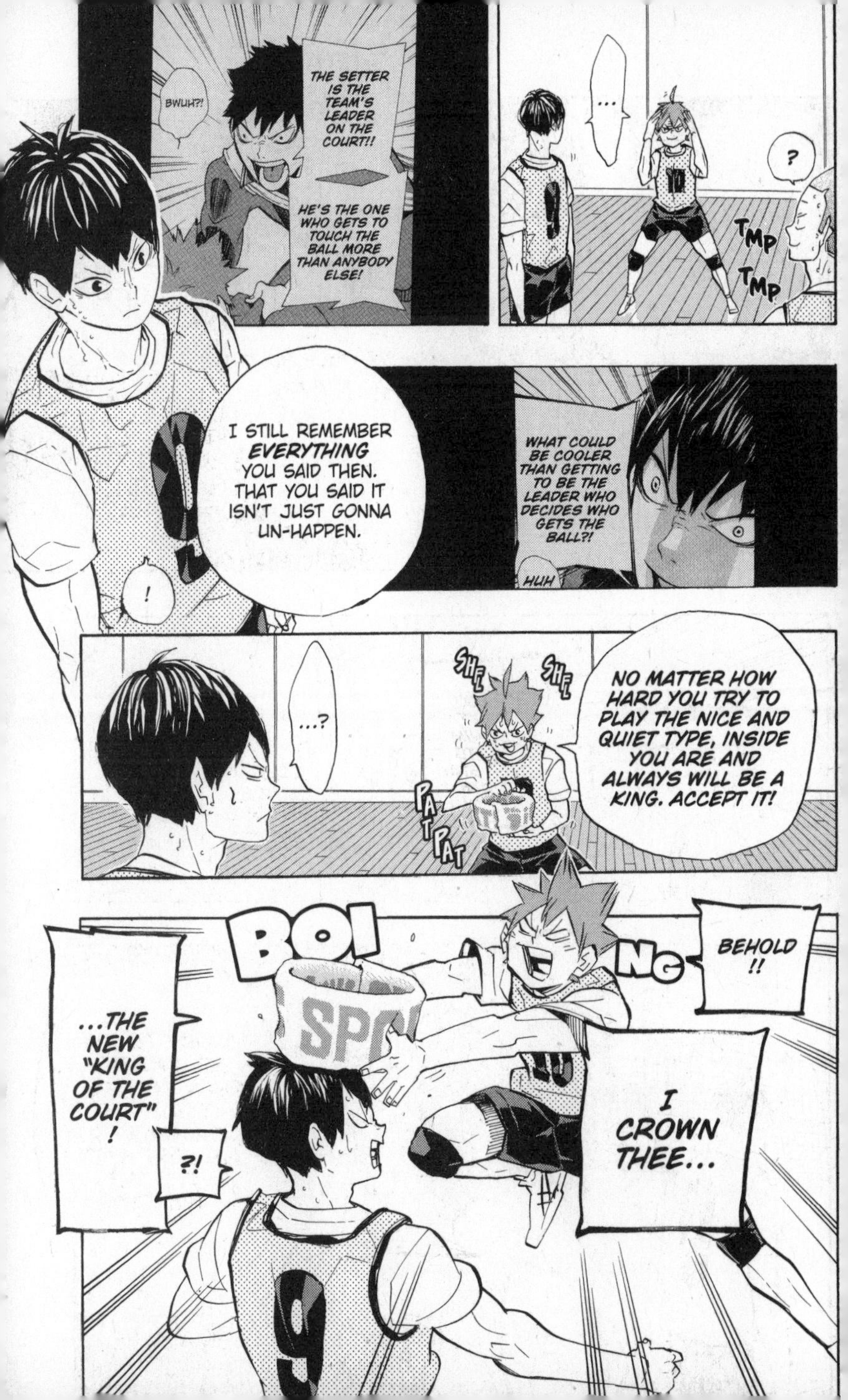
...
?
TMP TMP
THE SETTER IS THE TEAM'S LEADER ON THE COURT!!
BWUH?!
HE'S THE ONE WHO GETS TO TOUCH THE BALL MORE THAN ANYBODY ELSE!
WHAT COULD BE COOLER THAN GETTING TO BE THE LEADER WHO DECIDES WHO GETS THE BALL?!
HUH
I STILL REMEMBER *EVERYTHING* YOU SAID THEN. THAT YOU SAID IT ISN'T JUST GONNA UN-HAPPEN.
!
NO MATTER HOW HARD YOU TRY TO PLAY THE NICE AND QUIET TYPE, INSIDE YOU ARE AND ALWAYS WILL BE A KING. ACCEPT IT!
SHFL SHFL
PAT PAT
...?
BEHOLD!!
I CROWN THEE...
BOING
...THE NEW "KING OF THE COURT"!
?!

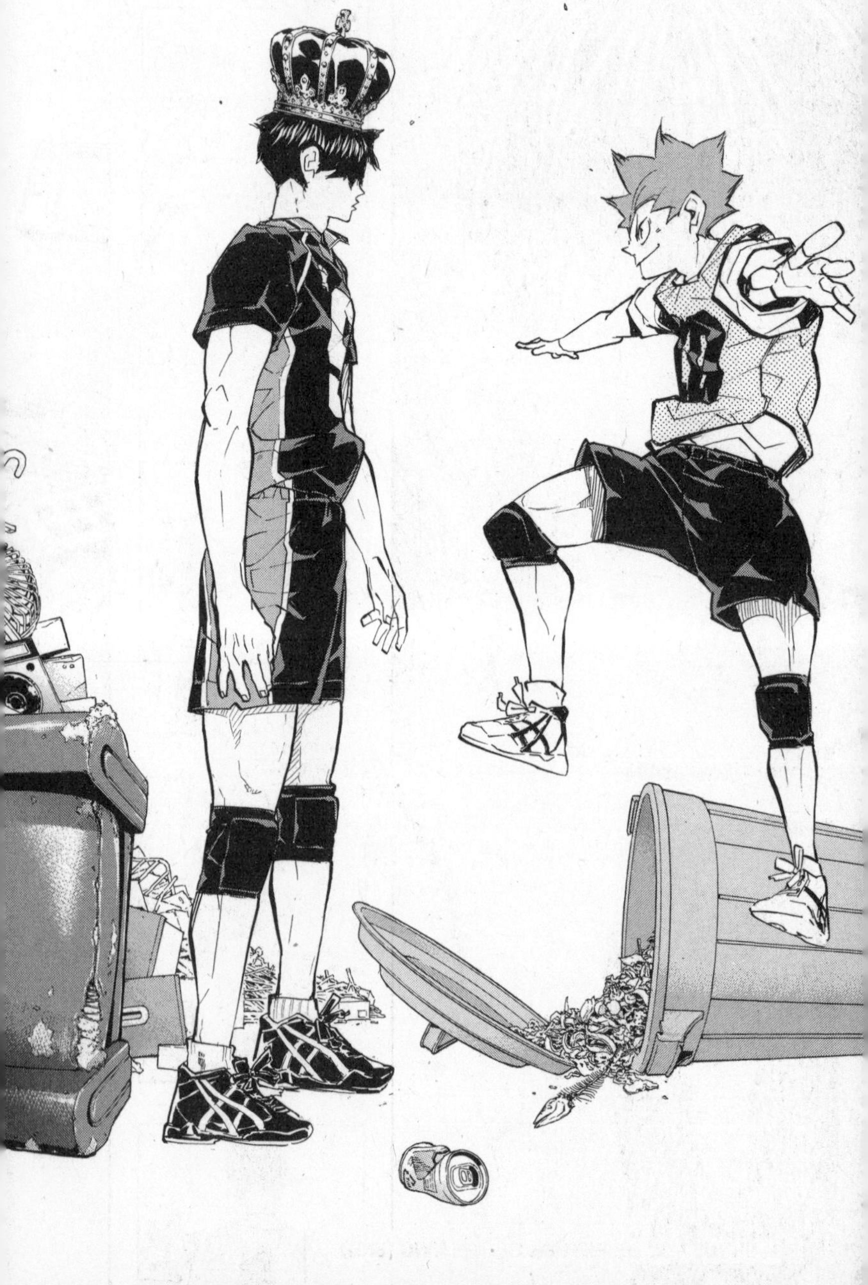

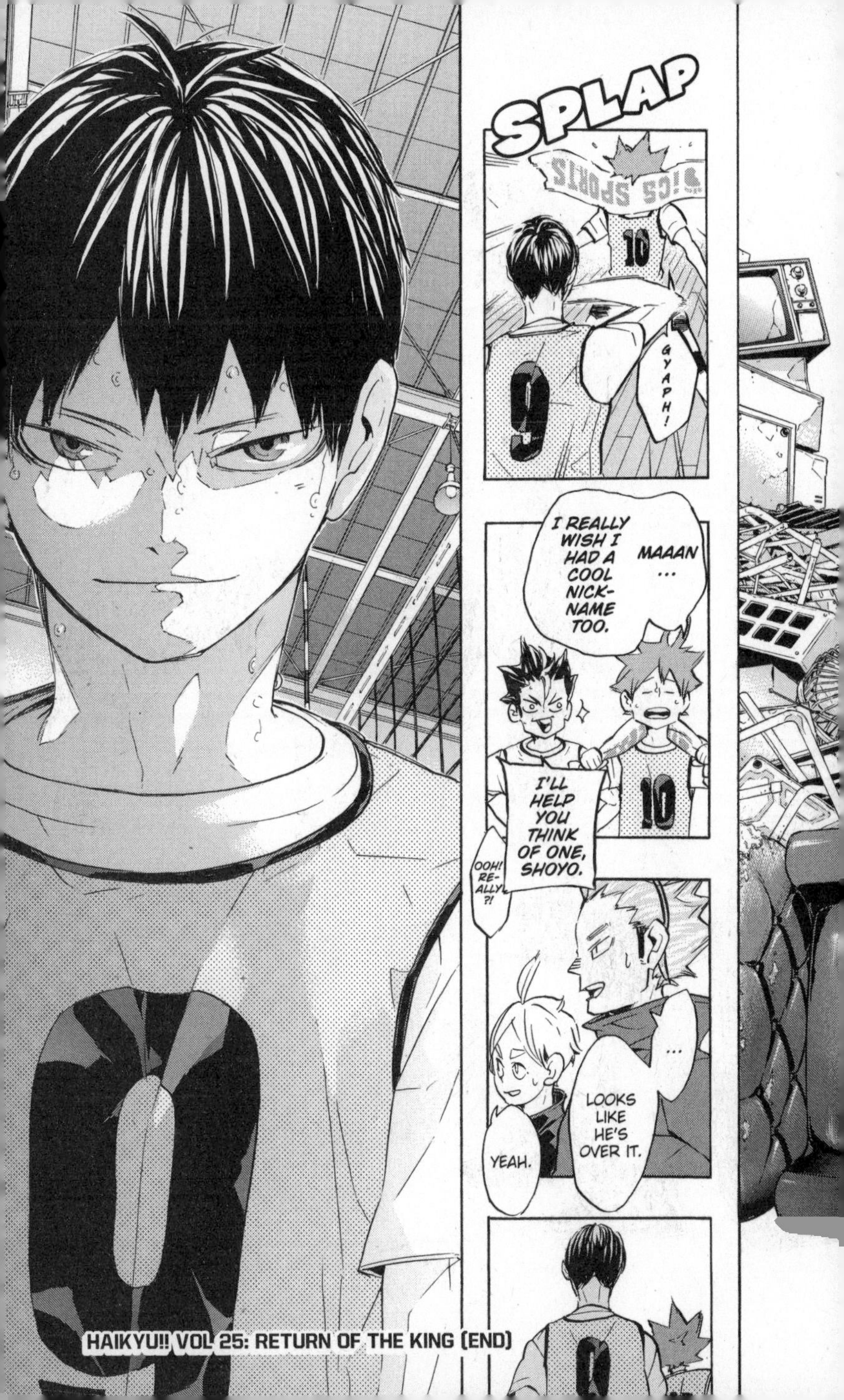
SPLAP
GYAPH!
MAAAN...
I REALLY WISH I HAD A COOL NICK-NAME TOO.
I'LL HELP YOU THINK OF ONE, SHOYO.
OOH! RE-ALLY?!
...
LOOKS LIKE HE'S OVER IT.
YEAH.
HAIKYU!! VOL 25: RETURN OF THE KING (END)

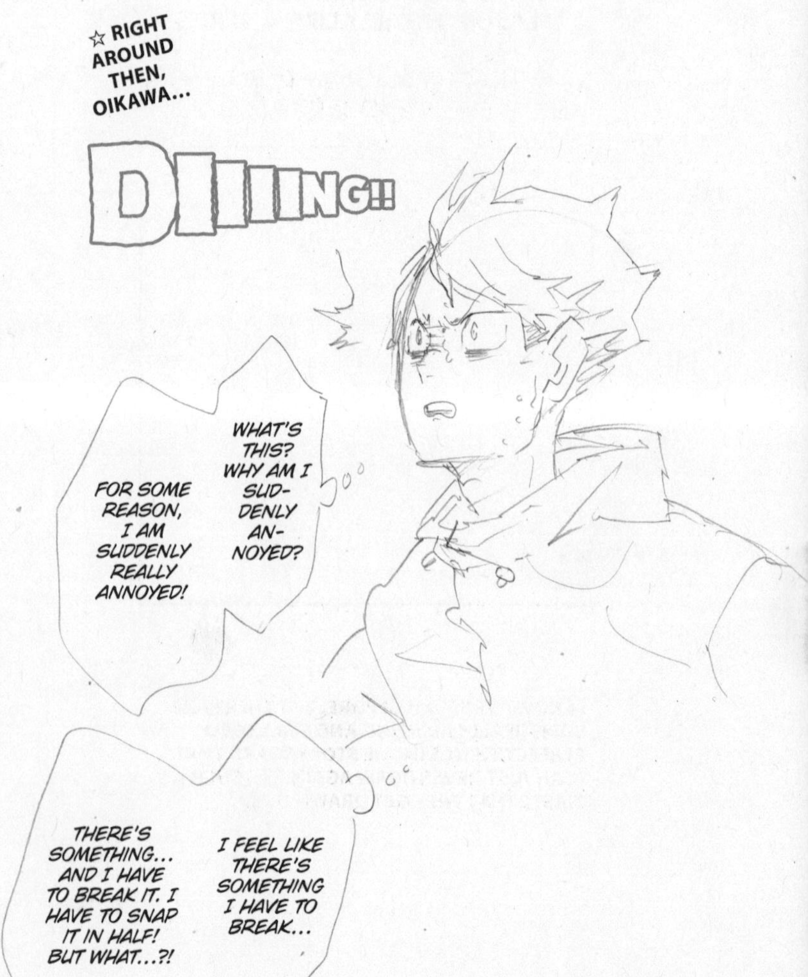
☆ RIGHT AROUND THEN, OIKAWA...
DIIIIING!!
WHAT'S THIS? WHY AM I SUD-DENLY AN-NOYED?
FOR SOME REASON, I AM SUDDENLY REALLY ANNOYED!
I FEEL LIKE THERE'S SOMETHING I HAVE TO BREAK...
THERE'S SOMETHING... AND I HAVE TO BREAK IT. I HAVE TO SNAP IT IN HALF! BUT WHAT...?!

☆ **THE STORYBOARD HAD THAT "FLAVOR" I REALLY LIKE ☆ SERIES!**

KAGEYAMA'S "WHOOPS, NOW I'VE DONE IT" FACE!

I KNOW I'VE SAID IT BEFORE, BUT THERE ARE SOME REALLY AMAZING AND STRANGELY PERFECT THINGS IN THE STORYBOARD THAT I CAN JUST NEVER DRAW AGAIN. IT'S SUCH A WASTE THAT THEY GET DRAWN OVER.

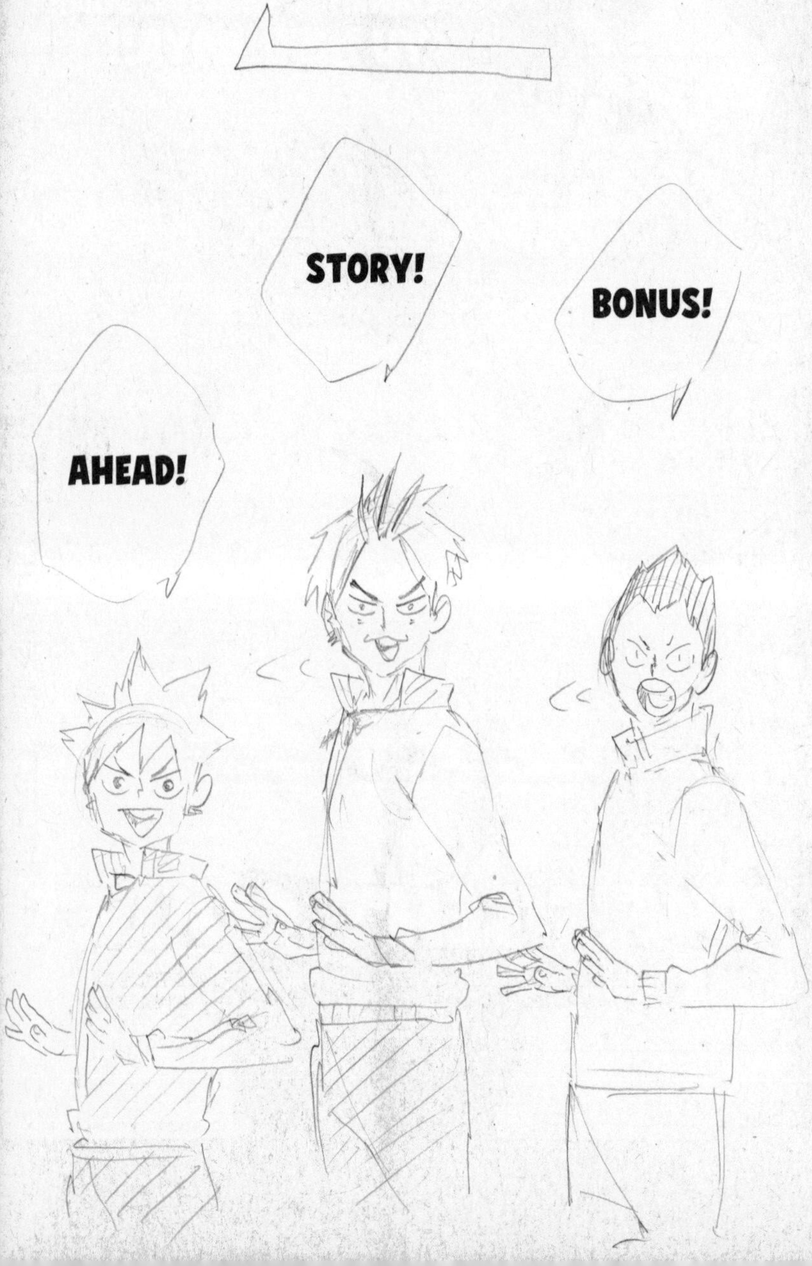
BONUS!
STORY!
AHEAD!

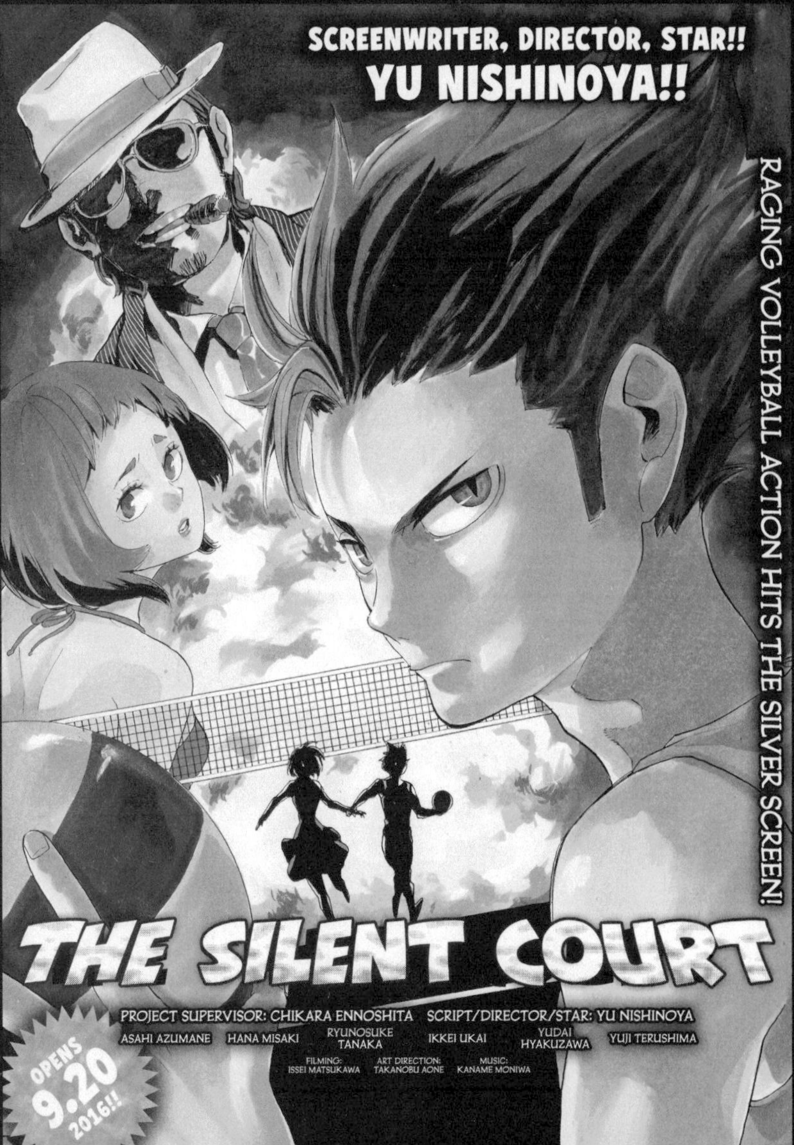
SCREENWRITER, DIRECTOR, STAR!!
YU NISHINOYA!!
RAGING VOLLEYBALL ACTION HITS THE SILVER SCREEN!
THE SILENT COURT
PROJECT SUPERVISOR: CHIKARA ENNOSHITA SCRIPT/DIRECTOR/STAR: YU NISHINOYA
ASAHI AZUMANE HANA MISAKI RYUNOSUKE TANAKA IKKEI UKAI YUDAI HYAKUZAWA YUJI TERUSHIMA
FILMING: ISSEI MATSUKAWA ART DIRECTION: TAKANOBU AONE MUSIC: KANAME MONIWA
OPENS 9.20 2016!!
2016 "THE SILENT COURT" PROJECT GROUP

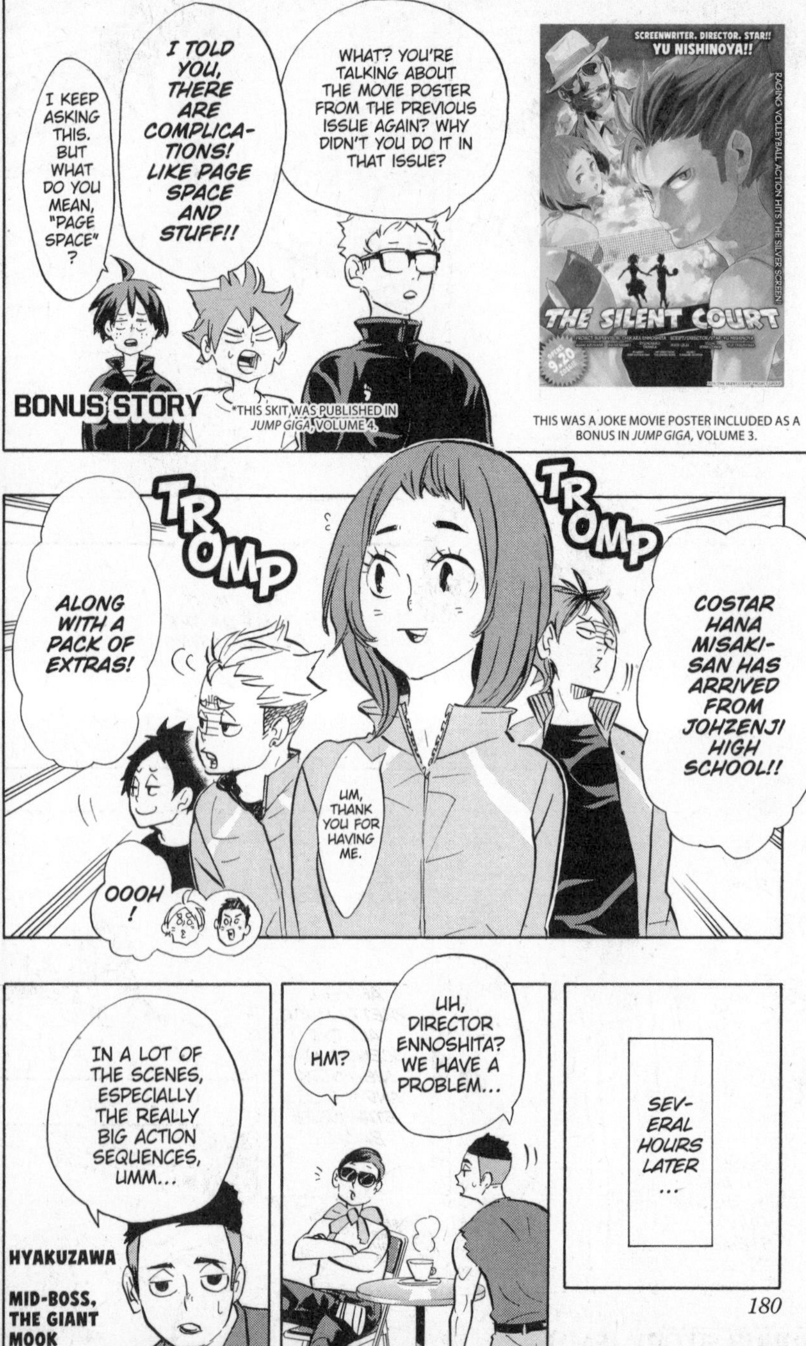
SCREENWRITER, DIRECTOR, STAR!! YU NISHINOYA!!
RAGING VOLLEYBALL ACTION HITS THE SILVER SCREEN!
THE SILENT COURT
OPENS 9.20
THIS WAS A JOKE MOVIE POSTER INCLUDED AS A BONUS IN *JUMP GIGA*, VOLUME 3.
WHAT? YOU'RE TALKING ABOUT THE MOVIE POSTER FROM THE PREVIOUS ISSUE AGAIN? WHY DIDN'T YOU DO IT IN THAT ISSUE?
I TOLD YOU, THERE ARE COMPLICATIONS! LIKE PAGE SPACE AND STUFF!!
I KEEP ASKING THIS. BUT WHAT DO YOU MEAN, "PAGE SPACE"?
BONUS STORY
*THIS SKIT WAS PUBLISHED IN *JUMP GIGA*, VOLUME 4.
TROMP
TROMP
COSTAR HANA MISAKI-SAN HAS ARRIVED FROM JOHZENJI HIGH SCHOOL!!
UM, THANK YOU FOR HAVING ME.
ALONG WITH A PACK OF EXTRAS!
OOOH!
SEVERAL HOURS LATER...
UH, DIRECTOR ENNOSHITA? WE HAVE A PROBLEM...
HM?
IN A LOT OF THE SCENES, ESPECIALLY THE REALLY BIG ACTION SEQUENCES, UMM...
HYAKUZAWA
MID-BOSS, THE GIANT MOOK

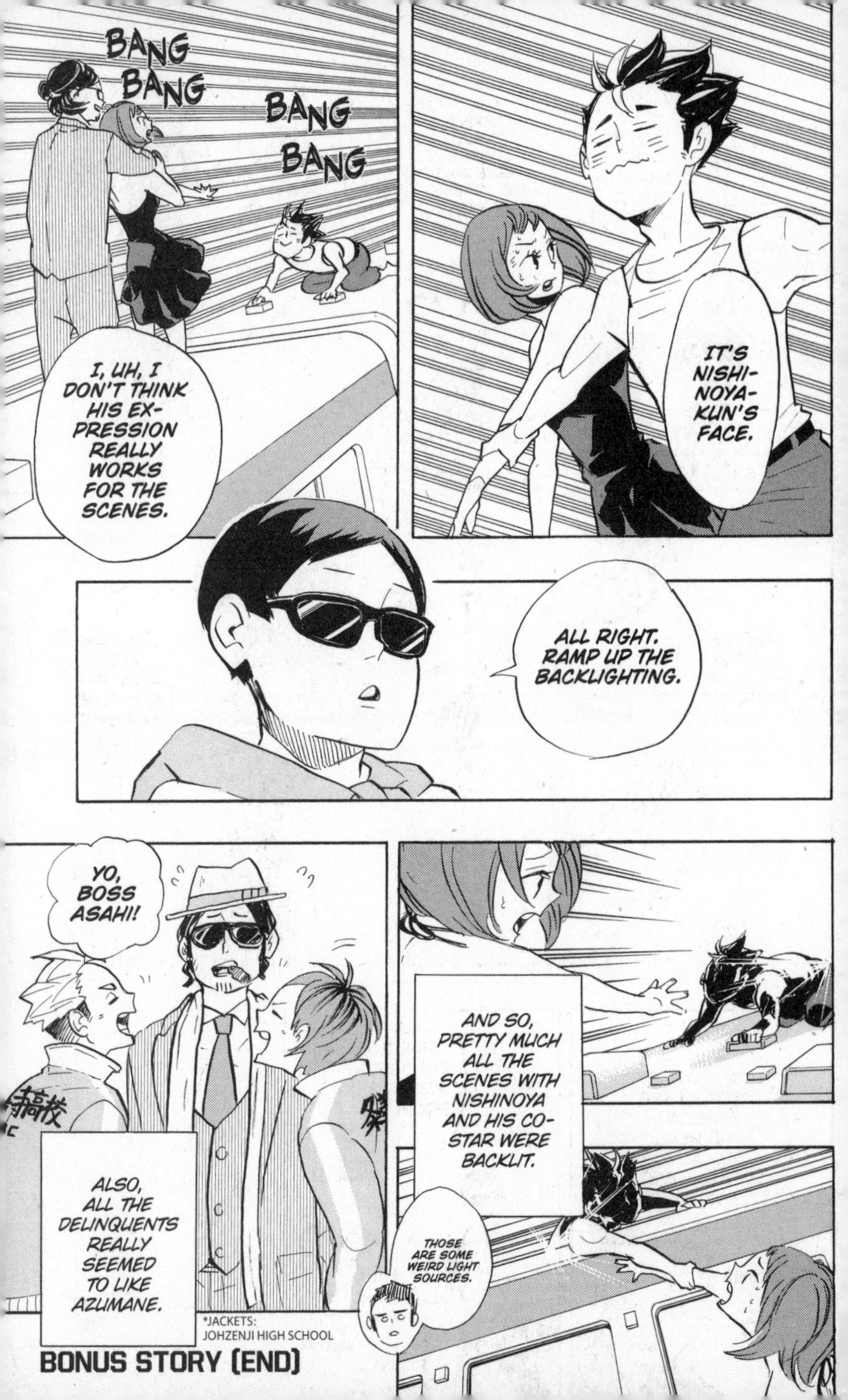
IT'S NISHINOYA-KUN'S FACE.
BANG BANG
BANG BANG
I, UH, I DON'T THINK HIS EXPRESSION REALLY WORKS FOR THE SCENES.
ALL RIGHT. RAMP UP THE BACKLIGHTING.
AND SO, PRETTY MUCH ALL THE SCENES WITH NISHINOYA AND HIS CO-STAR WERE BACKLIT.
THOSE ARE SOME WEIRD LIGHT SOURCES.
YO, BOSS ASAHI!
ALSO, ALL THE DELINQUENTS REALLY SEEMED TO LIKE AZUMANE.
*JACKETS: JOHZENJI HIGH SCHOOL
BONUS STORY (END)

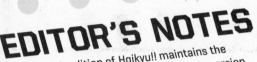

EDITOR'S NOTES

The English edition of Haikyu!! maintains the honorifics used in the original Japanese version. For those of you who are new to these terms, here's a brief explanation to help with your reading experience!

When saying someone's name in Japanese, a suffix is often attached to indicate how familiar the speaker is with the person. Some are more polite and respectful, while others are endearing.

1 *-kun* is often used for young men or boys, usually someone you are familiar with.

2 *-chan* is used for young children and can be used as a term of endearment.

3 *-san* is used for someone you respect or are not close to, or to be polite.

4 *Senpai* is used for someone who is older than you or in a higher position or grade in school.

5 *Kohai* is used for someone who is younger than you or in a lower position or grade in school.

6 *Sensei* means teacher.

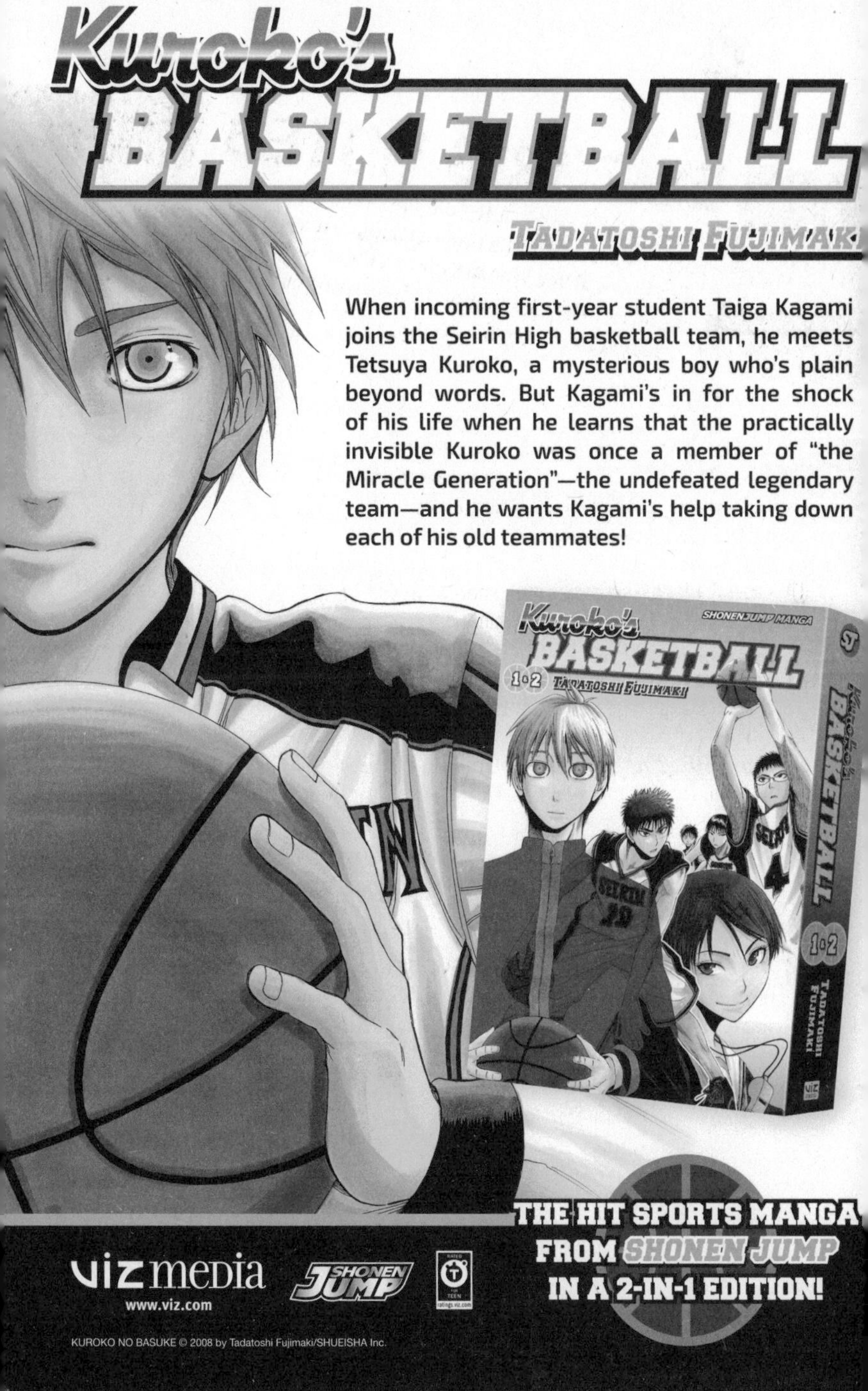
Kuroko's
BASKETBALL
TADATOSHI FUJIMAKI
When incoming first-year student Taiga Kagami joins the Seirin High basketball team, he meets Tetsuya Kuroko, a mysterious boy who's plain beyond words. But Kagami's in for the shock of his life when he learns that the practically invisible Kuroko was once a member of "the Miracle Generation"—the undefeated legendary team—and he wants Kagami's help taking down each of his old teammates!
Kuroko's BASKETBALL
SHONENJUMP MANGA
1•2
TADATOSHI FUJIMAKI
THE HIT SPORTS MANGA
FROM SHONEN JUMP
IN A 2-IN-1 EDITION!
viz media
www.viz.com
SHONEN JUMP
RATED T FOR TEEN
ratings.viz.com

You're Reading the
WRONG WAY!

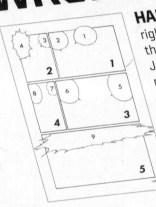

HAIKYU!! reads from right to left, starting in the upper-right corner. Japanese is read from right to left, meaning that action, sound effects and word-balloon order are completely reversed from English order.